Religious Rivalries in the Early Roman Empire and the Rise of Christianity

Studies in Christianity and Judaism /
Études sur le christianisme et le judaïsme : 18

Studies in Christianity and Judaism / Études sur le christianisme et le judaïsme publishes monographs on Christianity and Judaism in the last two centuries before the common era and the first six centuries of the common era, with a special interest in studies of their interrelationship or the cultural and social context in which they developed.

Studies in Christianity and Judaism /
Études sur le christianisme et le judaïsme : 18

Religious Rivalries in the Early Roman Empire and the Rise of Christianity

Leif E. Vaage, editor

Published for the Canadian Corporation for Studies in Religion/
Corporation Canadienne des Sciences Religieuses
by Wilfrid Laurier University Press
2006

This book has been published with the help of a grant from the Canadian Federation for the Humanities and Social Sciences, through the Aid to Scholarly Publications Programme, using funds provided by the Social Sciences and Humanities Research Council of Canada. We acknowledge the financial support of the Government of Canada through the Book Publishing Industry Development Program for our publishing activities.

Library and Archives Canada Cataloguing in Publication

Religious rivalries in the early Roman empire and the rise of christianity / Leif E. Vaage, editor.

(Studies in Christianity and Judaism / Études sur le christianisme et le judaïsme ; 18)
Includes bibliographical references and index.
ISBN-13: 978-0-88920-449-2
ISBN-10: 0-88920-449-7

1. Church history—Primitive and early church, ca. 30–600. 2. Christianity and other religions—Roman. 3. Rome—Religion. I. Vaage, Leif E. II. Canadian Corporation for Studies in Religion III. Series: Studies in Christianity and Judaism ; 18

BL96.R46 2006   270.1   C2006-900249-5

Cover design by P.J. Woodland. Cover photograph of the interior of the Pantheon in Rome courtesy of John Straube. Text design by Catharine Bonas-Taylor.

Printed in Canada

Contents

Acknowledgments

First of all, the editor wishes to thank all the contributors to this volume for their ready cooperation and sorely tested patience over the last few years; completion of the project has been "a long time coming," due, in part, to circumstances beyond my control, and I am exceedingly grateful to everyone who has awaited publication as generously as you all have. On two separate occasions, I received financial assistance from Emmanuel College (Centre for the Study of Religion in Canada) and Victoria University (Senate Research Grants) to pay for student support in preparing the manuscript, which I am eager here to acknowledge. My student assistants, Dr. Stephen Chambers and Ms. Karen Williams, able and professional in the performance of their various assignments, are both unrivalled in their cordiality and decency. Finally, I wish to thank Prof. Peter Richardson for his sustained commitment to the project and Prof. Stephen Wilson for his final "maieutic" nudging. In all these instances, the rivalries to which the volume as a whole is dedicated have been graciously absent.

Preface

This book is about religious rivalries in the early Roman Empire and the rise of Christianity. The book is divided into three parts. The first part debates the degree to which the category of rivalry adequately names the issue(s) that must be addressed when comparing and contrasting the social success of different religious groups in Mediterranean antiquity. Some scholars insist on the need for additional registers; others consider it important not only to contemplate success but also failure and loss; yet others treat specific cases. The second part of the book provides a critical assessment of the modern category of mission to describe the inner dynamics of such a process. Discussed are the early Christian apostle Paul, who typically is supposed to have been a missionary; the early Jewish historian Josephus, who typically is not described in this way; and ancient Mithraism, whose spread and social reproduction has heretofore remained a mystery. Finally, part 3 of the book discusses "the rise of Christianity," largely in response to the similarly titled work of the American sociologist of religion Rodney Stark. The book as a whole renders more complex and concrete the social histories of Christianity, Judaism, and paganism in the early Roman Empire. None of these groups succeeded merely by winning a given competition. It is not clear that any of them imagined its own success necessarily to entail the elimination of others. It does seem, however, that early Christianity had certain habits both of speech and of practice, which made it particularly apt to succeed (in) the Roman Empire.

The book is about rivalries in the plural, since there are many: sibling, imperial, professional, psychological, to name but a few. Each of these has its own characteristics, conditions, complications. All, however, share the same constitutive antinomy, which therefore may function here as a basic definition. In rivalry, one needs the other, against whom we struggle, from whom I seek to differentiate myself, over whom you hope to prevail, in order to know oneself as oneself. Religious rivalries in the early Roman Empire are no exception. Christianity, Judaism, and so-called paganism existed only through such a relationship with one another (although rivalry was hardly the only condition of their existence). It is not possible to understand any of these traditions without considering how each of them used the other(s) to explain itself to itself and, sometimes, to persuade another to become (like) one of them.

Rivalries. Not competition. Not coexistence. Even though not everyone who writes in this book finally thinks that "rivalries" is the best name for the diverse patterns of relationship among Christians, Jews, and others in different urban settings of the early Roman Empire. Nonetheless, to define these groups as somehow rivals with one another has served to keep together in conversation with one another the volatile codependency that characterized these groups' ongoing competition with each other; which is to say, the way(s) in which their undeniable coexistence included not infrequently and eventually the struggle for hegemony. By making rivalries the primary axis around which the various investigations of this book (and its companions) turn, it has become possible to give a better account of the particular social identity and concrete operational mode(s) of existence of each of these traditions in antiquity.

Religious rivalries...and the rise of Christianity: this book also discusses the different cultural destinies of Christianity, Judaism, and paganism in Mediterranean antiquity as a question of social rivalry. To which degree, and in which manner(s), did each of these traditions, in its variant forms, emerge, survive, and sometimes achieve social dominance by contending—competing, collaborating, coexisting—with its neighbours, specifically in urban contexts of the early Roman Empire? Under consideration here is the role of explicit social conflict and contest in the development of ancient religious identity and experience.

Part 1 of the book provides a number of different points of entry into the general topic of religious rivalries in the early Roman Empire. The first chapter is introductory. Written by Leif E. Vaage initially to suggest both a rationale and some further lines of inquiry for a seminar of the Canadian Society of Biblical Studies (CSBS), the essay asks a series of leading questions, taking early Christianity as its primary example, and seeks to encourage the production of alternate histories, especially if and when these are derived from more intimate knowledge of the fields of early Judaism and adjacent paganism. In the second and third chapters, Philip Harland and Stephen Wilson respectively begin such a revision, by qualifying what religious rivalry concretely meant. In the case of Harland, this is done by discussing the ongoing vitality of ancient civic life, in which the practices of rivalry between different social-religious associations were less a sign of significant social transformation and more a measure of continuing local health. In the case of Wilson, both why and how early Christians, Jews, and other pagan groups lost members through apostasy or defection is examined. In both cases, the precise social shape or contours of ancient religious rivalry is brought more clearly into focus through greater specification.

By contrast, in the fourth chapter, Reena Basser explores ancient religious rivalry as a constitutive ambiguity. At least, this seems to be the best way to understand early rabbinical efforts to imagine a particular form of Jewish religious life in a social context that was both their own, economically, and yet perceived by them nonetheless to be inherently incompatible, ritually, with this way of life. Developing Basser's work further, Jack Lightstone then inquires, in the fifth and final chapter of this section, whether the explicit focus on rivalry, in fact, does not skew or obscure our understanding of ancient social life. This includes, of course, the practice of religion, which certainly had its tensions and turmoil but also, in Lightstone's view, other more co-operative or *laissez-faire* aspects. In fact, Lightstone inquires, why not consider these other more congenial aspects to be at least as important as rivalry in shaping daily life and the diverse forms of relationship among different religious groups in antiquity?

The first and final chapters by Vaage and Lightstone define a theme that recurs throughout the book, namely, the degree to which the category of rivalry adequately names the issue(s) that must be addressed when comparing and contrasting the social destiny of different religious groups in antiquity. Is the category of rivalry ultimately a telling one for research in this area? Or does such a category, more or less immediately, require qualification through other considerations? Since the editor of the book and the author of this preface also wrote the first chapter, my presentation of the question is hardly impartial or objective. Suffice it to say that I chose the term "rivalry" to name an issue I thought could be intriguing and productive for collective inquiry. This issue, in a word, was the role that social power—both its imaginary pursuit and concrete conquest—played in shaping the diverse destiny of various religious groups in the early Roman Empire. By the pursuit and conquest of social power, I meant the stratagems developed and deployed by a given religious group to attain and secure its

immediate social survival as well as, sometimes, an enduring political presence, if not eventual dominance. Of course, I also chose the term to provoke
debate. Such debate quite properly includes an exploration of the limits of
the category itself.

In part 2, the reader has before her three quite different chapters, each
of which takes up the question of the category of mission as part of the standard vocabulary of scholarly discourse about Christian origins and the history of other religious groups in the early Roman Empire. In the first chapter
of the book, it was proposed that the category of mission be abandoned altogether. Neither Terence Donaldson nor Steve Mason in their respective
chapters on Paul and Josephus has been willing to do so. At the same time,
both Donaldson and Mason take care to define clearly, viz. redefine what
exactly they mean by mission.

In the case of Paul, to his own surprise, Donaldson admits that he did
not discover the explicit missionary sensibility he thought that he would
find in Paul; instead, Donaldson discerns a more modest or subdued list of
apostolic things to do. If Paul had a mission, it was not apparently at the
forefront of his consciousness, nor of the discourse Paul used about himself. Moreover, to describe the specific content of this understated mission
and its scope is said to require more exegetical work. One might wonder why
the apostolic robe has proven to be so threadbare on this point.

By contrast, Mason argues, quite directly, that Josephus *was* a missionary: for Judaism, in Rome. This puts Mason at odds with more than one
scholarly stereotype or conventional opinion, for example, the belief that
there were no Jewish missionaries in antiquity; that Josephus was a traitor to Judaism rather than an advocate for it; that a religious mission would
properly be something other than what Josephus practised. The rhetorical
advantage Mason derives from this use of "missionary" to characterize
Josephus can hardly be denied: it cuts to the heart of any number of mis-
conceptions and misrepresentations of the man. The question, however,
whether "missionary" is finally the best term to describe who Josephus
was and what he was doing in Rome, is not thereby resolved—at least, not
automatically. Much depends, for Mason, on the specific purpose of Josephus' late writing, *Contra Apionem*.

The third chapter in this second section of the book, by Roger Beck, does
not use the category of mission to describe the way(s) in which ancient
Mithraism maintained and reproduced itself socially. Indeed, the purpose
of Beck's essay is precisely to underscore how utterly "un-missionary"
ancient Mithraism appears to have been. Nonetheless, Beck makes a significant contribution to the debate about mission in the early Roman

Empire, insofar as he makes plain that such activity was *not* necessary for at least one ancient and genuinely religious tradition to succeed in propagating itself over time. The fact that such social reproduction evidently occurred in the most ordinary of ancient ways is instructive.

In part 3, under discussion is the evident "success" of early Christianity in becoming the dominant religion of the later Roman Empire. The four chapters that make up this section of the book are hardly the first writings to consider the topic; indeed, it appears to have become somewhat of a cottage industry among scholars of various stripes. Nonetheless, the topic obviously belongs to a discussion of religious rivalries in antiquity, and is addressed here for that reason. Each of the essays represents a response to one or more aspects of Rodney Stark's *The Rise of Christianity* (which the second half of the title of this book is meant to echo). Stark's work aims to provide a strictly sociological explanation for early Christianity's emergence as, in the words of the subtitle of the paperback edition, "the Dominant Religious Force in the Western World in a Few Centuries." Much could and has been written about Stark's analysis, both as sociology of religion and as history. The four essays in Part Three are meant to be illustrative and telling, not exhaustive, in their treatment of the topic.

The first essay, by Adele Reinhartz, reviews Stark's representation of the early Christian "mission to the Jews," which is chapter 3 of *The Rise of Christianity.* (The depiction of Judaism before Christianity, as discussed in the first chapter of the book, is one of the more evident weaknesses in the pioneering work of both Gibbon and Harnack.) Reinhartz does not ask the categorical question, whether there ever was a mission to the Jews, but, rather, inquires about evidence; namely, the degree to which, if at all, there can be found in the historical record indicators of the kind of mission Stark postulates as necessary or most probable for sociological reasons. As case in point, Reinhartz examines the Gospel of John, since this text otherwise seems to reflect the very sort of situation Stark takes to be constitutive of the origins and subsequent rise of early Christianity. Not surprisingly, the Gospel of John, as Reinhartz describes it, does not confirm Stark's straightforward scenario of multiple generations of Hellenized Diaspora Jews finding greater satisfaction in early Christianity.

The second essay, by Steven Muir, discusses health care and other practices of early Christian charity as a contributing factor to its social success. This topic was the theme of Stark's fourth chapter in *The Rise of Christianity.* Muir is appreciative of the fact that such a "mundane" explanation is possible but, again, wants to test the proposal against the historical evidence. Moreover, it is not clear that Stark accurately represents the nature and state of ancient health care before the advent of Christianity. In the end, it seems to Muir that the Christians did nothing especially new in this regard. At the same time, they did practise widely and with notable determination the kind of mutual aid and care for others, which ancient persons considered essential to religious satisfaction.

The third chapter in this section, by Roger Beck, also is appreciative of Stark's overall effort to account sociologically for the rise of Christianity in the religious marketplace of the Roman Empire. What bothers Beck is the way in which this account fails adequately to represent the pagan competition. Christianity's success becomes, in Stark's depiction of the ancient world, at best a triumph over a straw man and, at worst, a nonsensical set of assertions. Stark may well describe, even persuasively, various aspects of early Christianity through comparison with new religious movements in modern North America and Europe. But because Stark fails to grasp key aspects of especially public paganism in the Roman Empire, his explanation of Christianity's success in this realm is deemed not to be entirely successful.

The final essay, by Leif E. Vaage, does not discuss, in any detail, a specific aspect of Stark's work or its possible improvement. Rather, in explicit contrast to the sociological explanations favoured by Stark and his theoretical co-religionists, an essentially discursive reason for Christianity's success as the chosen faith of Roman rule is suggested. Without denying the role that sociological and other factors undoubtedly played in constructing the historical script of emerging Christian hegemony, these elements were able to contribute to such an outcome, it is proposed, only because such a script was already sufficiently composed and operative in the centuries before titular domain finally was achieved. The main purpose of this concluding chapter is to argue that it was especially how earliest Christianity *resisted* Roman rule, which made it such a probable successor to the eternal kingdom.

Abbreviations

AJAH	*American Journal of Ancient History*
AJP	*American Journal of Philology*
ANF	The Ante-Nicene Fathers
ANRW	*Aufstieg und Niedergang der römischen Welt,* ed. H. Temporini and W. Haase. Berlin: Walter de Gruyter, 1972–.
ARW	*Archiv für Religionswissenschaft*
BDF	Blass, Debrunner, and Funk's *Greek Grammar of the New Testament*
BETL	Bibliotheca Ephemeridum Theologicarum Lovaniensium
BibOr	Biblica et orientalia
BJS	Brown Judaic Studies
CBQ	*Catholic Biblical Quarterly*
CErc	*Cronache Ercolanesi*
CP	*Classical Philology*
CRAIBL	*Comptes rendus de l'Académie des inscriptions et belles-lettres*
CSCT	Columbia Studies in the Classical Tradition
EA	*Electronic Archive of Greek and Latin Epigraphy*
EMA	Europe in the Middle Ages
ERT	*Evangelical Review of Theology*
ESCJ	Studies in Christianity and Judaism / Études sur le christianisme et le judaïsme
HCS	Hellenistic Culture and Society
HTR	*Harvard Theological Review*
HUCA	*Hebrew Union College Annual*
IEJ	*Israel Exploration Journal*
JAAR	*Journal of the American Academy of Religion*
JAC	*Jahrbuch für Antike und Christentum*
JBL	*Journal of Biblical Literature*

JECS	*Journal of Early Christian Studies*
JEH	*Journal of Ecclesiastical History*
JMS	*Journal of Mithraic Studies*
JQR	*Jewish Quarterly Review*
JRA	*Journal of Roman Archaeology*
JRS	*Journal of Roman Studies*
JSJ	*Journal for the Study of Judaism in the Persian, Hellenistic and Roman Period*
JSNT	*Journal for the Study of the New Testament*
JSNTSup	*Journal for the Study of the New Testament,* Supplement Series
JSOT	*Journal for the Study of the Old Testament*
JSPA	Jewish Publication Society of America
JSPS	*Journal for the Study of the Pseudepigrapha,* Supplement Series
JTSA	Jewish Theological Seminary of America
JTS	*Journal of Theological Studies*
LEC	Library of Early Christianity
MDAI(A)	*Mitteilungen des deutschen archäologischen Instituts. Athenische Abteilung*
NovT	*Novum Testamentum*
NovTSup	*Novum Testamentum* Supplements
NTS	*New Testament Studies*
OLZ	*Orientalistische Literaturzeitung*
PCPS	*Proceedings of the Cambridge Philological Society*
PG	J. Migne, *Patrologia graeca*
PRS	*Perspectives in Religious Studies*
REG	*Revue des études grecques*
RelSRev	*Religious Studies Review*
RevExp	*Review and Expositor*
RIBLA	*Revista de interpretação bíblica latino-americana*
SBLDS	Society of Biblical Literature Dissertation Series
SBLSP	Society of Biblical Literature Seminar Papers
SBT	Studies in Biblical Theology
SJLA	Studies in Judaism in Late Antiquity
SNTSMS	Society for New Testament Studies Monograph Series
SPB	Studia Post Biblica
SPCK	Society for Promoting Christian Knowledge
SR	*Studies in Religion / Sciences religieuses*
TDNT	*Theological Dictionary of the New Testament*
ThLZ	*Theologischen Literaturzeitung*
TJT	*Toronto Journal of Theology*
TWNT	*Theologisches Wörterbuch zum Neuen Testament,* ed. Gerhard Kittel and Gerhard Friedrich, 11 vols., Stuttgart: Kohlhammer, 1932–79
WUNT	Wissenschaftliche Untersuchungen zum Neuen Testament
ZEE	*Zeitschrift für Evangelische Ethik*
ZNW	*Zeitschrift für die Neutestamentliche Wissenschaft und die Kunde der Alteren Kirche*
ZPE	*Zeitschrift für Papyrologie und Epigraphik*
ZST	*Zeitschrift für systematische Theologie*

Part I

RIVALRIES?

1

Ancient Religious Rivalries and the Struggle for Success

Christians, Jews, and Others
in the Early Roman Empire

Leif E. Vaage

INTRODUCTION

This chapter was initially written in 1994 to suggest both a rationale and a few possible lines of inquiry for a seminar of the Canadian Society of Biblical Studies (CSBS), which would focus on the question of religious rivalries in different urban settings of the early Roman Empire. The chapter is thus essentially a list of leading questions. It will also become apparent that my own particular interests and competencies lie in the field of earliest Christianities. This angle of vision is certainly not the only perspective, and conceivably not even the best one, from which to define such a conversation. Nonetheless, because a decidedly Christian, viz. Protestant view of things has shaped historical research in the area, it has still seemed useful to introduce the following studies with a critique of certain stock features of that traditional perspective.

EDWARD GIBBON

The eventual success of Christianity in becoming the official religion of the Roman Empire is an historical phenomenon that has been variously celebrated and lamented but still remains inadequately understood. Typically, the fact of Christianity's emergence as the empire's dominant persuasion is construed *mutatis mutandis* either as the inevitable triumph of a compelling truth (albeit initially ignored and benightedly disparaged) or as due to the opportunistic chicanery of politically astute but otherwise quite conventional believers (a.k.a. the deceived and the deceivers). Edward Gibbon's well-known magnum opus, *History of the Decline and Fall of the Roman Empire* (1776–1788), specifically, the two chapters (15–16) in Volume One dedicated to "the progress and establishment of Christianity," may well serve as a symbolic point of departure for an assessment of this modern scholarly tradition.

Understanding Gibbon himself is not my purpose here. Nonetheless, it is clear that an assessment of Gibbon's own social history would be relevant to any critical examination of his view of Mediterranean antiquity. In my opinion, for example, a notable contrast exists between Gibbon's general enthusiasm for life in the Roman republic and early Roman Empire (under the Antonines) and the rather fussy genteelness of Gibbon's own personal existence (beyond what Gibbon writes in his autobiography, see, e.g., Joyce 1953; de Beer 1968). Gibbon's own account of how he conceived the project that became his *History of the Decline and Fall of the Roman Empire* is remarkably short and uninformative (see Bonnard 1966, 136f); though, on more than one occasion, Gibbon did revise this account for maximum symbolic effect (Bonnard 1966, 304f; the significance of these revisions has been dismissed by Ghosh 1997, 283).

Writing with evident irony—yet, in my judgment, very much within the reigning convictions that Gibbon affected no longer seriously to entertain—the renowned historian proposed:

A candid but rational inquiry into the progress and establishment of Christianity may be considered as a very essential part of the history of the Roman Empire....Our curiosity is naturally prompted to inquire by what means the Christian faith obtained so remarkable a victory over the established religions of the earth. To this inquiry an obvious but satisfactory answer may be returned, that it was owing to the convincing evidence of the doctrine itself and to the ruling providence of its great Author. But as truth and reason seldom find so favourable a reception in the world, and as the wisdom of Providence frequently condescends to use the passions of the human heart and the general circumstances of mankind as instruments to execute its purpose, we may still be permitted (though with becoming submission) to ask, not indeed what were the first, but what were the secondary causes of the rapid growth of the Christian church? It will, perhaps, appear that it was most effectually favoured and assisted by the five following causes: I. The inflexible and, if we may use the expression, the intolerant zeal of the Christians—derived, it is true, from the Jewish religion but purified from the narrow and unsocial spirit which, instead of inviting, had deterred the Gentiles from embracing the law of Moses. II. The doctrine of a future life, improved by every additional circumstance which could give weight and efficacy to that important truth. III. The miraculous powers ascribed to the primitive church. IV. The pure and austere morals of the Christians. V. The union and discipline of the Christian republic, which gradually formed an independent and increasing state in the heart of the Roman Empire. (Saunders 1952, 260–62)

Each of the secondary causes that Gibbon ascribes to Christianity's eventual success can be debated. Certainly, for example, Gibbon's characterization of "the Jewish religion" as having a "narrow and unsocial spirit which, instead of inviting, had deterred the Gentiles from embracing the law of Moses," is completely unacceptable and has generally been reversed in modern scholarship. In his description of ancient Judaism, Gibbon appears merely to repeat traditional-contemporary European-Christian stereotypes. At the same time, Gibbon elsewhere observes with abiding perspicacity:

> There is the strongest reason to believe that before the reigns of Diocletian and Constantine the faith of Christ had been preached in every province and in all the great cities of the empire; but the foundation of the several congregations, the numbers of the faithful who composed them, and their proportion to the unbelieving multitude are now buried in obscurity or disguised by fiction and declamation.…The rich provinces that extend from the Euphrates to the Ionian Sea [i.e., Syria and Asia Minor] were the principal theatre on which the apostle of the Gentiles displayed his zeal and piety. The seeds of the Gospel, which he had scattered in a fertile soil, were diligently cultivated by his disciples; and it should seem that, during the first two centuries, the most considerable body of Christians was contained within those limits. (Saunders 1952, 309–10)

> The progress of Christianity was not confined to the Roman Empire; and, according to the primitive fathers, who interpret facts by prophecy, the new religion, within a century after the death of its Divine Author, had already visited every part of the globe.…But neither the belief nor the wishes of the fathers can alter the truth of history. It will remain an undoubted fact that the barbarians of Scythia and Germany, who afterwards subverted the Roman monarchy, were involved in the darkness of paganism, and that even the conversion of Iberia, of Armenia, or of AEthiopia was not attempted with any degree of success till the sceptre was in the hands of an orthodox emperor. Before that time the various accidents of war and commerce might indeed diffuse an imperfect knowledge of the Gospel among the tribes of Caledonia and among the borderers of the Rhine, the Danube, and the Euphrates. Beyond the last-mentioned river, Edessa was distinguished by a firm and early adherence to the faith. From Edessa the principles of Christianity were

easily introduced into the Greek and Syrian cities which obeyed the successors of Artaxerxes; but they do not appear to have made any deep impression on the minds of the Persians, whose religious system, by the labours of a well-disciplined order of priests, had been constructed with much more art and solidity than the uncertain mythology of Greece and Rome. (Saunders 1952, 316–17)

However foreign or distressingly familiar the cultural mindset may be within which Gibbon first penned these remarks, the transparency of his prose and the directness of his reasoning yet raise as effectively as any later historian's work a series of still unanswered questions. For example:

- What is the significance of the fact that, for at least two centuries (until approximately 180 CE) and effectively well into a third, there is no extant material (apart from literary) evidence of Christianity as a distinct socio-religious phenomenon, since the first two centuries of self-definition and growth remain "buried in obscurity or disguised by fiction and declamation"?
- Was Christianity during the first two centuries essentially, as Gibbon proposes, a religion of Asia Minor and (northern) Syria and, therefore, properly should be described in these terms, namely, as another—though by no means the most obvious or most vigorous—instance of the variable religious life of the diverse civic cultures of this region?
- If Gibbon is correct that until "the sceptre was in the hands of an orthodox emperor," Christianity did not succeed in establishing itself beyond the bounds of the ancient civilized (non-barbarian, Roman) world—perhaps because no serious effort had been made to promote it elsewhere—what conclusions, if any, should be drawn from this fact vis-à-vis the reputed missionary character of early Christianity?
- Does Gibbon's statement about the introduction of Christianity among the barbarians also hold true for Christianizing the Roman Empire, namely, that it was simply "the various accidents of war and commerce" which first "diffuse[d] an imperfect knowledge of the Gospel" throughout the Mediterranean basin before Constantine?
- What made it possible, or even likely, that a city like Edessa should be "distinguished by a firm and early adherence to the faith" in the midst of an otherwise disinterested culture? Was Christianity's success within the Roman Empire (versus, say, among the Persians) ultimately due to "the uncertain mythology of Greece and Rome"; in the words of Arthur Darby Nock, the fact that there was "in these [pagan] rivals of Judaism and Christianity no possibility of anything which can be called conversion" (1933, 14)? Nock, however, goes on to observe: "In fact the only context

in which we find [conversion] in ancient paganism is that of philosophy, which held a clear concept of two types of life, a higher and a lower, and which exhorted men to turn from the one to the other" (1933, 14). Perhaps we should seek another reason.

ADOLF VON HARNACK

In the preface to his seminal work, *The Mission and Expansion of Christianity in the First Three Centuries,* Adolf von Harnack claimed: "No monograph has yet been devoted to the mission and spread of the Christian religion during the first three centuries of our era" (1908, vii). Before Harnack's work, it is said, there were only myths of origin: "The primitive history of the church's mission lies buried in legend; or rather, it has been replaced by a tendentious history of what is alleged to have happened in the course of a few decades throughout every country on the face of the earth....But the worthless character of this history is now recognised on all sides" (1908, vii, slightly modified; cf. MacMullen 1981, 206n. 16: "so far as I know [Harnack's work] is the last [devoted to this subject]—certainly still standard").

This claim is patently ridiculous, once we acknowledge that the nineteenth-century German liberal academic understanding of the past is every bit as much "a tendentious history" as are, for example, the narrative of Christian beginnings in the canonical Acts of the Apostles or the triumphal account of Christian origins by Eusebius of Caesarea. Nonetheless, Harnack's claim to originality underscores the relative recentness of the scholarly recognition that early Christianity's success within the Roman Empire was hardly as assured as Gibbon's earlier (however ironical) reference to "the convincing evidence of the doctrine itself and...the ruling providence of its great Author" plainly, if playfully, presupposed. Furthermore, Harnack's claim also makes clear why Gibbon's so-called "secondary causes of the rapid growth of the Christian church" have now become of primary interest.

Unlike Gibbon's characterization of the Jewish religion as "narrow and unsocial," Harnack a century or so later begins his work by describing "the diffusion and limits" of Judaism as the crucial historical factor that both made possible and underwrote early Christianity's eventual success. The language of mission is used by Harnack as though it were a self-evident category for historical description:

> To the Jewish mission which preceded it, the Christian mission was indebted, in the first place, for a field tilled all over the empire; in the second place, for religious communities already formed everywhere in the towns; thirdly, for what Axenfeld calls "the help of materials" fur-

nished by the preliminary knowledge of the Old Testament, in addition
to catechetical and liturgical materials which could be employed without much alteration; fourthly, for the habit of regular worship and a
control of private life; fifthly, for an impressive apologetic on behalf of
monotheism, historical theology, and ethics; and finally, for the feeling
that self-diffusion was a duty. The amount of this debt is so large, that
one might venture to claim the Christian mission as a continuation of
the Jewish propaganda. "Judaism," said Renan, "was robbed of its due
reward by a generation of fanatics, and it was prevented from gathering in the harvest which it had prepared." (Harnack 1908, 15)

To nascent Christianity the synagogues in the Diaspora meant more
than the *fontes persecutionum* of Tertullian's complaint; they also formed
the most important presupposition for the rise and growth of Christian
communities throughout the empire. The network of the synagogues furnished the Christian propaganda with centres and courses for its development, and in this way the mission of the new religion, which was
undertaken in the name of the God of Abraham and Moses, found a
sphere already prepared for itself. (Harnack 1908, 1)

It is surprising that a religion which raised so stout a wall of partition
between itself and all other religions, and which in practice and prospects
alike was bound up so closely with its nation [*Volkstum*], should have possessed [in the diaspora] a missionary impulse of such vigour and attained
so large a measure of success. This is not ultimately to be explained by
any craving for power or ambition; it is a proof that Judaism, as a religion, through external influence and internal transformation was already
expanding, and becoming a cross [*Mittelding*] between a national religion
[*Volksreligion*] and a world-religion (confession of faith and a church).
(Harnack 1908, 9; modified)

The duty and the hopefulness of mission are brought out in the earliest Jewish Sibylline books. Almost the whole of the literature of Alexandrian Judaism has an apologetic and propagandistic tendency. (Harnack
1908, 9n. 3; slightly modified)

While all this was of the utmost importance for the Christian mission
which came afterwards, at least equal moment attaches to one vital
omission [*empfindliche Lücke*] in the Jewish missionary preaching: viz.,
that no Gentile, in the first generation at least, could become a real son
of Abraham. His rank before God remained inferior. Thus it also
remained very doubtful how far any proselyte—to say nothing of the
"God-fearing"—had a share in the glorious promises of the future. The
religion which repairs this omission [*diese Lücke ausfüllen*] will drive
Judaism from the field [*aus dem Felde schlagen*]. (Harnack 1908, 12–13)

Again, Harnack's description of ancient Judaism is hardly sufficient. To suggest, for example, as Harnack does in the last citation, that Christianity succeeded where Judaism failed, is, to say the least, a lamentable lapse into the worst sort of traditional dogmatic Christian historiography. Also dubious is Harnack's assumption (though hardly his alone) that there actually was such a thing as a Jewish mission. Harnack presumes that the presence of Jewish communities throughout the ancient Mediterranean world as well as the fact that some Gentiles did become Jews, the possibility of proselytes, and the writing of apologetic literature, all support such a conclusion. None of this is self-evident, however, not to mention the Hegelian conception of history, which seems to lurk within Harnack's reference to early Judaism as "a cross [*Mittelding*] between a national religion [*Volksreligion*] and a world-religion (confession of faith and a church)."

FORGET "MISSION"

The simple and unchecked use of terms such as mission, missionary, and preaching for conversion does not account for the eventual spread and social advancement of early Christianity within the ancient Mediterranean world. In this section, I focus my critique on use of the category of mission. Equally dubious, however, are other correlate notions as well. The use of such terminology assumes that there was a special Christian message (*Botschaft*, gospel, *kerygma*) to be proclaimed. Again, this is hardly self-evident. In what follows, I hope to demonstrate why such assumptions are historically dubious. A number of other questions will then become pressing. For example:

• How would we tell the story of the prolonged—and, in many ways, never resolved—internecine struggles between Jews, Christians, and other religious groups during the first two centuries CE, if we were self-consciously to eliminate or bracket out of our narrative and explanatory vocabulary all references to a mission of any sort on the part not only of pagans and Jews but also of early Christians?
• In which ways would a social history of the diverse relations between Jews, Christians, and other religious groups, in different cities of the early Roman Empire, shorn of all teleological assurances, change our description of this formative phase?

One result of recent research into Jewish and Christian beginnings is a renewed awareness of so-called paganism's continuing appeal and ongoing vitality in late antiquity (e.g., Lane Fox 1986). The polemic of early Christian and Jewish writers against the ritual practices and social mores of their cultural counterparts no longer appears to historians of the period to be especially representative of life on the ground for most persons—Christians, Jews, and others—in the ancient Mediterranean world. According to Ramsay MacMullen and Eugene N. Lane:

> The emergence of Christianity from the tangled mass of older religious beliefs, eventually to a position of unchallenged superiority, is surely the most important single phenomenon that can be discerned in the closing centuries of the ancient world. In its impact on the way life was to be lived thereafter in the West, it outmatches even the decline of Rome itself....It must be said in criticism of [previous books on this subject], however, that they make little or no mention of the body in which Christianity grew—as if obstetrics were limited to passing references in a handbook on babies. How about the mother? Will she not help determine the manner in which the child enters the world and, to some extent, its shape and nature? (MacMullen and Lane 1992, vii)

Regarding Harnack's *The Mission and Expansion of Christianity in the First Three Centuries,* MacMullen observes: "It is justly admired for its scholarship. Among its thousands of references to sources, however, I can find not one to a pagan source and hardly a line indicating the least attempt to find out what non-Christians thought and believed" (1981, 206n. 16). Already Nock in his seminal study, *Conversion,* had contended:

> We cannot understand the success of Christianity outside Judaea without making an effort to determine the elements in the mind of the time to which it appealed....In the first place, there was in this world very little that corresponded to a return to the faith of one's fathers as we know it. Except in the last phase of paganism, when the success of Christianity had put it on the defensive and caused it to fight for its existence, there was no traditional religion which was an entity with a theology and an organization. Classical Greek has no word which covers religion as we use the term. *Eusebeia* approximates to it, but in essence it means no more than the regular performance of due worship in the proper spirit, while *hosiotes* describes ritual purity in all its aspects. The place of faith was taken by myth and ritual. These things implied an attitude rather than a conviction [viz., conversion]. (Nock 1933, 10)

> *Soteria* and kindred words carried no theological implications; they applied to deliverance from perils by sea and land and disease and darkness and false opinions [and war], all perils of which men were fully aware. (Nock 1933, 9)

> These external circumstances [of conquest and invasion and contact between foreign groups] led not to any definite crossing of religious

frontiers, in which an old spiritual home was left for a new once and for all, but to men's having one foot on each side of a fence which was cultural and not creedal. They led to an acceptance of new worships as useful supplements and not as substitutes, and they did not involve the taking of a new way of life in place of the old. This we may call adhesion, in contradistinction to conversion. By conversion we mean the reorientation of the soul of an individual, his deliberate turning from indifference or from an earlier form of piety to another, a turning which implies a consciousness that a great change is involved, that the old was wrong and the new is right. It is seen at its fullest in the positive response of a man to the choice set before me by the prophetic religions [i.e., Judaism and Christianity]. (Nock 1933, 6–7)

Nock immediately continues: "We know this best from the history of modern Christianity" (1933, 7). Then, at the beginning of the next paragraph, Nock refers to William James, whose theoretical framework in *The Varieties of Religious Experience* (1902) is certainly psychological, if not simply modern American Protestant. To his credit, nonetheless, Nock swiftly notes: "We must not, however, expect to find exact analogies for [James's description of the experience of conversion] beyond the range of countries with a long-standing Christian tradition" (1933, 8). In fact, a subsequent essay by Nock, "Conversion and Adolescence," demonstrates how the association "in modern times" between adolescence and "some sort of moral and religious crisis" (i.e., conversion) was not true for Greco-Roman antiquity (1986).

The correlation of conversion with adolescence is actually not explicitly a postulate of James but, rather, had been suggested earlier by Edwin Diller Starbuck (1915, 28–48) on the basis of data that are decidedly American Protestant (evangelical) in nature. Even so, Starbuck himself noted that inductions made on this basis "are not necessarily true for savages or statesmen or Catholics or persons living in a different historical epoch" (1915, 13).

Nock is at his best, it seems to me, when he describes the specific cultural concerns and the open-ended or unorchestrated aspects of the different social and religious practices of ancient paganism. Nonetheless, Nock is quite untrustworthy, in my opinion, in his evaluation of the significance of the difference between these concerns and practices and those of "the prophetic religions" of Judaism and Christianity; if only because of the psychological theory of religion, which appears to inform Nock's critical assessment of ancient paganism's relative strengths and weaknesses, as well as the lingering Christian bias of Nock's use of the category of prophetic (cf. Nock 1933, 10, 15–16). According to Nock:

This contrast is clear. Judaism and Christianity demanded renunciation and a new start. They demanded not merely acceptance of a rite, but the adhesion of the will to a theology, in a word faith, a new life in a new people. It is wholly unhistorical to compare Christianity and Mithraism as Renan did, and to suggest that if Christianity had died Mithraism might have conquered the world. It might and would have won plenty of adherents, but it could not have founded a holy Mithraic church throughout the world. A man used Mithraism, but he did not belong to it body and soul; if he did, that was a matter of special attachment and not an inevitable concomitant prescribed by authority. (Nock 1933, 14)

In reply to Nock, we might agree that, indeed, it is wholly unhistorical to compare Christianity and Mithraism *as Renan did*. But, it seems to me, to observe that Mithraism before 325 CE "might and would have won plenty of adherents"; to compare the means and manner of this appeal to those of Christianity; and to analyze the reasons why one group (Christianity) finally came to garner imperial favour, while the other (Mithraism) did not, especially in light of the close link of the latter to the Roman military, is about as properly historical an investigation as one could imagine. Moreover, is the way in which "a man used Mithraism" finally so different from the way(s) in which most men and women in antiquity "used" Christianity or Judaism?

In this regard, the only significant difference between Mithraism and the so-called prophetic religions of Judaism and Christianity might be the fact that those in Judaism and Christianity, such as Paul or the rabbis, with a putatively special attachment to their faith, succeeded in having their specific claims to authority and their conviction of the need to "belong body and soul" to their particular persuasion preserved in writing through an enduring social institution. Conversely, the conceivably similar schemes and desires of other pagan priests and cultic leaders—that they, too, would continue to enjoy the active loyalty of their devotees; that these persons would participate regularly in the life of a given cult and contribute financially to its ongoing maintenance; that their group would obtain and retain wider social recognition ranging from a certain minimal respectability and local influence to a more generalized hegemony or monopoly—simply failed to leave a comparable trace.[1]

---

1 Cf. *P.Lond.* 27101. 14, which forbids a member of the cult of Zeus Hypsistos "to leave the brotherhood of the president for another" (*meid' ap[o]chôreise[in ek] tês tou hêg[ou]menou phratras eis heteran phratran*). See, further, Roberts, Skeat, and Nock (1936, 52) for discussion of the term *phratra* in this inscription.

To suggest that Judaism and Christianity were distinguished by "the adhesion of the will to a theology, in a word, faith, a new life in a new people," utterly obscures the fact of active or, at least, interactive participation by members of both groups in the regular round of ancient urban life. Far from being an exceptional case or merely a problem of neophyte misunderstanding, the situation faced by Paul, for example, in 1 Corinthians 8–10 with the question of food-offered-to-idols eloquently testifies to the ongoing cultural ties that still existed between some early Christians and their non-Christian, non-Jewish neighbours in ancient Corinth. These ties, moreover, likely were less a function of the general ubiquity of so-called idols than of the enduring human desire, unabated under Roman imperial rule, to eat well whenever possible. Likewise, Paul's letter to the Galatians attests a similar proximity between some early Christians in this region and the cultural traditions of early Judaism. In his letter to the Romans, Paul reveals his own lingering sense of identification with the same tradition.

On the other hand: "Of any organized or conscious evangelizing in paganism there are very few signs indeed, though it is often alleged; of any god whose cult required or had anything ordinarily to say about evangelizing there is no sign at all" (MacMullen 1981, 98–99). There is, perhaps, some evidence of debate with other perspectives, the effort to persuade, a certain self-promotion, even the advertisement of assorted wares for sale. But, again, none of this reveals more than ordinary human social life. One can hardly speak of a pagan mission in antiquity; unless, maximally, as Nock notes: "in the last phase of paganism, when the success of Christianity had put it on the defensive and caused it to fight for its existence" (1933, 10).

One might ask: What, then, made the social-religious practices of paganism and, specifically, participation in and identification with the group-life of different voluntary religious associations, so appealing to their members? One obvious answer is *philotimia* (cf. 1Thess. 4:11; Rom. 15:20), i.e., the opportunity these groups and their diverse habits gave to acquire honour to persons who apparently did not or could not hope to succeed so otherwise. Other possible motivations include the ubiquitous desire for "salvation" or bodily health and healing as well as personal improvement, including vengeance, justice, the avoidance of natural and other disasters, increased social power, even consolation in the face of death. In addition, there were sometimes explicit economic benefits: a guaranteed loan, if needed, and burial, when needed (though not likely in excess of actual financial contributions). To be a priest in a given cult was evidently profitable. At least, the purchase and resale of these activities were routinely regulated, suggesting some sort of marketable commodity. Finally, it has been suggested: "The reasons why people found associations attractive were doubtless many, but we should never underestimate the basic and instinctive desire of most people to socialize with those with whom they share things in common—devotion to a deity, a trade or skill, a similar background, or even just a love of eating and drinking in good company" (Wilson 1996, 14).

After the destruction of the temple in Jerusalem and the subsequent failure of the Bar Kochba rebellion, both early Judaism and early Christianity stood at the beginning of a protracted struggle to define, defend, and reproduce themselves in the face of other cultures, within which the adherents of these religions were obliged to live. Although the process was certainly marked by growing Christian claims to constitute the new "true Israel," including how properly to read the sacred scriptures shared between these two traditions, there is also evidence in rabbinic literature of another ongoing debate between the emergent arbiters of Jewish identity and the surrounding pagan culture(s) as well. The following questions suggest themselves:

• What do the repeated polemical references in rabbinic literature to "Epicureans," or the multiple Greek and Latin loan words in Talmudic Hebrew, suggest about the types of cultural conversations in which developing Judaism was engaged at the time (see, e.g., Fischel 1969; Luz 1989)?
• Is there a Jewish apologetic literature written after 132 CE with only a pagan audience—i.e., no Christians—in view? If not, why not? If so, how does Jewish apologetic literature compare with parallel Christian efforts to persuade Jews and pagans, viz. other early Christians of the truth and righteousness of (orthodox) Christianity?
• Is there any evidence of a desire on the part of early Judaism to increase the number of persons identified as Jews by attracting adherents from "all the nations" in which communities of Jews could then be found? If not, why not?

Martin Goodman's seminal article, "Jewish Proselytizing in the First Century" (1992; cf. Goodman 1994), argues: "On examination...the evidence for an active mission by first-century Jews to win proselytes is very weak. I think that it is possible to go further and to suggest that there are positive reasons to deny the existence of such a mission" (Goodman 1992, 70). According to Goodman, this is to be contrasted:

> with developments within Judaism later in antiquity. At some time in the second or third century [not unlike paganism on the defensive, as

Nock described it] some Jews seem to have begun looking for converts in just the way they were apparently not doing in the first century....The missionary hero in search of converts for Judaism is a phenomenon first attested well after the start of the Christian mission, not before it. There is no good reason to suppose that any Jew would have seen value in seeking proselytes in the first century with an enthusiasm like that of the Christian apostles. The origins of the missionary impulse within the Church should be sought elsewhere. (Goodman 1992, 74–77)

Whether or not Goodman is correct in his statements about "the Christian mission"—Goodman's conventional claims in this regard merely serve as a foil for his more competent and balanced description of early Judaism— he does make a compelling case against the earlier assumption by Harnack and others that:

the idea of a mission to convert was inherited by the early Jesus movement from contemporary Judaism. I should make it clear that I do not doubt either that Jews firmly believed in their role as religious mentors of the Gentile world or that Jews expected that in the last days the Gentiles would in fact come to recognize the glory of God and divine rule on earth. But the desire to encourage admiration of the Jewish way of life or respect for the Jewish God, or to inculcate general ethical behaviour in other peoples, or such pious hope for the future, should be clearly distinguished from an impulse to draw non-Jews into Judaism....It is likely enough, then, that Jews welcomed sincere proselytes in the first century. But passive acceptance is quite different from active mission. (Goodman 1992, 53–55)

Thus, pagans, according to MacMullen, did not evangelize, and, according to Goodman, there is no history of a Jewish mission. Nonetheless, it remains self-evident to these and other scholars that early Christians somehow did evangelize and had such a mission. For example, MacMullen nonchalantly writes: "With Gnosticism, however, we approach the Judaeo-Christian tradition, in which despatch of emissaries from a central organization, and other formal aspects of missionary activity, were perfectly at home" (1981, 98). And Goodman begins his essay with the confident assertion: "Other religions spread either because worshippers moved or because non-adherents happened to find them attractive. Christianity spread primarily because many Christians believed that it was positively desirable for non-Christians to join their faith and accrete to their congregations. It is my belief that no parallel to the early Christian mission was to be found in the ancient world in the first century" (1992, 53; cf. Goodman 1994, 91–108).

Is this, in fact, true? Not whether there is any parallel in the ancient world to "the early Christian mission" but, rather, whether there ever was such a thing as "early Christian mission." It is clear that, virtually from the beginning, early Christianity did find adherents across the customary ancient divides of social class or status and ethnicity. Within a generation, early Christianity appears to have included, among its diverse constituencies, persons of disparate origin. The concrete reasons for this state of affairs, however, remain to be determined.

I have tried to formulate the preceding paragraph as precisely as possible. For it is not at all obvious, at least to me, however zealous later Christians may have been about the ultimate truth and authority of their particular view of things, that this persuasion, for the first century or two of its existence, programmatically sought or even thought about seeking to convert the known world or a significant percentage of it "to Christ." While Christianity plainly emerged, developed, and spread throughout the Mediterranean basin, that it did so, within the confines of the Roman Empire, intentionally or self-consciously as a particular social (political; philosophical) project, with the recruitment of new members as a founding feature of its official purpose, is anything but clear. Again, I say this because it is precisely this sort of unargued assumption that, in turn, tends to make self-evident the highly questionable historical judgments about early Christianity's predictable, inevitable, understandable, probable, reasonable subsequent success.

This would be true, in my opinion, also for Paul, who otherwise describes himself, albeit only in Galatians and Romans, as Christ's emissary to the Gentiles. Unfortunately, I cannot develop here the argument that will be required to dismantle the prevailing view of the apostle Paul as early Christianity's first great missionary. At the same time, the issue is obviously important—indeed, crucial—to the usual scholarly imagination of the different ways in which Jews, Christians, and others in the early Roman Empire related to one another and to the larger social world(s) surrounding them. For this reason, in my judgment, we ought to find extremely interesting and cause for further reflection what John T. Townsend reports in his article, "Missionary Journeys in Acts and European Missionary Societies" (1985). According to Townsend, there is no evidence, before the preface to Acts in the first edition of J.A. Bengel's *Gnomon Novi Testamenti* (1742), that any previous Christian reader or commentator on the narratives of Paul's travels in Acts ever thought to observe, in the sequence of Paul's various encounters and diverse experiences, a series of intentional missionary journeys:

What is true of ancient writers is also true of those belonging to a later age. Neither Erasmus (c. 1466–1536) nor John Calvin (1509–64) nor Theodore Beze (1519–1605) nor Cornelius à Lapide (1567–1637) nor Hugo Grotius (1583–1645) interpreted Acts in terms of the traditional [three-fold] missionary journeys. In fact, the earliest reference that I can find to these journeys is in the first edition of J.A. Bengel's *Gnomon Novi Testamenti*....In the years following the first edition of *Gnomon* most writers on Acts adopted a missionary-journey pattern. It found its way into the major commentaries, including those of J.H. Heinrichs, H.A.W. Meyer, and H. Alford. Thus, by the middle of the century the three-missionary journey system had become firmly established in the exegetical tradition of Acts. Why should a missionary-journey pattern have been imposed on Acts at this time? A likely answer is that commentators were reading their own presuppositions back into apostolic times. The eighteenth and nineteenth centuries saw an escalation of Western missionary activity. It was an era for founding missionary societies....Since it was standard missionary practice for evangelists to operate out of a home base, one should not be surprised at the exegetical assumption that Paul, the great missionary of the New Testament, had done the same. (Townsend 1985, 436–37)

Whatever the actual relations were between Christians, Jews, and others in the different cities of the early Roman Empire; however these groups and persons must have engaged in diverse and reciprocal struggles for social and religious success; it seems unlikely that any of them, including early Christianity, did so with any sort of mission in mind. What, then, each of these persuasions did imagine it was doing locally, and how each of them would have understood its defining activities vis-à-vis the parallel presence and similar endeavours of contiguous groups in a given urban environment, is one of the principal topics to be addressed in the investigations to follow.

WHAT IF...

No social group or movement succeeds in persisting without a certain critical mass of committed participants or adherents. In order to survive, all social groups and movements must attract and retain a certain number of persons willing and able to be identified, on a given occasion, as part of group x versus group y or z. If only for this reason, the demographic fact of an always limited number of potential and desirable participants (however great this number might be) in the life of a specific social group, together with the need to claim a minimum number of such persons as one's own in order to assure the group's continuing social reproduction, and the likely possibility that a greater number of members will mean heightened prestige and social power for the group, already account for a certain level of constant struggle and agonistic competition with other groups at the heart of every ancient (religious) group's social existence.

To acknowledge the presence of multiple persuasions in a given cultural context necessarily includes the affirmation of some constitutive conflict between them. What remains to be determined—this is, perhaps, the most important consideration ethically and historically—is exactly how the predictable clashes of desire and asserted propriety are concretely negotiated.

There is no such thing as a totally open social group without boundaries or some sense of who its others are; which is to say, the excluded, alienated, disinterested, despite whom and/or versus whom the group in question has been constituted as such. At the same time, it is obviously a matter of great consequence exactly how, in a given cultural setting, different social groups or subgroups choose to coexist or compete with one another. More specifically, to what degree is the ongoing existence of one group imagined to require or to benefit rather than to suffer harm from the restriction or defeat or even the extinction of the others? How much unresolved or explicit difference between groups is perceived to be socially sustainable or desirable in a given place?

One way in which to address this topic—the generic problem of alternate social (religious) identities—has been to discuss it as a question of religious propaganda (see, e.g., Wendland 1972, 75–96; Schüssler Fiorenza 1976). To the extent that use of the category of propaganda effectively means mission, all further discussion along these lines necessarily reverts to the analysis of the previous section. The topic of propaganda could be understood, however, as a question of self-representation: both how a given group imagined that it ought to be seen by others (apologetics) as well as how others are habitually represented by it, which is to say, how the group imagines that those not itself ought to be viewed (polemics).

Regarding apologetic literature, I find it quite unlikely that such writing ever actually has as part of its original readership many persons beyond the group whose specific interests it so obviously articulates and defends. Apologetic literature customarily is written, of course, with an inquiring or hostile outsider as its ideal interlocutor, whose questions ostensibly set the agenda of the discussion. But the logic of the reasoning and the adequacy of the answers given in these texts are generally compelling only to those already committed in some fashion to the truth of the apologetic position. Justin Martyr's *Dialogue with Trypho,* for example, hardly appealed to Jews, let alone persuaded them to practice Christianity. In this regard, religious propaganda is essentially a means of self-definition; and its social success, a function of efficacy, by doing the job best which people want done in this or that way. Thus we might ask: What made Christianity or Judaism or any other ancient religious group the more satisfying option, in a given moment, for their committed practitioners?

In this vein, yet another way in which to address the issue of shifting social success by Christians, Jews, and others in the early Roman Empire has been to focus on how change in allegiance or taste occurred, sometimes described (unhelpfully, in my opinion) as conversion. Why did a particular group or person, at a given moment in their social life, choose identification, more or less exclusively, with a new religious practice instead of merely trying it out and/or assimilating it to a prior pattern of behaviour? According to Nock:

> The success of Christianity is the success of an institution which united the sacramentalism and the philosophy of the time. It satisfied the inquiring turn of mind, the desire for escape from Fate, the desire for security in the hereafter; like Stoicism, it gave a way of life and made man at home in the universe, but unlike Stoicism it did this for the ignorant as well as for the lettered. It satisfied also social needs and it secured men against loneliness. Its way was not easy; it made uncompromising demands on those who would enter and would continue to live in the brotherhood, but to those who did not fail it offered an equally uncompromising assurance. (Nock 1933, 210–11)

Personally, I find this explanation of Christianity's success to beg more questions than it answers. Some of these, nonetheless, warrant pursuit. For example:

- Why, in a given city, did more than a few persons, namely, diehard pagans and faithful Jews, not only remain not attracted to Christianity but become self-consciously opposed to it?
- What made paganism or Judaism continue to be the better option for their adherents, even when Christianity was politically triumphant?
- Did one group's success inevitably imply the failure of everyone else?

2

The Declining *Polis*?

Religious Rivalries in Ancient Civic Context

Philip A. Harland

INTRODUCTION

Any attempt to understand religious rivalries in the ancient Mediterranean world must take into account the social and political structures within which such phenomena took place. Such structures influenced or constrained in various ways the activities and behaviours of the individuals, groups, and communities that attract our historical interest. Thus, it is the city or *polis* of the Greek East, and the larger power structures of which the *polis* was a part, that should frame our investigations. It is important, of course, to remember that, in focusing on the *polis,* we are glimpsing only a small portion of social-religious life in antiquity; we are not studying life in the countryside and villages, concerning which the evidence is, unfortunately, far less abundant. Our understanding of the nature and characteristics of the *polis* and empire will have an impact on our assessment of social and religious life. For this reason, it is very important to be self-conscious about the models and presuppositions that have not only informed past scholarship in this area but also, for better or for worse, continue to shape our perceptions of civic life in regions like the Roman province of Asia.

It is common, in discussions of the *polis* under Hellenistic and Roman rule, to read about the corrosion of civic spirit or identity, about interference by ruling authorities, about the hollowness of civic institutions and structures, which are supposed to have accompanied a fundamental decline. In recent years, some scholars have begun to question key aspects of this traditional scenario of decline. As we shall soon see, theories concerning the degeneration of the *polis,* including its religious life, are based more on a debatable selection, interpretation, and employment of evidence—informed by an underlying model of decline—than they are by the weight of the evidence itself. Indeed, I shall argue that despite changes and developments in the Hellenistic and Roman periods, we can properly speak of the continuing vitality of civic life, especially in its social and religious aspects.

I begin by discussing and questioning notions of decline in the study of the *polis* (Models of Decline in the Study of the *Polis*), before outlining ways in which this notion has influenced studies of ancient religious life in this context (Models of Decline in the Study of Social-Religious Life). I then provide evidence for the continuing vitality of civic life by using the inscriptional evidence for small social-religious groups in the cities of Roman Asia (Evidence for the Vitality of the *Polis* in Asia Minor). This evidence gives us a glimpse into the importance of networks of benefaction, and provides a picture of the *polis* as a locus of identity, pride, co-operation, and competition among various levels of society. Finally, I discuss how this overall picture of the *polis* might inform our discussion of religious rivalries (Implications for the Study of Religious Rivalries).

MODELS OF DECLINE IN THE STUDY OF THE *POLIS*

Pausanias, the ancient travel guide, makes a sarcastic statement which provides us with a rare description of how an ancient Greek defined the *polis:* "From Chaironeia it is two and a half miles to the *polis* of Panopeus in Phokis: if you can call it a *polis* when it has no civic offices, no gymnasium, no theatre, and no market-place, when it has no running water at a fountain and they live on the edge of a torrent in hovels like mountain huts. Still, their territory has boundary stones, and they send delegates to the Phokian assembly" (Pausanias, *Descr.* 10.4.1; trans. adapted from Levi 1971). Evidently, Pausanias viewed the buildings and related institutions that accompanied civilized Hellenistic life as the essence of a Greek *polis,* and he qualifies his sarcasm by noting that Panopeus did, at least, participate in its regional political assembly. Conspicuously absent from Pausanias's description, however, is something that seems to be the focus of many modern attempts to define what is or is not a real *polis:* the idea that without true autonomy, or genuine democracy on the model of classical Athens, there is no *polis* at all, or at best only a *polis* in decay.

According to the common view, changes that took place in the fourth century BCE led to the failure of the Greek *polis,* followed by a steady degeneration of virtually every political, social, cultural, and other facet of civic life in the Hellenistic and Roman periods (cf. Tarn and Griffith 1952, 47–125;

Ehrenberg 1969 and 1965; Mossé 1973; Kreissig 1974; Ste. Croix 1981). A particular interpretation and employment of two interrelated developments form the basis for this view. First, the Hellenistic Age was a period in which the authority of the kings over their territories brought true freedom to an end and seriously undermined local autonomy through the rulers' policy of active interference in internal civic life. In this view, autonomy in its strict sense is the essential ingredient without which the *polis* becomes an empty shell, causing a corresponding decay in other dimensions of civic life (cf. Finley 1977, 306–307; Thomas 1981, 40; Runciman 1990).

More often than not, the turning point of the loss of autonomy and, hence, the beginning of the end of the *polis,* is placed either at the battle of Chaironeia in 338 BCE—echoing Lykurgos's statement that, "With the bodies of [those who died at the battle] was buried the freedom of the other Greeks" (*Leoc.* 50)—or at the beginning of the Hellenistic Age, at the death of Alexander in 323 BCE (cf. Thomas 1981, 40). Other scholars, such A.H.M. Jones (1940), argue that, although the Hellenistic era saw the beginning of limited interference by the kings in civic life, thereby undermining self-government to some degree, such interference was limited and indirect. Jones places the climax of such control and intervention five centuries or so later than most other scholars, under the Roman emperors, especially emphasizing its negative impact on civic life from the second century CE onward.

Second, most scholars who speak of decline also focus on the supposed degeneration of democracy and the declining role of the assembly (*ekklêsia*) of the people (*dêmos*) (Ste. Croix 1981, 300–306, 518 ff., is representative). While democracy in the classical period is thought to have permitted the real participation of all strata of the population, giving even the lower classes an avenue of political activity and a sense of belonging, there is often presumed to have been a gradual disintegration of democracy in the Hellenistic era, with a corresponding detachment, by the majority of the population, from civic structures. The interfering policies of the Hellenistic kings and, even more, the Roman emperors—especially their active favouring of the establishment of oligarchic rule in the cities—assisted the local elites in taking real power away from the people. Democracy by means of the assembly of the people was already in "full decay" by the beginning of the Roman era and, shortly thereafter, died out altogether, as G.E.M. de Ste. Croix argues. Corresponding to the death of democracy was the detachment of most inhabitants from civic identity or pride, especially in the lower social strata of society.

There are several respects in which this overall scenario of decline is exaggerated and inadequate. For this reason, some scholars have begun to deconstruct it. First of all, it seems that a broad set of assumptions and value judgments plays a role in many scholars' implicit plotting of historical developments as the tragic decline and fall of the ancient city from the glorious days of classical Athens. Seldom is the underlying plot line or meta-narrative as explicit as when Kathleen Freeman states that the history of Greece "reads like a tragedy in three acts": the glorious emergence of city states like Athens; the intellectual and political achievements of science and philosophy in the fifth and early fourth centuries; and the unfortunate "break-up of the city-state system" in the later fourth century which brought with it the end of the distinctive thought and work of ancient Hellas (Freeman 1950, xv–xx).

Quite often, it seems to be an idealization of classical Athens—a reflection of scholars' value judgments—that serves as the archetype against which the inferiority of cities in Hellenistic and Roman times is established. Rarely are the value judgments that accompany the idealization of the classical *polis* as blatant as when Ernest Barker laments that "those who have been touched by the tradition, and educated by the philosophy, of the Greek city-state may be permitted to stand by its grave and remember its life; to wonder what, under happier auspices, it might have achieved" (1927, 535). In a critique of Ste. Croix's affirmation of the popularity of the Athenian empire, Donald W. Bradeen perceptively notes: "most of us ancient historians have a sympathy for Athens and her Empire; no matter how impartial we try to be, our whole training as classicists, and possibly our political bent as well, incline us that way" (1975, 405).

Classical Athens itself, however, may not have lived up to the scholarly ideal. Arlene W. Saxonhouse's recent study suggests that scholars "still bring to the study of ancient democracy our conceptions of democracy as it has emerged in the nineteenth and...twentieth centuries," often allowing modern values to shape a romantic view of Athenian democracy (1996, 7, 1–29). We must also be cautious about assuming that classical Athens was typical, since it is the only *polis* of that era for which substantial evidence survives; as P.J. Rhodes points out, a variety of different constitutions were adopted by other cities in the classical era, some of which included varying combinations of democracy, oligarchy, and monarchy (1994, 579; cf. Pecirka 1976, 6–7).

Even if democratic Athens was, in some respects, typical of the earlier forms of the *polis,* and even if the decline-scholars are justified in the degree to which they emphasize the loss of autonomy and democracy in subsequent years, such historical developments do not demonstrate the precipitous decline in civic life and identity scholars usually presume. Changes in one specific area, such as political participation, do not always equal degeneration in all others. A trend toward oligarchy, for example, does not mean that the lower social strata (which play less of a role in official political life) will necessarily feel dislocated and isolated from the social and religious facets of the *polis,* or lack a sense of identity in relation to civic structures.

Moreover, recent years have seen the beginning of a shift away from the overall paradigm of decline, although the wake of such a shift has not yet reached disciplines such as our own. The shift is evident, for example, in a comparison of the first and second editions of *The Cambridge Ancient History.* Whereas a contributor to the 1927 edition concluded his discussion of politics in the fourth century BCE with a section entitled, "The end of the *polis,"* P.J. Rhodes's corresponding article in the 1994 edition concludes with a conspicuously interrogative section entitled, "The failure of the *polis?"* Louis Robert, whose knowledge of the inscriptions of Asia Minor remains unparalleled, states: "la cité grecque n'est pas morte à Chéronée, ni sous Alexandre, ni dans le cours de toute l'époque hellénistique" (1969, 42). Robert goes on to say that although cities such as Athens and Sparta no longer possessed their former power in international affairs, the internal structures of civic life in most cities remained largely unchanged: "La vie de la cité continue dans le même cadre et avec les même idéaux" (1969, 42). What was relatively new, however, was the emerging system of benefaction (see below, Models of Decline in the Study of Social-Religious Life).

P.J. Rhodes (1994), Walter Eder (1995), Mogens Herman Hansen (1993, 1994, 1995), Erich Gruen (1993), and others question many of the key interpretations of previous scholars concerning the early crisis and decline of the *polis,* emphasizing instead the vitality of civic life in the Hellenistic and Roman eras, despite changes and developments (see, e.g., Gauthier 1985, 1993). Stephen Mitchell argues that, despite the loss of complete autonomy for cities in Asia Minor, there was still considerable continuity from earlier times: the cities continued as effective centres of administration and, perhaps more importantly, the cities were, in a very positive sense, communities (1993, 1:199).

These and other recent studies call into question many scholars' specific historical interpretations concerning both autonomy and democracy, which are in need of considerable qualification or, in some cases, rejection. Most scholars who speak of decline hold in common a definition of the *polis,* which emphasizes autonomy (*autonomia*) or sovereignty as its essential ingredient; hence, dependence on an outside power such as a king or emperor means loss of identity as a genuine *polis,* and subsequent decline. This definition of the *polis,* however, is largely a product of modern scholarship, as Hansen's recent studies convincingly show. No ancient discussion of the nature of the *polis* mentions autonomy as a defining characteristic; furthermore, *hypêkoos* ("dependent") is the opposite of *autonomos,* yet the term *hypêkoos polis* is well attested, which would be a nonsensical statement if ancients considered autonomy an essential ingredient (Hansen 1993, 18–20; 1994, 15–17; 1995). Moreover, Hansen states, every "city-state would of course have preferred to be autonomous, but obviously a city-state did not lose its identity as a *polis* by being subjected to another city-state or, for example, to the king of Persia, or Macedon, or a Hellenistic ruler, or Rome" (1993, 19; cf. Brunt 1990, 272).

Furthermore, many scholars have overstated the degree to which the Hellenistic kings and Roman authorities actively interfered in the affairs of the cities. Recent studies of the nature of Roman rule by scholars such as Fergus Millar (1967, 1977, 1984) and G. P. Burton (1975) point to its passive and reactive character. G.P. Burton (1993, 24–25) points to some of the "severe constraints" and practical limitations on the effective power of proconsuls and other Roman officials: the province of Asia, for example, included about 300–500 civic communities, under the direction of only the proconsul, three legates and a *quaestor.* Keith Hopkins (1980, 121) estimates that, in the middle of the second century, there was one elite official (of senatorial or equestrian rank) for every 350,000–400,000 subjects. Seldom did Roman emperors or authorities actively interfere in civic affairs, unless public disorders could not be handled locally or action was requested from below. As Peter Anthony Brunt states: "it was not the practice of the Romans to govern much. The governor had only a small staff, and he did little more than defend his province, ensure the collection of the taxes and decide the most important criminal and civil cases. The local communities were left in the main to run their own affairs" (1990, 116–17).

Such a picture of Roman rule contradicts, for example, David Magie's argument that the self-government of the cities in Asia Minor was fundamentally undermined by active interference through a requirement for the governor's approval in connection with civic decrees (1950, 1:641, 2:1504n. 21). As James H. Oliver (1954) convincingly argues, the inscriptional evidence which Magie interprets as support for this view in fact represents quite a different situation: cities were not regularly required to gain permission from Roman authorities for their enactments, but rather sought occasional support from Roman governors, who were otherwise hesitant to get involved.

It is against this background that the passages in Plutarch's *Political Precepts* ought to be understood: with Plutarch not so much protesting the active interference of Roman authorities as exhorting Menemachos to avoid the practice of other civic officials who actively and unnecessarily seek their governor's involvement, thereby forcing "the governors to be their masters more than the governors wish" (814e-815a; translation by Oliver 1954, 163). Certainly there are other passages, in which Plutarch laments the loss of total freedom by the *polis,* for instance, when he cautions Menemachos to beware of the "boots of Roman soldiers just above your head" (813e). But, shortly thereafter, he advises Menemachos to foster friendships with Roman officials in order to further the welfare of the *polis* (814d). Plutarch evidently believed that the continued success of Roman rule was a consequence of divine providence; to struggle against it was to challenge the will of the gods. To categorize him as either anti- or pro-Roman, as Simon Swain points out, is to oversimplify a far more complex picture (1996, 135–86).

The second main point cited in support of a theory of decline, which is in need of qualification, is the degree to which the typical *polis* of the Hellenistic and Roman periods represents the degeneration of an earlier form of democracy. I have already noted that many scholars uphold an ideal vision of Athenian democracy, which is shaped by modern values and does not accurately reflect the reality of the ancient situation. For example, it is quite common for scholars to stress the increasing importance of the wealthy in political life, and the emerging dominance of oligarchy in the Hellenistic and Roman eras. Already in classical Athens, however, the wealthy, rather than average citizens, seem to have been dominant in the important political positions (Rhodes 1994, 566, 573; cf. A.H.M. Jones 1940, 166–69). Scholars such as Hansen (cf. Ste. Croix 1981, 284) also question the degree to which we can speak of ancient democracy in terms of the majority vote of all citizens when, in fact, the evidence concerning the number of citizens who could actually attend meetings of the assembly in classical Athens suggests otherwise (e.g., the seating capacity of the Pnyx accommodated only one-third to one-quarter of the citizen population in the fourth century BCE; see Saxonhouse 1996, 5–6).

Even so, as Rhodes states in reference to Ste. Croix's theories, "the failure of democracy would not be the same thing as the failure of the *polis,* and it is not obvious that either occurred" (Rhodes 1994, 189n.102). There is evidence that the assembly of the people could continue to play a significant role, in the Hellenistic and Roman eras, despite the prominence of the wealthy in civic affairs. Gruen points to the surviving attendance records for the Hellenistic era in various cities of Asia Minor and states that, contrary to the clichés in scholarship, "popular participation in the Hellenistic city-states did not consist merely in empty slogans, but rather involved the participation of citizens in the various legislative and judicial activities alongside honorary ones" (1993, 354). Furthermore, scholars such as Stephen Mitchell and Guy MacLean Rogers have begun to question the common view that, in the Roman era, the council so completely usurped the role of the people that the latter possessed very little, if any, real power, but merely approved lists of candidates for office.[1]

These various new studies mount a fundamental challenge to key interpretations of historical developments that have served as the basis of the theory of decline, which itself rests on questionable value judgments, models, and assumptions. Although important changes and developments definitely did take place under Hellenistic and Roman rule, these changes are not best understood in terms of a broad notion of decline. Further positive evidence for the continued vitality of the *polis* will be presented shortly. But first, the implications of the theory of decline for the study of social, cultural, and religious facets of civic life needs more attention, especially in light of our focus on religious rivalries.

MODELS OF DECLINE IN THE STUDY OF SOCIAL-RELIGIOUS LIFE

Unfortunately, the model of civic decline has often been used to explain other social and cultural phenomena in the Hellenistic and Roman eras. Many scholars correlate this decline with a degeneration of traditional religious life. As S.R.F. Price notes, "the conventional model, which has been applied to both Greek and Roman cults, posits an early apogee followed by a long and continuous decline, until the last embers were extinguished by Christianity" (1984, 14). As we shall see, the application to these other social and religious developments of both the model of civic decline and its related assumptions can produce misleading and exaggerated conclusions. One can also discern the role of modern value judgments in such scenarios; parallel to some scholars' use of classical Athens as a foil against which all subsequent developments are evaluated in negative terms, an ideal view of Christianity serves as a measure of genuine religion, over against which most, but not all, preceding phenomena are evaluated as superficial, less than genuine, and therefore in decay.

---

1 For the common view, see A.H.M. Jones 1940, 177; Magie 1950, 1:640–41 (cf. Lane Fox 1986, 51; Sheppard 1984–1986, 247); also Mitchell 1993, 1:201–4; Rogers 1992. Regarding activities of the assemblies in the Roman era, see C.P. Jones's discussion (1978, 97–98) of passages in Dio's orations, which indicate the working of the assembly (40.1, 5–6; 45.15–16; 47.12–13); also A.H.M. Jones 1940, 177–78, 340–41, and Oliver 1970, 61–63, who argues for considerable continuity in the constitution of Athens from classical times up to the time of Marcus Aurelius.

W.S. Ferguson's outline (1928) in *The Cambridge Ancient History* of the leading ideas of the Hellenistic Age reflects widespread views evident in the works of such influential scholars of Greco-Roman religion as Martin P. Nilsson (1961; 1964), André-Jean Festugière (1954; 1972), Eric Robertson Dodds (1959, 179–206, 236–69), and those who depend on them, such as Peter Green (1990, 382–413, 586–601).[2] According to these scholars, the vitality of traditional Greek religion was bound to the effectiveness of the autonomous and democratic *polis* in such a way that the decline of the *polis*, between the fourth and third centuries BCE, brought about the downfall of the civic religious system, leaving an "empty shell" having little vestige of "genuine religion," so that, in Nilsson's words, "the ancient gods were tottering" (1964, 260–62, 274–75, 285; cf. Murray 1935, 106–108, 158–63). More recently, Luther H. Martin claims to discern a parallel between the modern condition and that of the Hellenistic age: "Both are shaped in periods of transformation characterized by…altered sociopolitical systems…[by] the influx of strange new gods from the East. For both, the traditional gods might well be termed dead" (1987, 3). It seems, however, that this is less recognition of actual similarities between the ancient situation and the modern one than it is an imposition of modern concepts and historical developments on the description of the ancient world.

Even if individuals continued to participate in traditional religious ceremonies, it is assumed that their feelings and attitudes were no longer involved. Some scholars appear to possess additional knowledge, beyond what the evidence of continued participation in traditional forms of religion suggests. Festugière, for example, asserts that the decline of civic religions is an "undeniable fact." What it comes down to is that this "undeniable fact" is based on Festugière's claim to be able to distinguish between the "outer form" of the cults, which, he admits, continued to function largely unchanged, according to the only evidence we have, and the "feelings" and "attitudes" of those who participated, which, Festugière asserts, were no longer attached to the civic cults and, correspondingly, to the *polis* (1954, 37–38; cf. Dodds 1959, 243–44; Carcopino 1941, 137–44; P. Green 1990, 587). Nilsson similarly discounts the evidence for the continued vitality of

---

2 Peter Green favourably cites or footnotes both Nilsson and Dodds on a regular basis; cf. Guthrie 1950. My discussion, in what follows, is based on views shared by W.S. Ferguson, Nilsson, and Festugière, and echoes earlier evaluations by L.R. Farnell (1912), G. Murray (1935), and Tarn and Griffith (1952, 325–60). Nock (1933, 65, 99–121) has a similar view of the decline of traditional religion, though he states it more moderately. Some of the essential aspects of this view are still presented, albeit in modified form, by recent scholars (cf. J.K. Davies 1984; L.H. Martin 1987).

civic religion by categorizing it as a sign not of continued vitality but of an historical interest from a romantic and sentimental background characteristic of an age "weary of its culture" (1964, 295).

The decline of civic structures also led to other important trends, including the rise of individualism, which was "the dominant feature of the age" (W.S. Ferguson 1928, 4; cf. Nilsson 1964, 282–83, 287; Farnell 1912, 137, 140–41, 147–50, who speaks of the rise of a spirit of individualism and a corresponding waning in the old religion; Guthrie 1950, 256, 334). Tarn and Griffith state: "Man as a political animal, a fraction of the *polis* or self-governing city state, had ended with Aristotle; with Alexander begins man as an individual" (1952, 79). Luther H. Martin seems to have had a change of mind on the issue of individualism (contrast 1987 and 1994). Moreover, individuals in the Hellenistic era suffered from a general malaise characterized by feelings of detachment, isolation, and uncertainty: "loneliness and helplessness in a vast disintegrating world" (W.S. Ferguson 1928, 35), which led them to seek substitutes for the attachment they had previously felt toward the *polis* and its social and religious structures. Scholars who hold these views often explain and group together various religious phenomena in the Hellenistic world, including the addiction to foreign cults or mystery religions, the supposed preoccupation with Tyche, the popularity of both magic and astrology, and the rise of ruler cults, as (often misguided) responses to a social and spiritual vacuum, as relatively new compensatory phenomena.[3]

It is worth pointing out the place of ruler cults in this overall scenario, since it reveals some of the underlying assumptions and value judgments involved. For Nilsson and others, ruler cults were the epitome of faltering religious life, and foreshadowed the fall that was yet to come: "The origin of the cult of men in Greece is to be sought in the convulsions of the dying religion" (Nilsson 1964, 288, italics mine; cf. W.S. Ferguson 1928, 13–22). Nilsson's opinion is the same in his very influential *Geschichte der griechischen Religion,* where he states: "dass der Herrscherkult eine Verfallserscheinung der griechischen Religion ist, der es an wirklich religiösem Gehalt mangelt" (1961, 182). Lily Ross Taylor gives a similar assessment of the imperial cult when she states that "the inclusion of a mortal among the gods would not bring to the men of the day the same shock that it would have

---

3 For a recent restatement of the view, see P. Green 1990, 396–413, 586–601, esp. p. 396. Green is clearly reiterating the perspectives of Dodds and Nilsson. Such questionable conceptions of individualism and widespread deracination have also influenced the study and interpretation of Greco-Roman novels (see Swain 1996, 104–109, for a critique of associated assumptions and theories).

caused in a time when the native religion was strong" (1931, 54). According to Dodds, such cults were "expressions of helpless dependence; he who treats another human being as divine thereby assigns to himself the relative status of a child or an animal" (1959, 242).

Through such cults, rulers became a somewhat superficial replacement for the "old gods," whose importance was waning. Nilsson's strictly negative evaluation of ruler cults, within his overall story of a "dying religion" (which is paralleled in the works of other scholars, e.g., P. Green 1990, 396–413), evinces the convergence of the two modernizing concerns—the one regarding superior political life (i.e., the idealized picture of classical Athens) and the other regarding genuine religion (i.e., the idealized picture of Christianity)—which together serve as the basis for evaluating whether something is degeneration, rather than simply change or development. On the one hand, ruler cults involved the inhabitants of the *polis* in the worship of the same outside, interfering power that was already undermining their freedom and democracy. On the other hand, they also embodied a strictly outward, state-supported, and artificial form of religion, far removed from the personal religion that otherwise might have evoked the genuine feeling of individual participation. Nilsson and other scholars have similar things to say regarding imperial cults in the Roman era, which ostensibly had very little meaning for those who were involved and "lacked all genuine religious content" (Nilsson 1948, 178; cf. 1961, 385; for discussion and criticism of such oversimplifications, see Pleket 1965; Price 1984; Harland 1996, 2000). Once again, value judgments, informed by modern concerns rather than the weight of the evidence, play a significant role in the development of this overall scenario of a tragic decline, with a touch of romance being added to the plot through reference to the forthcoming triumph of Christianity. In chapter 1 of this book, Vaage gives examples of how similar assumptions by historians have shaped perceptions of early Christianity and its competitors.

According to the common view, one of the most important responses to feelings of deracination was the rise of what scholars such as Nilsson and Festugière call private or personal religion. This was, supposedly, a replacement for the outward and in many ways artificial public or civic religion, which no longer evoked the feeling of the individuals who participated. As traditional civic religious structures declined, private clubs, mysteries, and associations (which often involved not only the individual's personal choice, but also some notion of salvation) were the most successful social-religious units (Festugière 1954, 40; Dodds 1959, 243). This was because they responded to feelings of helplessness, isolation, and uncertainty by providing a replacement for the sense of belonging and attachment that individuals previously had felt toward the civic community and its social structures, including the household. In the case of the mysteries, they offered a religious system of salvation from uncertain conditions; in this sense, they were similar to Christianity.

Many scholars who hold similar views would stop short of explicitly stating, as George Herbert Box does, what seems to underlie such evaluations concerning the notion of a preparation for the triumph of Christianity: "[The mysteries] and the religious brotherhoods which made purity of life a condition of membership are genuine manifestations of the religious spirit, and may be regarded as a real preparation for Christianity" (1929, 45). Many scholars who suggest that the mysteries approached the status of a genuine religion (i.e., Christianity) are also careful to assert Christianity's difference from contemporary mysteries. The mysteries serve a twofold function in such theories: establishing preparation for, and serving as a foil against which, the superiority and uniqueness of Christianity is established (cf. Gasparro 1985, xiii-xxiii; J.Z. Smith 1990).

In the preceding scenario, associations are viewed as a compensatory phenomenon or symptom of decline, which accordingly should be defined in contrast with social structures of the *polis*, sometimes in subversive terms; according to John Kenyon Davies, for example, these groups "ran counter to city-based religion and society" (1984, 318). This view of associations as a compensation for the decline of the *polis* is widespread in scholarship (see, e.g., Ziebarth 1896, 191–93; Poland 1909, 516; Tod 1932, 71–73; Guthrie 1950, 265–68; Dill 1956, 256; Herrmann, Waszink and Kötting 1978, 94; J.Z. Smith 1978, 187).

Only a few of the general problems with the notion of religious decline can be mentioned here. The most fundamental problem is the evidence to the contrary. Some recent, as well as older, studies of civic religious life, namely, those that do not begin with an a priori model of decline, have convincingly interpreted the evidence quite differently. Moreover, as Johannes Geffcken saw in 1920 (1978), and both Ramsay MacMullen (1981) and Robin Lane Fox (1986) have vividly demonstrated more recently, the weight of the evidence demonstrates that Greco-Roman religion, traditional and otherwise, far from showing signs of deathly illness already in the third century BCE, thrived at least into the third century CE, even though there were certainly changes, developments, and differences from one region to another. MacMullen points out the quality of our evidence: "Religion, like many another aspect of life, rises and falls on the quantity of surviving evidence like a boat on the tide. Highs and lows of attestation, if they only follow the line on the table, indicate no change at all" (1981, 127).

Second, theories regarding widespread social-religious decline share the problems of the parallel notion of the decline of the *polis* (which is assumed rather than substantiated), including, for example, the tendency to neglect the possibility that innovations are not always negative, nor signs of degeneration, but simply changes (North 1976, 10–12).

Third, it seems that some scholars impose on the ancient evidence concepts and models of historical development (cultural and intellectual) borrowed from the modern era, which are not appropriate for the study of the Greco-Roman world. For example, such scholars claim to find in the Hellenistic Age the rise of individualism and corresponding feelings of detachment and uncertainty. The tendency to look for parallels, in the ancient world, to modern developments is perhaps most obvious in Dodds's *The Greeks and the Irrational* (1959): besides his emphasis on the rise of individualism, he sees in the fifth and fourth centuries BCE the Greek "Enlightenment" and "the rise of rationalism," to which many later developments in the Hellenistic era are viewed as an irrational response (for a critique of Dodds's views, see Gordon 1972b; also Paul Veyne 1990, 41).

A developed concept of individualism, however, and the related concepts of private versus public did not emerge until the sixteenth century, and developed fully only with the European Enlightenment; such concepts are, accordingly, inappropriate for studying pre-modern societies. The developments that W.S. Ferguson, Festugière, Dodds, and others claim to find in the ancient world, and emphasize the most, are precisely those that came with the European Enlightenment and modern individualism: the individual's detachment from the larger community, freedom of choice, cultural mobility, critique of traditional forms of religion, and affinity for privatized, mystical religion. Take, for example, the imposition of many such details on the ancient world in the article about "Individualism" by Lawrence Hazelrigg in the *Encyclopedia of Sociology* (1992), and compare this description with what scholars such as Festugière like to find in the Greco-Roman world.

Hazelrigg rightly emphasizes the contrast between pre-modern societies, in which social relations are largely organic, corporate, and group-based, and the individualism of the modern era. Furthermore, as Peter Brown observes: "many modern accounts of religious evolution of the Roman world place great emphasis on the malaise of life in great cities in Hellenistic and Roman times. Yet the loneliness of the great city and the rapid deculturation of immigrants from traditionalist areas are modern ills: they should not be overworked as explanatory devices for the society we are studying. We can be far from certain that [as Dodds states] 'such loneliness must have been felt by millions'" (1978, 2–3). Consider also Jonathan Barnes's comment: "life in Hellenistic Greece was no more upsetting, no more at the mercy of fickle fortune or malign foes, than it had been in an earlier era" (1986, 365).

Festugière's tendency to see in the ancient context parallels to the modern is evident in his statement: "la civilisation gréco-romaine est déjà une civilisation de grandes villes. Dans ces grandes villes la majorité des habitants vivent comme aujourd-hui" (cited in P. Brown 1978, 3; cf. P. Green 1990, 404). La Piana's study of immigrant groups in Rome likewise tends to see parallels between the situation of immigrants in the ancient and modern context; he alludes to a universal experience, which he imagines that all immigrants in all times, at least to some degree, shared (1927, 201–205, 225–26). In their enthusiasm to find important connections or similarities between the ancient Greco-Roman world and our own, such historians sometimes implicitly impose (rather than discover) structural and developmental parallels between the modern and ancient situations. This tendency is perhaps related to the fact that the Greco-Roman world is considered formative for the development of Western culture, and is thus closely connected with the values and sentiments of such historians. This factor is especially evident in Luther H. Martin's introduction to Hellenistic religions (1987, 3).

Another problematic aspect of this overall scenario of decline in religious life is that an anachronistic approach sometimes plays a role, modernizing and Christianizing the conception of religion. Because the civic cults of paganism eventually "lost" to the adopted religion of empire (=Christianity), such cults must have been inadequate in addressing people's needs, and accordingly began their inevitable decline long before. Any religious activity during this age of decline, which can be construed as private, personal, individualistic religion, involving genuine feelings or notions of salvation, i.e., any religious activity approximating what such scholars understand Christianity to have been (according to a modern Jamesian definition of genuine religion), is viewed as more vital than, or superior to, other traditional forms of religious life, though still inferior to Christianity, which was in other ways unique.

What seems to underlie, for example, Festugière's notion of personal or genuine religion closely resembles William James's definition of religion as "the feelings, acts and experiences of individual men in their solitude, so far as they apprehend themselves to stand in relation to whatever they may consider the divine" (1902, 50; cf. Festugière 1954, 1–4; Dodds 1959, 243; 1965, 2; Nilsson 1961, 711–12; P. Green 1990, 588). Festugière is not alone in adopting such a limited definition of religion; it is not hard to see how the application to the ancient world (or to any non-western culture, for that matter) of such a modern, western, Christian, individualist conception of religion can obscure the vast majority of religious life, categorizing it (*a priori*) as artificial and less than genuine.

Hence the misguided and all-consuming focus, in some scholarship, on the mystery religions. Giulia Sfameni Gasparro (1985, xiii–xxiii) and Walter Burkert (1987), among others, question the Christianizing interpretations of the mysteries that were previously prevalent. As Burkert points out, mysteries were an optional activity within the broader context of traditional religious forms, not a separate movement or religion over against the *polis* and its structures. Associations and groups that engaged in mysteries were often fully integrated into the complex structures of family and *polis* (Burkert 1987, 32) rather than being their replacements.

EVIDENCE FOR THE VITALITY OF THE *POLIS* IN ASIA MINOR

Now that we have challenged some scholarly portraits of the *polis,* we can go on to discuss more positive evidence concerning the continuing vitality of civic life. I begin by addressing the significance, for the *polis,* of social networks of benefaction in the Hellenistic and Roman eras; then, I continue by using inscriptional evidence for associations in Roman Asia as an indication of involvements in, attachments to, and identifications with numerous dimensions of the *polis* on the part of its inhabitants from various social strata.

Social Networks of Benefaction

One can see important continuities within many of the central political, social, and cultural institutions and structures of the *polis,* from the classical period into the Hellenistic and Roman eras. The constitutions of cities that were founded on the model of the Greek *polis* continued to consist of the two main bodies of civic authority: the council (*boulê*), which usually numbered between two hundred and five hundred members; and the people (*dêmos*), which included the citizen body divided according to tribes (*phylai*), along with various civic official positions and boards (whose titles could differ from one city to the next). Social-cultural institutions, including some mentioned earlier by Pausanias, remained prominent in civic life. Yet one of the most significant developments in the structure of the *polis* in the late-Hellenistic and Roman eras, which is also essential for understanding competition, rivalry, and co-operation between different groups, was the emergence of a systematic pattern of benefaction (euergetism), which relied upon social network connections and was accompanied by a particular cultural world view.

By the time the regions of western Asia Minor were incorporated into the Roman province of Asia (ca. 133 BCE), this system of benefaction—an elaboration and systematization of conventions that characterized the Greek *polis* in earlier times—had become a prominent structural element with special relevance to the social system and economic well-being of the cities. Space does not permit a discussion of the origins of this system of benefaction or euergetism (see Veyne 1990; 1987, 95–115; Gauthier 1985; 1993; cf. Wallace-Hadrill 1990, 150–54; Mitchell 1993, 1:210; Sartre 1991, 147–66). Basically, Veyne differs from Gauthier in emphasizing a sharp caesura between the classical/democratic and the Hellenistic/non-democratic period, in connection with the emergence of euergetism as a system in Hellenistic times. Gauthier, on the other hand (correctly, I believe), puts emphasis on the continuing importance of democracy, and suggests that euergetism flows naturally from the competitive ethos of democracy; he sees the era of full-fledged euergetism from the second century BCE onward. Wallace-Hadrill discusses ways in which "the Romans absorbed the Greek honorific idiom gradually, almost without realising it" (1990, 166).

This system involved webs of reciprocal relations within social networks marked by a clearly differentiated hierarchy, though the potential for relations was quite fluid at all levels. The most prominent characteristic of these reciprocal relations within social networks was the exchange of benefits or gifts of numerous kinds (e.g., protection, financial contributions for various purposes) in return for appropriate honours. The system was reciprocal, in the sense that both the benefactor and the beneficiary (whether gods, individuals, groups, or institutions) stood to gain from the exchange, whether the benefit was tangible or otherwise. The system was also self-perpetuating, in that a benefaction was followed by fitting honours, which in turn ensured the probability of further benefactions from the same source in the future, as well as benefactions from others who might seek to outdo their competitors in the pursuit of honour.

The appropriateness of the honours depended on both the nature of the benefits conferred and the position of the benefactor and the beneficiary within the overall hierarchy of relations. Failure fittingly to honour a benefactor resulted in shame (*aischynê*); as Dio of Prusa suggests, this was akin to impiety (*asebeia*) toward the gods (*Or.* 31.57, 65, 80–81, 157). Correspondingly, failure of the wealthy to provide such benefactions appropriately was a threat to the position they strove to maintain within society: in this sense, benefaction became an obligation, not simply a voluntary action. The provision of benefactions and the granting of honours reaffirmed the relative positions of both the benefactor and the beneficiary within the social system of the *polis* and cosmos.

At the top of this hierarchy, as powers external to the *polis,* were both the gods and the rulers, whose ongoing protection and benefaction ensured the well-being of the *polis* and its constituent groups. The deities' protection of the *polis* and its inhabitants, holding off earthquakes, famine, and other natural disasters, while providing safety (*sôtêria*), stability, and peace, was deserving of the utmost honours, especially cultic. Dio Chrysostom, for example, describes the role of the gods in causing (or preventing) such natural disasters (*Or.* 38.20). A deadly plague in various cities of Asia in the mid-second century CE led the city of Hierapolis to consult Apollo at Klaros, whose oracular response advised that sacrifices be made to several gods in order to appease their wrathful displeasures (Parke 1985:153–54). When natural disasters occurred, it was assumed that the gods had not been fittingly honoured; Jews or Christians accordingly became more likely to face local harassment and sporadic persecution (cf. Tertullian, *Apol.* 40.1–2). By the Roman era, the rulers' relation to the *polis* was considered to be parallel to that of the gods, and rulers whose beneficence and provision of stability were comparable to those of the gods were thought to be equally deserving of cultic honours. Examples of this parallelism between the roles of the gods and of the rulers can be drawn from various upper-class authors from Asia Minor, for instance, Artemidoros, who says: "rulers, like gods, also have the power to treat people well or badly" (*Onir.* 3.13).

Scholars who think that cultic honours given to rulers epitomize the failure of the *polis* and represent the utter debasement of its ideals and values fundamentally misunderstand the meaning and function of such honorary activities (cf. Price 1984; Friesen 1993; Harland 1996). Instead, the incorporation of emperors within the existing framework of the *polis* actually served to reinforce the ideals, values, and structures of civic society, rather than to undermine them (cf. Price 1984; R.R.R. Smith 1987; Wallace-Hadrill 1990, 152–53). What this incorporation of the emperors also means, as Fergus Millar (1993) stresses, is that having a relationship with the distant emperor was very much a part of what the *polis* was in Roman times.

The gods and emperors may have been at the top of the social networks upon which the system of benefaction rested, but they were certainly not the only important players. Imperial officials in the provinces also held sufficiently high positions within this hierarchy that local elites and groups were sure to cultivate contacts with these powerful figures. Per-

haps more importantly for the everyday life of the average *polis*, the wealthy
elites and other inhabitants or groups in the cities were expected to provide
various services and benefactions for the well-being of the *polis* and its
inhabitants. Such contributions could take the form of official liturgies or
magistracies, both of which required considerable financial outlay (which
led to a blurring between the two). But, apart from these official roles,
inhabitants could also make benefactions to the *polis* or its constituent
groups in the form of financial contributions for the establishment of buildings, festivals, statues, and other structures that were dedicated to honour
civic institutions, gods, or emperors. Benefactions could also take the form
of banquets or food distributions in times of famine, such as the provi-
sions made for the inhabitants at Termessos in Pamphylia by a wealthy
woman named Atalante (*TAM* III 4, 62). The beneficiaries of such actions
were expected to reciprocate with appropriate honours, such as the erection of an inscription of gratitude or a statue, in honour of the benefactor.
Gratitude for the benefaction of a festival could be shown in less tangible
ways; a statement by Petronius well sums up this mentality: "He gave me
a spectacle, but I applauded it. We're even: one hand washes the other"
(cited in Veyne 1987, 113).

This leads to the question of what motivated such contributions to the
life of the *polis*, thereby ensuring the stability of this systematic pattern of
benefactions. Motivations naturally differed from one person and situation to the next, but three main components tend to stand out. First, the
role of genuine feelings of civic pride should not be discounted. Second, honour (*timê*) was highly valued in and of itself, and its pursuit (*philotimia*) was
among the most highly praised virtues. The desire to have one's benefactions or deeds remembered after death, in order to preserve one's reputa-
tion for posterity, was accordingly significant (cf. Dio, *Or.* 31.16; Polybius
20.6.5–6; Laum 1964 [passim]; Woolf 1996, 25–27).

A third motivating factor, however, must not be forgotten: the wealthy
elites' fear of what might happen if conspicuous donations were not made.
There was a set of values and expectations which made such benefactions
virtually a duty; failure to meet these expectations, especially at critical
times, could result in angry mobs seeking revenge against the wealthy, as
happened during a food shortage in Prusa, when an angry mob came after
Dio and his neighbour (*Or.* 46, 7.25–26; cf. Philostratos, *Vit. Apoll.* 1.15).
Contributions by the wealthy on a regular basis ensured the maintenance
of their position and prestige within the city, while also limiting the potential for social conflicts when the contrasts between rich and poor, ruler and
ruled, were particularly stark (Mitchell 1993, 1:206).

It is not hard to see how competition and rivalry, as well as co-operation, played important roles within ancient social systems. Competition
for pre-eminence among wealthy elites was matched by competition among
the potential recipients of such benefactions. The constituent groups of
the *polis* were in many ways competitors with one another in their attempts
to maintain contacts with and receive ongoing support from important
persons within social networks. Beneficiaries also had something to gain
from publicly advertising, through the medium of honorary inscriptions,
their connections: namely, the advantage that such connections accrued,
in their competition for prestige within the civic context. In setting up an
honorary inscription, for example, an association or guild was not only
honouring its benefactor but also making a claim regarding its own place
within society, reaffirming in a very concrete way its ties within the networks of the *polis* (cf. Woolf 1996, 29; Harland 1999).

Yet co-operation was also essential to the system. Individual inhabitants
of the lower social strata—such as a purple-dyer alone, for instance—were
not very likely to gain the attention and benefaction of a wealthy imperial
or civic official. But by co-operating together in the form of an association,
united purple-dyers could ensure the possibility of such relations within the
social networks of the *polis* and empire. On a broader scale, too, apart from
its own intramural competitions, the sense of civic pride and identity,
belonging to the *polis* as such, meant that its inhabitants as a whole co-oper-
ated together in broader-scale competitions and rivalries with other cities
(cf. Dio, *Or.* 38–39).

Associations and the Civic Framework

Now that we have a framework within which to discuss the *polis* in Roman
times, we can provide some concrete examples of the working of this system of benefaction and the nature of social relations within it. I have chosen to use as a starting point for this discussion the epigraphic evidence for
small social-religious groups or associations in Roman Asia (for abbreviations for primary sources in this section, see G.H.R. Horsley and Lee 1994),
not only because it happens to be the area with which I am most familiar
(cf. Harland 1996, 1999, 2000), but for two other reasons as well. First,
associations play a key role in common scholarly scenarios of civic and religious decline; second, many of these groups represent the lower strata of
society which many scholars of the decline-theories think were the far-
thest removed from civic identity and participation. Therefore, if an investigation of the actual evidence for these groups shows signs of continuing
attachments to the civic community and its institutions and structures,

along with a sense of belonging among their members, then the theories of decline are questionable from another angle.

Strong feelings of civic pride and identification with the *polis* or homeland (*patris*) are clearly evident not only among wealthy benefactors or elite authors, such as Aristides of Smyrna, Dio of Prusa, Artemidoros of Daldis, and Strabo of Amaseia, but also among various other segments of society, including those represented within occupational and other associations. Regarding the first group, Aelius Aristides delivered an epideictic speech in praise of his homeland, Smyrna, speaking of the *polis* as "the very model of a city," which "recommends a love of itself among all mankind" (*Or.* 17.8). When an earthquake heavily damaged Smyrna, Aristides mourned over this catastrophe that had struck the most beautiful city, "the eye of Asia"; his letter to Marcus Aurelius requesting support for rebuilding was a success (*Or.* 18, 19, 20). Dio's epideictic speech in response to the honours that his homeland of Prusa granted him is full of references to his pride and attachment in relation to the *polis* (*Or.* 44). Artemidoros dedicates Book Three of his dream interpretations to Daldis, "his native land…in gratitude for my upbringing" (*Onir.* 3.66). Strabo is sure to specify that Amaseia is his city and homeland (*patris*), and his description is wholly positive (*Geogr.* 12.3.15.39).

Individuals or groups could express their sense of belonging to the *polis* or homeland through their involvement in benefactions for (or dedications to) the *polis* and its institutions, either as benefactors or as beneficiaries. The association of fishermen and fishmongers at Ephesus, for example, representing a spectrum of social-economic levels, built and dedicated the fishery toll-office to the imperial family of Nero, the people (*dêmos*) of the Romans, and the people of the Ephesians (*IEph* 20; mid-first century CE; cf. *IEph* 1501; G.H.R. Horsley 1989). The guild of silversmiths and goldsmiths at Smyrna expressed both its piety toward the goddess Athena and the civic pride of its members by repairing her statue "for the homeland" (*ISmyrna* 721; ca. 14–37 CE). The dyers at Hierapolis (Lykos valley) who set up a statue of personified Council (*Boulê*) evidently identified with the institutions of their *polis* (*SEG* 41, 1201; ca. 100–150 CE). Several civic officials and some groups at Smyrna, including theologians (*theologoi*), an association of hymn-singers (*hymnodoi*), and, likely, an immigrant group of Judeans (*hoi pote Ioudaioi*), displayed civic-mindedness by joining together to provide financial contributions toward a project of the *polis* in the early second century (*ISmyrna* 697; ca. 124 CE).

Civic inhabitants might also express their identification with the *polis* by honouring an individual who acted as a benefactor and showed goodwill toward the homeland. Examples of occupational and religious associations participating in this aspect of the civic networks of benefaction could be cited for many cities in Asia.[4] An inscription from Smyrna, for example, involves the sacred *synodos* of performers (*technitai*) and initiates (*mystai*) gathered round Dionysos Breseus, who are honouring Marcus Aurelius Julianus, a civic official and benefactor, "because of his piety towards the god and his goodwill towards the *polis*" (*ISmyrna* 639; mid-late second century CE).

What is perhaps even more telling, concerning the involvement and participation of various segments of society within these networks of civic life, is the degree of co-operation and contact between such groups and important civic and imperial officials and institutions. There is abundant evidence for associations honouring on their own important civic officials, thereby maintaining connections with powerful citizens of the *polis,* such as when the *therapeutai* of Zeus honoured a foremost leader of Sardis for his piety toward the deity (*ISardBR* 22; ca. 100 BCE).[5]

The institutions and inhabitants of the cities often maintained important links with Roman imperial officials of equestrian or senatorial rank (who could also be local notables). The involvement of associations in imperial aspects of the honorific system further attests to some of the ways in which they cemented their relationship with the *polis,* identifying with its interests (see Harland 1999). In various cities, for example, several associations honoured members of the prestigious Julius family, who were descendants of Galatian royalty, entered imperial service as equestrians, then became senators as early as the late first century CE. Julia Severa, at Acmonia, was a high priestess in the local imperial cult, who acted as benefactor to both the local elders' association (*gerousia*) and the group of Judeans, for whom she built a synagogue (*MAMA* VI 263, 264; mid-first century CE). Her relative, C. Antius Aulus Julius Quadratus, was a prominent Pergamene, who reached consular rank and held important imperial posi-

---

4 Attaleia (near Pergamon; *IGR* IV 1169, leather-workers); Hierapolis (*IHierapJ* 40, second-third century CE, wool-cleaners); Miletos (*SEG* 36, 1051-1055, linen-workers and sack-bearers devoted to Hermes); Temenothyrai (*AE* [1977], no. 802, late first century CE, clothing cleaners); Thyatira (*TAM* V 932, 933, 986, 989, 1098, slave merchants, linen-workers, tanners, dyers, *Juliastai* association devoted to a hero); Tralles (*ITrall* 74, third century CE, *mystai*).
5 Cf. *IEph* 425 (ca. 81–117 CE): The silversmiths honour T. Claudius Aristion, *grammateus* of the people and imperial high priest; *TAM* IV 33 (late first century CE): The shippers at Nikomedia (in Bithynia) honour a leader of the *polis* and high priest; *TAM* V 955 (third century CE): The hymn-singers (*hymnodoi*) of the Mother of the gods honour a civic magistrate and liturgist.

tions in various provinces of the Greek East, including the proconsulate of Asia; he was honoured as a benefactor by various cities, including Pergamon. But he was also the benefactor of local associations at Pergamon, including the young men (*neoi*) and the Dionysiac dancing cowherds, who honoured him on more than one occasion (early second century CE).[6] One of his cousins, Julius Amyntianus, likely the brother of C. Julius Severus of Ankyra, was a member in the Panhellenion institution of Athens and also, for a time, the priest of Isis and Sarapis at Tralles, for which the initiates (*mystai*) honoured him with a monument (*ITrall* 86; post-131 CE). Evidently, associations and the spectrum of inhabitants who belonged to them were very much involved in the webs of relationships that characterized civic life and linked the *polis* to the empire.

Yet what is even more striking, and indicative of widespread participation in the life of the *polis,* are the numerous examples of various types of associations and guilds collaborating together with the principal civic institutions (the council and the people) in honouring eminent citizens and benefactors. This is true of the groups of Roman businessmen throughout the cities of Asia who evidently became well integrated within the life of the *polis,* as well as the various age-group organizations officially attached to the gymnasia.[7] Yet even less official occupational and other associations joined with the political institutions in honouring benefactors.

At Smyrna, for example, the council and the people joined with a *synodos* of initiates (probably devoted to Demeter) in honouring two female theologians for their display of piety toward the goddess in providing their services at a festival of the group (*ISmyrna* 653; first-second century CE). At Thyatira, the *dêmos* and the *Juliastai* joined together to honour posthumously Julius Xenon, a prominent hero and member of the *polis* (*TAM* V 1098; first century CE). At Erythrai, the homeland (*patris*) and the sacred theatrical *synodos* joined together in honouring Antonia Tyrannis Juliane, the *agônothetis* of the great Hadrianic games (*IErythrai* 60; 124 CE). At Tralles, the provincial league of Asia joined with the *dêmos* of Tralles and the Dionysiac performers in honouring the association's high priest (*ITrall* 65; first century CE).

Similarly, it was common for guilds and associations to set up honours for a benefactor on behalf of the civic institutions, often in accordance with

---

6   For the former, see *IPergamon* 440; for the latter, *IPergamon* 486, and Conze and Schuchhardt 1899, 179, no. 31. On Quadratus and his family, see *PIR* I 507 (with family tree).
7   Cf. Adramytteion (*IAdramytt* 19); Acmonia (*IPhrygR* 533); Assos (*IAssos* 13–14, 19–21, 28); Apameia (*IGR* IV 785–786, 788–791); Iasos (*IIasos* 90); Tralles (*ITrall* 80).

a specific provision in a decree or decision of the *polis* (see, e.g., *IEph* 728, 3079, guilds at Ephesus; *IGR* IV 788–791, guilds at Apameia; *IGR* IV 907, leather-workers at Kibyra; Quandt 1913, 177, *mystai* at Sardis; *ITrall* 74, *mystai* at Tralles). Some scholars, such as Ramsay (1895, 105–106), A.H.M. Jones (1940, 15, 17, 43–44), and those who follow them, even suggest that the constitutions of civic communities in Lydia may have been organized by guilds instead of tribes (*phylai*); but this is not a certainty.

Even those citizens who left their native *polis* to pursue business and other activities in other parts of the empire could count on the continuation of attachments to their homeland and its institutions. The city from which one came very much defined who one was in the Greco-Roman world, as Bruce J. Malina and Jerome H. Neyrey emphasize in their 1996 study of the ancient personality. The very existence, throughout the empire, of associations based on common geographic or ethnic origin, with corresponding names, attests to the continuing importance of both civic and regional identity.[8] When the council and the people of Nysa (east of Ephesus and Tralles) passed a decree honouring their wealthy benefactor, T. Aelius Alkibiades, for his love of honour (*philotimia*) and benefactions, they were also sure to single out for mention his benefactions to an association (*kollêgion*) of Nysaian citizens living in Rome, who evidently maintained contacts with the wealthy elites and institutions of their homeland (ca. 142 CE).[9]

This evidence of positive involvement by inhabitants of various social-economic levels with civic institutions in Roman Asia suggests that the situation in Tarsus, Cilicia, toward the end of the first century CE, is more

---

8 For example, Sardians (*IGR* I 88–89 [Rome]); Ephesians (*IGR* I 147 [Rome]); Smyrnians (*IMagnSip* 18 [Magnesia near Syplos]); Asians (*IGBulg* 480 [Montana, Moesia], *IG* X.2 309, 480 [Thessalonika, Macedonia]); Phrygians (*IG* XIV 701 [Pompeii]); Pergaians (*ILindos* 392 [Rhodes]); Alexandrians (*IGR* I 604 [Tomis, Moesia], I 800 [Heraklea-Perinthos, Thracia], I 446 [Neapolis, Italy]); Tyrians (*OGIS* 595 = *IGR* I 421 [Puteoli, Italy]). Numerous inscriptions from Delos could be cited involving Tyrians, Berytians, Egyptians, and others (cf. *IDelos* 1519, 1521, 1774). On associations of Romans, see Hatzfeld 1919. See La Piana (1927) for a discussion of various immigrant groups at Rome, including Phrygians and Judeans.

9 Alkibiades was also a benefactor of the Roman and Asian branches of the worldwide Dionysiac performers; their honorary inscription to him is found on the other side of the same stone. Side A includes the Dionysiac performers' honorary decree; and side B, the decree of the Nysaian *polis* (see Clerc 1885 for both sides, *IEph* 22 for side A only). This man was likely the son of Publius Aelius Alkibiades, a freedman who was prefect of the bedchamber for emperor Hadrian, who granted him Roman citizenship (see *PIR*[2] A134, Robert 1938, 45–53; cf. *FGrHist* II 257.1–34: the father commissions P. Aelius Phlegon of Tralles to write a history).

an exception than the rule. There, linen-workers were consciously excluded from participation in the *polis*. Dio's response (*Or.* 34.21–23) indicates that this was not a regular practice in most other cities. There certainly were occasions when involvement by an association or a guild in certain activities was perceived by either civic or Roman officials to be subversive. Examples of such incidents in Asia Minor include the proconsul's edict regarding the riots of bakers in Ephesus (*IEph* 215, mid-second century CE; cf. Acts 19 and, further, below) and Pliny the Younger's dealings with associations in the cities of Bithynia-Pontus during his special appointment as governor there in the early second century CE (*Ep.* 10.33–34, 92–93, 96–97). In general, however, these sporadic incidents have been overemphasized by many scholars (see Harland 1999, 153–93). Ste. Croix, for example, discusses the involvement of associations in lower-class forms of protest, such as strikes and other disturbances, and the resulting Roman suspicion toward them; he does not mention at all the sort of positive relations between such groups and both civic and imperial officials which are so well attested in the inscriptional evidence (1981, 273, 319–20). Paul J. Achtemeier correctly looks to associations for understanding the social context of the Christian groups addressed by 1 Peter, but wrongly oversimplifies his portrait of associations in stating that they were a "constant problem to the governing authorities" (1996, 25–26; cf. Balch 1981, 65–80).

The preceding evidence clearly shows that the members of many different types of associations, representing a spectrum of social-economic levels within society, from the more prestigious occupations of Roman businessmen and silversmiths to the less desirable professions of dyers and clothing cleaners, actively participated in the networks of civic life and, in important ways, closely identified with the *polis* and its structures. So much, then, for the widespread scholarly view that associations and guilds were a replacement for the declining structures of the *polis,* and the equally untenable view that they were a consistently subversive element in society, removed from civic identity and involved primarily in negative relations with imperial and civic authorities.

This attachment to the institutions of the *polis,* and the accompanying sense of civic identity or pride, is evinced in various other ways as well, besides involvement in civic networks of benefaction. Some of the principal social-cultural institutions of the *polis,* often built or renovated through the benefactions of the wealthy, were marketplaces, baths, gymnasia, stadiums, and theatres. Here, too, there is clear evidence of active participation by inhabitants of the cities. The age-group organizations of girls or boys (*paides*), youths (*ephêboi*), young men (*neoi*), and elders (*gerousia*) were a very prominent feature of gymnasium life for members of citizen families. Jews also could participate in the life of the gymnasia in Asia: there was a group of "younger Judaeans" (*neoteroi Ioudaioi*) at Hypaipa (*CIJ* 755), and several Jewish names are included in lists of *ephêboi* from Iasos and elsewhere (see Robert 1946, 100–101). Guilds of performers and athletes were similarly active in the gymnasia, stadiums, and theatres, where they competed during the various festivals held in honour of gods or emperors.

Yet ordinary associations and guilds also had a place (often in a literal sense) within these institutions of the *polis*. The stadiums at Aphrodisias, Didyma, and Saittai, for example, included bench reservations for guilds and associations of various kinds (*IAphrodSpect* 45; *IDidyma* 50; Kolb 1990). Several latrines at the Vedius bath-gymnasium complex at Ephesus were set aside for groups of bankers, hemp-workers, wool-dealers, and linen-weavers, all of whom evidently frequented the place (*IEph* 454). Quite well known is the Jewish synagogue contained within the bath-gymnasium complex at Sardis in the third century CE, right next door to the imperial cult hall. Such groups could also have special seats reserved for them in the theatre where the assembly of the people, as well as various theatrical and other performances, took place; the theatre at Miletos included reservations for guilds such as the "emperor-loving goldsmiths" and the "Judaeans (or Jews) and God-fearers," who sat just a few rows from the front, right next to the benches reserved for the "friends of the Augusti" (*philaugustoi*).[10]

Discussion of these kinds of social-cultural institutions leads us to another important aspect of civic life, which attests to the vitality, not the decline, of the *polis* and its social-religious life: festivals, processions, and related activities.[11] As we noted earlier, the gods, rulers, and emperors were an integral part of the webs of relations that characterized the social systems of the cities; festivals were one means by which appropriate honour could be shown to these godly benefactors, who protected the *polis* and its inhabitants. Thus, Plutarch, who was quite emphatic about the need for moderation in the pursuit of honour (*philotimia*), felt that the best pretext for benefaction was one "connected with the worship of a god [which]

10 Unfortunately, most of the *topos*-inscriptions from the theatre at Miletos are as yet unpublished; on some of these inscriptions, including the Jewish one, see Kleiner 1970, 18–20. The theatre at Aphrodisias included a bench for the butchers, alongside others (*IAphrodSpect* 46).
11 For a general discussion of festivals (especially those in honour of emperors), and their importance for all strata of society, see Price 1984, 101–32. For an excellent study of festivals and foundations in the cities of Asia Minor, focusing on the recently discovered Hadrianic inscription from Oenoanda (one of the most extensive festival-foundation inscriptions yet found), see Wörrle 1988 and Mitchell 1993 (with English translation).

leads the people to piety; for at the same time there springs up in the minds of the masses a strong disposition to believe that the deity is great and majestic, when they see the men whom they themselves honour and regard as great so liberally and zealously vying with each other in honouring the divinity" (*Mor.* 822b).

The pan-Hellenic festival established by Magnesia in honour of Artemis Leukophryene in the second century BCE, after an epiphany of the goddess and a consultation of the oracle of Apollo at Delphi (cf. *IMagnMai* 16, 17–87, 100), is paralleled by similar festivals, both local and regional (pan-Hellenic or provincial), which were established in cities throughout the Hellenistic and Roman periods. The proliferation of associations of athletes and performers in the Hellenistic and, especially, Roman eras is just one clear indication of the continuing popularity and importance of festivals, and the gods and goddesses they honoured.

To cite just one example from the Roman era, Salutaris gave a substantial financial foundation to Ephesus in 104 CE (*IEph* 27). The council and the people decided that the income from the funds would be used for processions expressing various elements of civic identity. Several groups participated, most prominently the youths (*ephêboi*), who carried images not only of Artemis and the Ionian and Hellenistic founders but also of the emperors. As Rogers (1991, 80–127, 136–51) convincingly argues, the composition of the biweekly procession was an expression of the multi-faceted identity of the city, not only encompassing the Roman imperial family and regime but also reaffirming the Ionian origins and sacred identity of Ephesus as the city of Artemis. The procession, in fact, began and ended in her sanctuary.

There is varied evidence for the continuing importance of gods and goddesses (whose popularity was not dying, as some scholars imagine) in the life of the *polis,* especially in connection with civic identity and pride. Virtually every city chose a particular deity as benefactor and protector, to whom proper honour was due. The relation between the civic community and the gods was taken seriously, and any threat to this relationship was a grave offence. The account, in Acts (19:21–41), of the silversmiths' riot at Ephesus, whether documenting an actual event or not, realistically portrays the attachment that inhabitants felt to their patron deity (cf. Oster 1976). In reaction to Paul's preaching that gods made with hands are not gods, the silversmiths are said to have gathered together a considerable crowd of other craftsmen and local inhabitants in the theatre, shouting (for two hours), "Great is Artemis of the Ephesians!" The more important of the motives Acts mentions for this protest relates to the need appropriately to honour the goddess: "There is danger…that the temple of the great goddess Artemis will be scorned, and she will be deprived of her majesty that brought all Asia and the world to worship her" (Acts 19:27; cf. *IEph* 24 [ca. 160 CE]).

The official patron deity was not the only deity, however, to whom honour was due. Temples and altars for various gods and goddesses, both foreign and local, dotted the cities of Roman Asia. At Ephesus, for example, there is surviving evidence of cultic activity for Zeus, Aphrodite, Apollo, Asklepios, Athena, Demeter, Dionysos, Cybele, Isis and Sarapis, and others; a similar array of evidence has been found at Pergamon (cf. Knibbe 1978; Oster 1990; Ohlemutz 1968). As well, possession of an official provincial imperial-cult temple could be a source of rivalry among cities in Asia, as illustrated by one particular incident Tacitus relates from the reign of Tiberius (*Ann.* 4.55–56). Other local shrines or cults of the emperors, including cultic activities practised within associations, likewise attest to the importance of the emperors as gods within the civic system (cf. Pleket 1965; Price 1984, 190–91; Harland 1996).

The foundation and continuation of cults or associations in honour of gods other than the patron deity of the *polis* were also bound up with civic identity and well-being. An inscription from the second century CE, claiming to be an ancient oracle, records the myth of the introduction of Dionysiac associations (*thiasoi*) to the city of Magnesia (*IMagnMai* 215). It tells a story about the people of Magnesia sending messengers to consult the god Apollo at Delphi concerning a miraculous sign and epiphany of the god Dionysos, which happened at Magnesia "when the clear-aired city was founded but well-cut temples were not yet built for Dionysos" (lines 19–21). The oracular response implied that the well-being of the Magnesians depended upon an obedient response to the will of both gods, Apollo and Dionysos, that associations devoted to Dionysos should be founded. This oracle may have been a useful weapon in establishing the pre-eminence of these particular Dionysiac associations within the context of religious rivalries at Magnesia at the time.

IMPLICATIONS FOR THE STUDY OF RELIGIOUS RIVALRIES

Reference to competition, of course, brings us back to the focus of this book. I think it appropriate to conclude this chapter by outlining a few of its main implications for the study of different religious rivalries within ancient civic contexts. First, when discussing and explaining religious rivalries, we must avoid adopting models of decline and broad notions of degeneration, even though such assumptions have been widespread in this area of study in the past. Hopefully, I have shown how pervasively and frequently the predominant model of decline has, in the past, shaped our picture of the *polis* of the Hellenistic and Roman eras. Many recent scholars, however, are beginning to deconstruct this scholarly edifice and build instead a more complex picture with regard to the continuing importance and vitality of the *polis,* despite changes, developments, and regional variations.

Yet conceptions of the decaying *polis* have also been the basis upon which various other questionable theories have been built regarding social-religious life and the general milieu of the Greco-Roman world—theories and assumptions that must no longer be unquestioningly employed in our attempts to understand and explain religious rivalries. I have tried to show ways in which problematic modern concepts and models of historical development have played a significant role in the formation and acceptance of many such theories. The inscriptional evidence from Asia, which I have discussed, has further challenged, in several ways, broad notions of decline. To begin with, it has provided concrete illustrations of the continuing importance of the *polis* and its structures as a locus of identity, co-operation, and competition for members of various strata of society. At the same time, it has also further undermined some of the more commonly accepted theories regarding the effects on religious life of supposedly widespread feelings of detachment from the civic community. Many scholars have thought that such deracination led directly to the emergence of the private religion of the individual, including mystery religions or associations, as a functional replacement for civic structures. But we have found that, far from being a replacement for attachment to the *polis,* many small social-religious groups could be integrated, though some more than others, within the *polis* and its standard structures.

The second main implication of the present study is this: that the practice of competition, or rivalry, was a natural consequence of living within the social system of the *polis.* Even more, the agonistic culture that constituted this social system made rivalries (as well as co-operation) essential to its continued vitality. Within such a context, both rivalries themselves and the potential disturbances that sometimes accompanied them should be understood as signs of vitality, not decline.

Third, it is evident that inhabitants who joined together on a regular basis to form small social-religious groups could indeed find the *polis* to be a home. They could find their place within the *polis,* cement their relationship with its structures, and identify with its interests in a variety of ways, including participation in civic networks of benefaction, direct relations with the political organs, and participation within social and cultural institutions, including gymnasia and theatres. We also found that emperors and imperial officials were incorporated within the civic system and its webs of relations to such an extent that the relation of a *polis* to the emperors was an important component of civic identity in the Roman era. The participation of inhabitants or groups in imperial aspects of civic life provided another way for people to stake a claim regarding their particular place(s) within society.

Fourth, the vitality of both traditional and other forms of social-religious life means that groups of Jews or Christians, like others, would have to work hard to establish and to maintain their place within the *polis*. Despite their peculiarities, the most important of which may have been a firm rejection of many features of polytheistic cultic life, Jewish and Christian groups, like other associations, could not utterly reject all participation in and involvement with at least some of the varied social, economic, and cultural features of civic life; at least, not if they hoped to persist. Those Jewish groups that found a place (literally) within the bath-gymnasium complex at Sardis, and within the theatre at Miletos, illustrate some of the possibilities, even for putatively exclusive Jewish and Christian groups, of finding a home within the social structures of cities in the Roman Empire.

ACKNOWLEDGMENT

I would like to thank Professor Roger Beck (University of Toronto), the members of the University of Waterloo/Wilfrid Laurier University Biblical Colloquium, and the CSBS Religious Rivalries Seminar, for their comments on earlier versions of this chapter.

3

Rivalry and Defection

Stephen G. Wilson

INTRODUCTION

The general topic of this book is religious rivalry. It has become apparent, however, that "rivalry" does not cover all the evidence for social relations between different religious groups in the ancient Mediterranean world, so that some scholars prefer terms such as "competition," "interaction," and the like in order to avoid the implications of the former term. It has perhaps not been spelled out clearly what is meant with this change of terms, but the gist of it seems to be that rivalry carries with it notions of antagonism, or hostility, or a type of head-on conflict, which we do not often see in the materials we have studied. Jews and pagans are thought to have been largely indifferent toward Christianity, at least early on, and the Christian view of Jews and pagans, when it expresses antagonism or hostility, is often understood to be a rhetorical construct designed to meet the inner needs of Christian communities rather than an expression of real social conflict with their competitors.

I suspect that things were not so simple. For one thing, if such rhetoric was designed to secure a sense of self-identity or to deflect members from the attractions of the alternatives (two explanations commonly given), then a sense of rivalry is already built in, even though the conversation is going on primarily within one community. For another, not all of the evidence we have looked at points this way, and some of the examples I will look at below can be as appropriately described in terms of rivalry as by any of the milder terms we might care to employ. Moreover, we need to note that

we can speak of friendly rivalry as we can of intense competition or interaction, and that a lot depends on the nuance we give to the terms. Perhaps
all we need to recognize is that whichever term we use, it must retain sufficient flexibility to encompass all the evidence we wish to consider. Thus
we could think of intense, modest, and friendly rivalry as a sort of scale that
may comprehend a fair amount of our evidence, even if it does not cover
it all. This is not to claim, of course, that rivalry was the only way that religious groups interacted. In the ancient urban setting, in particular, co-
operation on some levels may have been unavoidable and equally important
for success (see Lightstone, chapter 5; Harland, chapter 2).

    From the start, the notion of mission has been held up to scrutiny. In
chapter 1 of this book, Leif E. Vaage programmatically subjects Adolf von
Harnack's classic description of the "Mission and Expansion" of Christianity to a severe critique. This is an important move, and it throws out a
number of issues for us to ponder. One is the importance of mission itself.
The image we get, from Paul and Acts, of Christianity as an aggressively
evangelistic movement has too often been allowed to colour our picture of
subsequent centuries where, in fact, there is very little evidence to sustain
it. Likewise, the notion of mission within Judaism has recently been critically appraised by a number of scholars, with the result that, at least before
the fourth century CE, there appears to be remarkably little evidence for a
proselytizing mission. At the most, we can speak of a centripetal movement of some interested Gentiles toward Judaism, but not of a centrifugal
mission out from it (see also Donaldson, chapter 6).

    There is some evidence for peripatetic philosophers plying their wares
in the towns and villages of the Mediterranean world, and it is clear that
some of them hoped to influence the behaviour of the public at large. In general, however, pagans did not aggressively propagate their philosophies
and cults. Martin Goodman (1994) has brought some refinement to the discussion by differentiating between informational, educational, apologetic,
and proselytizing missions, defining the latter as the desire not only to
change the behaviour of, but also to recruit, complete outsiders. Perhaps this
broader understanding of the concept of mission can accommodate those
who wish to retain the notion (see, e.g., Mason, chapter 7) while allowing
that the critique of Harnack's view has considerable force.

    A related issue then arises. If religious groups in Mediterranean antiq-
uity did not extend their membership through aggressive missionary activity, how did they survive and grow, in particular, at a time when the options
were so many and the clamour for people's attention so confusing? Recent
work on the spread of cults in the modern world has provided one key,

which has been applied to the early Christian movement, most notably by Rodney Stark (1996). In essence, Stark argues, Christianity spread through networks of family and friends. Intimate social relations (together with several other factors that, Stark thinks, favoured Christianity over its rivals) were more likely to influence a person's religious affiliation than anything else, including the solicitations of a rabid evangelist. Some aspects of Stark's argument are questioned in this book (see Reinhartz, chapter 9; Muir, chapter 10; Beck, chapter 11), but Stark's general notion of growth through networking remains largely unscathed.

If this is true, then, for some people in antiquity, such would have posed a problem, because their social and religious loyalties did not always coincide. What, for example, of those who had married someone with other loyalties? And what of those whose decision to join one group was constantly undermined by nagging ties with their former life? Such cases were common, and we shall see several examples where social and familial bonds had a profound effect not only on what people chose to affiliate with but also what they chose to disaffiliate from. Yet we should note, too, that the proper recognition of the importance of social ties should not blind us to the role of individual curiosity and inner impulse, which in some cases may have been paramount in the changing of religious allegiance.

When we seek to understand religious affiliation, we often call on the notion of conversion. This is understandable, since a great deal of attention has been paid to conversion in the ancient world (notably by Nock 1933), and even more so in the sociological study of religion in the modern world. That the term "conversion" appropriately describes a handful of famous examples (Paul, Justin, Augustine, the royal house of Adiabene) need not be questioned. Yet, in some ways, the notion of conversion is tied to the notion of mission, and may need to be used with equal caution. It may have limited value in explaining religious loyalties for all but a handful of examples (though there were undoubtedly others we don't hear about), since many people presumably either accepted the tradition into which they were born or were persuaded by family and friends to change their allegiance without undergoing a dramatic *volte-face*. Moreover, the notion of conversion points our attention, rightly, to those things that attracted religious adherents. It looks at the moment of entry.

There is another side to this, however, on which the present chapter will focus: the moment of exit. For, if many joined religious groups, some left them. These defectors or apostates point our attention not to the attractions of joining but to the attractions of leaving. (The term "defector" is perhaps less theologically loaded than the term "apostasy," and I will thus prefer it.) This can become complicated, because one group's defector could become another's convert, in which case defection and conversion were part of the same process. Yet we can still isolate for attention the two different moments: joining and leaving. Nor were these moments always conjoined, since, as far as we can tell, some people seem to have drifted away from their religious commitments without actively associating with an alternative religious community, even though, in the pervasively religious world of antiquity, some sort of religious activity was probably unavoidable.

There are few studies of defection or apostasy in the ancient world. The Jewish evidence has been most discussed, though often in a peremptory fashion.[1] The Christian evidence has rarely been considered, and possible analogies within the pagan world, not at all (Harvey 1985; Marshall 1987). There is, in fact, a considerable amount of evidence in all three areas, even though defectors do not tend to advertise their position and ancient authors would have had little reason to dwell on them, since they are not a success story. In view of this book's theme and the issues that animate it, I shall dwell on the few examples that most sharply raise the questions associated with rivalry, competition, interaction, that is, those where we have fairly clear evidence that there was a desire, a tug, or even a political imperative to move from one affiliation to another. These are, conveniently, the cases where defection is fairly blatant, so that there is little doubt about what we are dealing with.

DEFECTION FROM JUDAISM

One of the clearest examples of defection from Judaism occurred in Antioch during the Jewish War. A Jew named Antiochus threw over the traces, denounced his fellow Jews, and accused them of setting the city centre on fire. To prove the sincerity of his own conversion (*metabolê*) and his detestation of Jewish customs, he sacrificed in the Greek fashion, denounced (*enedeiknyto*) his father and other Jews, and forced as many as he was able to abandon their customs and follow his lead (Josephus, *B.J.* 7.46–52). As a result, some Jews were apparently forced to apostatize under severe pres-

---

1   For example, Tcherikover 1957, 1:37; Hengel 1974, 1:31; 2:25n. 224; Williams 1990, 200n. 22; Grabbe 1992, 2:536–37. For Alexandrian Judaism, see Wolfson 1947, 1:73–85; Feldman 1960, 227–30; 1992, 65–83. H. Green (1985, 155–69), under the heading "Assimilation and Apostasy," in fact gives little evidence for apostasy, more for assimilation. Schiffman (1985, 41–49) discusses some of the rabbinic evidence. See, also, Stern (1994, 105–12). Useful encyclopedia articles are found in *JE* 1901–1906, 1:12ff; *EJ* 1971–1972, 3:202–15; *EOJ* 1989, 69–70; *Enc.T.* 1969, 2:404–409. The best discussion, both for its range and sophistication, is now Barclay (1995a, 1995b, 1998, and at various points in his survey of Diaspora Judaism, 1996).

sure, but Antiochus, at least, did so willingly. We do not know why. Jose-phus says that Antiochus was the son of a prominent Antiochene Jew and that his defection took place when Jews were hated everywhere. While rebellion against parents is not unknown as a cause of apostasy, it is per-haps more likely that Antiochus was affected by immediate political pres-sures; perhaps, a conviction that the Jews were doomed, and a fear that he would go down with them.

Others appear to have been more highly pressured, such as the Alexan-drian Jews who succumbed to the persecution instigated by Ptolemy IV Philopater, accepted initiation into the Dionysiac mysteries, and thereby gained Alexandrian citizenship (3 Macc. 2:31–33; 3:23; 7:10–15). For this they were despised and ostracized by their fellow Jews and, when the tables were turned, the king gave permission for the defectors, numbering three hundred according to 3 Maccabees 7:15, to be hunted down and put to death. The defectors acted out of fear, a desire to enhance their reputa-tion with the king (2:31), and, more obscurely, "for the sake of their belly" (7:11). The overall implication is that they were responding to external pressure but also acting out of self-interest. What they gained (temporar-ily) was Alexandrian citizenship, but only at the price of apostasy and the loss of solidarity with their fellow Jews.

The same work (3 Macc. 1:3) mentions Dositheus, a Jewish servant of the king, "who changed his religion and apostatized from the ancestral traditions (*metabalôn ta nomima kai tôn patriôn dogmatôn apellotriomenos*)." From papyri we know of a Dositheus who was a scribe and priest in the royal court of Philopater IV (Modrzejewski-Mélèze 1993, 82–85), who may be the same man as the Dositheus in 3 Macc. 1:3, and we may not be far wrong in supposing that social and political ambitions lay at the root of his defec-tion. Ostensibly these events took place in Philopater's reign (222–203 BCE), but the work in which they appear comes from the first century CE (though it has often been dated to the first century BCE), perhaps during the reign of Gaius Caligula (38–41 CE; thus J.J. Collins 1983, 104–11, who notes, how-ever, that the fit with events in Alexandria during Caligula's reign is loose and more like the account of Philo in *Legatio ad Gaium* than what is known from other sources), and this work may be alert to contemporary prob-lems as well.

The case of Philo's nephew, Tiberius Julius Alexander, of whom it was said that he "did not continue in the customs of his forefathers (*tois patri-ois ou diemeinen ethesin*)" (Josephus, *A.J.* 20.100), is of interest, too. His suc-cessful military career included spells in Egypt (military commander of Upper Egypt in the forties, prefect of Egypt in the sixties), Judea (procu-

rator 46–48 CE, second-in-command to Titus at the end of the Jewish War),
and, perhaps, the prefecture of the Praetorian Guard (Turner 1954, 61–64).
Once launched, his military career, and any ambitions he harboured,
depended on absorption into the military ethos. Part of his routine military
and political duties would presumably have involved participation in civic
cults (when he was prefect of Egypt, for example), and there is evidence of
him dedicating a relief to the emperor and pagan deities (Turner 1954,
56–57). That is, he not only left behind Jewish traditions, but also took on
those of the typical Roman aristocrat.

We can speculate about the factors that led Tiberius Alexander to drift
away from his Jewish roots. Education in a Greek gymnasium, a common
training for military officers and, in some periods, a favoured route to
advancement for wealthy Alexandrian Jews, was probably one. Wolfson
(1947, 1:79) thought that Jews did not attend the gymnasia, but the evidence points in the other direction. There is no convincing evidence for
specifically Jewish gymnasia in Alexandria. Louis H. Feldman (1960,
222–26) gives a useful summary and notes the serious compromises that
a gymnasium education involved for Jews (see also Sandelin 1991, 112–13,
138–42). Philo condemns those who used education for social advancement (*Leg.* 3.164–165) or socio-economic mobility (*Spec.* 2.18f). Of course,
attending a gymnasium or otherwise taking part in Hellenistic cultural
events did not inevitably lead to apostasy, as the case of Philo himself
clearly shows (see, further, Kerkeslager 1997, for the case of a Hellenized
Jew who participates in a theatrical mime, but in a way that only accentuates his Jewish identity).

Philo tells us (in *De providentia* and elsewhere) that he had discussed the
problem of divine providence and theodicy with a man called Alexander,
whom many identify with Philo's nephew (*pace* Hadas-Lebel 1973, 23, 46).
If this identification is correct, we may suppose that the nephew had some
philosophical problems with Judaism. Moreover, Alexander probably began
his official career at the time his father—a well-connected and influential
Alexandrian Jew—was freed, when Claudius took the place of Gaius as
emperor (Turner 1954, 58). Alexander's drift away from Judaism was thus
probably caused by a combination of Greek education, philosophical doubt,
worldly ambition, and family gratitude.

Was Tiberius Alexander an apostate? Josephus doesn't precisely say
this, but he would have had reason to tread lightly in his description of an
ally of Vespasian. Note as well the similarity between Tiberius "not remaining in (*diemeinen*) the customs" and the proselytes who do "remain"
(*emeinan*) as distinct from those who "leave" (*apestēsan*), in Josephus, *Con-*

tra Apionem (2.123). John M.G. Barclay (1995a, 120) observes that Josephus may have considered it politic not to label Tiberius Alexander an apostate until after he was dead (i.e., in *Antiquitates judaicae,* but not in *Bellum judaicum*). Though we don't have Tiberius Alexander's view on the matter, to describe him merely as a non-observant Jew seems not to catch the flavour of his career and, if he did not openly renounce Judaism, he appears to have followed a path which steadily drew him toward the practices, ideals, and politics of the non-Jewish world (contra Feldman 1993a, 81). S. Applebaum (1976, 705) suggests that Tiberius was, "if not actually a renegade, at least a studious neglecter of Judaism," while Barclay (1995a, 120) raises the interesting hypothetical question whether Alexander would have been viewed differently if he had been able to be of advantage to the Jews in Egypt and Judea. We can only guess. Pursuit of a political career may also have led to the deracination of Herod's great-grandchildren, who are said to have abandoned (*ekleipô*) Judaism in favour of the Greek way of life (Josephus, *A.J.* 18.141).

That Josephus was concerned about contemporary problems of Jewish assimilation and apostasy is indicated by the way he recasts two biblical narratives: (i) the seduction of Israelite men by the Midianite and Moabite women, which led to the eating of forbidden foods, worship of foreign gods, murder of an apostate Jew (Zimri=Zambrias in Josephus) and his pagan consort by the zealous Phinehas, and further punishment of Israel by a plague (Num. 25; Josephus, *A.J.* 4.126–155); and (ii) Solomon's downfall (1 Kgs 11:1–13, Josephus, *A.J.* 8.190–198) when he took foreign wives and began to worship their gods. In the first story, the arguments used by Zambrias, which Willem Cornelius van Unnik has called a "rationale for apostasy," may very well reflect the views of Jewish defectors who had succumbed to intellectual arguments in favour of the pluralism of pagan religion (1974, 261; in this paragraph, I summarize van Unnik [1974], who is followed by Borgen 1995, 33–36). The pressure on Jews to join in pagan worship is indicated in Josephus, *Antiquitates judaicae* 12.125–126; 16.58–59; *Contra Apionem* 2.66. In the second case, "the story dramatically highlights the on-going contemporary problem of assimilation vis-à-vis fidelity to 'ancestral customs'" (Begg 1997, 313; van Unnik [1974, 251] also connects this story with Josephus's account of Num. 25). In both instances, Josephus seems particularly alert to the dangers of exogamy and the ease with which transgression of food laws can lead down the slippery slope to apostasy.

Philo is a rich source of information about Jews who drifted away from their community. In *De virtutibus* 182, he speaks of "rebels against the holy laws" (*tous tôn hierôn nomôn apostantes*) who favour instead strong drink, delicate foods, and the enjoyment of another's beauty (*eumorphias*), the last of which may refer to marriage to a Gentile. By following their natural appetites, eating forbidden food, and marrying forbidden people, they have thus sold their freedom (*eleutheria*), and do "the gravest injury to both body and soul." In *De praemiis et poenis* 152, Philo alludes to Jews who are like the well-born man who "debases the coinage of his noble birth" (*parakompsas to nomisma tês eugeneias*), which may also allude to intermarriage as well as a more general abandonment of Jewish laws. In the first passage, the Jewish apostates are contrasted pointedly with faithful proselytes; and in the second, their fate, to "be carried into Tartarus itself and profound darkness," is contrasted with that of virtuous proselytes who will be especially prized in heaven. In each case, the allusion to intermarriage is oblique, but Harry Austryn Wolfson (1947, 1:73–77) has made a case for this interpretation, as he has for distinguishing the Jews alluded to here from the "Yom Kippur" Jews (*Spec.* 1.186–187), who sat lightly on religious observance but once a year, and from those who were lured by the attractions of the Gentile world but made no deliberate break with their community (an interpretation originally followed by Feldman [1960, 227] but not recently [1993a, 79–82]). The language Philo uses to describe these apostate Jews, the dire fate he envisages for them, and the contrast between them and faithful proselytes suggest that they were of a different order from the casually unobservant.

Feldman (1993a, 80) denies a reference to intermarriage and thinks that Philo is speaking not of apostates but of those who do not keep the commandments—part of Feldman's overall tendency to minimize the incidence of apostasy. Feldman refers, unconvincingly, to the concern for repentance in *De virtutibus,* and the rabbinic view that apostates remain, in some sense, Jews. It is the context, rather than the terms themselves, which might support Wolfson. *Eumorphia* literally means "beauty of form" (cf. Josephus, *A.J.* 10.186; 15.23), and is used by Philo of men (*Opif.* 136; *Ios.* 40, 268), animals (*Leg.* 2.75), slaves (*Spec.* 2.34; *Flacc.* 149), and idols (*Spec.* 1.29), as well as of women (*Post.* 117; *Sobr.* 12; *Abr.* 93). It probably refers to beautiful women in *De specialibus legibus* 4.82: one of those things (like money and power) which uncontrolled appetites desire. Apart from Philo, *Testament of Judah* 14:3 conveys the sense of promiscuous sex. Thus, desire for beautiful women, rather than marriage to foreign women, is all that the terminology suggests. Elsewhere, however, Philo specifically mentions the dangers of intermarriage, especially as it affects offspring (*Spec.* 3.29; cf. *Jub.* 30:11). When recalling biblical instances of intermarriage, Philo takes a benign view and minimizes the foreign element in the relationships. Is this because it was not a pressing issue for him (Feldman 1993a, 77–79), or because it was sufficiently significant that the wise course was to take a gentle line and hope for the conversion of the pagan partner (Mendelson 1988, 73–74)? Philo sees the food laws as a form of moral discipline (*Spec.* 4.100ff.). In a number of writings (e.g., 4 Macc. 5:6ff.), adherence to the food laws epitomizes faithfulness to Judaism. "Debasing the coinage" is a common metaphor in Philo, and alludes to the transgression of various personal or civic ideals (*Conf.* 159; *Fug.* 171, 208; *Spec.* 3.38, 176; 4.47; *Contempl.* 41). A reference to intermarriage in *De praemiis et poenis* 152 is, at most, a possibility.

In a vivid passage in *De specialibus legibus* (1.316), Philo asserts that if false prophets, friends, or relatives "bid us to fraternize with the multitudes, resort to their temples, and join in their libations and sacrifices," they are to be treated as public enemies, whose death it is a religious duty to seek. Here, defection means not only abandoning Jewish practice but also embracing pagan worship—and that with the encouragement of prophets, relatives, and friends, presumably fellow Jews. Note, too, *De praemiis et poenis* 162, where Philo speaks of the punishments he has described for those "who disregard the holy laws of justice and piety, who have been seduced by the polytheistic creeds (*polytheiois doxais*) which finally lead to atheism (*atheotês*), and have forgotten the teaching of their nation and their fathers." Is Philo here thinking merely theoretically or letting his imagination run away with him as he meditates on biblical stories? I think not, and it reminds us pointedly of the influence of social and familial networks.

Most of these examples concern defection from Judaism to paganism. Proselytes could also move in this direction since, even though they had made a difficult choice in once joining the Jewish community, not all of them stayed. Josephus (*C. Ap.* 2.123) tells us specifically that "many of them [Greeks] have agreed to adopt our laws; and some of them have remained (*emeinan*), while others, lacking the necessary endurance, have again seceded (*hoi tên karterian ouch hypomeinantes palin apestêsan*)." Thus, while Josephus, like Philo, was proud of Gentile converts, he admits that not all of them stayed the course.

Finally, we also have some inscriptional evidence for Jews defecting to Christianity. From North Africa in the fourth century (le Bohec 1981, nos. 1, 66, 75):

Mos[e]s (with chi-rho)

Sabbatiolus (with chi-rho)

In memory (with chi-rho) of the blessed Istablicus, also called Donatus. Installed by his brother Peregrinus, also called Mosattes, once a Jew (*de Jude[i]s*)

These epitaphs appear to be for men who once had been Jews but now were Christians. Their Jewish origin is indicated by their names in the first two cases and by the declaration that they were *de Judeis* in the third. Yann le Bohec thought the first and third examples were Jewish converts to Christianity. The second he thought to be a converted pagan Jewish sympathizer, though it could as easily refer to a Jew (Figueras 1990, 205) or to a Christian Judaizer (Kant 1987, 707). The Christian element in each case is the appearance of the chi-rho symbol. It is not certain that Jews commonly used the name of Moses at this time, and a name is not always a reliable indicator of origin. Tomasz Devda (1997, 257–60) thinks that Jews did not use Moses until the late Byzantine period. Margaret H. Williams (1997, 274) counters with examples from the fourth century on, though the name is not always certainly transcribed (on use of names as indicators in inscriptions, see G.H.R. Horsley 1987). Le Bohec argues, on the other hand, that non-Jews were unlikely to use this name at a time when anti-Semitism was rabid in North Africa. Even so, the third example remains clear.

From Italy around the same time (fourth to fifth century CE) we have a fairly uncomplicated example (*CIJ* I2 643a=Noy 1993/1995:1.8):

> Here lies Peter, also called Paprio, son of Olympus the Jew, and the only one of his family (*gens*) who has deserved to attain the grace of Christ.

There is no doubt that this is an example of Jewish conversion to Christianity. That Peter truly was the only one of his family (*gens* could also mean nation) to convert is likely, given the other evidence we have for Jewish converts in the post-Constantine era. The timing of these defections—during the period when Christianity was becoming increasingly dominant as the official religion of the empire—should be noted. There is nevertheless no reason to suppose that these changes of loyalty were cynical acts of convenience. Many other things may have motivated them, but, as usual, the epitaphs remain frustratingly silent.

Of course, a much earlier, but more controversial, example would be Paul—worth a large section alone, but one that would deflect us too far from our overall theme. Most scholars judge Paul to have been an apostate from Judaism (Gaston 1987, 76–79; Segal 1990, 223, 290; Barclay 1995a; though for a different view, see Dunn 1998). Many other Jewish Christians would likewise be grist for our mill, if we knew about specific cases beyond the first few decades of Christianity, but we do not. Moreover, for the purposes of this chapter, the period when Christianity was still largely a sectarian movement within Judaism is less important.

DEFECTION FROM CHRISTIANITY

For our first Christian example, we may appropriately start with an unusual group: the Jewish Christians who got caught up in the Bar Kochba rebellion. Justin mentions that some of them were put to death for refusing to recognize the claims of Bar Kochba (1 *Apol.* 31.6; *Dial.*16; cf. Eusebius, *Hist. eccl.* 4.6.2), but we may have a fuller, if cryptic, account in *The Apocalypse of Peter* (2:8–13):

> (8) They will promise that, "I am the Christ who has come into the world." And when they see the wickedness of his deed, they will follow after them. (9) And they will deny him whom they call the Glory of our Fathers, whom they crucified, the first [?], and Christ. And when they have rejected him, he will kill with the sword and many will become martyrs…(11) This is the house of Israel only. They will be martyrs by his hand…(12) For Enoch and Elijah will be sent that they might teach them that this is the deceiver who must come into the world and do signs and wonders and deceive. (13) And on account of [?] those who die by his hand will be martyrs and will be reckoned with the good and righteous martyrs who have pleased God in their life.

The most recent commentary on this passage (Bucholz 1988, 283–89, 408–12; see also Bauckham 1998), which dates the work to ca. 132–135 CE, detects the following allusions to the reaction of Jewish Christians to Bar Kochba: some Christians, presumably Jewish (v. 11), joined the cause of the false messiah (v. 8), which amounted to a denial of Christ (v. 9); when they realized that he was not the messiah, they abandoned him, and he, in turn, persecuted and killed them (vv. 10–11); messengers are promised who will confirm that he is the deceiver and that these are the end times (v. 12); the one-time defectors, now martyrs, will be counted among the righteous (v. 13). This is an attractive interpretation and fits well with the concern elsewhere in *The Apocalypse of Peter* with signs of the end and false messiahs (1:2–5), those who die in their sins without having observed the laws of God (1:2), the fate of Israel (2:1–13), and the certainty of resurrection (4:1–13).

If this view is correct, these Jewish Christians are, in the eyes of the author of *The Apocalypse of Peter,* guilty of a double defection: first, by supporting the Bar Kochba movement, they defected from the Christian community; second, by subsequently denying that Bar Kochba was the messiah, they defected from the Jewish community or, at least, from that part of it which supported Bar Kochba. In both instances, the position of the defectors seems to have been taken voluntarily, and they may not have accepted the author's judgment that their initial support amounted to a denial of Jesus Christ. At first, they may have thought that they were merely supporting a Jewish liberation movement, and it may have been precisely the pressure to recognize Bar Kochba's messianic status which led to their withdrawal and subsequent execution. It was rare for divisions within Judaism to turn so critically on questions of messiahship, and even rarer for Christian Jews to be treated so severely by other Jews. But the passions and tensions aroused by the Bar Kochba rebellion, and the temporary overthrow of Roman rule in a small part of Judea, produced a situation in which both the definition and the punishment of defection took an unusual turn.

The author of Hebrews refers obliquely to a problem with Christians, who, in his eyes, had reneged on their Christian commitment. They had already tasted the benefits of membership in the Christian community: knowledge of the truth, heavenly gifts, experience of the Spirit, and the goodness of God's word. Yet now they had fallen away (*parapesontas,* 6:6), and had—to use the unusually strong language of the author—spurned or re-crucified the Son of God and made a mockery of his death. Repentance for such renegades is out of the question, and their punishment will be severe, even more severe than the punishment for those who breach the Mosaic Law (6:4–8; 10:26–31; cf. "drifting away," 2:1, "falling short," 4:1, "shrinking back," 10:39). These defections appear to lie in the past at the time of writing; but, although the author expresses confidence in his readers (6:9), the issue is raised presumably because the possibility of a recurrence was not out of the question. What led to the defections is not clear, but the allusion to past experiences of persecution, public harassment, confiscation, and imprisonment may be the best clue (10:32–34).

A number of other things remain unclear. The persecution may have been instigated by Jews, but is perhaps more likely an allusion to state harassment during the reign of Nero or Domitian. Anthony Ernest Harvey (1985, 89) thinks in terms of synagogue discipline. But did Jewish courts have the right to confiscate and imprison? The date (whether before or after 70 CE) and the setting of Hebrews have been much discussed, but for our purposes are not very important. David A. deSilva (1996) likens apostasy to a client spurning a patron. The readers are commonly thought to have been Jewish Christians. The deep concern to establish the supersession of Jewish traditions, especially those related to the cult, together with the exhortation to "go to him [Jesus] outside the camp and bear the abuse he endured" (13:13), certainly suggests that the author of Hebrews is trying to wean his readers from their hankering after Jewish thought and practice. It is also possible that they were Gentiles, who had previously formed an attachment to Judaism and were now wondering if they had left too much behind when they allied themselves with the Christians. Whether Jewish Christians or Gentile Judaizers, the defectors probably, but not certainly, headed back to the Jewish community.

If this reconstruction is correct, we may surmise that those who defected from the Christian community did so because of both persecution and an unsatisfied longing for aspects of the Judaism they had earlier left. Whether they thought this involved abandonment of their Christian beliefs is not clear, though the author of Hebrews is in no doubt that it did. A similar situation may be implied by Revelation, which speaks of "those who say they are Jews but are not" (2:9; cf. 3:9). These were more likely Jewish Christians or Gentile Christian Judaizers than Jews (Wilson 1992, 613–14), and the reasons for their defection are the perception of a hostile Roman state and a hankering for their former association with Judaism.

The Shepherd of Hermas twice mentions apostates and considers their fate. They are the "apostates and traitors (*apostatai kai prodotai*) to the church, who by their sins have blasphemed the Lord, and in addition were ashamed of the Lord's name, by which they were called" (Herm. *Sim.* 8.6.4); and "apostates and blasphemers (*apostatai kai blasphêmoi*) against the Lord and betrayers (*prodotai*) of God's servants" (Herm. *Sim.* 9.19.1). They are presumably the same persons as those elsewhere who "fell away [*apestêsan* or *apôlesan*] completely" (Herm. *Sim.* 8.8.2,5). For such, there is no possibility of repentance, unlike the "hypocrites and false teachers" or "teachers of evil," for whom repentance is possible.

Asked why this is so, considering the similarity of the two groups' deeds, Hermas answers that the latter "have not blasphemed their Lord nor become betrayers (*prodotai*) of God's people" (Herm. *Sim.* 8.6.5; 9.19.2–3; cf. 6.2.3). In addition, one individual, Maximus, is singled out as someone who had denied his faith in the past and might do so again (Herm. *Vis.* 2.3.4). The charge of blasphemy reminds us of the sacrifice and curse required of those denying Christian allegiance in Bithynia (cf. Herm. *Sim.* 9.21.3; Freudenberger 1969, 147).

The severe judgment passed in Hermas on apostates and betrayers matches that of the author of Hebrews, and it may have something to do with the fact that they had not only apostatized and blasphemed but had also betrayed their fellow Christians. For while "betrayal" could mean simply that these people had abandoned the community, a mere synonym for defection, it might more precisely mean that they had become informers (Jeffers 1991, 129).

Hermas is usually thought to come from Rome some time in the second century CE, but recently a good case has been made for an earlier date toward the end of the first century CE (see Maier 1991, 55–58). The circumstances in which apostasy and betrayal occurred are not given, but two things are discussed which may shed some light on the matter. First, there are references to persecution, either past or to come (Herm. *Vis.* 2.2.7; 4:1.6–9; Herm. *Sim.* 8.6.4; 8.8.2). This could relate to the time of Domitian, Pliny, or any similar second-century CE situation in which Christians were publicly arraigned and required to confirm or to deny their faith. Second, denial and defection are often associated with the problem of riches, a recurrent theme of the book (Herm. *Vis.* 1.4.2; 2.2.6–8; 3.6.5; Herm. *Sim.* 1.4–6; 6.2.3–4; 8.8.2; 8.9.1–3; 9.19.3). Wealthy Christians, some of whom became wealthy as Christians (Herm. *Sim.* 8.9.1), and many of whom were probably benefactors and/or leaders of the house churches, found themselves pried from the Christian community by their social and financial connections to the outside world and the pressure to live according to pagan standards (Herm. *Sim.* 8.8.1; 8.9.1–3; 9.20.2; Herm. *Mand.* 10.1.4–5; thus Maier 1991, 66–67; also P. Lampe 1987, 71–78, who thinks Hermas's notion of a second repentance, and the concession that the rich can be involved in one business rather than many, are designed to entice the rich back to the church and to ensure that the poor are taken care of). It is probable that Hermas himself had once been rich, but was not so now (likely because of imprisonment and confiscation), so that he knew some of the pressures at first hand. James S. Jeffers (1991, 171–72), however, separates the problems of apostasy and wealth. In any case, it seems, some continued in the faith even if they didn't do the works of faith, but others were absorbed entirely into their pagan environment (Herm. *Sim.* 8.9.1–3, 8.10.3).

The problems of the wealthy seem to have been constantly on the mind of the author, no doubt because assimilation was a constant temptation and, in itself, accounted for some of the defections. But the acid test often came in times of persecution. For while the Romans did not authorize any official or widespread persecution, when Christians were brought to their attention by informers or by their own activities, these same Christians were invariably faced with a stark option: confess and die, or deny and live. In addition, the families stood to lose all their property through confiscation.

For some of the wealthy and well connected, it seems, allegiance was too great a price to pay. Hermas (*Vis.* 3.6.5) speaks of those who "have faith, but also have the riches of this world. Whenever persecution comes, they deny their Lord because of their riches and their business affairs."

And when they defected, they may well have dragged other Christians into difficulty by betraying them to the authorities.

Hermas thus presents us with a quite rich array of material, albeit sometimes oblique: different degrees of assimilation among the wealthy, ranging from mere neglect of the Christian poor to total absorption in pagan life (the latter condition being considered to be beyond the pale, and those found in it to be defectors, even if they are not called apostates/ betrayers in the text); and different degrees of denial under pressure, rang- ing from the merely hesitant who come through in the end (Herm. *Sim.* 9.28.4), through those who deny but can repent (when divested of their wealth, Herm. *Vis.* 3.6.5–6; *Sim.* 9.21.3), to those called apostates/betrayers/ blasphemers, whose uncompromising denial and betrayal of others seems to place them beyond redemption. In addition, Hermas highlights the effect that the pressures of family and friends, social status, and threats from the ruling order could have on defection.

Another snippet of evidence comes from Justin's discussion of the relationships of various Jewish Christian groups with Gentile Christians and the synagogue communities (*Dial.* 46–47). At the end of his discussion, Justin alludes to erstwhile Christians who have defected to the synagogue and who openly deny their previous Christian beliefs (*Dial.* 47.4). These may have been Jewish Christians, but the statement that they "switched over to" (*metabainô*) rather than "returned to" the synagogue perhaps sug- gests that they were Gentiles. We are not told what motivated them, only that they defected "for some reason or other," but the general context suggests that a significant role was played by Jewish persuasion (Wilson 1992, 609–10). If so, we gain a glimpse of yet another element in the process of defection: active enticement from another quarter, in this case Judaism.

Finally, we turn to the later stories of Christian martyrs (Musurillo 1972; Droge and Tabor 1992). Our richest source is Cyprian's *De Lapsis,* in which he defends his rigourist line on dealing with the "lapsed" who had succumbed during the Decian persecution in 250–251 CE, but who subse- quently wanted to return to the church. In the course of his argument, Cyprian gives a vivid picture of the reaction of Christians in Carthage, where he was the newly appointed bishop. In an attempt to encourage unity and the honouring of traditional gods, the Romans required a pub- lic confession that involved sacrifice to pagan gods in front of a usually "scoffing crowd" (2.8–17; 28.15–20). Cyprian describes the following groups:

- the confessors, some of whom were martyred, some of whom survived their torture, others of whom broke (2–3);

• the fugitives, like Cyprian himself, who went into hiding, had their property confiscated, but made no public denial (3, 4, 10);
• the ordinary faithful (*stantes*), who were not cowed but were saved by the bell (2.23–34; 3.1–5);
• the potential *lapsi*, who considered denial but were not required to make a decision (28.107);
• the *libellatici*, who got a false certificate of sacrifice through bribery (27.1–5)—what Cyprian calls a "confession of apostasy" (*professio denegantis*);
• the *sacrificati*, who acceded, many of them rushing to offer sacrifice before they were arrested, encouraging their friends to join them, dragging along their children, and generally behaving like eager defectors (7–9); these are the "apostates and renegades" (*apostati, perfidis*, 33.16).

Cyprian defends his rigorous conditions for accepting back the defectors against a softer line supported by surviving confessors. This, together with his own flight, put him in a weak position at the time, though he was later to soften his views in the face of a devastating plague and the threat of new persecutions. He provides a number of insights into defection. For some defectors, the impression is that ties to friends and the desire to protect families were paramount (9.1). In chapter 6, Cyprian details the signs of a church gone slack. Among these signs are marriage to pagans, which would have posed a dilemma in times of public pressure, and the accumulation of property and wealth, fear for the loss of which was one of the main reasons for defection (11.1ff). Clearly, too, some Christians (the *lapsi*) later wished to recant their public defection and return to the church, which, with appropriate acts of repentance, they were allowed to do. Defection, that is, was not necessarily final.

Another intriguing example crops up in the account of the *Martyrdom of Pionius*, which took place around 250 CE, where it is recorded that there were deserters (10.5–6, 12.2, 20.3), some of whom voluntarily offered sacrifice (4.3) and others of whom, like the leader Euctemon, tried unsuccessfully to persuade the rest to follow him (15.2, 16.1, 18.13–14; Musurillo 1972, 137–67). Pionius himself despised learned pagans, and warns against Jews who, in his view, took advantage of Christians in distress by inviting them to take shelter in the synagogue. He deeply suspected their motives, and warned Christians against consorting with the killers of Christ. But that may be no more than an expression of his ingrained suspicions, and the Jews may kindly have been offering a refuge to Christians in a time of peril.

What the motives of these Jews were, we cannot know. Harking back to the accounts of Jewish involvement in the death of Polycarp a century earlier (Lane Fox 1986, 481–82)—accounts which are deeply suspect for their mirroring of the Gospel accounts of Jesus' death—sheds little light on events a century later. At any rate, we have in the *Martyrdom of Pionius* an example of some sort of rivalry: either two-sided (Christians and pagans, with Jews ameliorating) or three-sided (Christians and pagans, with Jews taking advantage). The circumstances are abnormal—persecution of Christians was only sporadic—but the pattern of interaction may not have been.

DEFECTION FROM PAGANISM

Evidence for pagan defectors is harder to come by, as we might expect. Indeed, some might say that the absence in Greco-Roman culture of the principle of exclusive commitment or firm boundaries, such as characterized Jewish and Christian communities (even if the reality was somewhat different), seems to exclude at the outset the notion of defection/apostasy. Yet we do find examples that look very much like the phenomena we have already surveyed in Jewish and Christian texts, some of which, interestingly, suggest that boundaries were sometimes firmer and more exclusive than our usual picture of *laissez-faire* syncretism would lead us to expect.

One of the more interesting examples is Peregrinus, the publicity-hungry philosopher lampooned by Lucian. Peregrinus late in his career took the name "Proteus," which Lucian sarcastically suggests was appropriate in view of his constant transformations. According to Lucian, Peregrinus was an adulterer and a corrupter of youth, who had to leave his homeland after killing his father. He turned up in Palestine and joined the Christian movement, where he became a renowned "prophet, cult-leader, and head of the synagogue." Imprisoned—by whom and for what reason is not said—his fame increased, and many gullible Christians supported him with gifts and money, revering him as a "new Socrates" second only to their Christ. Running into difficulties, apparently for eating idol food, he abandoned the Christians, went to Egypt for ascetic training, and returned to Italy a Cynic, promoting a blend of Cynicism and popular religion. Expelled from Italy, he ended up in Athens, where, eventually, egged on by his followers, he publicly demonstrated his indifference to death in an act of self-immolation. Soon after, an oracle and statues were erected in his memory.

We need to dig beneath Lucian's satirical veneer, of course, but if we accept the broad outline of his version there is little doubt that Peregrinus was both a convert to and an apostate from Christianity. What motivated him to join and defect was probably a lot more complex than Lucian allows us to see. Perhaps his defection was simply a matter of unacceptable behaviour (consuming idol food); perhaps the gullible began to suspect his sincerity; or perhaps Lucian is close to the truth and he was an egomaniac who obsessively sought the limelight. We cannot know with any certainty. Yet Peregrinus is a fascinating example of a figure who shifted allegiance more than once, apparently with both plausibility and success, and who did so perhaps not because he was enticed by the missionary efforts of others but because he was following his own quest for religious satisfaction.

Many examples arise in connection with the disputes and divisions in philosophical schools. Timocrates, like his brother Metrodorus, once a dedicated Epicurean, eventually abandoned the Epicurean school and became its implacable opponent (*Diog. Laert.* 10.6–8). Both Metrodorus and Epicurus wrote refutations of Timocrates' polemical attacks on their school, but Timocrates still became an influential source for the anti-Epicurean tradition (see Sedley 1976). Among the reasons for the split, Diogenes Laertius lists the following: Epicurus was a glutton, in poor health and largely chairbound; Epicurus had only limited knowledge of philosophy and real life; Epicurus and Metrodorus encouraged courtesans to join their school; Timocrates was tired of the "midnight philosophizing" and the "secrets of the confraternity" (*tên mystikên ekeinên syndiagogên*); and Epicurus had few original thoughts, expending his energy as a dismissive and satirical critic of his philosophical predecessors and contemporaries.

It is hard to get beyond the polemical slant of this exposé. Some Epicurean positions were easy to distort, such as their qualified hedonism, or their encouragement of philosophical training for women, and Timocrates took full advantage of this weakness. In general, his criticisms concern two things: communal lifestyle and intellectual pretension. David Sedley (1976, 153n. 34) suggests that a fratricidal split was at the root of things. He also thinks that Timocrates may have joined the Academy (see also Frischer 1982, 50–52). Some things may have been rankling for a while and may genuinely have precipitated his defection, but a lot of it looks like *post facto* justification and polemics, too. It is not unusual for a certain type of defector—those who become active opponents of the group they have abandoned—to exaggerate the shortcomings of the community they have left, and give to everything a negative twist.

Epicureans were far more communally minded than other philosophical schools. They lived together in well-ordered communities that resembled miniature states. The religious element included commemorative festivals, common meals, honouring the founder (the "sole saviour" Epicurus), and the extensive use of statues of their masters (Glad 1995, 8–9; Frischer 1982, 52–70). Diskin Clay notes the broad similarities between Epicureans and Christians to outsiders, something observed as early as the second century by Lucian: "Both groups were charged with atheism, separateness and secrecy, misanthropy, social irresponsibility, the disruption of families, sexual immorality and general moral depravity" (Clay 1986, 9n. 16). Timocrates' departure is thus a notable example of defection. What we do not know is whether Timocrates joined up elsewhere or simply became an independent, obsessive critic of the Epicureans.

Other philosophical dissidents, such as Metrodorus of Stratonicus (*Diog. Laert.* 10.9–11), transferred their allegiance, or, like Stilpo of Megara, founded their own school (*Diog. Laert.* 2.113–114). Together, all these cases add an interesting refinement to our notion of rivalry: conflicts between subgroups within the larger categories that we more typically use. A similar situation, but a quite different context, is suggested by a fascinating inscription from Sardis, dated to the first or early second century CE (see G.H.R. Horsley 1981, 21–23). The inscription instructs the temple-warden devotees in a cult of Zeus the Legislator to desist from participation in the mysteries of Sabazios, Agdistis, and Ma (*CCCA* 1.456; trans. G.H.R. Horsley 1981, no. 3:21–23):

> In the thirty-ninth year of Artaxerxes' reign, Droaphernes son of Barakis, governor of Lydia, dedicated a statue to Zeus the Legislator. He [Droaphernes] instructs his [Zeus'] temple-warden devotees who enter the innermost sanctum and who serve and crown the god, not to participate in the mysteries of Sabazios with those who bring the burnt offerings and [the mysteries] of Agdistis and Ma. They instruct Dorates the temple-warden to keep away from these mysteries.

This text is apparently a Greek rewriting of an earlier (Aramaic?) edict (ca. 365 BCE) relating to the cult of Zeus Baradates (Legislator)—a Greek translation of the name of a Persian deity (Ahura Mazda)—suggesting an originally Iranian association that had taken on a Greek form. The prohibition is here updated to bring into line one Dorates, who had transgressed it, though precisely who was laying down the law remains obscure. While the edict seems to apply only to the functionaries of the cult and not to the general membership, it nevertheless provides a fascinating glimpse of a religious exclusivity and conservatism, which flies in the face of the generalized notion of relaxed and casual religious syncretism in the pagan world. The inscription is, at most, an example of temporary defection (unless Dorates defied the edict), but it does alert us again to the issue of rivalry between groups within one of the larger categories (in this case, paganism) with which we tend to operate. Rivalry, that is, occurred not only between but also within the "big three."

A quite different example, only briefly related in our sources, is the shift of allegiance attributed to Flavius Clemens and his wife Domitilla. They were accused of "atheism" and "drifting into Jewish ways" (*Dio* 67.14.1–3) and, as a result, Clemens was executed and his wife exiled. Some scholars have argued that these two had drifted toward Christianity rather than Judaism, which is a possible understanding of the accusations, since Christians were indeed accused of atheism and could broadly be said to have adopted Jewish ways. Eusebius, later, refers to a Domitilla who was the niece of Flavius Clemens and who was exiled under Domitian "as a testimony to Christ" (*Hist. Eccl.* 3.18.4). If the two Domitillas are conflated, then she was a Christian, but there is no good reason to do so, and no evidence that Flavius Clemens was moving toward Christianity rather than Judaism.

Thus we may have the following: Flavius Clemens and his wife, moving from paganism toward Judaism, and their niece moving from paganism (or Judaism?) toward Christianity. In each case, we are dealing with Roman aristocrats, whose defection would have been seen as a serious matter at the best of times, but since Flavius Clemens and his wife were also the parents of Domitian's designated heirs, political concerns would have been paramount. Perhaps this, rather than their religious predilections, was the real problem; some have suggested that the charge of Judaizing was merely a pretext in a dynastic and political struggle. Yet it remains interesting that defection from paganism—to Judaism or to Christianity—could plausibly be used as a charge, and could provoke such a severe reaction from the emperor.

CONCLUSION

What, then, do these defectors tell us about religious rivalry? Certainly not that, as fast as converts came in one door, apostates left by another. Yet there was a significant enough number of defectors to alert us to the phenomenon of losing, as distinct from gaining, adherents, and this adds an important element to our broader consideration of religious rivalries. It shows, at least, that religious cults did not always satisfy the needs of their adherents. Moreover, with few exceptions, there was an element of rivalry between them, at least in the sense that the defectors were pushed or tugged in the direction of one or more of the competitors. Tiberius Alexander the aristocratic Jewish-Roman general and Timocrates the philosopher may be exceptions, but in most cases the move out of one religious context also involved a move into another. In some instances, for both Jews and Christians, there was strong political pressure to shift allegiance, for example, the Jews in 3 Maccabees and the Christians in Hebrews and Hermas, but in other instances this was not the case. Usually only two of the major players are in view—when Jews shift to paganism or Christianity, or Christians to Judaism or paganism—but in at least one instance (Pionius) we see all three groups interacting at the same time. We also have some evidence (Timocrates and the Zeus association) that encourages us to broaden our concept of religious rivalry to include competition within the larger entities that we typically take as our points of comparison.

Mostly, there is little hint of missionary activity, though Justin's reference to Christian defectors may imply such activity on the part of the synagogue. As expected, the pull of social and family networks had a considerable effect, as can be seen in the warnings against intermarriage in Philo and Josephus, in Philo's depiction of the solicitations of family and friends to join in pagan worship, and in the dilemma faced by wealthy Christians in Hermas. In some cases, the attraction is clearly a previous form of religious life, as with Josephus's proselyte defectors and the Christians in Hebrews. In addition, it is worth noting that a few of our examples appear to be people on a highly individual quest: Peregrinus with his switching from one thing to another, and Tiberius Alexander following his intellectual doubts and his advancing career.

The reasons given for defection are quite varied, ranging through hostile pressure, career advancement, social attachments, prior religious experience, and intellectual doubt: a rich enough array to alert us to the manifold circumstances and motives that could prompt people to change their religious allegiance. This warns us never to ignore the complexity of the phenomena we study. The answer to the questions of how religious and quasi-religious groups interacted and why some of them eventually gained the upper hand will have to be as complex and as nuanced as the explanations we can offer for defections. And since the reasons for defection, given in ancient and modern sources, are, as some have noted, often a mirror image of the reasons for the attraction and retention of converts, studying the one may be an indirect way of studying the other.

4

Is the Pagan Fair Fairly Dangerous?
Jewish-Pagan Relations in Antiquity

Reena Basser

INTRODUCTION

Fairs in the life of ancient Israel touched every facet of society. Many people were involved in the life of the fair, because it was the place in which goods and services were sold and purchased. The fair included luxury as well as small, inexpensive goods; land was sold, and slaves and animals bought. This institution included many characteristics that were considered offensive by the authors of the seminal literature of the Sages: the *Mishnah,* the *Tosefta,* and both the Jerusalem and Babylonian Talmuds. However, many of the prohibitions against participating in the fair were removed by the simultaneous introduction of ways in which Israelites could be involved in this economic aspect of daily life.

Most secondary discussions of fairs and their meaning aim to demonstrate how the Sages permitted the Israelites' involvement in the fair after the Bar Kochba revolt. Missing in the scholarly literature, however, is a survey of attitudes toward the fair in general. To what are the Sages objecting? Do these objections parallel the general opposition to idolatry in Christian literature of the same period? Drawing on the work of Russian formalists (in particular, Bakhtin) and a modified formalist (Canetti), we will seek to contextualize the underlying assumptions that the Sages held toward surrounding non-Jewish culture through the life of the fair.

CHARACTERISTICS OF FAIRS

Yarid is the common term employed in the *Tosefta* and the Talmuds for the fair.[1] According to Z. Safrai's work on the subject, this term is comparable to a rare and antiquated meaning of the Greek term, *katabainô*, "to descend" (1984, 139–58). In Greek, it was more common to use *pangypis* or, at times, *agora*. Latin employs *nundinae* or simply *mercatus* (analogous to *shuk*[2] in Hebrew), which are not found in rabbinic literature. The Talmudic corpus also employs *atlaz* (especially in relation to the fair held at Aza), which is equivalent to the Latin *atelus,* a place "free of taxes." *Shuk* is used in the Talmud to signify a more localized market.

Features of the ancient Mediterranean fair are known primarily from Greco-Roman sources. Ramsay MacMullen wrote an article on the subject, using information culled from ancient central Italy (1970, 333–41). He noted that the fairs operated at set times of the year. Taxes at these fairs were waived or greatly reduced. We are not certain as to the amount of this reduction, but it was significant. A wide variety of items were available, many of them luxuries. Religious worship was connected with the fair. MacMullen claims that "the most important factor of all was the connection between religion and commerce. A particularly clear illustration lies in the worship of Jupiter Nundinarius or Mercurius Nundinator, by persons known to be merchants" (1970, 336). The shrines of various gods, most notably those of Jupiter and Mercury, provided ready-made sites for crowds and fairs to gather. Many other festivals were associated with the sale of commercial goods.

The fair also served social functions, and sexual activity took place. The fair was held in or near a city (*polis*) or in an open area in a village. The fair was accorded prestige by the king under whose authority it fell. At times, a fair was arranged to complement the beginning of a king's reign. Official acts also took place: laws were passed, judgments granted, and so on.

Such aspects of the fair, which are indeed varied, were not only functional but also introduced by the king, landowner, or magnate (or other

---

1   Manuscript evidence for the *Tosefta* suggests that *yarid* is also written *yarud. Tosefta Avodah Zarah* has three manuscripts: Vienna, Erfurt, and *editio princeps.* Vienna (Lieberman's choice of text in his *Tosefta*) is more reliable and reads *yarud,* but the other two witnesses (Erfurt, used in Zuckermandel's 1888 edition) record *yarid.* I have employed the more familiar and contemporary *yarid.*

2   *Shavakim* were better established than fairs; the former took place on Monday and Thursday. Public fast days and some forms of legal activity were also typical at marketplaces. The *shuk* was characterized by these and by many other elements common to the fair (e.g., worship, sale of all kinds of goods), but one important distinction must be recognized: the *shuk* did not have a decrease in taxes, a feature discussed below.

sponsor of the event) in order to attract merchants. All fairs during the later empire had to receive permission from the emperor (MacMullen 1970, 334). The sponsor of the fair, including the king, prevented other fairs from being held in the same locale in order to reduce competition. One proconsul of Asia, for instance, announced that in Tetrapyrgia "an *agora* [was established] for goods for sale on the fifteenth of the month. Let no other city whatsoever in Maeonia anticipate Tetrapyrgia in holding a market" (*SEG* 13, 518; ca. 250/270 CE, as cited in MacMullen 1970, 335n. 10). The reason for this prohibition was that a fair's success depended upon the presence of vendors, and a wide range of elements needed to be included in order to enrich the gathering. MacMullen writes: "Efficiency required that they [vendors] be brought together in large numbers, whether once every seven, or eight, or thirteen, or thirty days, or less frequently still. To this end a variety of other purposes were adopted: assemblies for worship, spectacles and entertainments, elections, or assizes" (1970, 341).

RABBINIC TEXTUAL EVIDENCE

The period under investigation in this chapter is covered by the *Mishnah,* the *Tosefta,* and the Jerusalem and Babylonian Talmuds. Modern scholarship frequently treats the historical information in these documents with a high degree of suspicion, because it appears that the opinions presented are essentially ahistorical. Some material is presented anonymously, while some is associated with specific Sages. Even when we can locate these Sages historically between the first century BCE and the sixth century CE, accurate transmission of the sayings attributed to them is still debated.

A number of scholars assume that some Mishnaic sayings might be dated close to the time of their textual redaction. This view does not consider any saying secure until (at the earliest) the early third century CE, which is the accepted publication date for the *Mishnah*, although "publication" is a term debated by many scholars. It is unclear whether the *Mishnah* was committed to writing and disseminated widely by its assumed editor, Rabbi Judah the Prince, or whether he compiled one copy only. The manner of his editorial decisions, a murky subject introduced as early as the tenth century through the response of Rav Sherira Gaon from Babylonia, is also debated in the scholarly literature (see Weiss 1904, 87–89; Lieberman 1950, 81–99; Zlotnick 1988). In any case, other students of these texts are vehemently opposed to any such perspective. According to these scholars, if the text claims that a certain rabbi authored a particular saying, the accuracy of that claim should be accepted, in the absence of any proof to the contrary.

Scholars of Jewish-pagan relations in antiquity generally represent the more traditional approach.[3] Even if they are outspoken adherents of more contemporary trends, when it comes to analyzing the material for historical purposes, they tend to adopt the more traditional approach. For example, Sacha Stern (1994) outlines his grave concerns about reading rabbinic literature as history, but still assumes that it is true when it finally comes time to process its content. I shall approach the material under review here in a similar fashion.

Intertextual approaches, despite being widely used with little hesitation until very recently, have begun to be challenged. Whereas historians formerly used all material from approximately the same period to answer a given question, some scholars now dispense with this method, recognizing that each text has its own agenda, which disqualifies it from being read together with other texts, even those from the same period. Jacob Neusner has produced a large literature on the basis of this approach, treating each text independently in order to discern the particular philosophy or interest behind it. This method, however, which has some advantages and produces much interesting and valuable material, is occasionally questioned by Neusner himself (1981), and does on occasion fail to provide a satisfying interpretation of the text. Nonetheless, there is support for Neusner's approach: "[Neusner's] approach allows us to ascertain *what Mishnah says* and to separate this from what later documents and figures *claim it says*" (Porton 1988, 7; emphasis original).

Pagan-Jewish relations are discussed in the tractate *Avodah Zarah* (Idolatry), part of the order of "Damages" in the *Mishnah,* the *Tosefta,* and the Talmuds. *Avodah Zarah* can be translated literally as "strange service." This form of worship is contrasted with *avodah* as temple service. The term *zara* appears in the biblical episode of the "strange fire" offered by Nadab and Abihu, who died prematurely because of their offensive offering (Num. 26:61). W.A.L. Elmslie (1911) also likens the term (*avodah zara*) to the "strange incense" of Exodus 30:9. The term for idolater, *avodat kokhavim u-mazalot* (not found in the canonical writings), means star and planet worship. The Bible does employ *zar* to refer to something opposed to the correct worship of God (e.g., Lev. 22:10). Our study will omit most of what is said

---

3 "Pagan" is another term that has come under scrutiny. It is a derogatory term for an idol-worshipper, its Latin root meaning rustic or, more colloquially, country bumpkin. Heathen is obviously not preferable to pagan, and non-Jew and Gentile are terms too broad to be useful in the context of Greco-Roman divinities. Thus, scholarship has not yet found a more inventive and respectful term with which to refer to this broad group of persons.

in the Babylonian Talmud, because it often either draws on Jewish Palestinian texts or simply interprets concepts non-literally (thereby suggesting that the Babylonian predicament is not analogous to the Palestinian).

Mishnah Avodah Zarah's five chapters treat Jewish-pagan relations during the time of the pagan festivals. However, many of the regulations also concern prohibited items that were part of more generalized commercial enterprise as well, such as oil, food products, animals, weapons, and the practice of midwifery. The first chapter alludes to the fair:

> A town in which there is an idolatrous festival: outside it one is permitted [to trade]. If there was an idolatrous festival outside, then, inside trade is permitted. What about travelling? It is prohibited if the road leads only to the idolatrous place; but if you can go somewhere else, using that road, the road is permitted. A town which has an idolatrous festival, and there are stores with wreaths adorning them, but there are some without wreaths—[what is the ruling?]. This was a case in Bet-Shean, and the Sages said: the wreathed stores are prohibited and those without are permitted [trade]. (*Mishnah* 1:4)

Z. Safrai (1984) claims that (pagan) fairs are the referent of "a town in which there is idolatry." Other *mishnayot*, too, refer to the prohibition of trade relations at times when pagans would be likely to use the goods acquired for idol worship (*Mishnah* 1:1–3). Safrai assumes that the *Tosefta*, which introduces the term "fair" in no uncertain terms, functions as a gloss on the *Mishnah*. The Jerusalem Talmud, however, recognizes the lacuna in the text, and explicitly contextualizes the *Mishnah:* "Resh Lakish said we are referring to a fair." The Babylonian Talmud (*Avodah Zarah* 11b) also records the mention of the *atliza* of Aza by Resh Lakish (third century Palestinian Amora) as an example of this type of legal ruling.

Wreaths on stores were a characteristic feature of fairs in antiquity, because it was this sign that advertised to the public the reduced level of taxation such establishments offered. The tax paid, in these cases, went to support the pagan deity that was being sponsored. Elmslie (1911) glosses: "exaction of *octroi* duties, whereof a tithe goes to support the cult of the idol." Elmslie is uncertain whether this tax was paid at the market itself or at the gate of the city. The *Mishnah,* according to Elmslie, suggests the latter.

The *Tosefta* (1:5ff) not only mentions the *yarid* but also, in contrast to the *Mishnah,* adopts a more permissive attitude toward it. *Tosefta* 1:6, for instance, permits trade with wreathed stores inside and outside the city of a fair. The same text goes on to distinguish between a fair with idolatry and one that is "permitted because [it is] a government-sponsored fair, one sponsored by the capital city, or one sponsored by the leaders of the capital city."

INTERPRETING THE EXEMPTIONS

The contrast between the stricter Mishnaic approach and the material collected in the *Tosefta* and the two Talmuds has been noted by scholars, who categorize the later allowances as an attempt to relieve some of the strictures in the area of Jewish-pagan relations. Ephraim E. Urbach, for example, notes that relationships between Jews and their neighbours relaxed and became more lenient over the years, claiming that all kinds of goods were permitted because of economic necessity (1959, 189–205). The presence of zodiac mosaic floors (with sun-gods and other human images) in synagogues would reflect this relaxed approach to paganism. Saul Lieberman also thinks that economic necessity drove Jews to trade with pagans, even though some regulations were still maintained in order to "deter Jews from falling victims to it [idolatry] under duress or for lucrative reasons" (1950, 121). Safrai concurs with Urbach and Lieberman but introduces a more sophisticated approach, suggesting that it was only in the Ushan period (135–180 CE), following the Bar Kochba revolt (when, Safrai claims, the term *yarid* first appears in this literature), that the more relaxed approach to trade was announced. Safrai feels that it was only after substantial losses that the Jews accepted Roman rule, and reduced their criticism of fairs.

After Bar Kochba, Roman rule had more direct and dramatic effects on the land of Israel. For instance, the Romans introduced practices of paganism on the Temple site, and introduced or reintroduced many more fairs. Safrai notes that Rabbi Yohanan, in particular, abrogated prohibitions in the *Mishnah* (ca. 240 CE). There is also some textual evidence to suggest that Jews attended fairs, with the Jerusalem Talmud requiring, for instance, that purchased items must be destroyed (*Avodah Zarah* 1:4), and the *Tosefta* (1:8; see also Jerusalem Talmud 1:4) introducing a justification for the purchase of slaves: "[An Israelite] buys houses, fields, and vineyards, animals, slaves, handmaids from [pagans] because [his action is] considered as if he redeems [the property] from their hands. And he writes down [the binding documents] and deposits them in their courts." The Babylonian Talmud (*Avodah Zarah* 13a) is aware of this Palestinian explanation and, recording it, introduces another explanation: one is permitted to purchase these items from a regular householder because he (unlike a merchant) does not contribute tax to the fair.

R. Yohanan is said to have omitted other restrictions as well, so that it became possible to purchase items from an innkeeper (at fair time), particularly staple goods. Only certain fairs were still prohibited, like the well known one at Botna, also known as Bet-Elonim, which hosted a fair already during the Second Temple period. Herod fortified the town, which was destroyed by the Romans and rebuilt by Hadrian as a pagan settlement. Church Fathers refer to Jewish slaves being sold there cheaply. Coin discoveries reveal that the fair attracted traders from all over the empire. R. Yohanan even allows that one may purchase items in wreathed stores, providing the wreath is free of the myrtle plant (Jerusalem Talmud *Avodah Zarah* 1:4), and admits to uncertainty as to whether or not the commercial event at Aza should be considered a fair (Aza was revived as a fair by Hadrian). Safrai (1984, 149) also notes that non-Jewish writers such as Sozomenous and Epiphanius, who mentions having met at a fair a Jew named Jacob, speak of Jews participating in such gatherings.

The question of economics is central to the perspective of Safrai and Urbach. Did an impoverished situation in the land of Israel cause legal strictures against trade with pagans to be weakened? Daniel Sperber (1978, 160–76) offers support for this point of view, citing material from both Jewish and Roman sources to show that conditions in Palestine changed radically during that time. Land prices dropped, and much land was sold to non-Jews. Many of the laws dealing with adherence to the land seem to have been written in response to this difficult situation. Gary Porton also agrees with these views, providing a long list of items that could have been restricted, but which the *Mishnah* and the *Tosefta* in fact allowed to be traded freely. Porton claims an even wider-ranging economic rationale than the others. Few restrictions were placed on marketplace activity, and those restrictions that were in place are said to be "few and relatively innocuous" (Porton 1988, 335n. 67).

Porton is also concerned with another related topic: How was the idolater viewed in this literature? This question is relevant when we ask about the extent to which the restrictions embedded within Jewish legal literature were meant to reflect purely economic concerns, and the extent to which they expressed a desire to abstain from trading with a pagan on unapproved holidays. Was the pagan to be avoided at all times, or just during the time of his worship events? Porton thinks that the texts created times to avoid trade and times to engage in it: "Our authors differentiated between occasions when overtly religious activity within the spheres of social and economic life were evident and periods when they were not" (1988, 243). This implies that the writers did not in fact want their readers to refrain from all interactions with pagans, but only those that took place on certain significant days.

Saul Lieberman (1950) writes that the "principles of idols and idol worship" are omitted intentionally in Jewish literature, all forms of opposition toward pagan practices being curtailed because the Greco-Roman writers already recognized the flaws in their own system. Edwyn Bevan

(1940, 63f) already refers to the pervasive Cynic protests against idolatry. Although the secondary literature refers to scattered pieces of criticism against paganism (see, e.g., Wallach 1977, 389–404; Fischel 1977; Herford 1903), little of this evidence is drawn from *Avodah Zarah*. The general view, then, is that the tractate functions as an extended note on economic matters. The only scholar opposed to this point of view is Stern (1994:145).

THE FAIR AS A CROWD

Many of the topics in the Jerusalem Talmud, which recall our passage from the *Mishnah*, try to recover the impulse that governs the discussion of the *Mishnah*. "Why are these things prohibited?" asks the Jerusalem Talmud. One response refers to the tax-reduction and subsequent contribution to idol worship, which we have identified above. But there are other responses that discuss the compelling character of idol-worship by throngs of people.

The Jerusalem Talmud opens with a question that tries to quantify the amount of idolatry (i.e., statues) necessary to be considered *avodah zarah*. Resh Lakish (ca. 250) claims, rather opaquely, "we are referring to a fair." How does that answer the question? P'nei Moshe (Moses Margalit, an eighteenth-century Talmudic commentator) suggests that one statue will only attract a few worshippers, but many statues will attract many followers. In this light, Resh Lakish would mean that a fair is a place where there are many statues. But even more is being suggested. The throngs of people, things, and produce are characteristic of a fair. It appears that the crowd, and not only the reduction of taxes and the contribution to the god being honoured, is the dangerous element implied in his statement.

Elias Canetti's work may shed some light on the fears evident in the Talmudic material. For Canetti, the crowd is composed of four main attributes: "The crowd always wants to grow…within the crowd there is equality…the crowd loves density…the crowd needs a direction" (1978, 29). The crowd, according to Canetti, changes basic human behaviour. Normally, people fear being touched by strangers. But the crowd "is the only situation in which the fear changes into its opposite. The crowd needs density, in which body is pressed to body…he no longer notices who it is that presses against him. As soon as a man has surrendered himself to the crowd, he ceases to fear its touch. Ideally, all are equal here; no distinctions count, not even that of sex" (Canetti 1978, 15). Canetti's impassioned description is certainly applicable to our fair. We witness a social event—one that has, as its base, an economic-religious element—but, as Canetti notes, it is also a place where people need to be.

Bakhtin's work shares much regarding the nature of the crowd, viz. fair, which is analogous to Canetti's description. The carnivalesque quality of these events inverts the universe and enables people to assume different identities (Canetti: "all are equal there"). Thus, Bakhtin writes regarding "unofficial folk culture": "In the marketplace a special kind of speech was heard, almost a language of its own, quite unlike the language of Church, palace, courts, and institutions" (1968, 154). We can interpret Resh Lakish's statement in light of these formalists: the fair encompasses these dangers because it is a place where many congregate, and one must be careful for this reason.

The fear of the crowd is part of another Sage's concern: R. Abahu of the early fourth century CE (Caesarea). R. Abahu notes that one is permitted to attend the fair, but only in a circumscribed fashion: "R. Abahu prohibits the creation of a gang (*chavilah*) at a fair. And they taught:[4] do not exchange salutations in a significant place. If you find him [the pagan] anywhere else, exchange salutations [with him] respectfully."

The *chavilah* is a group, according to the commentator "Ridbaz," which grants weight to the event. The key to understanding this enigmatic Mishnaic proof-text resides in the term *be-makom she-mitchashev,* a difficult term, glossed by Moshe Margalit as, "like a market in public." (The term also appears in *Mishnah Oholot* 1:3, where "reckoning" is the appropriate translation.) The biblical text and commentators are relevant for interpretation of the phrase. The term *mitchashev* is found in Numbers 23:9, where Balaam, the prophet hired by Balak, is defining, in poetic form, the Israelites: "They are a nation who dwells alone; and among the nations *they are not considered*" (italics mine). There are a number of interpretations of this passage but, for us, the most helpful one is found in *Tanhuma Balak* 12: "When the Israelites are happy, no nation rejoices with them, but when the nations are well-off in this world, they eat with everybody and do not consider the Jews." This text is appropriate for the mood of the fair: celebrations, feasting, rejoicing, and so on. The passage reflects on our text: You must abstain from the fair because pagans, who are rejoicing, will consider that you, too, will participate with them. Simply passing by the fair must be done in a dignified and careful manner, lest the pagan read it another way.

---

4 In a Mishnaic ruling, namely, *Gittin* 5:6, and modified in *Tosefta Avodah Zarah* 1:2.

RELAXED PROHIBITIONS

Safrai claims consistently that R. Yohanan is one of the leaders in relaxing Jewish-pagan prohibitions. However, there is a substantial methodological weakness in this claim. Many of the laws associated with R. Yohanan are recorded in the *Tosefta,* which is a document contemporaneous with the *Mishnah,* if not earlier than it. For instance, *Tosefta* 1:8 records that you can purchase Jewish slaves in a fair "because you will save them from [pagan] hands." This ruling is taken up in a later text, the Jerusalem Talmud *Avodah Zarah* 1:4, although modified slightly. Another example: R. Yohanan is said to have ruled that an Israelite need not halt trade associations with pagans on the Kalends (January 1) with those pagans who participate in the festival. But *Tosefta* 1:4 already had recorded: "Kalends: Even though everyone participates [in the celebrations] only those who participate in worship are prohibited [from trade relations with pagans]."

The *Tosefta's* "even though" appears to challenge the stricter approach of the *Mishnah:* "For three days before the holidays of the pagans, it is prohibited to trade with them" (1:1). The holidays are defined in *halacha* number three as follows: "These are the [nation-wide] holidays of the pagans: Kalends, Saturnalia [December 17–23], Kratesim [31 August 30 BCE, the date that the Egyptians assigned to Octavian's victory over Antony and Cleopatra]," and so on. Again, the *Tosefta* predates R. Yohanan's saying. Safrai does not seem to trace back the sources of the Jerusalem Talmud. The *Tosefta* does not operate merely as a gloss to the *Mishnah;* as we see from our example, it could record laws that are contemporaneous with or predate the *Mishnah.* Safrai himself admits that much of the material is not datable (1984, 156).

Regarding methodology, just because a Sage from the period of Usha utters a law, does it mean that he was the first one to propose this? Most of the attributed sayings in the *Mishnah* come from the period of R. Akiba and his students (mid-second century CE). Does this mean that these discussions are only representative of that time: sacrifices, dietary laws, laws of cleanness? Impossible. Hence, it is difficult to say with any certainty that one period in particular meant to change these laws. Perhaps caution should rule in these matters and one should suggest that prohibitions were certainly relaxed at times, but one cannot say with certainty if a certain period ushered in these changes. Perhaps it was more a matter of localized changes, or changes that were made by certain Sages at different times throughout the period under discussion.

THE THREAT OF IDOLATRY: PHILO AND JOSEPHUS

Idolatry is treated in the Talmudic literature as if it were irrelevant after the destruction of the First Temple. A number of Talmudic Midrashim discuss the manner in which the threat of idolatry was weakened (*b. Yoma* 69b; *b. Sanh.* 64a). What emerges in Philo, Josephus, and even some other rabbinic material, however, differs greatly from these texts. Philo, for one, was wont to employ invectives against paganism, in contrast to Lieberman's claims that the Rabbis were loath to engage in this form of critique. Philo describes the pagan mystery cults as "imposture and buffoonery" and "mummeries and mystic fables." Philo objects to their secrecy, and suggests: "If these things are good and profitable, they should be put in the midst of the marketplace, where you might extend them to every man and thus enable all to share in security and a better and happier life" (*Spec.* 1.59, 319–320).

Josephus also objects to idolatry and idol worship at many junctures. He warns against trophies in the theatres, the banners of the Roman legions, the eagle at the gate of the Temple, and Caligula's statue in Jerusalem (for references, see Hoenig 1970, 70, who assumes that Josephus and the *Mishnah* are to be treated as contemporaneous witnesses). Josephus (*A.J.* 14.259–261) even claims that a separate meeting place and market (in Sardis) were requested from and granted by one of the Roman emperors (for a critique, see Rajak 1985, 19–35).

Idolatry, in these Jewish-Greek writers, appears to be a force to be reckoned with. It was not quenched, even if it were tortured, as the Midrash graphically claims, but its soul was still heard. Evidence for this exists also in the *Mishnah*. M. Sanhedrin refers to typical worship practices, in which Israelites might be involved: "The one who worships [will be stoned to death]: this includes the worshipper, the participation in activity at the altar, the incense, the libation, the prostration" (7:6–7).

CONCLUSION

The complicated area of Jewish-pagan relations is summed up by the *Tosefta Avodah Zarah:* "The murky area of idolatry: one should not do business with a pagan on the day of the pagan's festival because it would appear that one is taking part in idolatry" (1:13). How much is too much? The Talmudic literature tries to define this. The prohibitions and their requisite abrogation are not necessarily the product of the later generations of Sages. The *Tosefta* opens with a saying of Nahum the Mede (ca. first century BCE), who qualifies the strictures of the *Mishnah:* "In communities of the diaspora, one abstains from trade relations with pagans only for one day before their

[nationwide] holidays (as distinct from the Land of Israel's three day ban)."
Safrai, among others, is only willing to attribute such changes to a later
stage. But it is necessary to recognize that the texts cannot be categorized
into such neat layers of prohibition followed by permission. We must recognize that each generation of Sages could offer variant approaches.

Scholars also are anxious to credit all these changes to economic necessity. How could this be? After all, the *Mishnah* (*Avodah Zarah*) is motivated
by a host of other considerations as well. *Mishnah* 1:8, for example, names
various ways in which land is to be sold (or not sold) to pagans. If these
anonymous sayings are the product of the third century CE (a position
assumed by most scholars), then we must reckon with the phenomenon of
a wide takeover of Palestinian land by non-Jews. However, many of these
prohibitions seem to respond to such fears, seeking to keep Israelites in the
Land of Israel at all costs. Isaiah Gafni (1992), for one, believes that the regulations in question were motivated by this very reality, i.e., not only by economic necessity but also by ideology, theology, and the like. The question
of the fair, in Tannaitic and Talmudic literature, demonstrates the Sages'
multi-level approach to the issue of paganism, pagans, and the Israelite as
such. To this end, we must strive for a more nuanced view of the whole
murky relationship between these two groups, who, at times, stirred the
same pot (cf. Jerusalem Talmud *Avodah Zarah* 1:4).

5

My Rival, My Fellow
Conceptual and Methodological Prolegomena to
Mapping Inter-Religious Relations in 2nd- and
3rd-Century CE Levantine Society Using the
Evidence of Early Rabbinic Texts

Jack N. Lightstone

INTRODUCTION

This chapter locates the analysis of religious rivalry within a broader analytical framework. It views religious rivalry and the exclusion of the religiously other as only one dimension of inter-group relations, social formation, and self-definition within the pluri-religious and pluri-ethnic urban environment of the second- and third-century CE Levant. I begin unconventionally, by offering a full account of my conclusions at the outset. The remainder of the chapter is not, however, intended to be a probative argument for those conclusions. Rather, I present a sample of the evidence, principally from early rabbinic texts, meant to lend these propositions sufficient weight to warrant their further exploration and to suggest their utility. The chapter puts forward three main propositions, two conceptual and theoretical in nature, and one methodological:

1. By means of the analysis of several illustrative texts from third-century Galilean-rabbinic sources, the chapter propounds a particular conceptual framework. In this framework, rivalry, exclusion, and competition (which produce group cohesion and, at times, expansion) operate alongside other mechanisms in creating arenas for trans-group social co-operation, co-participation and social solidarity. In this framework, understanding religious rivalry and competition in context requires more than the identification of social spheres in which Jews, Christians, and adherents of other religions operated as rivals or practised mutual avoidance. In addition, scholars also need to attend to social spheres in which these same

actors interacted as fellow citizens. But this is already an overly simple account of the proposition.

Each of these groups inhabited a highly differentiated social world of its own construction. In that construction, the other had a defined, legitimate place, not infrequently as a friendly co-inhabitant. To be sure, there is nothing startling about this proposition; it has an air of self-evidence about it. But perhaps because of that self-evidence, we have given too little attention to its implications. Acceptance of this proposition invites us to think of a religious group's social formation and emerging identity as being worked out not only over against the other but also by means of mapping out a pattern of interaction with the neighbouring other. Such a perspective suggests that we remember that rivalry extends beyond the quest for group survival in the face of detractors among, or competition for membership from, the camp of the other.

Rivalry includes (perhaps foremost) competition and rivalry among religious communities living cheek-by-jowl in the narrow physical confines of the second- and third-century Levantine urban setting, each seeking to lay their respective mappings over the same urban social landscape. This landscape they must continue to cohabit, as well as divide amongst themselves, a core issue in any minority group's "struggle for success" (cf. Vaage, chapter 1). Moreover, as Philip Harland (chapter 2) reminds us, the social structures of the city constrained all religious communities, on the one hand, and, on the other, made both rivalry and cooperation a "natural" consequence of city life.

2. From this last-mentioned element follows an important conceptual corollary. A religious community's map of those social arenas in which the religiously other is a welcome co-participant will not necessarily result in a consistent fit with the neighbouring group's equivalent map. Consequently, an important area for inter-religious debate and conflict relates precisely to the categorization of social spheres as either competitive or co-operative arenas. That is to say, religious community A may welcome members of religious community B in zone X; indeed, A may expect and demand B's co-participation. But B's social map may not permit access to A in what in B's world corresponds to zone X. Much conflict between religious communities in the second- to fourth-century CE Levant derives from precisely this sort of asymmetry, and the conflicting expectations it causes.

Sometimes, those expectations surface as concern within a community about the potential for its members to drift into, or to be overly influenced by, the community of the other. This would result from the other's acceptance of members of one's own community into social arenas, which one's own community does not map as territory for co-participation. At other times, the conflict arises out of resentment over the non-participation of the other in social spheres, which one's own community either defines as being open to all or perceives as the basis of civil society. For a minority religious community, successfully managing this resentment is a key requisite to success. Community members must be adequately prepared to manage such resentment, and provided with norms for mitigating it, as they move through the urban landscape inhabited by the other. In part, a community's capacity to maintain loyalty among its members and attract new adherents depends upon its ability to do this.

As I will show, adopting the proposed conceptual framework permits us to make sense out of hitherto confusing, ambiguous, or contradictory evidence in the earliest rabbinic literature (particularly the *Tosefta*) from third-century CE Galilee. As a result, we might better glimpse the formal early-rabbinic social mappings, which underlie religious rivalry between early rabbinic guild members and their non-Jewish co-inhabitants of the south-central Levant.

3. The last purpose of this chapter lies in the methodological realm, rather than the conceptual-theoretical. I argue that the rhetorical and formal traits of those rabbinic documents that are our principal sources significantly affect the degree to which they are useful in helping us differentiate social spheres. This is an important preliminary consideration for any attempt to work within the conceptual framework here being espoused, because the degree of social differentiation permitted by the rules of rhetoric governing a particular document either facilitates or inhibits the study of inter-religious relations. This is not to say that the degree and direction of social differentiation mapped by a text is merely a matter of rhetoric, disconnected from its author's social mappings of the real world. After all, what counts as persuasive and authoritative (the core definition of rhetoric) is socially defined. The rhetoric of early rabbinic documents is the formalized representation of the expertise demanded of the rabbinic master, and in this sense it has everything to do with real-world spheres, in which the master acts (see Lightstone 1994; 1997). Rather, what I mean to suggest is that the degree of social differentiation reflected in the text is mediated by its rules of rhetoric, which is to say, by the guild's social definition of the mastery required of the rabbi.

CONCEPTUAL AND METHODOLOGICAL PROBLEMS

Scholars attempting social descriptions of ancient Judaism, early Christianity, and other Greco-Roman religious communities labour within a loop that is sometimes problematic (Mack 1996, 247–49; Lightstone 1997). On one side of the circle is literary evidence with severe limitations, given the questions we ask of it. On the other side of the circle is the attempt to provide conceptual and theoretical frameworks that help us frame our questions, to make sense of the literary evidence and use it to our specific ends rather than those of its authors. Sometimes we continue to travel around this loop in an unproductive fashion. Why? Because conceptual and theoretical frameworks for inquiry are not created *ex nihilo.* Rather, they emerge from some substantial knowledge of the phenomenon that is the subject of the inquiry. This knowledge, however, is largely derived from our literary evidence, the use of which depends upon the theoretical and conceptual frameworks we adopt. The problem is, then, that if the framework is so closely derived from the literary evidence it purports to analyze that it is merely an abstraction of what the texts themselves say, we are engaged in a tautological exercise with no explanatory force. Explanation, in the social and human sciences, relies on the capacity to conduct careful, systematic comparisons (J.Z. Smith 1982a, 19–35). Tautological restatements provide no basis for explanation. Yet if, on the other hand, our framework is imported "whole-hog" from an alien socio-historical context, we risk veiling the variety of the social and cultural formations we are trying to study, undermining meaningful comparisons in a different but equally unacceptable way. Scholarly virtue lies somewhere between these extremes.

In setting the Canadian Society of Biblical Studies' Religious Rivalries Seminar on its course, Leif E. Vaage (chapter 1) provided a set of framing questions and concepts for the work to follow. Subsequently, I sometimes felt perplexed by the evidence that was adduced regarding the general topic of the seminar, and uncertain about how I would proceed to make sense of it. By habit, my reaction is to step back and see if I can reframe or refine some of the conceptual and methodological issues. The purpose served by this looping back to theoretical and methodological matters, is not only to gain for myself better purchase on the evidence at hand; there is an intrinsic value to the exercise itself, as well. After all, the purpose of seeking to understand particular social formations in the first place is to learn more about what it is to be human, which is a theoretical and conceptual construct.

Whence my perplexity? Most often it derives from apparent contradictions in the evidence, even evidence from single communities within a relatively circumscribed geographical area and from a limited period of time. Perhaps differences in attitudes and practices exist at the micro-regional level, or communities' norms and perspectives shift significantly within a short time span, or members of the community disagree. All of these explanations are possible and may account for some apparent contradictions within the evidence. But is it methodologically or conceptually sound to rush to these easy explanations? The implied answer is no. And this cautionary no is my point of departure. It has significant implications for the construction of conceptual and theoretical models for understanding the nature of religious rivalries between neighbouring communities.

Let me both substantiate my negative response to this question and argue its theoretical and conceptual implications by considering a particular body of evidence for a specific community and geographical region. Ancient Judaism, particularly emergent Rabbinism, is my special interest, and so I will turn principally to rabbinic evidence, which, at first glance, often seems confusing and self-contradictory, both in its rulings about relations between Jews and non-Jews and in the attitudes and rationales sometimes attached to these rulings by their editors. Here, I am much indebted to Reena Basser's work (chapter 4) on early rabbinic attitudes to pagan fairs. The *Mishnah* and the *Tosefta,* out of which much of Basser's evidence is taken, were both authored and promulgated in the Galilee by the rabbinic guild, most likely within about a 75-year period. Both documents express the social, cultural, and cosmological mappings of the worlds of their authors by articulating rules, although the former was obviously authoritative for the latter. Many of the pericopes of the *Tosefta,* in turn, are found in parallel, but altered, form in the Palestinian and Babylonian Talmuds.

As Basser demonstrates, not only do the *Mishnah* and immediately subsequent rabbinic works register quite different, even opposing, rules about interacting with the religiously other, but stupefying contradictions are found even within some particular texts (for example, the *Tosefta*). Basser reviews the ways in which other modern scholars have accounted for these contradictions. Typically, they have opted for some version of the following stock response: Rabbinism's attitudes toward non-Jews simply changed, from rejection to a more benign openness (see Urbach 1959; Lieberman 1950; also Safrai 1984; Stern 1994; Porton 1988). Basser argues that the standard articulation of this shift is unsatisfactory, and I agree. It smacks of the type of case-by-case made-to-measure explanation, which lacks any of the elucidating power that otherwise derives from more appropriately formulated theoretical and conceptual constructs. Simply put, it invents a particular history, to account for a particular historical datum.

In principle, I do not favour rushing to offer a unique historical explanation tailored to a particular datum or set of data. It is a truism that each historical event is unique, but the truly unique is by definition incomprehensible. Thus, I offer the theoretical and conceptual propositions outlined at the beginning of this chapter and the accompanying methodological consideration as a means of making sense of the data without resorting to made-to-measure historical explanations. Ultimately, the real test of the utility of such propositions is the extent to which they are portable to other data concerning religious rivalries in the Levant in the first four centuries of the Christian era.

THIRD-CENTURY GALILEAN RABBINIC PERSPECTIVES ON JEWISH-GENTILE RELATIONS: *MISHNAH AVODAH ZARAH* 1 AND *TOSEFTA AVODAH ZARAH* 1–3

The *Tosefta* is a rabbinic legal document organized as an explanatory supplement and companion to the *Mishnah*. From the time of its promulgation in the early third-century CE rabbinic guild, the *Mishnah* became the guild's founding text. Most of the *Tosefta*'s materials, and perhaps even their redaction in the current extant document, are immediately post-Mishnaic. That is, they stem from the mid- to late-third century CE Galilean rabbinic guild, during the first hundred years of the pro-rabbinic patriarchate in that area.

The *Tosefta* may be subdivided into three literary categories, as Neusner (1991) has demonstrated. Toseftan pericopes either (1) cite and gloss the *Mishnah,* (2) complement Mishnaic passages in ways that demonstrate direct dependence on the *Mishnah,* or (3) provide material that supplants the *Mishnah*'s agenda altogether. The last-mentioned materials show little or no literary dependence upon the text of the *Mishnah*.

Elsewhere, I have attempted to demonstrate the pervasive influence of the *Mishnah*'s particular form of rhetoric (Lightstone 1997, 283n. 21; cf. Neusner 1981). Its lyrical, litany- and clock-like, permutative rhetorical features encourage the spinning out of hypothetical, highly laconic exempla, which are classified by specifying whether one rule or another applies. These exempla are ideal, in many senses of the word. Indeed, they sometimes appear to be generated more through rhetorical necessity or convention than because of their utility in differentiating even an ideal, divinely ordered world. Moreover, as a corollary, other hypothetical exempla that might serve as interesting bases for exploring the rabbinic legal principles of world mapping are often not dealt with, because the aesthetic of *Mishnah*'s rhetoric would be diminished in the process.

The *Tosefta,* on the other hand, does not replicate fully the *Mishnah*'s rhetorical features. Especially where it glosses or directly complements the *Mishnah,* the *Tosefta* does exhibit a tendency to explore, extend or even revise the *Mishnah*'s rulings by introducing new distinctions and differentiations without the limitations imposed by *Mishnah*'s rhetorical requisites. This is not to say that the *Tosefta*'s cases are any more reflective of real-world situations than are the *Mishnah*'s. We simply cannot know that. Rather, the *Tosefta* introduces a greater differentiation of its world, and is less limited and constrained in doing so, than is the *Mishnah*. Therefore, there seems to be more flesh on the bones in the *Tosefta*'s attempt to map the world rabbinically—i.e., a higher degree of verisimilitude, even though the *Tosefta* also may not be dealing with real cases.

Even if the cases themselves are not real, however, the *Tosefta*'s rhetorical penchant for greater social differentiation and verisimilitude may well represent a shift or development within the real life of the rabbinic guild. That shift could be characterized as a movement from an internally focused preoccupation with initial guild formation, cohesion, and continuity (as reflected in the *Mishnah*'s rhetoric and preoccupation with an ideal Temple-centred world) toward a greater participation, qua guild members, in the real life of the south-central Levantine world of the local Jewish population. The ideal world, which is the object of contemplation in Mishnaic rhetoric, was mapped as a series of concentric circles of holiness, cleanness, and increased exclusion of the other as one moved inward from the periphery. In such an imagined world, the non-Jew is a carefully managed minority relegated primarily to the periphery; perhaps, an apt homology of the initial social formation of the rabbinic guild. One might speculate that the increased use of members of the rabbinic guild by the patriarchate's administration of the Jewish communities of the south-central Levant occasioned the shift from Mishnaic to Toseftan rhetoric. Framed in terms of the third conclusion expressed at the beginning of this chapter, Toseftan rhetoric reflects an immediately post-Mishnaic evolution in the guild expertise required by the rabbis (again, I am indebted here to comments by Leif E. Vaage).

It is in light of the *Mishnah*'s and the *Tosefta*'s respective, and quite different, literary traits and rhetorical conventions that, once more, I have come to the methodological and conceptual propositions spelled out at the outset of this paper:

1. Religious rivalry is a subset of a larger category, namely, differentiation of the social world.
2. The way in which a text differentiates the social world does not necessarily reflect, and should not be confused with, the way in which its author(s), or the authorial community, differentiated the real social world.

3. A document's rhetorical or formal traits affect the level of social differentiation that it will introduce. In moving from one text to another within the same geographical-historical community, one should try to be sensitive to this fact before ascribing significantly different socioreligious perspectives to the texts, their authors, or their community.

In practice, what does this mean? For one thing, a document from a particular geographical-historical group may appear to say, "Jews ought to have nothing to do with pagans." Another document from the same group may appear to reflect quite a different view, such as: "In this array of activities, Jews ought to have nothing to do with pagans; but in these other activities, they may." Our first proposition urges us to look at statements about inter-religious relations within the larger context of how groups map or differentiate the social world. Even if a text does not give us much in the way of describing that greater degree of social differentiation, we ought not to assume that its author (or the author's community) failed to make such distinctions in the real world. Rather, we ought first to try to make a judgment about how the rhetorical or formal features of the text either promote or inhibit the introduction of these distinctions into the textual world. The distinctive views of two texts may have more to do with their different rhetorical-formal constraints than with any real difference or evolution of social perspective or policy. This, in turn, is a reflection of the second and third propositions working together.

The tractate *Avodah Zarah,* in both the *Mishnah* and the *Tosefta,* assumes the authority of the biblical prohibitions against idolatry: Israelites may not worship gods other than Yahweh; they may not use in the worship of Yahweh anything previously used in the worship of any other god; they may not marry persons who (continue to) worship other gods (see Deut. 5–13). I leave aside, for now, the proposition that these severely mapped boundaries between other gods and their worshippers, on one side, and Yahweh and Israelites, on the other, represented only a minority perspective until mid- or late-fifth-century (BCE) Judean society. Even if this proposal was known to the early rabbis, they would simply have ignored it (see Lightstone 1988, chapter 2).

The biblical prohibitions about co-participation in the worship of other gods, whether undertaken by Israelites on their own or together with those other gods' worshippers, is simply axiomatic for the Mishnaic and Toseftan authors. Therefore, *m. Avodah Zarah* starts *in medias res,* as is so often the case in Mishnaic rhetoric. Indeed, the (implicit) demands of Mishnaic rhetoric tend to bias its authors against the specification of axioms, even when these assumed perspectives are second- or third-stage developments above and beyond explicit biblical law. The *Tosefta* shares this tendency, to a significantly lesser degree, again, because of its own quite different rhetorical rules. *Mishnah Avodah Zarah* 1:1–2 (ed. Romm) follows (my translation):

M.1:1
A. [For] three days prior to the holy days of Gentiles,
B. it is forbidden:
C. 1. to buy [from] and to sell [to] them;
　　2. to lend [property to] and to borrow [property] from them;
　　3. to lend [money to] and to borrow [money] from them;
　　4. to pay back [a loan] or to require payment [of a loan] from them.
D. Rabbi Judah says:
E. They require payment [of a loan] from them,
F. because it is a vexation to him [i.e., the Gentile].
G. They said to him:
H. even though it is a vexation now, it is a [cause for] joy after a while.

M.1:2
I. Rabbi Ishmael says:
J. 1. For three days prior to them [i.e., the Gentiles' holy days]
　　2. and [for three days] subsequent to them
　　3. it is forbidden.
K. And sages say:
L. 1. Prior to their holy days
　　2. it is forbidden;
　　3. subsequent to their holy days
　　4. it is permitted.

This is typical *Mishnah:* laconic language; balanced repetition of phrases and clauses, varied by permutation and opposing operative terms (e.g., forbidden and permitted); disputes described by these balanced phrases, often as glosses of an antecedent list. There is little, or nothing, in the way of articulated principles, nor is the problem at issue spelled out. From *m. Avodah Zarah* 1:1–2, one gets a clear sense of how the literary tightness demanded by Mishnaic rhetoric restricts the opportunity for elaborate social differentiation, despite the rhetorical tendency to generate lists and permute phrases in order to create new circumstances. The passage cited thus lends weight to the methodological claims outlined earlier. But what of the conceptual claim: that inter-religious rivalry is, and should be viewed as, a subset of a larger system of social differentiation?

Despite the *Mishnah*'s laconic rhetoric, it is clear that the (unstated) issue is the appropriate degree of social separation—the definition of social boundaries and of rules about their permeability—between Jews and Gentiles (i.e., idolaters). Yet the issue is not social separation in an absolute sense, that is, over the entire spectrum of arenas constituting the socially constructed world. Rather, the *Mishnah* attempts to sort out rules where two social spheres overlap: the cultic, and the commercial.

The *Mishnah*, of course, assumes the biblical prohibition of worship, by Jews, of foreign gods. As noted, Jews may not engage in such worship themselves, as individuals or as a group. Nor may they do so in fellowship with non-Jews. Thus, with respect to the social category of foreign cults, a firm and impermeable social boundary exists. The *Mishnah* appears to assume, however, that Jews will still engage in commercial relationships with non-Jewish worshippers of foreign deities. In the commercial sphere, there is either no boundary at all between Jew and Gentile, or one that is highly permeable. So *m. Avodah Zarah* 1:1–2 implicitly works with two social spheres, foreign cultic and commercial. Social segregation or avoidance (and, perhaps, rivalry and competition) is assumed to apply generally to the first, but not to the second.

A third, unstated assumption is at work in *m. Avodah Zarah* 1:1–2. There is a certain range of human activities wherein the commercial and cultic spheres overlap, namely, commercial enterprise with non-Jews on the non-Jews' holy days. For the *Mishnah*, the distinction between commercial and cultic spheres blurs at this point, since, as subsequent passages and chapters of this tractate surmise, the cultic celebration invades commercial activity for non-Jews on these days. For Jews, the biblical prohibition of commerce on holy days means that their own cultic and commercial spheres are totally separate; but this is not so for Gentiles. Therefore, ironically, the Jewish prohibition of commerce on Jewish holy days is extended to a further prohibition of commerce with Gentiles on the Gentiles' holy days. However, the reason, left unstated in the *Mishnah*, seems to be that such commercial activity would amount to indirect participation in, or complicit fostering of, idolatrous cults.

Mishnah Avodah Zarah 1:1–2 is specifically concerned with definitional questions surrounding this issue. When does the overlap of the commercial and Gentile-cultic spheres begin and end? What activities are central to commercial activity? (In this regard, the reasoning of the contrived formulaic debate [1:1F following], which glosses the opinion attributed to Rabbi Judah [1:1D-E], misses the point: not an uncommon trait of Mishnaic passages cast in debate form.) *Mishnah Avodah Zarah* 1:3 (not cited above) carries the conversation further to consider what counts as a Gentile holy day. For example, does a personal holy day of a private person count? Finally, 1:4 (again, not cited, but dealt with extensively by Basser) considers the location of the spatial boundary in relation to the celebration of a Gentile holy day.

When? What? Who? Where? These are all simple and straightforward definitional issues pertaining to the identification of overlapping areas between the commercial and Gentile-cultic spheres. Whether or not the *Mishnah*'s definitions accord with any lived social reality is unknown and beside the point. These definitional issues are simply the logical-theoretical ones pertaining to overlapping social spheres; in each of which, considered separately, different and opposing rules about social segregation and boundary maintenance apply.

When we turn now to *t. Avodah Zarah* 1:1ff, it is important to note that the *Tosefta,* while imitating many aspects of Mishnaic rhetoric, falls far short of replicating it. As stated earlier, the practical consequence of this difference is that the *Tosefta* seems far less rhetorically restricted in the range of issues, information, and supplementary materials it may introduce at any one juncture. And, again, as noted above, Toseftan authors use this licence to engage in a much higher degree of social differentiation than their Mishnaic counterparts. Given the issues of primary interest in this book, the *Tosefta* is therefore a boon. *Tosefta Avodah Zarah* 1:1–3 (ed. Zuckermandel) reads as follows (my translation):

T.1:1

A. Nahum the Mede says:

B. [For] one day, in the Diaspora, prior to their holy days—

C. with respect to what are these things stated?

D. With respect to fixed holy days [i.e., with fixed calendar dates].

E. But with respect to their holy days which are not fixed,

F. It is forbidden [to buy from and to sell to Gentiles] only on that day exclusively.

G. And even though they said:

H. [For] three days, it is forbidden to buy [from] and to sell [to] them—

I. with respect to what are these things stated?

J. With respect to something which endures [that is, non-perishables].

K. But with respect to something which does not endure [that is, perishables],

L. it is permitted [to buy from or sell to Gentiles during the days prior to the holy day].

M. And even with respect to something which endures—

N. [if] one bought or sold [it during the three days prior to the holy day],

N. lo, this is permitted [after the fact].

P. Rabbi Joshua b. Korhah says:

Q. Any loan secured by written contract (שטבבשר)—

R. they do not claim repayment from him [that is, the Gentile, on the days prior to his holy day].

S. And that which is not secured by written contract [that is, made by verbal covenant only]—

T. they claim repayment from him,

U. because one is like one who rescues [something] from them [that is, the risk of permanent loss is higher].

T.1:2

A. One may not buy [from] and sell [to] a Gentile on the day of his holy day.

B. And one may not engage in frivolity with him.

C. And one may not inquire after their well-being in a [private] place, [that is,] where he [the Gentile] commiserates [with others].

D. But if he [the Israelite] happens upon him [the Gentile] on his way [in public], he [the Israelite] inquires after his [the Gentile's] well-being politely.

T.1:3

E. They inquire after the well-being of Gentiles on their holy days because of [the importance of promoting] peaceful co-existence.

A. Workers of an Israelite who are doing work for a Gentile [and it is the Gentile's holy day]—

B. [work being done] in the house of the Israelite

C. is permitted,

D. and [work being done] in the house of the Gentile

E. is forbidden.

F. R. Simeon b. Eleazar says:

G. If [the worker] is a [casual] day-laborer,

H. whether [the work is being done] in the house of the Israelite,

I. or [the work is being done] in the house of the Gentile,

J. it is forbidden.

K. If [the worker] is a contractor [that is, paid when the entire project is completed]—

L. [work being done] in the house of the Israelite

M. is permitted;

N. [but work being done] in the house of the Gentile

O. is forbidden.

P. With respect to immovable [i.e., real] property—

Q. whether one or the other,

R. [the work] is forbidden.

S. And [when the work is being done] in another city—

T. whether one or the other,

U. [the work] is permitted.

V.   And even though the worker [may have] completed [working with]
      his tools prior to [commencement of] his [the Gentile's] holy day,

W. he may not transport them on the day of his holy day,

X.   because he [the Israelite] gladdens him [the Gentile on his holy day].

Tosefta Avodah Zarah 1:1 thus functions as a commentary on *m. Avodah
Zarah* 1:1–2. *Tosefta* 1:2 and 1:3 complement and supplement, respectively,
the Mishnaic passage, introducing matters related to (but also extensive of)
the agenda set by the *Mishnah* itself. The *Tosefta*'s penchant for precisely
ramifying Mishnaic law by proffering a greater degree of differentiation of
social circumstances is clearly evident in *t. Avodah Zarah* 1:1, 1:2, and the first
statement of 1:3. To rehearse what the *Mishnah* does, *m. Avodah Zarah* considers the implications of the overlap between two socially differentiated
spheres: commercial enterprise (in which social interaction with Gentiles
is normally permitted) and cultic celebration of Gentile holy days (in which
interaction with Gentiles is normally forbidden). The *Mishnah* lists and
permutes circumstances dealing with definitional issues: What amounts to
commercial activity? What counts as a Gentile holy day?

   Tosefta Avodah Zarah 1:1 addresses, but also moves beyond, mere ram-
ification of *Mishnah*'s definitional questions. One standard rhetorical formula, which indicates that the *Tosefta* is about to engage in an exercise of
social differentiation beyond that contemplated by the *Mishnah,* is the stock
question, "With respect to what are these things stated (דברים אמורים
במה)?" After introducing an entirely new socially differentiated category
at *t. Avodah Zarah* 1:1A (namely, the territorial distinction between the Diaspora and the home territory of the land of Israel), the *Tosefta* moves on to
distinguish two subcategories of Gentile holy days: calendrical (public)
holy days, and those which are not calendrical. Within the category of the
commercial sphere, *Tosefta* further distinguishes financially risk-laden commercial activity and that which is not (or less) risk-laden.

   Tosefta Avodah Zarah 1:2 (including the first complete sentence of 1:3)
further differentiates the social map, adding the following categories
involved in mapping out the situation: play, commiserative or other more
intimate social interaction (versus the rather more episodic commercial
interaction); and the civil-private sphere (versus the civil-public sphere).
The remainder of *t. Avodah Zarah* 1:3 supplements the *Mishnah*'s agenda by
introducing quite another category of economic activity: contract work. In
this context, *t. Avodah Zarah* distinguishes the Israelite private sphere from
the Gentile private sphere (as opposed to the distinction between public and
private); real versus immovable property; and long-term contract work
versus short-term day labour.

In the above-listed binary distinctions, introduced by the *Tosefta* to complement and to supplement the *Mishnah*'s agenda, it is clear that the *Tosefta* is not simply engaged in a process of softening the *Mishnah*'s authoritative stance. Although the latter is the often proffered explanation for the differences between Mishnaic and Toseftan law on these particular issues, it is, in my view, clearly a category error to ask why the later Toseftan authorities have abandoned or moderated the *Mishnah*'s stance regarding Jews' interaction with Gentiles on the latter's holy days. What *Tosefta* is, in fact, asking is this: What does the *Mishnah*'s stance on commercial interaction with Gentiles on their holy days really mean, when one considers the fuller array of differentiated social spheres and social distinctions that are relevant to mapping the specific situation with which the *Mishnah*'s rulings deal?

For the *Tosefta,* the cultic sphere of Gentiles is definitely off limits, just as in the *Mishnah.* In the sphere of casual commercial exchange, however, generally speaking, there is no differentiation between Jewish and non-Jewish realms, but Jews and Gentiles are considered to inhabit a common world. So, too, in the case of the civil (not the civic) public sphere, where Jews and Gentiles are once again understood to be co-inhabitants, with full mutual responsibility for polite civil interaction. But the private sphere, for the *Tosefta,* is something else entirely. There is a strong Toseftan tendency to exclude Jews and Gentiles from one another's private domains, with flexible modalities for handling generally permitted commercial activity.

The differentiation between the territory of the homeland and that of the Diaspora, also introduced by the *Tosefta* in this context, seems to be parallel to the distinction between the private and public domains. The land of Israel is, in some sense, private to the Jewish people as a whole, although Gentiles clearly also inhabit it; which is, of course, not the case for the personal private domain of individual Jews. The Diaspora, interestingly, by contrast, is not akin to the private domain of the Gentile. Rather, it is a kind of public domain, in which peoples of various religious persuasions are equal co-inhabitants.

Mishnah Avodah Zarah 1:8–9 has preceded the *Tosefta* in distinguishing between the land of Israel, Syria, and other lands for the purposes of renting and buying real property. (Syria's status is intermediate because of the rabbinic conviction that the Davidic kingdom included much of Syria.) At issue specifically for the *Mishnah* is the Mishnaic-rabbinic notion that biblical law prohibits the sale of the biblical territorial inheritance of the Israelites to non-Israelites, and the application of the laws of tithing and heave offering to all the produce of the biblical land of Israel. Obviously, by the beginning of the third century CE, such a conception of the land of Israel totally within Israelite franchise is a utopian fantasy; it is doubtful that it could ever have been a historical reality. Again, the *Mishnah*'s utopian character comes to the fore. The distinction between the land of Israel and the Diaspora in *Tosefta Avodah Zarah* 1:1 seems to be unrelated to Mishnaic considerations of the biblical laws of territorial inheritance and agricultural gifts to the priestly and levitical classes.

This does not nearly exhaust the social spheres differentiated by the *Tosefta* in mapping out a world co-inhabited by Jews and Gentiles. Again, taking the *Mishnah* as its point of departure, the *Tosefta* differentiates within such spheres as medicine and wet nursing (that is, biophysical/nurturing service roles and institutions), civic and administrative institutions (public registries and courts for socio-economic regulation and suits), wayfaring and way-lodging (that is, travel between domains), military and penal institutions, institutions of public entertainment (*stadia* and circuses), and civil-public institutions of hygiene (e.g., bathhouses) and of leisure (e.g., parks and gardens). Within all of these social spheres, separately and in various degrees of overlap, the Toseftan authors must define the mode of relations between Jews and Gentiles as a pattern of either social avoidance or social co-participation.

Understanding inter-religious rivalry, competition, or avoidance within a larger socially constructed context comprising multiple, overlapping mapped spheres appears, then, to help us understand apparent contradictions within any one community's attitudes toward the other. This is so because, in some mapped spheres (such as cultic activity), total avoidance might be the norm, while in other spheres, other religious groups may be perceived as co-participants. Again, this was the key conceptual-theoretical point argued at the outset of this chapter. However, several corollaries follow from this point, and merit further discussion.

The first corollary derives from the observation that, for many religious communities, not all others are equal. Thus, the task of understanding inter-religious rivalry in any one time and place is not only best carried out within a methodological frame that views the socially mapped human and physical landscape as comprising many overlapping spheres, each with its own rules regarding interaction with or avoidance of the other; but it also requires each of various others to be differentiated from one another. How? By determining whether, in this particular sphere or that one, all others are equally to be avoided (or equally treated as co-participants), or whether some distinctions are made among them.

Again, the *Tosefta*, with its penchant for social differentiation, provides an apt example at *t. Avodah Zarah* 3:1–3, which complements *m. Avodah Zarah* 2:1 by contrasting the status of Gentiles and Samaritans with respect to the social spheres of contracting the care of animals, wet nursing, education and apprenticing. *Tosefta Avodah Zarah* 3:1–3 (ed. Zuckermandel) is as follows (my translation):

T.3:1

A. They billet an animal [of an Israelite] in [the stables of] inns of Cutheans [i.e., Samaritans],

B. even male [animal]s at [inns operated by] female [innkeeper]s,

C. and female [animal]s at [inns operated by] male [innkeeper]s,

D. and female [animal]s at [inns operated by] female [innkeeper]s.

E. And they hand over an animal [of an Israelite] to one of their shepherds [for care].

F. And they hand over to him a child in order to teach him reading and writing (ללמדו ספר),

G. and to teach him a trade,

H. and to be alone with him.

I. An Israelite woman performs midwifery and provides wet nursing for the child of a Samaritan woman.

J. And the Samaritan woman performs midwifery and provides wet nursing for the child of an Israelite woman.

T.3:2

K. They do not billet an animal [of an Israelite] in [the stables of] inns of Gentiles (גוים),

L. even male [animal]s at [inns operated by] male [innkeeper]s,

M. and female [animal]s at [inns operated by] female [innkeeper]s,

N. because the male [innkeeper] has intercourse with the male [animal],

O. and the female [innkeeper] has intercourse with the female [animal],

P. And there is no need to mention [prohibiting the billeting of] male [animals] at [the inns of] female [innkeeper]s,

Q. and female [animals] at [the inns of] male [innkeeper]s.

R. And they do not hand over an animal [of an Israelite] to one of their shepherds [for care].

S. And they do not hand over to him a child in order to teach him reading and writing (ללמדו ספר),

T. and to teach him a trade,

U. and to be alone with him.

T.3:3

V.   An Israelite woman does not provide wet nursing for the child of a Gentile woman (נברית),

W.   because she nurtures someone for idolatry,

X.   but a Gentile woman provides wet nursing for the child of an Israelite woman in her [the Israelite's] domain.

Y.   An Israelite woman does not perform midwifery for a Gentile woman,

Z.   because she delivers someone for idolatry,

AA. And a Gentile woman does not perform midwifery for an Israelite woman,

BB. because they [Gentiles] are suspect with respect to homicide (חשורים על הנפשות),

CC. the words of Rabbi Meir.

DD. And the sages say,

EE. a Gentile woman does perform midwifery for an Israelite woman,

FF. when others are standing by her.

Obviously, for both the *Tosefta* and the *Mishnah,* Samaritans are not Israelites. The *Tosefta,* like the *Mishnah,* assumes that an Israelite is not to participate in the Samaritan cult, among other restrictions. *Tosefta,* nevertheless, radically distinguishes Gentiles (that is, idolaters) from Samaritans with respect to other spheres. More to the point, the means by which these two non-Israelite groups are distinguished from one another is through different definitions, in sphere after sphere, as to whether co-participation with each is permitted or forbidden.

In my treatment of these passages, I have not given primacy to either the *Mishnah*'s or the *Tosefta*'s stated reasons for a particular ruling, but have rather advocated viewing individual rulings within a larger pattern of mapping that has its own implicit logic or rationality, apart from, and more determinative than, explicit reasons offered at any one juncture in the texts. This procedure stems from my own and others' research into the nature of the *Mishnah* and the *Tosefta,* which sees these documents' preoccupation with systems and systemic mapping as the fundamental and generative foundation of their content. I tend to view the proffering of individual reasons, including proof-texts, as secondary (both logically and generatively), even if they are not necessarily secondary accretions in literary terms.

Tosefta Avodah Zarah 3:1–3 thus permits us to see the variety and richness of the socially mapped landscape inhabited by oneself and a variety of others. This complexity and richness, in turn, suggests another conceptual-theoretical corollary, which was already prefigured at the outset of this chapter. A great deal of inter-group and intra-group conflict can be attributed to the high probability that different groups inhabiting the same geophysical space will map it differently. It is therefore unlikely that Galilean Gentiles (if there even was such a homogeneous group) mapped their pluri-religious world so that it was simply a mirror image of the *Tosefta*'s mapped social world. How surprising it would be if, in (mapped) sphere after sphere, Galilean Gentiles treated Toseftan rabbis as either co-participants or persons to be avoided, precisely where Toseftan rabbis similarly defined Galilean Gentiles! Indeed, the very substance of many Toseftan passages assumes that this type of mirror-image congruence did not happen. Moreover, methodologically speaking, it is this lack of congruent mirroring within geographical areas which should be one of the principal objects of our research.

APPLICABILITY ELSEWHERE

Theoretical and conceptual constructs pass muster when they may be use-fully employed beyond the body of evidence for which (and from which) they were initially derived. Otherwise, propositions and concepts cannot be deemed to have much theoretical force. A construct that cannot meet this minimum test is either a made-to-measure, one-time explanation of a unique body of evidence from a particular human community or, more simply, a mere descriptive translation of the data. For example, in John Chrysostom's first and eighth homilies entitled "Against the Jews" (*PG* 48; Meeks and Wilken 1978), the then-presbyter of fourth-century Syrian Antioch rails against those Gentile Christians among his congregation, whom he fully expects to attend synagogue on the Jewish New Year ("Trum-pets") and on the Day of Atonement. Chrysostom also admonishes those Gentile Christians among his congregation, who, apparently regularly, seek healing potions and incantations from Jewish practitioners operating out of the synagogues, and use Jewish courts, also housed in synagogues, to bring suits against other Gentile Christians. Chrysostom would have his con-gregants healed exclusively by Christian holy men, and their civil suits brought only to Roman courts. Presumably the Antiochene Jewish commu-nity, courts, and shamans saw nothing untoward about Gentile Christians patronizing Jewish communal liturgies and celebrations, judicial institutions and holy men. Jews, on the other hand, were likely prohibited by their own leadership from attending the Eucharistic liturgy, and Christian bish-ops of that era often barred all non-baptized persons from the church dur-ing the Eucharist.

It is obvious that the conceptual and methodological perspectives proposed earlier in order to come to grips with the Mishnaic and Toseftan evidence provides a useful grid to analyze what appears to have been happening in Chrysostom's Antioch. He and (at least) a minority of his Gentile Christian parishioners differed from one another with respect to their avoidance of, or co-participation with, Jews, in various socially differentiated spheres. Moreover, in several of these mapped spheres, Antioch's Jews sufficiently shared a set of mapping norms with Judaizing Gentile Christians to have permitted Gentile Christian attendance at communal liturgical rituals in the synagogue and to have allowed use by Gentile Christians of Jewish institutions of civil justice and of synagogue-based shamans. Chrysostom's alternate map of certain specific social spheres put him in conflict with both some of his own congregants and (some of) the Antiochene Jews. Had Chrysostom's recalcitrant congregants mapped the world as he did, or had the Jews themselves mirrored his map (by excluding Gentile Christians outright from the spheres in question), the basis for the indicated conflict would have been lessened.

Another example is Tertullian, who took great pains in his *Apology* to explain that, in many spheres, Christians saw themselves as complete co-participants with their non-Christian (pagan) fellow citizens: "[We Christians] live with you, enjoy the same food, have the same manner of life, and dress, the same requirements for life.…We cannot dwell together in the world, without the marketplace, without butchers, without your baths, shops, factories, taverns, fairs and other places of business. We sail in ships with you, serve in the army, till the ground, engage in trade as you do; we provide skills and services to the public for your benefit" (*Apol.* 42; trans. R.M. Grant 1980, 28). Why make this point? Tertullian was responding here to the anti-Christian charge that Christians did not contribute to the local economy. In response, Tertullian laid out his map of the economic social sphere, defining much of it as one in which Christians and pagans are co-participants.

Some authorities within the non-Christian Gentile community seem to have perceived Gentile Christians as propounding social avoidance in spheres where, in the opinion of these authorities, Christians ought to behave as fellow citizens. Indeed, some Christian authorities other than Tertullian may have held this (isolationist) view. But Tertullian is stating (pleading) otherwise. In any case, real or potential conflict due to inharmonious mapping of social spheres by different communities, including perhaps different subgroups within the Christian community, lies behind Tertullian's remarks. In fact, Judaizing Gentile Christians counselled avoidance by Christians of some of the very same socio-economic spheres that Tertullian defines as arenas of full co-participation with pagans. At issue for Judaizing Gentile Christians were likely meat, oil, and wine sold in pagan shops. In light of Philip Harland's work (chapter 2), one might also add that some aspects of Christian belief and life may have limited, or were perceived to limit, a Christian's participation in benefaction of his or her city, and that Tertullian seeks in his argument to gloss over this issue.

Such conflict is confirmed by the remainder of *Apology* 42, in which Tertullian admits to the accuracy of pagan claims that Christians do not participate in a number of aspects of life in the ancient urban setting. Tertullian manages the resulting resentment experienced by members of his community by showing that Christians economically compensate their non-Christian neighbours in other ways.

A third example is the early second-century CE work, *Diognetus*.[1] I strongly sense that similar social conflicts lie behind the following passage:

> The difference between Christians and the rest of mankind is not a matter of nationality, or language, or customs. Christians do not live apart in separate cities of their own, speak any special dialect, nor practise any eccentric way of life....They pass their lives in whatever township—Greek or foreign—each man's lot has determined; and they conform to ordinary local usage in their clothing, diet, and other habits....Nevertheless, the organization of their community does exhibit some features that are remarkable, and even surprising. For instance, though they are residents at home in their own country, their behaviour is more like transients; they take their full part as citizens, but they also submit to anything and everything as if they were aliens. For them, any foreign country is a motherland, and any motherland is a foreign country (*Diogn.* 5).

The author of *Diognetus* appears to be addressing pagan perceptions of Christians as inappropriately non-participatory in, and self-distancing from, a number of spheres of the ordinary social world. The apologist deals with this perception by asserting that Christians have a kind of dual nature, worldly and otherworldly, at one and the same time. Presumably, the author of *Diognetus* had confidence that this type of explanation would serve, at the very least, his Christian readers' need to justify and to appreciate their way of mapping the social world and their place in its various spheres. Whether he would have mollified the views of pagan critics is another matter.

---

1 For *Diognetus* not as an apology but as an example of *logos protreptikos,* see Steve Mason (chapter 7).

CONCLUSION

I am not prepared to offer a manual for the application of these conceptual, theoretical, and methodological perspectives to all bodies of evidence. I am not certain that such an enterprise is either possible or useful. Several general, differentiable spheres: public, private, civic, civil, cultic, commercial, educational, health- and welfare-related, leisure- and entertainment-oriented, would be useful analytic categories in almost any Mediterranean urban setting for examining inter-religious rivalry, avoidance, and co-participation. But beyond these, the researcher ought to be sensitive to discovering how the community or group under study differentiates the world into discrete spheres, and where, in various social situations, its spheres overlap.

The researcher will want to discover, as well, whether (or how) various communities in the same setting differently categorize the world (that is, divide the world into spheres), and how each neighbouring community defines its norms for interaction with the other in particular spheres. It is important to attend to the social consequences of symmetries and asymmetries across various communities' mappings of the same narrow urban landscape, and to ask how each community has dealt with these consequences in devising its strategy for success.

Finally, on the methodological level, I counsel attention to the rhetorical rules governing our sources, in light of the fact that authoritative modes of rhetoric are grounded in social definitions of authoritative speaking or with recognized mastery within specific social forums. Hence, the representation of social differentiation in texts is mediated by social definitions of masterful rhetoric. In the final instance, therefore, I am recommending not a particular method at all but, rather, the adoption of a general orientation toward these types of studies, in the belief that the underlying conceptual and theoretical perspectives here described will prove useful in guiding the development of specific research designs appropriate to the particular evidence at hand.

ACKNOWLEDGMENT

The chapter derives from ongoing research into the social meaning of the rhetoric of early rabbinic texts, which has been funded by a grant from the Social Sciences and Humanities Research Council of Canada and from Concordia University.

Part II

MISSION?

6

"The Field God Has Assigned"
Geography and Mission in Paul

Terence L. Donaldson

INTRODUCTION

The immediate focus of this chapter is the geographical framework of Paul's mission and, in particular, the possibility that there was a territorial dimension to his sense of apostolic calling, resulting in a discernible geographical strategy. As a contribution to the discussion concerning religious rivalries, however, this question is being pursued in the context of a larger question, viz. the extent to which the eventual success of Christianity was the result of a deliberate and organized program of mission.

Martin Goodman's recent work (1994) on mission in antiquity provides us with a convenient point of entry into the larger discussion. In this book, Goodman sets out to challenge the assumption (prevalent, in his view) that religions in the Roman Empire were missionary in nature and intent. His work is best known for its treatment of Judaism, particularly the rejection of the idea that Judaism was in any way a missionary religion (at least prior to 100 CE; for Rome, see, more convincingly, Mason, chapter 7). But Goodman's thesis is of more general application. With the exception of Christianity, Goodman argues, religions had little desire to win converts, and no interest in organized proselytizing efforts; the assumption that they did is to be seen as one aspect of "an unconscious Christianization of the study of ancient religions" (1994, 3). Indeed, "such a proselytizing mission" as is encountered in early Christianity "was a shocking novelty in the ancient world" (Goodman 1994, 105).

Goodman's work makes a highly significant contribution, and is of fundamental significance for the issues discussed in this book. For the moment, however, I am interested in his definition of what constitutes a missionary religion, and his argument that Christianity was successful precisely because it was such a religion. First, the definition: as Goodman (1994, 1–7) describes it, a missionary religion is characterized by at least three components (see also Vaage, chapter 1).

1. *A commitment to proselytization*: Members of such a religion share a self-conscious desire to make converts and to incorporate them into the group. In a helpful typology of mission, Goodman differentiates this proselytizing form of mission from three other types, namely, informative, educational, and apologetic.
2. *A universal scope*: Potential converts are not limited to any ethnic group or social class. The goal is to convert the whole world, or at least as many outsiders as possible.
3. *An organized and systematic program*: This universal goal is approached by means of a systematic and centrally coordinated missionary enterprise. A missionary religion, then, is one characterized by and committed to a universal program of proselytization.

Goodman believes that early Christianity is to be seen as a missionary religion in this sense (though not without some significant qualifications, to which we will return below), and that this is what accounts for "the phenomenal spread and eventual victory of the Church within the Roman Empire" (1994, 160). Further, this aspect of Christianity is due in large measure to Paul: "Only familiarity makes us fail to appreciate the extraordinary ambition of the single apostle who invented the whole idea of a systematic conversion of the world, area by geographical area" (Goodman 1994, 106). This view—that the ultimate success of Christianity in the Roman Empire is the result of an organized and systematic program of mission that goes back in significant measure to Paul himself—has been a commonplace in early church history. Take Harnack, for example, whose classic study of the expansion of Christianity devotes a whole chapter to "the Christian missionaries" (Harnack 1904, 398–461; cf. M. Green 1970, 166–93); or, more recently, MacMullen, who contrasts the attitudes within paganism with those of the "Judaeo-Christian tradition, in which despatch of emissaries from a central organization, and other formal aspects of missionary activity, were perfectly at home" (1981, 98).

As Leif E. Vaage argues in the first chapter of this book, however, there are good reasons to doubt such a picture of a systematic and centrally organized mission. Indeed, the case against the traditional view is made most forcefully by MacMullen himself, who, in a subsequent work (1984), has abandoned the position represented by the statement quoted in the previous paragraph. MacMullen points out that, after the end of the New Testament period, there are very few references to missionary activity. Further, the few references that can be invoked by supporters of the traditional view either are vague and indefinite, demonstrating nothing more than the belief that the earliest generations of Christianity had engaged in mission, or refer to itinerant teachers whose activity is directed toward the already converted (see *Did.* 11–13; Origen, *Cels.* 3.9). The two relevant passages in Eusebius (*Hist. eccl.* 3.37.1–4; 5.10.2) are strongly retrospective in tone. The first states that, in the time of Pantaenus, "there were still many evangelists of the word," suggesting that by Eusebius's day this had long since ceased to be the case; the second declares that there were many itinerant evangelists "in the age immediately succeeding the apostles," but names only those whose names were attached to writings (e.g., the decidedly non-itinerant Clement of Rome). MacMullen's conclusion is: "after Saint Paul, the church had no mission, it made no organized or official approach to unbelievers; rather, it left everything to the individual" (1984, 34). Accordingly, MacMullen argues for the informal spread of the faith through various social networks, laying particular stress on testimonies of healing and the like (see, further, Stark 1997; also, below, chapters 9 to 12). The plausibility of this conclusion receives inadvertent support from the fact that proponents of the traditional position, including Goodman himself, invariably recognize both the paucity of the evidence and the significance of informal or unorganized means of propagation.

This latter point should caution us not to exaggerate the difference between MacMullen and his predecessors. Nowhere was the idea of an organized, official, worldwide mission ever thought to be the sole, or even the most important, factor in the spread of Christianity. In contrast to the paucity of references to missionary activity, it is important to note that there is a wealth of references in early Christian literature to the geographical spread of the movement (see Harnack 1904, 147–82). Still, the belief that, in its earliest centuries, Christianity was characterized by such a mission is deeply and widely held, and it is striking to read MacMullen and to realize how little evidence there is to support it.

More precisely, MacMullen's position is that there is little evidence "after Saint Paul" (1984, 34). But what about "Saint Paul"? The traditional view that Paul "invented the whole idea of a systematic conversion of the world, area by geographical area" (Goodman 1994, 106), and bequeathed it to the church, has been called into question, at least on the latter point: if the church in the second and third century CE had no systematically organized mission, we cannot credit Paul with its origin. But what about the former point? Despite their differences with respect to the later period, Goodman and MacMullen (and Harnack, too, for that matter) are agreed in their assumption that in the case of Paul, at least, we have an example of this type of mission. But is this an accurate characterization of Paul's missionary activity and intentions? Might it be possible that here, too, a conceptual a priori has shaped our reading of the evidence?

GEOGRAPHY AND MISSION IN PAUL

Deconstructing Paul the Missionary?

In chapter 1 of this book, Vaage questions traditional scholarly approaches to the mission and expansion of Christianity, not only in the post-apostolic period but also with reference to Paul himself. Vaage claims, or at least implies, that it is possible to develop a comprehensive argument that would dismantle the prevalent view of Paul as the first Christian missionary. Unfortunately, Vaage does not provide us with any indication of how this massive program of deconstruction might be carried out. Nevertheless, there is heuristic value, I believe, in pressing the issue and asking what this claim might mean.

One aspect of the prevalent view has been dismantled already, i.e., the idea that Paul was the first missionary, in the sense that he was the prototype and model for an ongoing series of missionaries, whose work resulted in the conversion of the Roman Empire. Furthermore, anticipating observations to be made later in this chapter, one could easily envisage extending this process of demolition to the next stage—moving, as it were, from the upper storey to the ground level—and denying that it ever was Paul's intention to initiate a missionary enterprise that would carry on into the future. The eschatological framework within which Paul operated—his expectation of Christ's imminent *parousia,* in particular—tends to rule out any possibility that Paul saw himself as a pioneer, marking a trail for later generations of the church to follow. Confirmation of this impossibility can be found in the striking absence from Paul's letters of any attempt to mobilize his congregations for ongoing evangelistic activity, even in the present. Both of these points will come up again for further discussion (on the eschatological framework, see below, Eschatological Horizon; on the absence of any evangelistic injunctions, see Patterns of Selection).

But might Vaage's program be pushed even further to deny any element of mission whatsoever in Paul's apostolic self-consciousness, i.e., demolishing not only the superstructure but also the foundation as well? The answer depends, to a certain extent, on one's definition of mission. For my present purposes, it is probably the third element in Goodman's definition (as outlined above) that is most germane. Can we account for the pattern and sequence of Paul's church-planting activity without appeal to concepts of territoriality, planning, strategy, and so on? Can Paul's evangelizing movements be understood simply as the product of more mundane factors such as the availability of work, particular modes of travel, transportation networks, accepted patterns of itinerancy, the degree of reception or opposition to the message, etc.?

Such factors are certainly important, and we will return to them in due course (see below, The Gritty Realities). But first we need to acknowledge that several of Paul's own statements seem to bar the way to any such interpretation. Taken at face value, 2 Corinthians 10:13–16 and especially Romans 15:15–29 seem to suggest that, at least at this stage of his career, Paul was operating with some conception of an overarching territorial task to be completed: that is, he had a missionary consciousness, in the sense that we have defined the term.

Admittedly, these statements by themselves do not necessarily mean the end of Vaage's demolition project. Rhetoric is not necessarily reality. Rather than providing evidence for the self-understanding that produced and shaped Paul's work to this point, Romans 15, for example, might be accounted for without remainder simply in terms of the constraints of the rhetorical situation vis-à-vis Rome, e.g., as a retrospective conceptualization constructed solely out of Paul's desire to preach in Rome (cf. Rom. 1:15). Still, there is the desire itself to go to Rome (and thence to Spain), which represents a territorial goal of some kind. And Paul's justification of these plans raises questions that would need to be addressed before any assessment of the implications of Romans 15 might be made. In particular, how can Paul say that his work in the east is "complete" (vv. 19, 23)? How has the desire to preach in Rome (and Spain) emerged in the context of his previous work in the east? Romans 15 provides us with a convenient point of entry into the Pauline material.

Romans 15:19, 23: Tension between Claim and Reality

In Romans 15:19, as he looks back on his Gentile mission to this point, Paul makes a startling claim: "from Jerusalem around to Illyricum," he grandly declares, he has "completed the gospel of Christ" (*peplêrôkenai to euaggelion tou christou*). The language is as extravagant as it is equivocal; how the gospel can be said to be "filled up to completion" is not immediately clear. A few verses later, Paul repeats the claim in language that equally mixes the categorical and the ambiguous: Paul "no longer has room (*mêketi topon echôn*) in these regions" (Rom. 15:23). These are no mere passing comments. The statements are made in explanation of his decision to jour-

ney to Rome, and appear near the conclusion of a substantial and carefully considered letter written precisely for the purpose of ensuring that the
proposed journey is a success. Evidently, they are supposed to be taken
with all seriousness.

But the reality to which Paul refers is hardly commensurate with the
extravagance of the language used to describe it. His own letters provide us
with explicit evidence for ongoing churches in fewer than a dozen cities—
Thessalonica, Philippi, Corinth, Cenchreae, Ephesus, Colossae, Laodicea, and
the churches of Galatia (whose identification need not delay us here)—and
even if we were to include all of the additional references in Acts and the
Pastoral Epistles, we would not increase this total significantly (Meeks
1983, 40–42). Further, while membership estimates are difficult to come by,
the fact that a gathering of the whole church in Corinth could be accommodated in a single house (Rom. 16:23) suggests that we are dealing with
population totals in the lower four-digit range at most (Munck 1959, 278).
Even in those cities where churches had been planted, there was a great deal
of scope for ongoing evangelizing activity. Readers, both ancient and modern, of Paul's letter to the Romans could be forgiven for thinking that "from
Jerusalem around to Illyricum" the proclamation of the gospel was far
from complete, and that Paul had much more "room" for preaching "in
these regions."

Not surprisingly, modern scholarly readers have often taken note of
the striking disjunction between this claim and reality (Hultgren 1985,
131; Munck 1959, 277–78; Bornkamm 1971, 53–54; Meeks 1983, 9–10).
What is more surprising, perhaps, is the widespread assumption that it is
possible to discern from the evidence of the Epistles a coherent geographical strategy that would resolve it. Broadly considered, these reconstructions
of Paul's strategy are built up on the basis of two elements: (1) Paul's concentration on important cities, which he seems to understand in some way
as representative of larger geographical areas; and (2) the cumulative pattern of these larger areas themselves, understood to be the result not only
of the negative policy of avoiding areas where others have been active, but
also of several suggested positive patterns of selection. We will discuss each
of these in turn.

Cities as Representative   The urban character of Paul's mission is readily
apparent. His efforts were concentrated in cities, and any list of the important cities of the Roman world—important in terms of imperial administration, trade, transportation, intellectual life, size, and so on—would
invariably include those cities in which Paul was active. A striking indication of the way Paul thinks of these churches, however, is his tendency to

refer to them with the name of the Roman province in which they were found. Sometimes this is simply a matter of convenience, as when he wants to speak collectively of the "churches of" Macedonia (2 Cor. 8:1), or Asia (1 Cor. 16:19), or Galatia (Gal. 1:2), or when he wants to speak of all of the Christians in an area (e.g., "all the believers in Macedonia and Achaia," 1 Thess. 1:7; also 4:10). But something more than this is going on when, speaking of the collection project, Paul uses provincial names almost as a personification of the Christian groups present therein: "Macedonia and Achaia have been pleased" to contribute to the project (Rom. 15:26); "Achaia has been ready since last year" (2 Cor. 9:2). Something similar comes to expression when Paul speaks of the household of Stephanus as "the first fruits of Achaia" (1 Cor. 16:15), or of Epaenetus as the "first fruits of Asia" (Rom. 16:5). These passages seem to suggest that Paul conceived of his apostolic activity in provincial and representative terms: that is, his churches and converts would represent, in some way, the larger provincial entities in which they were located, with the provincial boundaries themselves providing the geographical framework within which his mission was to be carried out.

If this is in any way an accurate description of Paul's conception, it suggests a way of understanding how he could say that he had "completed the gospel" in a given area. Once the faith had taken sufficient root in one or more cities, the province in which they were located and which they represented could be said to have been "completed" (though the question would remain as to what constitutes sufficient "rootage"). Such a line of interpretation has been widespread in scholarly discussion, though with two distinct ways of understanding the mode of representation. First, there are those who understand the relationship between the cities and the provinces in terms of sober missionary strategy. Paul plants churches in particular cities with the expectation that they will function as missionary centres from which the faith will spread not only into the rest of those cities themselves but also into the surrounding territory. In Dunn's picturesque description: "Paul's vision then could be likened to lighting a series of candles at intervals in a curve around the northeastern quadrant of the Mediterranean; having lit them and ensured that the flame was steady, he left it to others to widen the pool of light while he went on to light more at further discrete centers of influence" (1988, 2:869; see also Allen 1962, 12; Bornkamm 1971, 53–54; Sanday and Headlam 1902, 409; M. Green 1970, 263).

Alternatively, it has been suggested (at least since the work of Munck) that Paul thinks in terms of nations, not individuals, and, moreover, that he does so within an eschatological framework. In Paul's usage, it is argued, *ethnê* has not lost its basic sense of "nations," so that the various Roman provinces function as the current manifestation of the *ethnê/goyim* over against which Israel's identity had always been forged. Further, in keeping with scriptural expectations about the eschatological salvation of the nations, Paul is thought to have understood his mission as that phase which occupied and defined the brief interval between the resurrection and the *parousia*. His congregations in Corinth, Ephesus or Philippi represented the larger nation, or province, of which they were a part. When all the nations had been evangelized in this representative way, Paul and the other Gentile missionaries would have accomplished the "full number of the nations" (*to plêrôma tôn ethnôn,* Rom. 11:25), which would precipitate the *parousia* and the end-time salvation of "all Israel" (Munck 1959, 277–78; Hultgren 1985, 127–37; Jewett 1992, 598; Aus 1979, 232–62; Knox 1964, 1–11). In this reading, the collection project functions as Paul's demonstration of the completion of the *plêrôma* in the east, the church representatives travelling with him functioning as a kind of representative universalism once removed (Munck 1959, 303–305; Nickle 1966, 129–42).

Patterns of Selection Even when full allowance is made for such notions of representation, however, a glance at the map will indicate that there were many provinces between Jerusalem and Illyricum without Pauline churches. Many scholars are content at this point to appeal generally to the negative principle enunciated in Romans 15:20–21, that is, Paul's declared policy of working only in areas where other missionaries have not already founded churches (cf. 1 Cor. 3:5–14; 2 Cor. 10:16). While Paul provides us with nothing in the way of detail, it is assumed that the reason he feels no need to delay his trip to Rome until after he has worked in Cappadocia, Bithynia and Pontus, Thrace, and other places in the east, is that other missionaries have founded churches in these areas (Dunn 1988, 2:868–69; Hultgren 1985, 131–32; Munck 1959, 52–54; M. Green 1970, 260).

A few scholars, however, go farther than this, proposing schemes that would account for Paul's choice of territory much more precisely and on the basis of more positive principles of selection. John Knox, for example, takes seriously and literally the word *kyklô* (in a circular manner) in its appearance in Romans 15:19. Spain was not Paul's final destination, in this reading; rather, he planned to go on from there to Africa, with the ultimate goal of planting representative churches in a string of provinces circling the Mediterranean (Knox 1964, 10–11; followed, at least tentatively, by Hultgren 1985, 132–33, Dunn 1988, 2:864, and others). In contrast, Roger D. Aus argues that Spain was Paul's ultimate goal. He presents two lines of argument in support of the idea that Paul would have seen his mission as complete, once he had evangelized all the way to Spain. One is that, in both Jewish and Greco-Roman contexts, Spain was commonly considered to be the "ends of the earth." The other is based on Isaiah 66:18–19, the only eschatological pilgrimage text to contemplate a mission going out to the nations. This passage lists several nations in particular, including Tarshish, which Aus takes to be a reference to Spain (*Tartessos*). In his view, when Paul can present Gentile converts from "Tarshish," the most distant of the nations listed in Isaiah 66:19, the full number of the nations can be said to be complete (Aus 1979; see also Jewett 1992).

Isaiah 66:18–19 figures prominently in two other detailed hypotheses concerning Paul's geographical strategy. The more precise of the two is that of Rainer Riesner (1994, 213–25), who argues that this passage provided Paul not only with the ultimate goal of Spain (referred to by "the coastlands far away," and not by "Tarshish," which Riesner links with Tarsus), but also with Paul's complete missionary itinerary (Tarshish=Tarsus, Put=Cilicia, Lud=Lydia in Asia Minor, Javan=Greece, and so on). While Riesner allows for other, more mundane factors also to play a role—indeed, he provides highly detailed treatments of road systems, sea travel, wintering practices, etc.—he nevertheless attempts to account for a whole range of detail concerning Paul's travels, in both Acts and the Epistles, on the basis of Isaiah 66:18–19 (Riesner 1994, 234–36, 261, 264, 271).

The same passage from Isaiah (66:18–19) plays a role, albeit not nearly as central a role, in one other interpretation of Paul's geo-missionary ideas and strategies. Building on a thorough study of Jewish conceptions of geography and ethnography, James M. Scott (1994; 1995) argues that the "table of nations" tradition developing from the lists of the descendants of Noah's three sons in Genesis 10—a tradition including Isaiah 66:18–19—provided the framework within which Paul and other Jewish Christian missionaries viewed the world. In this ethnogeographical conception, the world was divided, often with Jerusalem located at the centre, into three broad areas corresponding to the three sons of Noah: Judea, Mesopotamia and Arabia (Shem); Egypt and North Africa (Ham); northern and western lands, including Asia Minor and Europe (Japheth). J.M. Scott's argument is that Paul saw his missionary territory as comprising the lands traditionally associated with the descendants of Japheth, and his task as "preaching the gospel to a representative number of [each] Japhethite nation" (1995, 144).

Many scholars, then, are prepared to take Romans 15:19–24 more or less at face value, and to understand Paul's missionary travels to this point not as "sporadic, random skirmishes into gentile lands" (Hultgren 1985, 133) but, rather, as the outworking of a more deliberate "detailed strategy" and "vision" (Dunn 1988, 2:869). Nonetheless, without denying the validity of many of the insights contained in this literature (some of which will be picked up for more detailed examination in what follows), I am not convinced that they add up to a coherent strategy that would eliminate any perceived tension between claim and reality; which is to say, I am no longer convinced, since I began this study with the assumption that such a coherent underlying strategy could be ascertained. Let us look again, therefore, at the two broad areas discussed above.

We begin with Paul's provincial orientation. I agree fully that Paul thinks in terms of Roman provinces, and that he sees his churches somehow as representative of the provinces in which they are located. But significant questions can be raised about both of the ways in which such representation has been understood. First, there is no clear evidence that Paul saw his churches as centres of evangelism from which the gospel would spread into the surrounding territory. An examination of Paul's letters from this angle of perception produces a startling observation: nowhere do we find a single injunction to evangelize! This does not seem to be generally recognized, though Goodman (1994, 94) comments on the scarcity of detailed teaching on evangelism in the New Testament (see also Bowers 1991; Ware 1992; O'Brien 1995).

Injunctions of various kinds, of course, abound. Paul frequently urges his readers to hold firm, to live in a manner consistent with their Christian vocation, to uphold one another, to rejoice in the Lord, to continue in prayer, and so on. Occasionally, these injunctions concern outsiders: to work for the good of all (Gal. 6:10), to give no offence (1 Cor. 10:32), to live peaceably (Rom. 12:18), to maintain a good reputation (1 Thess. 4:11–12), to behave wisely and to speak graciously (Col. 4:5–6), to respond to persecution with blessing rather than cursing (Rom. 12:14, 19–21): in short, "to shine like stars in the midst of a crooked and perverse generation" (Phil. 2:15). But nowhere does Paul go on to say that the goal of such behaviour is to win outsiders to Christ, though there was plenty of opportunity for him to do so.

To be sure, this conclusion requires some elaboration, for arguments have been made that such injunctions are at least implicitly present in several texts, notably, Philippians 2:16 and Colossians 4:5–6 (O'Brien 1995, 109–31). In Philippians 2:16, while commentators generally recognize that *epechô* has the sense "to hold fast to" rather than "to hold forth, to proffer," some argue that Paul nevertheless is encouraging his readers to evangelize, pointing to the fact that what is being held onto is the "word of life" and that this is part of the way in which the Philippians are to shine in the darkness (O'Brien 1995, 118–19; Fee 1995). But the thrust of the whole passage (Phil. 2:12–18) has to do with perseverance, not mission; Paul will be able to boast on the day of Christ to the extent that they "work out [their] salvation with fear and trembling" (2:12), holding firm to the gospel until the end (Bowers 1991, 100). In Colossians 4:5–6, a stronger case can be made for evangelistic discourse of some kind. Here, part of the wise behaviour that Christians are to cultivate with respect to outsiders is a graciousness of speech, "so that you may know how you ought to answer everyone." But even if it be conceded that discourse with outsiders naturally would involve issues of faith, it is striking to note the responsive nature of such speech by Christians. The issue has to do with how to reply to the questions of outsiders (v. 6: *apokrinesthai*), not how to take evangelistic initiative. In neither case, then, do we have even an implicit injunction to evangelize.

Nor is it the case, as James Ware (1992) has argued, that active evangelization on the part of the Thessalonians is assumed in Paul's statement in 1 Thessalonians 1:8, "For the word of the Lord has sounded forth from you not only in Macedonia and Achaia, but in every place your faith in God has become known, so that we have no need to speak about it." It is highly unlikely that the clause, "the word of the Lord has sounded forth from you," implies that "the Thessalonians had not only received the gospel message, but were themselves active in communicating it" (Ware 1992, 127; cf. Bowers 1991, 97–99). A series of considerations tell against this conclusion: (1) In 1 Thessalonians 1:7, the Macedonians and Achaians who have heard what has "sounded forth" are *believers* already and thus not potential converts at all. (2) If 1 Thessalonians 1:8 refers to secondary evangelization, then the Thessalonians would need to have sent out missionaries of their own not only to Macedonia and Achaia but to "every place"—hardly a plausible scenario! (3) The clause in question in 1 Thessalonians 1:8a, i.e., "the word of the Lord has sounded forth," stands in parallel with "your faith in God has become known" in 1 Thessalonians 1:8b; the parallelism implies that, in each case, what is being spread abroad is the news of the Thessalonians' new faith, not the faith itself. (4) The content of what was "sounded forth" is articulated clearly in 1 Thessalonians 1:9, namely, "how you turned to God from idols, to serve a living and true God." Again, what has spread outwards from Thessalonica is the report of a successful mission there, not a program of secondary evangelization. Thus it is quite unlikely that 1 Thessalonians 1:5–8 provides evidence for such a practice.

Not that such evidence is wholly lacking: Paul holds open the possibility that non-Christian husbands or wives will be won by the deportment of their believing spouses (1 Cor. 7:16); he takes for granted the presence of outsiders at church gatherings, and is concerned that the Corinthians conduct their meetings in such a way that outsiders will turn to God (1 Cor. 14:23–25); he is aware that his imprisonment has encouraged "most of the brothers...to speak the word with boldness," resulting in the further spread of the gospel (Phil. 1:12–14). But such secondary evangelism is nowhere thematized. Evangelism does not appear, for example, in the lists of gifts (1 Cor. 12:4–11; Rom. 12:6–7); nor is it addressed in the parenetical sections of the letters. (The list in Ephesians 4:11–12 contains "evangelists," of course. But even if this can be taken as a reflection of Paul's thinking, it needs to be observed that a distinction is made here between the "saints," i.e., Christians in general, and those endowed with special gifts of church planting and leadership, including evangelists.) When Paul speaks of the work of local leaders, it is generally in terms of their ministry to the saints, that is, work directed inward rather than outward. For example, while Stephanus's household might represent the "first fruits of Achaia," since then "they have devoted themselves to the service of the saints," not to the task of bringing in the full harvest (1 Cor. 16:15; also Gal. 6:6; 1 Thess. 5:12). The closest we get to evangelism is the statement that Euodia and Syntyche "have struggled beside me in the gospel" (Phil. 4:3); but, even here, the reference is backward looking and devoid of any suggestion of independent evangelistic activity on the part of these two women. In short, there is nothing to suggest a strategy in which local congregations were mobilized to spread the gospel throughout the rest of the city and the surrounding territory.

Not that Paul was silent on the topic of evangelism, of course. But he tends to describe it as an apostolic activity: the work of himself, his travelling co-workers and other apostles, as distinguished from the members of a congregation in general. The Corinthian congregation is the plant or the building, Paul and Apollos the gardeners or the builders (1 Cor. 3:5–15); those who proclaim the gospel have a right to be supported by those who have received the gospel (1 Cor. 9:3–14); death is at work in the apostles so that life may be at work in their converts (2 Cor. 4:12; cf. the whole of 2:14–6:12), and so on.

This distinction between the evangelists and the evangelized might suggest an alternative, however: i.e., a strategy wherein Paul expected the gospel to spread outward from his churches through the agency not of the local congregations themselves but of other workers like Apollos, who came along afterward to water what Paul had planted, in the expectation that there might be divinely given increase (1 Cor. 3:5–14). In fact, this seems to be Dunn's point of view (see above). But such a modified version of the approach in question is equally unsupported by the evidence. Certainly the importance for Paul of co-workers, both localized and itinerant, is not to be underestimated; Paul needs to be seen not as a unique and solitary figure, but as part of a network of assistants, colleagues, and independent co-workers (not to mention rivals; see Ellis 1993, 183–89; Holmberg 1978, 58–76). And undoubtedly there were actual cases, like the work of Epaphras in Colossae, where the Christian movement did radiate outward from Pauline centres through the activity of people whom Paul would have called or considered co-workers.

But, again, there is no evidence of a deliberate strategy where, as Paul moves on to new territory, he leaves behind a cadre of evangelistic co-workers to spread the faith in this way. In the case of Apollos, Paul seems prepared to accept his activity in Corinth (at least once Paul has made the requisite distinction between the one master builder and the subsequent tradespeople [1 Cor. 3:10], or between the one father and the many guardians [4:15]!), but there is no evidence that Paul initiated it. Colossians (which I take to be authentic) provides more evidence for the fact that Paul considered this church to fall within his sphere of jurisdiction than it does for the idea that Epaphras had founded it under Paul's supervision. Of course, the issue is complicated here by a textual crux: Does the author of the letter see Epaphras as a "minister of Christ on our [*hêmôn,* i.e., Paul's] behalf" or "on your (*hymôn*) behalf" (Col. 1:7)? While the textual evidence is not compelling either way, at least it can be observed that nowhere else in the letter do we find evidence that Paul considered Epaphras to be his agent of secondary evangelism. Of the co-workers about whom most is known, i.e., Timothy and, to a lesser extent, Silvanus and Titus, it can be said that supplementary evangelism was clearly not one of their assigned tasks.

To ensure that my position is not misunderstood, let me emphasize that what is under discussion here is Paul's conscious strategy, not the actual realities on the ground. I have no doubt that Paul's churches did attract converts, and that the Christian movement spread outward from these churches into the surrounding territory. But this spread was probably due more to spontaneous expansion along natural lines than to any organized program of evangelization, and in any case—this is the important point—it was not planned or even anticipated by Paul as part of a conscious strategy. While he rejoiced in the spread of the gospel (2 Thess.

3:1; Col. 1:6), and celebrated those who were the "first fruits" of a new area (1 Cor. 16:15; Rom. 16:5), Paul nowhere gives us cause to believe that the reason he feels free to move on to a new province, once one or two churches have been established in a given region, is his expectation that these churches would become centres of evangelization for the province as a whole.

Arland J. Hultgren (1985, 135–36) speaks of Paul's churches as "first fruits" of a larger Gentile offering. But this is not in accordance with Paul's usage of the term. Paul never uses it with respect to the church in a given area, but only regarding initial converts. In other words, the "full harvest" implied in the metaphor is the church itself in the present, rather than any potential conversion of a larger proportion of the region in the future. The only possible counter-example is 2 Thessalonians 2:13. Here, though, for reasons clearly articulated by Ernest Best (1972, 312–13), the reading *ap' archês* ("God chose you from the beginning for salvation") is to be preferred.

If Paul's statement about his work in the east being completed cannot be accounted for in the preceding terms, what about the idea of representative universalism (Munck 1959, 278)? Does Paul really believe that his apostolic commission to proclaim Christ "among all the Gentiles" (Rom. 1:5; also Gal. 1:16) has been fully discharged in any given Roman province, once a few small congregations have been planted in this "nation"? This might appear to be the implication of Paul's statement in Romans 15. But it is not easy to see how it could be corroborated. The universal scope of the gospel is a common Pauline theme; in 2 Corinthians 5:14, for example, it is the conviction that "one has died for all" that drives Paul on (see also Rom. 3:22–24; 5:18; 10:11–15; 11:32; 1 Cor. 9:19–23; Phil. 2:10–11; Col. 1:28). While he can speak of the believers as having been chosen by God (e.g., 1 Thess. 1:4; 1 Cor. 1:27; Rom. 8:28–30), and so is fully prepared to accept the fact that not all will respond (cf. 2 Cor. 2:15–16), he gives us no reason to believe that, in his doctrine of election, the chosen are limited from the outset to a few cities (Philippi but not Dyrrhachium, Corinth but not Olympia, Ephesus but not Sardis). Further, despite the attempt by Aus (1979, 257) to find a background for this idea in Jeremiah 3:14 ("one from a city and two from a family"), it is difficult to see anything in Jewish traditions about the Gentiles which might have shaped Paul's thinking in this way. Jeremiah 3:14 has to do with a remnant from Israel; Old Testament passages looking ahead to the ultimate salvation of Gentiles, including those cited by Paul (see especially Rom. 15:9–12), tend to be more universal in tone and scope. Zechariah 8:23 might provide a counter-example. Still, the ratio of ten to one puts the stress on the multitude of Gentiles who join in the pilgrimage to Zion.

In my opinion, then, this notion of representative universalism simply begs the question. It accentuates the disjunction between the elaborate way in which Paul speaks of his mission and the much more modest scale of the reality, without really explaining it. All it does is describe how Paul himself negotiates the tension between vision and performance, without providing us with a coherent explanation of the Pauline reality itself.

Similar conclusions are to be drawn, I believe, with respect to the second element discussed above, namely, the various suggestions about Paul's selection of territories in which to work. We will consider first the situation in the east, before turning to a consideration of Paul's plans to go on to Rome and Spain. As we have seen, two justifications have been put forward for Paul's declaration that his work in the east was completed. The more common one builds on Paul's stated principle of working only in untouched territory; his statement that there is no more room for him in the east is then understood to mean that other Gentile missionaries are at work in the territories between "Jerusalem and Illyricum" untouched by Paul. The other is Riesner's argument that Isaiah 66:19 provided Paul with his itinerary.

Riesner's hypothesis is quite unlikely, and so needs to be treated only briefly (see J.M. Scott 1995, 145–46). First, as Riesner himself recognizes, the list of names in Isaiah 66:19 is variously interpreted in Jewish tradition, and cannot be correlated with any certainty with Paul's itinerary. To take one particularly telling example, Put is usually associated with Libya in Africa, not Cilicia (the LXX renders Put as Libya; see Jer. 46:9 [LXX 26:9]; Ezek. 27:10; 30:5; 38:5; Nah. 3:9; also Josephus, *A.J.* 1.132). Further, in Isaiah 66:19, those who are going out to these nations to proclaim God's glory are Gentiles—this is implied by Isaiah 66:19 (cf. Isa. 45:20, where the same word "survivors" (*palitim*) refers to the nations [see Westermann 1969, 425]; in the LXX, it is made explicit: *ex autôn sesômenous*)—and their goal is to bring the scattered Israelites back to Jerusalem as an offering to the Lord. It is difficult to see how Paul could find grounds in this text for his mission as a Jewish apostle to the Gentiles, especially if one also wants to find in this text the background for Paul's language about the "offering of the Gentiles" (Rom. 15:16; see Riesner 1994, 218–21; also Aus 1979, 236–41, though Aus's statement that Paul reverses the usual meaning of the text simply underlines the difficulty without removing it). A significant mental strain is required to take a project in which a Jew (Paul) brings an offering of Gentiles, and then to understand it as Paul's conscious attempt to realize a prophetic text in which Gentiles bring Jews. Finally, the fact that

Paul frequently quotes from Isaiah does not cancel out the opposing fact that he nowhere explicitly cites this text.

What, then, of the other, more commonly encountered, justification, building on Paul's stated preference for unevangelized territory? It, too, fails to convince. It may well have been the case that provinces standing somewhat outside the Pauline arc (e.g., Cappadocia, Bithynia and Pontus) had already been evangelized by others. Lack of information makes any judgment on the matter difficult, though the connection of these regions with the figure of Peter (1 Pet. 1:1) may be of some significance. But surely within Paul's territory there was plenty of scope for additional work. In fact, we know this to be true in the case of one city in particular, namely, Troas. Not long before he wrote Romans 15, Paul had left Troas in search of Titus, despite the fact that "a door was opened" for him there "to proclaim the gospel" (2 Cor. 2:12–13). In Troas, at least, there was room for more work to be done.

Looking at his eastern territory more generally, Paul's return to Ephesus, after having worked further west in Macedonia and Achaia, might be taken as evidence that Paul perceived Asia as a gap to be filled (Riesner 1994, 264–66). But even so, without any churches in Thrace, one cannot really argue for a series of contiguous provinces from Galatia to Achaia. Asia is not the only gap between Galatia and Macedonia. In any case, the absence of any substantial information about evangelistic results in Thrace, Moesia, and Illyricum itself suggests that these territories, apparently within the arc of Paul's provinces, offered plenty of room for additional work. What Romans 15 seems to suggest, then, is: (1) that Paul wants to go on to Rome and Spain, but (2) that for some reason, probably because of a sense of a grand territorial task entrusted to him, he feels constrained to convince himself and others that he is not heading off to Rome and Spain without finishing his work in the east.

What, then, of Paul's projected work in the west? Is it the case that Paul's intentions to evangelize in Spain form part of a discernible, coherent plan to complete the "fullness of the nations" (Rom. 11:25)? As I will argue in a subsequent section, I think it probably is the case that Spain's significance for Paul is its location at the "ends of the earth," to use a relevant Old Testament phrase. To this extent, then, I agree with Aus, Johannes Munck, and others. But it cannot be enough simply to evangelize in Spain. If this had been the goal, Paul could have headed there at the outset, and saved himself a lot of grief and trouble! No, if Spain will bring the Gentile mission to completion, it must be that Paul envisages the planting of churches in every province up to and including Spain, or at least in a string of contiguous provinces leading up to Spain.

Here is where attempts to discern a coherent Pauline strategy get fuzzy. Aus (1979, 242–49) claims that evangelistic work in "the most distant site" mentioned in Isaiah 66:19 (i.e., Tarshish=Spain) will complete the task of gathering "representatives from all the nations mentioned in Old Testament eschatological prophecy," but does not provide any real indication of how those nations to the east or south of Spain would be included. Munck (1959, 52), with greater consistency but without any supporting evidence from Paul himself, suggests that Paul intended to evangelize in Gaul and Britain as well. Gerd Theissen (1982b, 40) similarly assumes without further clarification that Paul will evangelize "all the way to Spain." Knox argues that, after reaching Spain, Paul planned to turn south and then east, completing the circuit of nations ringing the Mediterranean. But the single word *kyklô* is too slender a basis on which to construct such an elaborate itinerary. J.M. Scott (1995, 138) refers to examples where *kyklô* is used of a curving route, with no expectation of a complete circuit. Scott's own argument (1995, 138–40), that the term *kyklô* is used by Paul to refer to the arrangement of the nations in a circle around Jerusalem, is intriguing; but it is hard to square this with Scott's belief that Paul's own mission, which after all is what is being described in the verse, is to be carried out in the nations of Japheth alone. Even if this could be demonstrated, it would not eliminate the problems faced by all such attempts to fit Paul's projected Spanish mission into a coherent strategy: most especially, the absence of any reference to evangelizing work in the territory between Rome and Spain, but also (even if it could be assumed that Paul's plans were to do for the territory between Rome and Spain what he had already done from Jerusalem to Illyricum) the vastness of the territory in question and the considerably greater difficulties involved (e.g., the language barrier, the absence of Jewish communities, etc.: see Jewett 1988, 143–47).

Thus, it is even more difficult to discern a coherent geographical strategy behind Paul's plans to head to Spain than it was regarding his already accomplished work in the east. This tends to confirm the tentative interpretation of Romans 15 suggested above. For reasons yet to be ascertained, Paul wants to head westward, to Rome and ultimately Spain. But, at the same time, he feels compelled to present his work in the east not only as completed but also in grandly comprehensive terms. And so, in my opinion, the tension in Romans 15 between grand claim and gritty reality must be allowed to stand.

This, however, is not a negative conclusion. It suggests, rather, an alternative model for interpreting the rich and confusing data emerging from Paul's letters: the dialectic, if you will, between a grand vision and a set of hard realities. On the one hand, I believe that Paul does have a grand and lofty vision of a universal mission entrusted to him as apostle to the Gentiles. On the other hand, any attempt to carry out such a vision would inevitably run headlong into a whole range of stubborn *realia* on the ground: the vastness of the territory, the activity of others with territorial claims of their own, the difficulties of travel, and so on. The pattern of Paul's missionary activity, such as it was, should be seen as the contingent product of the combination of these two conflicting sets of forces.

The Grand Vision

Scattered throughout Paul's letters are statements and comments which, taken together, reflect a lofty conception: a divinely ordered mission, embracing the whole Gentile *oikoumenê,* in which Paul himself plays the central human role. The relevant passages can be considered within four categories.

Paul's Own Role   Paul's boldest and most unambiguous claim to uniqueness is found in his account of the Apostolic Council (Gal. 2:1–10). Despite the fact that he was present as part of a delegation, of which Barnabas was undoubtedly the senior member, when Paul comes to describe the actual agreement, he dispenses with the first person plural and claims the Gentile mission for his own: "when they saw that I had been entrusted with the gospel for the uncircumcised…when [they] recognized the grace that had been given to me" (Gal. 2:7, 9). The right hand of fellowship might have been extended to both Barnabas and Paul, but in the agreement, as Paul presents it here, he himself, on the Gentile side of things, is the sole counterpart to Peter. Whatever the nature of the actual agreement may have been (for a shrewd discussion, see Holmberg 1978, 58–67), Paul understands it as simply confirming what God had already ordained and, more significantly, entrusted to Paul alone.

Outside the highly charged, self-defensive environment of Galatians, Paul is more guarded in his claim about himself. Still, a similar attitude can be seen in several other texts. In Colossians 1, as Paul introduces himself to the Colossians, he says that God has given him a commission for "you" (i.e., you Gentiles) to "fill to completion" (*plerôsai*) the mystery of the inclusion of the Gentiles (1:25–26). In the previous verse (to which I shall return), Paul declares himself to be the one—the only one, apparently—who is "completing what is lacking in Christ's afflictions for the sake of…the church" (1:24). In Romans, the rhetorical situation of the letter: Paul's desire to win acceptance by a church that he did not found and which has some questions about his gospel, necessitates a certain measure of tact and diplomacy. Still, Paul describes himself as "called to be an apostle" in order "to bring about the obedience of faith among all the Gentiles" (1:1, 5). Later in the same Epistle, speaking of the Gentile mission and its place in the divine scheme of things, while Paul refers to himself anarthrously as "an apostle to the Gentiles" (11:13) and "a minister of Christ Jesus to the Gentiles" (15:16), he nevertheless gives no indication that he is to be seen simply as one among many. Indeed, given the fact that both terms are found in the predicate of sentences with *einai,* it would be possible to render them as articular, namely, the apostle, the minister (as do several translations in the case of Romans 11:13; for the construction with *einai,* see BDF § 273). Perhaps the ambiguity of this construction—the fact that these terms could have been read either way—was in keeping with Paul's rhetorical purposes here. Munck's comment on Romans 15 is apropos: while Paul acknowledges that others have worked among the Gentiles, "he alone is the priest who is to prepare the Gentiles' offering" (1959, 52).

Paul's Sense of Territory   Paul seems to have a sense of territory commensurate with this elevated view of his own role. Indeed, such a sense would almost necessarily be implicit in the apostolic agreement of Galatians 2:1–10, as Paul understands it. A claim to have been entrusted with "the gospel for the uncircumcised" carries with it definite territorial implications. As for the agreement itself, it is not clear whether the division agreed to by Peter, Paul, and the others was understood ethnically (Jews/Gentiles) or territorially (the land of Israel/the land outside Israel); commentators are divided on the issue (for the ethnic reading, see, e.g., Betz 1979, 100; for the territorial, E. W. Burton 1921, 97–99). Probably there was a degree of ambiguity in the agreement from the outset (Bruce 1982, 125). In any case, what is more significant for our present purposes is how Paul understood it.

The nature of the evidence requires a nuanced answer to the question. On the one hand, it seems clear that Paul thinks more in territorial terms. In his missionary activity, he seems to have no compunction about preaching to Jews (1 Cor. 9:20). Further, in an important passage in 2 Corinthians 10:13–16, he speaks explicitly of a geographical sphere of jurisdiction that God has assigned to him. In and of itself, the terminology in 2 Corinthians 10:13 is somewhat obscure: *kata to metron tou kanonos hou emerisen hēmin ho theos metrou.* But the spatial terms in what follows: "we were not overstepping our limits when we reached you," "we were the first to come all the way to you," "so that we may proclaim the good news in lands beyond you," seem to require a territorial reading of the term *kanôn.* Victor Paul Furnish renders it "jurisdiction," an appropriate term in that it combines the ideas of territory and of an authority operative in that territory (1984, 471–73, 480–83; see also R.P. Martin 1986, 319–24). On the other hand, Paul's is not an unqualified territorial claim. He raises no objection to the activity of Peter outside Judea (Gal. 2:11; 1 Cor. 9:5). Further, Paul limits his territory by restricting himself to areas where others have not worked and churches have not yet been founded (2 Cor. 10:13–16; Rom. 15:20–21). Thus, Paul's claim to Gentile territory does not seem to be absolute.

At the same time, however, it needs to be recognized that the principle enunciated in Romans 15:20, i.e., the one of restricting his evangelizing activity to areas "where Christ has not already been named," is not absolute, either. We have one case, or perhaps two, where Paul seems prepared to press his apostolic claim, even though others have already done the foundational work. The less certain of the two is the case of Colossae, where the relationship between Paul and Epaphras and the circumstances of the founding of the church (not to mention the question of the letter's authenticity) are problematic. While it is not impossible, there is nevertheless no definite indication, as was observed already, that Epaphras had founded the church while working under Paul's authority. In any event, despite the fact that the church in Colossae was founded by someone else, so that, in the strictest sense, Paul's letter represents an attempt to build on a foundation already laid by someone else, Paul writes in the full authority of his role as apostle to the Gentiles, treating the church there as part of his own jurisdiction (see esp. Col. 1:24–25; 2:1, 5).

The clearer case, however, is that of Rome itself. Paul's intentions vis-à-vis Rome are, of course, hotly debated (see Donfried 1991). The case cannot be discussed in detail here, but it seems clear to me that, despite the statement in Romans 15:20, Paul has every intention to "proclaim the good news" (cf. Rom. 15:20) in Rome (1:5–6, 13, 15). Further, this proclamation of the gospel is not to be carried out somehow independently of the church already there; Paul desires "to proclaim the gospel to you also who are in Rome" (1:15). The statement of Romans 15:20 is sometimes used to blunt the plain sense of such verses (Hultgren 1985, 131; Stuhlmacher 1991, 231–42). But, in context, this statement is oriented totally to the work already carried out in the east, not to the projected work in the west. That is, Paul presents this policy as a way of explaining why he has not been able to get to Rome before this point: there was too much work to do in the east. He shows no awareness whatsoever that the policy might be taken to imply that Rome was off limits. Indeed, as A.J.M. Wedderburn (1988, 97–102) has cogently argued, the clear implication of statements such as Romans 1:5–6, 11 and 15:15–16 is that, because of his apostolic commissioning "to bring about the obedience of faith among all the Gentiles, among whom are you also" (1:5), Paul has legitimate authority to exercise the same apostleship in Rome as well, even if the circumstances require a certain measure of tact (see, e.g., 1:12). The Epistle as a whole can thus be read as Paul's attempt to claim Rome as part of his own apostolic territory. To quote Wedderburn, the church in Rome, since it was in Gentile territory, "was therefore in principle one of his churches, for which he was responsible, and which was responsible to him" (1988, 142).

What is being suggested here is that Paul's principle of working in fresh territory (Rom. 15:20; 2 Cor. 10:15) is to be seen as a tactical concession, rather than a fundamental element in his territorial consciousness. That is, Paul believes that, because of his calling as the apostle to the Gentiles, he has jurisdiction in the whole Gentile world; although, for the sake of his mission's overall success, Paul chose to restrict his activity to unevangelized areas. The reasons are varied, though interrelated: avoidance of conflict, independence, justification for objection to others working in his territories, etc. Even so, there are circumstances in which this tactical policy is set aside and overridden by his more fundamental territorial assumptions. This tactical policy should be seen, therefore, as one way in which Paul's grand vision was accommodated to certain hard realities, rather than as a fundamental territorial principle.

Eschatological Horizon   The third indication of Paul's grand vision is the eschatological framework within which his Gentile mission is perceived. This aspect of Paul's self-understanding has been well established by Munck (1959) and needs only brief mention here. It is based on two observations. First, there is Paul's expectation of Christ's imminent *parousia*. As is well known, Paul's early letters, at least, indicate that he expected the *parousia* to occur during his own lifetime (1 Thess. 4:17). While Paul subsequently had to reckon with the possibility of his own death (2 Cor. 1:8–10; Phil. 1:20–24), he nevertheless continued to believe that "the night is far gone, the day is near" (Rom. 13:11–12; also 1 Cor. 7:29; Phil. 4:5). The second observation concerns the Gentile mission. The significant thing is not simply that the Gentile mission takes place in the period between the resurrection and the *parousia* but, furthermore, that it defines this interim period. It is the completion of the "fullness of the Gentiles" that is supposed to trigger the salvation of Israel, the coming of 'the Deliverer,' and the resurrection of the dead (Rom. 11:15, 25–26).

As the one primarily charged with the mission to the Gentiles, Paul, in his own perception, "becomes the central figure in the story of salvation" (Munck 1959, 49)—at least, in that part of the story occupying this interim period. Paul's mission gives the present age its raison d'être; this mission's completion will bring the present age to an end. Paul's grand vision includes a temporal as well as a spatial dimension, though the concern for *to plêrôma tôn ethnôn* (Rom. 11:25) carries with it a definite territorial dimension as well.

Scriptural Background   Finally, the grandness of Paul's missionary vision is indicated by the scriptural terms in which he views it. We begin with Aus (1979), who argues, as we have seen, that Paul's desire to evangelize in Spain was driven by Isaiah 66:18–21 (see above, Patterns of Selection). This argument rests on two considerations: one, that Paul understood Tarshish as equivalent to Tartessos and thus as a reference to Spain; and two, that Paul would have seen Spain as the end of the earth. Thus, Aus's argument is that Paul would have seen his mission as completed when he had won converts in the most distant territory mentioned in Isaiah 66:19.

While the Tarshish-Tartessos connection is not implausible, it is nevertheless one that is not made by any ancient writer. Josephus (*A.J.* 1.127), for example, reads Tarshish as Tarsus. Further, Paul nowhere cites Isaiah 66:18–21, which deprives the argument of much of its force. It is important to note, however, that the idea of the end of the earth figures prominently in a set of texts that Paul does mention, and which are important for his self-conception as apostle to the Gentiles. The texts in question are all drawn from Isaiah 49, 52 and 53, and thus are linked to the Servant figure of Deutero-Isaiah. Paul's references to these texts, which strongly suggest that Paul's view of his own mission was shaped by the perspective of the Servant, are as follows. The account of Paul's call, in Galatians 1:15, echoes the call of the Servant in Isaiah 49:1. In 2 Corinthians 6:2, Paul quotes Isaiah 49:8 in the context of a discussion of Paul's own ministry, linking the day of salvation announced by the Servant to the time of Paul's own missionary proclamation. In Romans 15:21, Paul justifies his policy of working only in untouched territory by citing Isaiah 52:15; here, at least, Paul seems to understand the Servant as a reference to Christ, since "him" in Romans 15:21 must refer to Christ, though in Isaiah 52:15 it refers back to the Servant. Still, the significant point is that here, too, Paul draws upon Servant texts in order to explain and make sense of his mission. A similar phenomenon is at work in the more general quotations in Romans 10:15 (Isa. 52:7) and Romans 10:16 (Isa. 53:1). A citation of Isaiah 52:11 also appears in the problematic passage 2 Corinthians 6:14–7:1 (i.e., 6:17).

This material deserves more attention than can be given to it here (see Donaldson 1997, 253–55; Munck 1959, 24–35; Stendahl 1976, 7–23; Sandnes 1991; Dunn 1988, 1:7–8; 2:866; Bruce 1977, 146). Certainly, in view of the nature of the citation in Romans 15:21, it would be pressing the matter too far to say that Paul thought of himself, without qualification, as the Servant. Still, the evidence is sufficient to indicate that Paul understood his own mission against this background: in Dunn's words, as "completing the Servant's mission by taking the light of the gospel 'to the nations' (Isaiah 49:6)" (1988, 2:866). Incidentally, might this shed light on the puzzling statement about "completing what is lacking in Christ's afflictions" (Col. 1:24)?

This being so, it is worth completing the passage (Isa. 49:6) to which Dunn refers: "I will give you as a light to the nations, that my salvation may reach the end of the earth" (also attributed to Paul in Acts 13:47). The saving ministry carried out by the Servant has a territorial dimension, reaching to the end of the earth. Such language recurs repeatedly in this section of Isaiah. Two terms appear in the MT: *qatseh* and *efes*; the LXX uses *akron* and *eschaton*. Because of the Servant's ministry, God's praise will be sung "from the end of the earth" (Isa. 42:10); the exiles will return "from the end of the earth" (43:6); God's call goes out to the nations, "turn to me and be saved, all the ends of the earth" (45:22); the proclamation of redemption is sent forth "to the end of the earth" (48:20); "all the ends of the earth shall see the salvation of our God" (52:10). References to "the coastlands" (42:4, 10, 12; 49:1; 51:5) establish a similar territorial expanse for the promised salvation. The frequency of such territorial language in a portion of Isaiah of such apparent significance for Paul's own self-conception as apostle to the Gentiles is highly suggestive and worthy of further consideration.

While the phrase "the end of the earth" was often used in antiquity as a vague and general reference (see Aus 1979, 244–45; J.M. Scott 1994, 507–27 [passim]; Barrett 1994, 1:80; van Unnik 1973, 386–401), there is sufficient evidence to indicate that someone who, like Paul, was pointed westward would understand the term "the end of the earth" as a reference to Spain. The territory divided between Noah's three sons, in *Jubilees* 8–9, stretches from Eden in the east (8:16) to Gadir (= Cadiz in Spain) in the west (9:26). Rehearsing the same material, Josephus describes Japheth's territory as extending "in Europe as far as Gadeira" (*A.J.* 1.122; similarly, in *B.J.* 2.363, Gades is the westernmost limit of the Roman Empire). In a probable reference to Paul's plans to visit Spain, Clement speaks of him as reaching "the limits of the west" (1 Clem. 5.7). Spain might be in view, in *Psalms of Solomon* 8:15, in the reference to Pompey as one coming "from the end of the earth," though Rome is also possible. Except for the quotation of Psalm 19:4 in Romans 10:18 (which also contains Paul's only use of *oikoumenê*), the phrase "the end of the earth" does not appear in Paul's writings. Nonetheless, Paul quotes frequently from a section of scripture where this term is common, especially in connection with a proclamation of salvation to the nations; Paul seems to be compelled to continue westward until he reaches Spain; and the connection between Spain and "the end of the earth" is a natural one. Thus, there are good reasons to believe not only that Paul understood his own Gentile mission in terms of the Servant's mission among the nations, but also that the territorial scope of the Servant's mission (to the ends of the earth) provided Paul with the territorial dimensions of his own apostolate. At the very least, it can be said that this provides a much more plausible scriptural background to Paul's territorial imperative than any other that has been suggested thus far.

To sum up: these four factors strongly suggest that Paul operated on the basis of a grand missionary vision. Called by God and entrusted with the gospel "to the uncircumcised," Paul was thereby commissioned to complete the Servant's task of announcing salvation to all the nations to the ends of the earth, an enterprise which, when completed, would usher in Christ's *parousia* and the consummation of salvation. The vision is breathtaking in its scope. The grandness of its territorial dimension is fully in keeping with the loftiness of Paul's own personal role and the finality of the temporal framework within which it is placed.

The Gritty Realities

A grand vision is one thing; work in the field, quite another. Without yet raising the question of how the grand vision might have influenced Paul's actual plans and itinerary, we need to take note of the gritty realities that he inevitably encountered as a travelling missionary and which shaped his mission in significant ways. Given the constraints and the concerns of this chapter, we will have to be content with what amounts to little more than a list of these, though a full study of them would be very fruitful.

Geographical Expanse   Perhaps the basic constraining reality is the sheer geographical expanse of the territory that Paul saw as properly his own. The call to extend God's salvation to "the end of the earth" (cf. Isa. 49:6) has a noble ring to it. But the end of the earth, i.e., Spain, stands some 4,000 hard-slogging kilometres distant from a starting point at Antioch on the Orontes. Broadening coverage outward from this narrow ribbon of territory would add hundreds of kilometres more. And this is only a portion of the Roman *oikoumenê*.

Travel   The fact that Paul could even contemplate travels of such magnitude is due to the *Pax Romana* and the mobility it made possible (Riesner 1994, 273–82; Meeks 1983, 16–18; Hock 1980, 27–29; Rapske 1994). A network of roads stretched outwards from the golden milestone in Rome throughout the empire; commercial ship traffic criss-crossed the Mediterranean; and Roman administration kept both roads and sea relatively free of bandits and pirates. Still, travel cost money, even on foot, and was not without its attendant dangers, as the catalogue of hardships in 2 Corinthians 11:25–27 attests. Inevitably, the configuration of the transportation network would affect Paul's choice of cities in which to work, and—especially when factors such as the need to winter are taken into account (Riesner 1994, 274–75)—would also constrain his subsequent travel plans (see, e.g., 1 Cor. 16:5–6).

Subsistence Missionary activity is inevitably shaped by the need for subsistence, and Paul's decision to support himself as an artisan had definite consequences (Hock 1980; Theissen 1982a, 27–67). On the one hand, Paul's trade was portable, could probably be plied in any significant Greco-Roman city, and offered a ready-made social network in which to evangelize. On the other, the work was long and hard (1 Thess. 2:9), and carried with it a certain social stigma (Hock 1980, 25–26; Ariès and Duby 1987, 117–37).

Degree of Acceptance and Local Opposition Receptivity played a definite role in determining Paul's mission locales. He extended his time in Ephesus because of a "wide open door" (1 Cor. 16:9; cf. 2 Cor. 2:12–13; Col. 4:3). Presumably this was a factor leading Paul to spend lengthy periods of time in some places (e.g., Corinth, Ephesus) but not in others (e.g., Athens). Opposition also played a role, whether stiffening Paul's resolve to stay and support the church (1 Cor. 16:9; cf. 1 Thess. 2:17–3:3) or sometimes forcing him to move on (1 Thess. 2:2, 16, 18). Imprisonment opened up new possibilities as well (Phil. 1:12–14; Col. 4:3–4), with probable implications for the shape of subsequent work.

Other Missionaries As has already been observed, Paul was by no means the only missionary at work among the Gentiles. Conflicts with Peter and others over the terms and status of the Gentile mission (Gal. 2:11–14) seem to have resulted in a severing of connections with Antioch and the development of a more independent mission (Holmberg 1978, 34; Becker 1993, 94–99, 125–26). The need to defend this turf against various interlopers (see, e.g., Galatians; 2 Cor. 10–13) absorbed a great deal of time and energy. The collection project itself was initiated, at least in part, to defend the legitimacy of Paul's churches in the eyes of Jerusalem and Jewish Christianity. Both the break with Antioch and the tensions with other missionaries probably contributed to a decision to work in fresh areas and, consequently, to push further west.

Church Maintenance Paul's westward drive was countered by a consider-able retarding force, namely, the ongoing "daily pressure because of [his] anxiety for all [his] churches" (2 Cor. 11:28; on the determinative role played by these "two opposed currents" at work in Paul's missionary compulsions, see Bornkamm 1971, 57). No hit-and-run evangelist, Paul evidently felt that ensuring the ongoing viability and loyalty of his congregations was part of his apostolic responsibility. This had obvious effects on his travels (see, e.g., 2 Cor. 1:15–17; 2:1–2), and probably had the side effect, as well, of opening up new areas of work (cf. 2 Cor. 2:12).

Personal Factors Everything mentioned to this point had a personal dimen-sion, of course. But, in addition, we can note several instances where Paul's choice of territory was influenced by factors of a more purely personal nature. In Galatians 4:13–15, he refers in passing to a physical ailment that somehow created the occasion for his preaching to the Galatians. In addi-tion, there is presumably some connection between his lengthy time in Cilicia (and Syria; Gal. 1:21–2:1) and Paul's reported origins in Tarsus (Acts 9:11; 21:39; 22:3). Finally—a point to be developed further in the next sec-tion—there are good reasons to believe that it was his first brush with mortality (2 Cor. 1:8–11) that spurred Paul on to the west.

This catalogue is not exhaustive. Undoubtedly there were additional fac-tors at work in determining the territorial dimensions of Paul's mission (e.g., the presence of Jewish communities). But this is sufficient to illus-trate the degree to which the actual shape of Paul's mission was deter-mined by very mundane realities.

Between the Vision and the Realities

My thesis is that the geographical shape of Paul's missionary activity is to be seen as emerging between two poles: his grand vision of a mission among all the nations to the end of the earth, and the gritty realities impinging on an itinerant Christian missionary in the first century CE Roman world. It remains to say something about the nature of the interplay between the two.

On the one hand, it is not possible to see the actual shape of the mis-sion simply as the outworking of a coherent strategy arising from the vision. The vision that occasionally can be glimpsed, especially in Paul's need to present the evangelization of the east as complete (Rom. 15:19, 23) and in his drive toward Spain, is much too grand in scope (grandiose, even) for anyone to think realistically of fulfilling it, especially with the expectation of Christ's imminent *parousia* as a component part. Further, the length of time spent in Syria and Cilicia suggests that there was no westward terri-torial imperative from the outset (Bornkamm 1971, 49).

On the other hand, I do not think that the grand vision can simply be seen as something arising out of the mission as it developed on the ground, with the forces that were pushing Paul into independent work, further and further west, somehow, at the same time, leading him to conceive of his mission in universal and unique terms. For Paul seems to be aware of a unique call to "proclaim [Christ] among the Gentiles" from the very beginning of his apostleship (Gal. 1:15–16). Of course, one has to reckon with the possibility that this is a retrospective view, Paul collapsing into the moment of conversion a process of realization that stretched over a longer period (Fredriksen 1986, 3–34). But without denying the possibility of development, Paul's (evidently evangelistic) activity in Arabia (Gal. 1:17) seems to indicate that he was conscious of a mission to Gentiles from a very early point. This is the most probable explanation of Aretas's annoyance with Paul (2 Cor. 11:32–33; cf. Acts 9:23–25; see Betz 1979, 74). This is not to say that Paul had from the beginning the specific intention of evangelizing all the way to Spain, nor that he always understood his call in terms of the Servant missionary of Deutero-Isaiah. Nevertheless, from a very early point Paul believed himself to have been called by God to a unique mission among the *ethnê,* which means that the grand vision was present, already then, in implicit or embryonic form.

My suggestion is that the nature of the relationship between grand vision and gritty reality falls somewhere in between these two extremes. For the most part, I think that they operated at different levels: the grand vision providing the horizon within which Paul carried out his mission, and the actual course of that mission being governed largely by the more mundane realities on the ground. But, at certain points, events unfolded in such a way as to bring the two factors into a more dialectical relationship: Paul's actual experiences serving to bring dimensions of the grand vision into clearer focus, on the one hand; the imperatives of the vision impinging upon his actual plans for the future, on the other.

In particular, I believe that we have evidence for two such dialectical moments. The first is the break with Antioch and the beginning of Paul's independent missionary activity. Up to this point, Paul seems to have been content to work in and around Antioch, or, at least, outward from Antioch as a home base. The conflict with Peter and the break with Barnabas seem to coincide with the beginning of Paul's push to the west, first to the Greek peninsula and then, in intention at least ("at last" [Rom. 1:10]; "often intended" [Rom. 1:13]), to Rome. It is at least plausible to suggest that these developments pushed Paul to a clearer perception of the territorial dimensions of his apostolic call, and perhaps to the belief that the shape of his call was already prefigured in that of the Servant of Deutero-Isaiah (if this belief was not present already).

The second moment—to return to our point of departure—becomes apparent in the decision to push on to Rome and then to Spain. This plan needs to be seen as more than just the next step in a sequence of territorial stages; the land distance between Corinth and Spain is probably twice that covered up to this point between Antioch and Corinth. There is a dimension—finality—to the projected journey that requires explanation. My suggestion is that it is linked to Paul's brush with death in Ephesus (2 Cor. 1:8–11). Confronted for the first time with the real possibility of his own death before Christ's *parousia*, Paul is made urgently aware of both the magnitude of the task yet to be accomplished and the limits of his own time. Hence the pressing desire to push on, as directly as possible, to Rome and then to the end of the earth.

And so, the plans Paul announced to the Romans are not to be seen as part of a realistic strategy fully to spread the Gospel "from Illyricum to Spain," just as he had already done "from Jerusalem to Illyricum." Attempts to account for the pertinent material in Romans 15, i.e., the statement that the work in the east is complete and the announced travel plans, on the basis of some putatively coherent territorial strategy, are misguided. Both elements are to be seen instead as the result of a dialectic between vision and reality, which is to say, Paul's attempt to accommodate the grandness of the vision to the stubborn facts of his own real experience; or, better, by sheer will and rhetoric, to force the untidy contingencies of reality to fit the grand pattern of the vision.

CONCLUSION

At the beginning of this chapter, I raised several questions concerning Paul's mission. Two of them: whether Paul had a sense of territory assigned to him, and the extent to which his actual missionary activity was shaped by an overarching sense of mission, have been sufficiently discussed and require no further comment. But what about the third question? What can we say about Paul's legacy to the Christian movement? What did Paul contribute toward the eventual success of Christianity?

As observed already in the first section of this chapter, Paul was not the originator, either deliberately or inadvertently, of a missionary movement, for which he would be the prototype, and which eventually was successful in its project of Christianizing the Roman Empire. After the first century, professional itinerant missionaries seem to have played no significant role in the spread of the movement. This is due, at least in part, to the fact that the movement had been planted, already by the end of the first century CE, in significant centres throughout much of the empire (at least on the northern shore of the Mediterranean; information on Egypt and North Africa is harder to come by) from which it could spread through more spontaneous, informal, or ordinary means.

Paul's contribution to this spread is not to be underestimated. The major centres of Pauline Christianity (Ephesus, Philippi, Thessalonica, Corinth) continued to be important into the second century CE and beyond. Still, the facts (1) that the Christian movement was able to take root in Rome without any apparent apostolic initiative, and (2) that what was pushing Paul westward, at least in part, was the increasing activity of other missionaries in the east, suggests that sooner or later the movement would have arrived in these cities as well. Instead, Paul's most significant contribution to the spread and ultimate success of the Christian movement was undoubtedly the letters that he wrote, with the vision contained therein of a gospel "bearing fruit and growing in the whole world" (Col. 1:6; also 2 Cor. 2:14) and of the church as a trans-local fellowship spreading out into the *oikoumenê* (1 Thess. 1:8; 1 Cor. 1:2; 4:17; 7:17; 11:16; Rom. 1:8), thereby constituting a third race ("to Jews or to Greeks or to the church of God," 1 Cor. 10:32). There is a certain irony in this, of course, in that what produced these letters in the first place was precisely those backwards-looking circumstances of church maintenance that slowed down Paul's missionary advance. Still, the greatest of these letters arose out of Paul's compulsion to move forward: to push on to Spain, and thus to complete his mission to the end of the earth.

7

The *Contra Apionem* in Social and Literary Context

An Invitation to Judean Philosophy

Steve Mason

INTRODUCTION

One of the baseline problems posed in this book by Leif E. Vaage's programmatic chapter 1 and engaged also by Terence Donaldson in chapter 6 concerns the place of mission in ancient religions, and especially in Judaism. Was Judaism, during the Greco-Roman period, a missionary religion? Through more than a century scholars occasionally debated the issue, but the dominant view was that Judaism encouraged proselytism (e.g., Schürer 1973–1986, 3:1, 150–76; Bamberger 1968; Braude 1940; Leon 1960, 250–56; Georgi 1986; Simon 1986). Evidence was adduced from Greek and Latin authors who reflected upon Jewish proselytizing, from Jewish literature that seemed to welcome converts, from the expulsions of Jews from Rome on charges of proselytism, and from early Christian texts. In recent years, however, the question has been reopened with vigour. In this recent flurry of activity, the decidedly stronger current holds that Judaism was not a missionary religion (McKnight 1991; Will and Orrieux 1992; Cohen 1991, 1992; Goodman 1992, 1994; Kraabel 1994). On this view, texts that extol the virtues of Judaism were read almost exclusively by Jews. And, in any case, the Jewish literature does not advocate proselytism, even if it welcomes the occasional self-motivated convert. In holding to the view that ancient Judaism was a missionary religion, Louis Feldman (1993a) has become something of a lone voice. Shaye J.D. Cohen, himself a recent proselyte to the non-missionary hypothesis, sees a "new consensus" in the making (1991, 166; but cf. 1987a, 49–58).

Although these debates have been helpful in some ways, I see little point in asking whether Judaism was a missionary religion. All of the key terms are problematic: Judaism (which kind? represented by whom?), missionary (does mission require a central body or charter?), and religion (how was ancient religion in these contexts distinct from ethnic culture? from philosophy?). Further, we cannot penetrate through the surviving texts to uncover such psychological motives as missionary zeal. We shall only progress, therefore, if we narrow the question to particular places, times, documents, and individuals. In such local conditions, did Gentiles embrace Judean culture in any significant numbers, and, if they did, how is that process best explained?

Accordingly, this chapter deals with one author, one text, one place, and one time: Josephus's *Contra Apionem,* written for Gentiles in Rome at the end of the first century CE. This document, I shall argue, is best understood as an invitation to already interested Gentile readers to embrace Judean philosophy. Of course, the text does not plainly say this, so anyone who insists that texts tell us everything we should like to know about them, will not find the argument convincing. But the author and first readers shared extratextual resources that were critical to their communication. In an effort to recover those resources, the best that we can do is to sketch out what is known of Josephus's broad social context in postwar Rome and of the immediate (personal) literary context provided for *Contra Apionem* by Josephus's earlier works. Taking into account both the context and the content of *Contra Apionem,* I shall argue that the closest parallels to this work are among the so-called *logoi protreptikoi,* or discourses and dialogues intended to promote "conversion" to a philosophical community.

SOCIAL CONTEXT: ATTRACTION AND AVERSION TO JUDEAN CULTURE IN ROME

Attraction

Fortunately, some germane features of Judean-Roman relations in Rome are well attested. On the one hand, Judean culture attracted considerable interest among Romans, even to the point of a conversion that was perceived to involve the renunciation of one's native tradition. This conclusion does not depend on courageous inference from a jug handle, but is the only reasonable explanation of an array of evidence. It raises problems from a sociological perspective, for how could a Roman plausibly adopt the ways of another ethnic group and truly forsake his or her own (Goodman 1994, 1–37)? But we must bracket that question while we survey the sources. Because they have been widely discussed elsewhere, and my conclusions here are not meant to be controversial, I discuss only what seems to me to be the most telling evidence.

Literary Evidence   The fullest extant portrayal of Judeans by a Roman author is that of Tacitus, who attempts to describe the Judean character in order to create a context for his account of the revolt in 66–73 CE (*Hist.* 5.1–13). That Tacitus is familiar with many traditions about the Judeans is clear, both because he says so and because his account intersects with various remarks made in other authors. Tacitus thus provides something of a compendium of contemporary literary perspectives on the Judeans.

The dominant theme here, in keeping with Tacitus's purpose, is Judean misanthropy: they oppose the rest of humanity in their values. It is striking, however, that the first item mentioned by Tacitus in his proof of Judean depravity is the fact that "the worst rascals among other peoples, renouncing their ancestral traditions, always kept sending tribute and contributions to Jerusalem." Tacitus continues: "those who are converted (*transgressi*) to their ways follow the same practice [circumcision], and the earliest lesson they receive is to despise the gods, to disown their country, and to regard their parents, children, and brothers as of little account" (*Hist.* 5.5). Clearly, Tacitus did not invent the phenomenon of conversion to Judaism; he can only try to explain it away as the actions of the worst people (*pessimi*— presumably, the lower classes).

The perception by Tacitus that the Judeans invite life-changing conversion is confirmed by other Roman authors. It is remarkable, since these others have so very little to say about Judeans, that conversion should figure so largely in what they do say. For Epictetus (ca. 100 CE), according to Arrian's notes, it was already proverbial that, "Whenever we observe someone caught in two directions, we are in the habit of saying (*eiothamen legein*), 'He is not a Judean, but only plays the part' (*hypokrinetai*). But when he takes upon himself the attitude of the one who has been immersed and made his choice (*haireomai*), then he really is, and is called, a Judean" (*Diatr.* 2.9.20). This is the only place in which Epictetus singles out Judeans for special mention (though twice he mentions their food laws alongside those of other nations [*Diatr.* 1.11.12–13; 1.22.4] by way of illustration). Interest in and conversion to Judean culture are common enough that Epictetus can cite a proverbial saying in support of his point about being a true philosopher.

We get the same impression from another contemporary, Juvenal, who satirically illustrates the potentially corrupting example of a parent with the example of a Judean sympathizer whose son goes as far as conversion by "putting aside his foreskin." Juvenal (*Sat.* 5.14.96–106) assumes, as do

Epictetus and Tacitus, that this kind of conversion involves the complete repudiation of one's traditional piety. Elsewhere, Juvenal makes only passing references to Judeans begging in Rome (*Sat.* 1.3.14; 2.6.543–547). Their attraction of converts thus stands out as a noteworthy feature.

Other literary allusions to Judean attraction of proselytes—by Horace (*Sat.* 1.4.139–143), Seneca (*Superst.*, in Augustine, *Civ.* 6.11), and Celsus (*True Word,* in Origen, *Cels.* 5.41.6)—could be discussed, but their interpretation is more controversial. The three that I have introduced are valuable because they show us independent Roman writers reflecting commonplace assumptions about the Judeans: they commonly attract sympathizers and also full converts, who renounce native traditions in order to join them. Since these remarks are incidental, adduced as given in the service of some other point, it is not likely that the authors invented or exaggerated the phenomenon of conversion.

Particular Cases   In addition to these observations by Roman authors concerning the state of their society, we have several names of individuals in Rome, from the first to third centuries CE, who either expressed strong interest in Judean culture or actually made it their own. Some of these appear on funerary inscriptions from Judean cemeteries. According to Harry J. Leon, seven Jewish epitaphs are of "indubitable proselytes" (1960, 254); though one might have doubts about the three-and-a-half-year-old Irene. These proselytes were sufficiently welcomed by the community to be given proper Judean burials. Non-Judean sites have, in addition, turned up the epitaphs of four "reverers" (*metuentes*), who apparently associated themselves in some way with Judaism but, to borrow Epictetus's distinction, were not considered proper Judeans.

In terms of social status, it is noteworthy that one of the *metuentes* was a Roman knight; that two of the proselyte inscriptions at Nomentana were carved on marble, whereas most were simply painted on the grave closures; that five of the proselyte inscriptions are in Latin, although the vast majority of the Judean inscriptions are in the Greek of newcomers to Rome; and that at least one of the proselytes—Veturia Paulla, who was buried in a sarcophagus and was the "mother" of two synagogues—seems to have been a woman of substance. Although this evidence is hardly decisive, in view of the small sample, it militates against Tacitus's rhetorical charge that converts to Judaism were of the basest sort.

That only five or seven of Leon's 534 inscriptions—little more than one per cent—certainly come from proselytes should not be taken as evidence of their insignificant numbers. First, many of those buried may not have wished to record for posterity their conversion. Even in a Judean cemetery, social pressures may have encouraged converts to assimilate to the group as quickly as possible and not advertise their new status. Moreover, conversion was a capital crime from Hadrian's time onward (van der Horst 1991, 72), the period from which most of these inscriptions come. Second, we may indeed have other proselytes behind such epithets as *Ioudaios* and *Hebraios,* and in the statement that a woman lived both well and "in Judaism" (Leon 1960, 129). Third, the surviving family members who proudly recorded their loved one's conversion may well have been proselytes as well. In view of these mitigating factors, it is impressive enough that the Judean inscriptions of Rome preserve any physical evidence of conversion.

Although most converts would not have become famous, we also know from the surviving literature the names of a few high-profile Roman proselytes. Josephus mentions a prominent senator's wife, during the reign of Tiberius, named Fulvia. Having embraced the Judean ordinances (*nomimois proselêlythuian tois Ioudaikois, A.J.* 18.81), Fulvia was reportedly defrauded of gifts intended for the temple in Jerusalem. Josephus further alleges that Nero's consort and wife, Poppea Sabina, was a God-fearer (*A.J.* 20.195), who twice intervened on behalf of Judean interests. Josephus had no evident reason to claim Poppea's sympathies so long after Nero's rule, when the memories of both husband and wife were odious. Finally, Dio claims that Domitian executed the consul Flavius Clemens (95 CE) and exiled his wife Flavia Domitilla, although she was a relative of Domitian, on charges of "atheism" (*Hist. Rom.* 67.14.2). Dio immediately explains that this was the charge Domitian levelled also against "others who had drifted into Judean customs" (*es ta tôn Ioudaiôn ethê echokellontes*). The nautical verb "to drift" perhaps implies that there was a current of proselytes at the time. That there was at least significant interest in Judaism, is also suggested by Suetonius, who claims that Domitian collected the Judean tax with the utmost severity, even from "those who lived as Judeans without professing Judaism" (*Dom.* 12: *inprofessi Iudaicam viverent vitam*).

Because Suetonius and Dio indicate that Domitian eliminated enemies on mere pretexts, and because another version of the story has Domitilla embracing Christianity (Eusebius, *Hist. eccl.* 3.18; cf. P. Lampe 1989, 166–72), we should not insist upon the real conversion of Clemens and Domitilla. Nevertheless, Dio's incidental notice about the others who adopted Judean ways must point to some kind of real condition at that time, because he goes on to say (*Hist. Rom.* 68.1.2) that one of Nerva's first policies was to stop admitting accusations of either impiety or adopting a Judean life (*oute asebeias oute Ioudaikou biou*). Since Dio has already mentioned

Nerva's reversal of the impiety charge (*Hist. Rom.* 68.1.1), this repeated reference must be linked to the charge of adopting Judaism. Evidently, Dio assumes that adopting a Judean life results in impiety with respect to Roman tradition. That impression fits with the remarks of Tacitus, Epictetus, and Juvenal.

The Legal Situation of Judeans in Rome The question of Nerva's policy brings us to the third kind of evidence for significant proselytism in Rome, namely: throughout the entire period of our interest, a Judean propensity to seek proselytes is assumed in Roman legislation. In describing the three occasions on which disciplinary measures were taken against Roman Judeans, later writers typically allege proselytizing efforts as causes. Thus, both of the Byzantine epitomizers of Valerius Maximus's *Memorable Words and Deeds* (i.e., Paris and Nepotianus) claim that the Judeans were expelled from Rome in 139 BCE for trying to transmit to the Roman people their sacred rites (described by Paris as "the cult of Jupiter Sabazius"). And everyone who writes about the expulsion of Judeans from Rome in 19 CE connects it in some way with proselytism. Josephus claims that the affair resulted from the defrauding of the aristocratic convert Fulvia (*A.J.* 18.81). Dio says that the Judeans, having flocked to Rome in great numbers, "were converting many of the natives to their ways" (*Hist. Rom.* 57.18.5a). Suetonius couples Judeans with Egyptians, and claims that Tiberius ordered all who had "embraced these superstitions" to burn their religious symbols (*Tib.* 36). Tacitus likewise groups Judeans and Egyptians, and says that those who had been "infected" with these superstitions had to leave (*Ann.* 2.85).

Finally, in the 40s CE, Claudius undertook some kind of disciplinary action, possibly more than one, against the Roman Judeans. Although Suetonius has him expelling those Judeans "who were continually rioting at the instigation of Chrestus" (*Claud.* 25), Dio claims that Claudius could not expel the Judeans because of their great numbers, but only forbade them to hold meetings; they were permitted to preserve their ancestral way of life (*Hist. Rom.* 60.6.6). Dio does not give an explicit reason for Claudius's action, but his opening notice that their numbers had "once again increased greatly" seems to direct the reader's attention back to his earlier remarks about Judean proselytism. In this context, permission to follow their ancestral ways would be an imposed limitation: they should stop trying to induce others to follow those ways as well.

Later emperors would remain concerned about conversion to Judaism, apparently seeing it as a significant factor in the perceived weakening of Roman traditions. Domitian's reform, according to which conversion to

Judaism became a capital offence, though rescinded by Nerva, became law again with Hadrian's general prohibition of circumcision. If, as many think, Hadrian did not mean to proscribe Judaism per se, but only conversion, then his successor Antoninus Pius got it right when he prohibited the circumcision of non-Judeans. Proselytism evidently continued to merit legislation, however, for Septimius Severus imposed severe penalties on converts (*Script. Hist. Aug.,* Sept. Sev. 17.1). A century later, the jurist Paul prescribed the death penalty for those who circumcised non-Judeans, and exile for those who converted (*Sent.* 5.22.3–4). These prohibitions, as is well known, became a standard part of later Christian legislation. Whereas the central government was generally tolerant of foreign traditions, and may even have been conspicuously benevolent toward Judean communities around the empire, proselytism in Rome was evidently an ongoing problem for it.

In the face of such diverse evidence, the only reasonable hypothesis seems to be that Gentile attraction and also full conversion to Judaism were easily observable phenomena during Josephus's residency in Rome at the end of the first century CE. Since that much is admitted not only by scholars who have accepted the notion of a Jewish mission but also by those who seem to have little at stake in the issue (Smallwood 1981, 201–16; Leon 1960, 250–56) and even by some who deny a Jewish mission—Scot McKnight curiously suggests that the Roman situation was exceptional (1991, 74)—we may leave the issue as provisionally settled. Cohen (1993, 26–27) holds that the evidence for conversion to Judaism in Rome is "abundant and unequivocal." Although some of the evidence is post-Hadrian, there seem to be clear lines of continuity. Attraction and conversion to Judaism were readily observable in postwar Rome.

Aversion

There was, of course, another side. Not everyone in the world capital of that time was eager to convert. Roman literati tended to disparage Judean culture, partly because they disparaged all foreign cultures in Rome and partly because Judeans had exclusivist traits that smacked of misanthropy. Egyptian accounts of Judean origins appear to have had some influence in Rome, perhaps through the activities of Apion and other resident Alexandrians. These slanders have now been thoroughly documented, and we need not reproduce the evidence. Our interest is in the particular postwar situation in which Josephus found himself: Was the image of Judean culture in Rome affected by the revolt?

We do not have much direct literary evidence, but we can piece together some clues. First, the highly visible postwar celebrations must have had an impact on Roman observers: after Vespasian's glorious return from his

Judean campaign to become emperor in 69 CE (Josephus, *B.J.* 7.63–74) came the spectacle of Titus's triumphal march, with Judean rebel leaders being led through the streets to their execution; the sudden influx of Judean slaves; the issue of a commemorative (*Judea Capta*) coin series; and the erection of the monumental Arch of Titus in the city centre. These displays can only have made life uncomfortable for Roman Judeans and sympathizers. We do not know whether there were reprisals against Judeans in Rome itself during or after the war, but it should not surprise us if there were, for Josephus claims that "hatred of the Judeans was everywhere at its height" when the war began, and in other major centres this hatred had resulted in massacres (*B.J.* 7.51, 57, 367–368).

Our clearest evidence for anti-Judean sentiments in Rome is the simple fact that Josephus devoted so much energy, immediately after his arrival there, to writing an account of the revolt that would refute current anti-Judean stories. Josephus claims that, before his own history, the only accounts in circulation were written by people who either flattered the Romans or hated the Judeans (*B.J.* 1.2), which meant in either case an anti-Judean bias. Josephus writes because he considers it "monstrous" (*B.J.* 1.6) that the truth should be lost to these writers, who were doing outrage to the truth (*B.J.* 1.4). Josephus elaborates: "They desire to represent the Romans as a great nation, and yet they continually depreciate and disparage the actions of the Judeans. But I fail to see how the conquerors of a puny people deserve to be accounted great" (*B.J.* 1.7–8).

To find out more about these other accounts, which are all lost, perhaps the best we can do is to read *Bellum judaicum* in a mirror, so to speak. This is a dangerous practice for particulars, but it should work for the main themes. It turns out that Josephus is greatly concerned (a) to dissociate the revolt from the national character, by blaming it on a small handful of aberrant rebels who have now been punished, and (b) to show that it was the Judeans' own God who punished the nation for the rebels' impiety. We might reasonably suppose, therefore, that the Roman authors in question had argued the reverse: the revolt was symptomatic of the national character, and the outcome was a victory of the Roman gods.

In fact, these very themes appear in later Roman authors who deal with the revolt. Tacitus disparages the Judean character as the context for his story of the revolt (*Hist.* 5.1–13). Philostratus's Euphrates likewise complains, in relation to the war, that, "The Judeans have long been in revolt, not only against the Romans, but against humanity" (*Vit. Apoll.* 5.33). Celsus, in the footsteps of Cicero (*Flac.* 28.69) long before him, appeals to the Judean defeat in refutation of Judaism's claims to know a uniquely powerful God (in Origen, *Cels.* 5.41). Minucius Felix's Caecilius contends that the Judean god had so little power he is now enslaved by the Roman gods (*Oct.* 10; cf. 33). Since we find such views in later authors, since they are predictable responses to the war, and since Josephus confronts them directly in his account, we may conclude that they were already present in the lost histories of the revolt by Josephus's contemporaries. The image of Judeans in Rome suffered, in both popular and literary circles, as a result of the war.

If we try now to paint a rounded picture of the Judean situation in Rome after the war, we end up with something like this. Ever since its arrival in Rome, Judean culture proved attractive to Gentiles of different ethnic backgrounds and social strata; most of the evidence for conversion seems to involve native Romans or romanized elements of the population. This is not the place to speculate on the reasons for this attraction, but it seems that attraction and full conversion, with a conscious repudiation of one's native tradition, were well known. On the other hand, the revolt seriously tarnished the Judean image. The war and its aftermath must have had social and psychological effects on sympathizers and would-be proselytes even before Domitian's prosecution of Judaizers. We should like to learn a great deal more about Josephus's social context, but these general and secure observations must suffice for our present purposes as background to his *Contra Apionem*.

LITERARY CONTEXT: THE *ANTIQUITATES JUDAICAE*

When Josephus writes *Contra Apionem* at the end of the first century CE, he appeals directly to his earlier *Antiquitates judaicae:* the new work, Josephus says, will try again to do what his magnum opus had failed to do (*C.Ap.* 1.1–5). If we are to assess the purpose of *Contra Apionem,* we must therefore have in mind some notion of the purpose and scope of *Antiquitates judaicae.* Fortunately, we enjoy almost universal agreement on the main themes of this work: Josephus writes *Antiquitates judaicae* to defend Judean history and culture before a Gentile audience. His apologetic motive has been amply demonstrated by studies of particular passages, most notably, Louis Feldman's investigations of how Josephus portrays biblical characters (listed in Feldman 1993a, 594–96). These studies have shown that Josephus carefully reworks his sources, in part to refute common slanders about Judean origins and misanthropic tendencies. Explicitly apologetic statements appear also in his justification for including the pro-Judean decrees (*A.J.* 14.1–3, 186–187; 16.175). Agreement about Josephus's apologetic motive in *Antiquitates judaicae* is so widespread that even those who follow

Laqueur's cynical view (1970) of *Bellum judaicum* as a piece of Roman propaganda must posit either that Josephus repented between the two works
or that he found a new way of serving his political interests (e.g., M. Smith
1956, 74–79; Cohen 1979, 148–51, 237–38; Schwartz 1990, 170–208).

I would like to suggest, however, that the apologetic motive, which is
obviously present, does not satisfactorily explain *Antiquitates judaicae*. Having completed the urgent task of exonerating Judeans from complicity in
the revolt (in *Bellum judaicum*), why expend so much energy—and Josephus
admits his weariness (*A.J.* 1.7)—writing another twenty volumes? Simple
refutation of slanders about Judean origins could have been done more
compactly. Moreover, nearly half of *Antiquitates judaicae* (from Book 13
onward), including four volumes on Herod and a detailed account of the
emperor Gaius's death, has nothing to do with ancient Judean history.

What then? Did Josephus extend *Antiquitates judaicae* to twenty volumes in order to match Dionysius's famous *Roman Antiquities,* as Henry St. J.
Thackeray suggested (1967, 69)? Did Josephus haplessly wander through
the post-biblical period, cutting and pasting large chunks of undigested
source material? Such views were popular during the heyday of extreme
source criticism, but they have long since been proven untenable (e.g.,
Laqueur 1970; Attridge 1976; Franxman 1979; Feldman and Hata 1988;
Krieger 1994). Was the apologetic of *Antiquitates judaicae,* then, meant to serve
some urgent political goal, perhaps to ingratiate Josephus with the emerging rabbinic coalition at Yavneh? Such an interpretation runs afoul of the
text itself and its implied audience at every turn: Josephus writes for Gentiles a rambling narrative that is mostly hostile toward the Pharisees and
evinces no obvious rabbinic connections (see, e.g., Mason 1988, 1991, 1992).
Thus, the identification of an apologetic motive with respect to Judean origins, though accurate as far as it goes, does not explain Josephus's gargan-
tuan effort in composing the 60,000 lines of *Antiquitates judaicae* (20.267).
It seems to me that the lengthy preface to *Antiquitates judaicae* promises
much more than an apologetic. Indeed, a defensive posture is remarkably
absent. The whole body of the work sustains a positive appeal to Gentile
readers, to which the defensive elements are entirely subordinate.

The Preface (A.J. 1.1–26)

After recalling his account in *Bellum judaicum* (1.1–4), Josephus claims that
he is now writing *Antiquitates judaicae* in the belief that the "whole Greek-
speaking world" will find this translation of the Judeans' political history
and constitution "worthy of serious pursuit" (1.5). That Josephus's global
ambition is highly exaggerated should not blind us to its tone; he does not
suggest that he is out primarily to combat false presentations, as he had

done in *Bellum judaicum* (1.3, 6, 9). Josephus allows that he had intended to include some ancient Judean history in his earlier work. As he now phrases it, his goal would have been to describe Judean origins and fortunes, "the great lawgiver under whom they were trained in piety and the exercise of the other virtues," and all of their (noble) wars before the unfortunate conflict with Rome (*A.J.* 1.6). Josephus assumes the reader's interest in things Judean.

Josephus next introduces his patron Epaphroditus, who serves as a paradigm for the implied reader: he is a curious and beneficent Gentile. It was because of his persistent eagerness to support the producers of "beneficial and beautiful work" that Josephus persevered in this noblest undertaking (*A.J.* 1.9). There is no hint of defensiveness here. That Josephus really did expect an interested Gentile readership, and that this is not merely a superficial rhetorical ploy, is confirmed by an abundance of incidental notices throughout *Antiquitates judaicae* (e.g., 1.128–129; 3.317; 14.1–3, 186–187; 16.175; 20.262) and its appendix, *Vita* (1, 12c).

Josephus's outward-looking tone continues when he proposes that the translation of the LXX was a model for his own work. He ponders whether, before his time, any Greeks had been eager to learn Judean history, and whether Judeans had been willing to share it. On the one side, he cites the keen interest of Ptolemy II in the Judean laws and constitution and, on the other, claims that the high priest Eleazar did not jealously keep from the king "the enjoyment of a benefit" (*A.J.* 1.11). Indeed, Eleazar's willingness to share the laws reflected the Judean tradition not to make a secret of good things (1.11). Josephus, therefore, will imitate the high priest's magnanimity, since in his own day there are also many lovers of learning (1.12). The tone of the preface to *Antiquitates judaicae* thus differs markedly from that of the preface to *Bellum judaicum:* Josephus no longer seems preoccupied with refuting falsehood; his work is described only as a boon to interested readers.

Josephus now moves to state the thesis of his work. It is that those who conform to the will of God, and do not venture to transgress laws that have been excellently laid down, prosper in all things beyond belief, and for their reward are offered happiness by God; whereas, in proportion as they depart from the strict observance of the laws, things practicable become impracticable, and whatever imaginary good thing they strive to do ends in irretrievable disasters (*A.J.* 1.14).

This lesson is interesting for at least two reasons. First, there is no limitation to Judeans of the principle involved. Whoever follows the laws of God will prosper, and whoever does not will suffer. How can this be? In the following sentences, Josephus ties the Judean laws very closely to the laws of nature. Indeed, he says that Moses first treated the creation of the world before disclosing his legislation precisely so that his laws would be seen to be based upon the construction of the universe. Josephus downplays or omits material from his sources dealing with Israel's special election and covenant (Attridge 1976, 78–92; Daniel 1981; Amaru 1980–1981; Bailey 1987; contra E.P. Sanders 1992, 279). This is in keeping with Josephus's view that the Judean laws reflect universal law. His detailed account of the emperor Gaius's death shows the efficacy of divine retribution across national lines (*A.J.* 19.201–204). This view of history is not meaningful to Judeans alone, therefore, but will be clear to "any who care to peruse" Josephus's work (1.14).

The second outstanding feature of Josephus's thesis is related to the first: namely, conformity to the Judean laws promises happiness! He will repeat the point in *A.J.* 1.20: those who follow God, the father and Lord of all, who beholds all things, find a happy life. The word *eudaimonia* in these passages is worthy of close attention, because it was the recognized goal of philosophical schools in Josephus's day (see, e.g., Aristotle, *Eth. Nic.* 10.6.1; Epictetus, *Diatr.* 1.4.32; cf. Weiss 1979, 427–28). Two generations after Josephus, Lucian would take pleasure in exposing the philosophers' competing and contradictory recipes for happiness (e.g., *Vit. auct., Hermot.*). But his many satires on this issue are only effective because philosophers promised *eudaimonia* to their adherents.

In that context, it is noteworthy that Josephus presents Judaism much more as a philosophy than as an ethnic cult. The remainder of the preface is taken up with philosophical reflections on nature, reason, and law, which Josephus concludes by saying that, if anyone wishes to search further, he will find the inquiry "profound and highly philosophical" (*A.J.* 1.25). This is not merely an ad hoc device for the preface, for he will portray some of the key figures in Judean history, notably, Abraham, Moses, Solomon, and Daniel, as peerless philosophers in their own right. And, of course, Josephus presents Pharisees, Sadducees, and Essenes as schools within the national philosophy (*A.J.* 13.171–173; 18.12–18). Further, he introduces the word *eudaimonia* some forty-seven times into his biblical paraphrase, though it is missing from the Greek Bible. Evidently, he means to present Judaism as an option, the preferred option, in the philosophical marketplace.

Josephus's positive advocacy of Judaism seems confirmed, finally, by a series of direct appeals to the reader. For example: "At the outset, then, I exhort those who engage these volumes to place their thought in reliance upon God and to prove our lawgiver, whether he has had a worthy conception of God's nature and has always attributed to Him behaviour appropriate to His power, keeping his teaching concerning Him free of all the grotesque mythology current among others" (*A.J.* 1.15). This forthright challenge to discover for oneself the superiority of the Judean constitution fits precisely with what we know of the implied reader via Epaphroditus, with the paradigm of the LXX translation, and with Josephus's repeated claim that the Judean laws bring happiness to anyone who follows them. He takes the offensive, here, by employing a polemical contrast (*sygkrisis*) with all other traditions—including the native traditions of the implied readers! He does not write, then, as a member of a beleaguered community trying desperately to fend off slander. Rather, he expects a friendly Gentile audience.

Josephus's appeal to "taste and see" governs also the excursus on Moses (*A.J.* 1.18–26). Josephus remarks that, whereas other legislators have credited the gods with disgraceful human practices, and so have provided a poor example to the wicked, Moses' noble conception of God carries with it the encouragement of human virtue and the severe punishment of human vice (1.22–23). Josephus therefore advocates Judean culture as a practicable system for dealing with human behaviour; he is not merely discussing antiquity. Again, Josephus entreats the reader to make a careful examination of his work regarding this thesis of the superiority of Judean culture (1.24). He then closes the extension of the preface with the expectation that there will be those who wish to search out the reasons for every aspect of the culture, though he cannot deal with those now (1.25). Again, Josephus evidently expects an eager Gentile readership.

Body of **Antiquitates judaicae**

Space does not permit a proper treatment of the body of *Antiquitates judaicae.* Fortunately, I can defer to the many studies of Josephus's biblical paraphrase (Books 1–11), which show that he has carefully rewritten his source material to convey the themes of the preface (e.g., Attridge 1976; Franxman 1979; Feldman 1990; Begg 1993). What I would emphasize here, in distinction from the studies mentioned, is that the solicitous tone of the preface is also sustained throughout the work. Josephus wants to show that the key figures of Judean tradition represent the oldest, noblest, and most excellent features of human civilization. Thus it was Abraham who first conceived of God as one and taught the elements of science to the Egyptians (*A.J.* 1.154–168), Moses who laid down the best constitution ever known (3.223), and Solomon who was the wisest philosopher-king in human history (8).

In his synthesis of the Midianite Balaam's four prophecies concerning Israel (cf. Num. 22–24; Feldman 1993b), Josephus takes the opportunity to reinforce his theme: the Judean nation is singularly happy, Balaam says, indeed happier than all other nations, because it alone has been granted God's providence as an eternal guide (*A.J.* 4.114). In the future, Balaam continues, Judeans will dominate the entire earth by population and by fame (4.115–116). That Josephus fails to mention proselytism here does not (*pace* Cohen 1987b, 421–22) imply his distaste for conversion. On the contrary, his continued assertion before interested Gentile readers that Judeans are uniquely happy would presumably have the effect of encouraging conversion.

The sacred writings of the Judeans—notably, those of Moses, Isaiah, Jeremiah, and Daniel—have predicted the entire course of human history, and this fact was happily admitted by the famous kings Cyrus, Artaxerxes, and Alexander. Innocent of Porphyry's insights into Daniel, Josephus truly believes that the predictions of the Judean prophets have been verifiably fulfilled (*A.J.* 10.276–281). He is eager to share this knowledge with his Gentile readers. He exults also in the fact that Judeans continue to exercise Solomonic powers of exorcism and have the ability to predict the future (*A.J.* 8.44–49). Thus, although Josephus does incidentally defend Judean antiquity from current slanders, his defensive strategies serve a more comprehensive advocacy of Judean culture.

Conversion in Antiquitates judaicae

Cohen (1987b) is the only critic who has tried to work out a comprehensive picture of Josephus's attitude toward conversion. In the article in question, Cohen does not seek to explain the motives of *Antiquitates judaicae* and *Contra Apionem;* though in his earlier work Cohen accepted Morton Smith's view (1956) that Josephus wrote *Antiquitates judaicae* and *Vita* in order to throw in his lot with the rising fortunes of the Pharisees at Yavneh after the war (Cohen 1979, 148–51, 237–38).

Cohen contends that, of seven instances of conversion recounted in *Antiquitates judaicae,* six have strongly negative overtones: three forced conversions of neighbouring peoples by the Hasmoneans (*A.J.* 13.257–258, 318–319, 397), two unfortunate conversions to facilitate marriage of Herodian women (20.139, 145), and the conversion of Fulvia, who was duped by some Judean charlatans (18.81–84). Cohen concedes (1987b, 421) that Josephus does look favourably on Gentile adherents to Judaism, as distinct from converts, who appear in the narrative. Nevertheless, writes Cohen, "In his [Josephus's] view, Judaism is not a missionary religion" (1987b, 423). The zeal for conversion reflected in the seventh episode, concerning the royal house of Adiabene, is therefore peculiar in *Antiquitates judaicae;* it should be explained either as Josephus's careless inclusion of an uncongenial source or, better, on the ground that the story "concerns the propagation of Judaism outside the Roman empire in a kingdom which resisted the Parthian kings, the enemies of Rome" (Cohen 1987b, 425). But I do not understand this suggestion, and Cohen does not clarify it.

Having concluded that *Antiquitates judaicae* (minus the Adiabene episode) is opposed to conversion, Cohen must also isolate *Contra Apionem*, which warmly welcomes converts, as atypical of Josephus's perspective. On the basis of some well-known parallels with Philo's writings, Cohen proposes that Josephus took over the latter tract more or less bodily from another author and that its perspective is that of "an Alexandrian Jew of the first half of the first century" (1987b, 425). Cohen is apparently willing, in this case, to override his usual axiom that "Josephus was not a mindless transcriber of sources" (1987b, 425).

Seth Schwartz deals with *Contra Apionem* in a similar way, though for different reasons. Schwartz's recent attempt to read all of Josephus's other writings as efforts to carve out for himself a place in the postwar Judean political world leads him to dismiss *Contra Apionem* as basically non-Josephan (1990, 23, 56n. 127), since it cannot easily be reconciled with a picture of Josephus as a self-serving opportunist.

I cannot debate Cohen's argument point by point here, but it seems to me that he makes dubious assumptions about Josephus's "negative overtones" and ignores important clues in the preface and structure of the whole work of *Antiquitates judaicae*. Cohen's excision—on the ground that it is unrepresentative of Josephus's views—of the Adiabene episode, which is by far the most extensive conversion account in the whole narrative, is unpersuasive. Cohen's cavalier assignment of *Contra Apionem* to another hand is an improbable stratagem. The language and major themes of that tractate—e.g., the contrast between Greek and oriental historiography, the strong priestly bias, and the itemization of anti-Judean slanders—are fully anticipated in Josephus's earlier works.

Of the seven references to conversion in *Antiquitates judaicae,* only the first and last are described in any length; the other five are incidental to the narrative. First, Josephus retells at length the story of Haman's failed plot to annihilate the "entire Judean nation" (*A.J.* 11.184, 211–212). Like his earlier account of Daniel, this story allows Josephus to show how God has preserved, in spite of all human designs, those who follow the laws. Josephus joyfully reports that Haman and his co-conspirators ultimately suffered the violent death that they had planned for the Judean people (11.266–267, 281–293; cf. 11.212). Further, once Mordecai had been shown favour by the king, many Persians converted to Judaism in order to avoid reprisals (11.285; cf. Esth. 9:17). So the wicked Persians were forced to adopt the very way of life that they had tried to eradicate. The whole story is triumphantly told, and Cohen's supposition (1987b, 422) that Josephus opposed these conversions is hard to credit. Josephus's editorial remarks (11.268) and the king's letters on behalf of the Judeans (11.272–283) make Josephus's points clearly enough.

In his narrative of Hasmonean history, Josephus incidentally mentions the forced conversions of Idumea and Iturea by John Hyrcanus and Aristobulus I, respectively. Cohen cites a passage from *Vita* (113), in which Josephus himself allows Gentile refugees to remain uncircumcised during the war, to argue that Josephus must therefore have opposed these forced conversions by the Hasmoneans (Cohen 1987b, 423). The problem is that all of the contextual indicators in the Hasmonean story point in the opposite direction. Hyrcanus's action is recounted as part of Josephus's glowing tale of his virtuous reign, which culminates in the author's famous declaration of the prince's unique favour with the deity (*A.J.* 13.299–300; cf. 13.282, 284, 288). Aristobulus's conversion of the Itureans similarly receives explicit praise in Josephus's closing remarks on his reign (13.319). Josephus's comment, in *Vita,* concerning his own command of the Galilee, reflects an entirely different rhetorical and historical situation. His stated reason for not circumcising his guests is that they should be able to make their own choice to worship God and not be forced to do so, lest they regret having fled to the Judeans (*Vita* 113). This reasoning certainly leaves open the prospect of conversion, and fits well with Josephus's whole project of persuasion in *Antiquitates judaicae, Vita,* and *Contra Apionem.* It has no bearing on the Hasmonean golden age.

Closer to his own time, Josephus incidentally mentions the conversion of the Roman aristocrat Fulvia (*A.J.* 18.82), in order to explain the awkward fact that Judeans had been expelled from Rome by the otherwise gentle Tiberius (18.84). Josephus also mentions the voluntary circumcision of two Gentile kings who wished to marry Herodian princesses (20.139, 145). Cohen is quite right that none of these stories turned out happily for the converts in question, but his inference that Josephus therefore means to discourage conversion again runs counter to the narrative indicators. Josephus only mentions the defrauding of Fulvia by some Judeans in Rome in order to isolate them as aberrant specimens of the nation (18.81); he laments the punishment of all Roman Judeans for the actions of these few miscreants (18.84). He surely does not mean to say to his readers: If you convert, you may be defrauded as well! The moral lies elsewhere, namely, in explaining the expulsion under Tiberius, to which Fulvia's conversion is mere background.

Similarly, the circumcisions of Azizus, king of Emesa, and Polemo, king of Cilicia, to marry Drusilla and Berenike, respectively, are mere scenery for Josephus's main points. In the first case, we are told that Azizus married Drusilla after another king had turned down the marriage because he was unwilling to convert (*A.J.* 20.139). Azizus's willingness to convert, by contrast, provides a foil for the main story. Felix, the new Judean governor, is so overcome with passion for Drusilla that he induces her to leave Azizus and marry him, although he does not intend to make the slightest concession to Judean tradition. Josephus's verdict on this arrangement is perfectly clear: in marrying Felix, Drusilla "transgress[ed] the ancestral laws" (20.143). Josephus immediately notes that the unfortunate child of this marriage was killed in the eruption of Vesuvius (20.144), presumably as a token of divine retribution (cf. the earlier story of David and Bathsheba), and goes on to detail Felix's other impieties (20.162–163, 182). No criticism of the jilted convert Azizus is implied; unlike the evil Felix, he did the right thing.

Likewise, Josephus is scandalized by Berenike's persuasion of Polemo to be circumcised and marry her only so that she can quash the rumours of her incestuous relations with her brother (*A.J.* 20.145). Both of these cases come in a section of Volume 20 in which Josephus is piling up examples of divergence from the laws, which finally brought about God's punishment in the destruction of the temple (20.160, 166–167, 179–180, 184, 207, 214). He does not mean to suggest, of course, that future converts to Judaism also run the risk of abuse by Herodian princesses. There is no moral in the background information that certain people converted. That Josephus could cite these conversion stories as background without explanation does imply, however, that conversion to Judaism was a common enough occurrence to be easily understood by his readers.

A Closing Story with a Moral: Conversions in Adiabene

The decisive proof that Josephus warmly welcomed converts is the only full conversion story in *Antiquitates judaicae*. It concerns the royal family of Adiabene, and is the longest single episode in Volume 20, occupying about one quarter of its text (*A.J.* 20.17–96). Its position in the narrative constitutes a massive contextual rebuttal of Cohen's attempt to tease an anti-conversion stance out of the incidental references to conversion in Volume 20. The Adiabene story precedes, and completely overshadows, those incidental notices.

This story has been widely read for what it might reveal historically about the mechanics of conversion, or about Josephus's sources (Neusner 1964; Schalit 1975; J.J. Collins 1985, 177–80; Schiffman 1987; Segal 1990,

99–101). Our interest, however, is with the literary question: What does Josephus hope to achieve by including this lengthy story? The account is plainly his, for it is shot through with his language and evocations of his earlier narratives. How does it serve Josephus's purpose?

Against this view, Schiffman (1987, 294) argues that the unfulfilled cross-references here (*A.J.* 20.48, 53, 96) indicate that Josephus copied some source with extreme carelessness ("did little, if anything, to modify this passage"). My response is:

a) the cross-references are to anticipated passages, and may indeed be partially fulfilled within the narrative (see, e.g., 20.48 in 20.69–91). They may also reflect Josephus's own unfulfilled plans, of which he had many (20.267). In any case, these forward-looking references are characteristic of *Antiquitates judaicae* 20 (144, 147) in material that clearly does not come from the putative Adiabenian source.

b) More serious problems in Josephus are unfulfilled references to material already (allegedly) covered, which occur fairly often in the earlier parts of *Antiquitates judaicae* (13.36, 108). But even in these cases, one cannot claim that Josephus has taken over his source undigested (cf. Gafni 1988 on 1 Macc., the source in question for the passages cited from *A.J.* 13). In general, those narratives have been shown to bear the clear marks of Josephus's authorial hand.

c) Evidence of Josephus's hand in the Adiabene story includes: the characteristic Josephan introduction (20.17); the emphasis on God's *pronoia,* which is one of the main themes of *Antiquitates judaicae* (Attridge 1976, 67–70; cf. *A.J.* 20.18, 91); a characteristic emphasis on Roman invincibility and fortune (20.69–71); the characteristic claim that success engenders "envy and hatred" and the corresponding evocation of Josephus's own Joseph story (20.19–22; cf. 2.9–10); the reprise (20.25) of the notice in *Antiquitates judaicae* 1.92–93 about the story of Noah's ark; typical use of other characteristic language (e.g., *akribeia dokein* in 20.43; *eusebeia* in 20.75); and the deliberate restatement of Josephus's central thesis within this story (20.48).

The basic message is clear. Josephus begins with a statement of the subject: "Helena, queen of Adiabene, and her son Izates changed their way of life to accord with the customs of the Judeans" (*eis ta Ioudaiôn ethê ton bion metebalon, A.J.* 20.17). If we have rightly understood the bulk of *Antiquitates judaicae,* the royal family's action should not occasion surprise, for conversion would be the logical consequence of having discovered the noblest set of laws in existence. But a curious reader might well ask: How could such highly visible Gentile rulers adopt a foreign way of life, when I myself would face all sorts of social obstacles if I converted? That is the question Josephus answers, and he does so emphatically.

Under the influence of his wives and a Judean merchant, we are told, the prince Izates first began to worship God according to the tradition of the Judeans (*A.J.* 20.34). When Izates found out that his mother had also been attracted to Judean ways (20.38), through a different teacher, Izates became eager to convert fully (*metatithêmi*). He desired this, even though he knew that to become a real Judean would require circumcision (20.38). Tension builds in the story as we read that both his mother and his Judean teacher agreed that, in his case, circumcision would be most dangerous because of public perceptions. The reader's question becomes: Will Izates do it, and if he does, will he survive?

Josephus makes it clear that if any would-be convert had a reason to refrain from circumcision, it was Izates (*A.J.* 20.38–42; cf. 20.47), who could certainly be assured, in such circumstances, of divine pardon for omitting the rite (20.42). Josephus makes this alternative perfectly reasonable, and allows that the pious Izates was content with it for a time. But when another teacher, whose precision in the laws Josephus respects (20.43), insisted that conversion required circumcision, Izates immediately complied (20.46). After noting that Izates's mother and former teacher became afraid, Josephus editorializes: "It was God who was to prevent their fears from being realized. For although Izates himself and his children were often threatened with destruction, God preserved them....God thus demonstrated that those who fix their eyes on Him and trust in Him alone do not lose the reward of their piety" (20.48).

We are still only halfway through the story, and Josephus takes the remainder to illustrate the beneficial effects of Izates's conversion on world affairs, and the divine protection of his family. Izates prospered and was universally admired (20.49); he and his mother supported the needy of Jerusalem during a famine (20.53); he used his influence to restore the Parthian king Artabanus to his rightful throne (20.66); Izates himself was protected by God from the Parthian Vardanes (20.72) and then from two separate plots instigated by the nobles of Adiabene (20.76–91). In these last cases, Josephus emphasizes that although Izates's conversion to Judaism was the cause of hatred (20.77, 81), Izates entrusted himself to God (20.85). Indeed, the Arab king enlisted by the nobles makes the issue a contest between his own power and that of Izates's God, saying that "even the God whom he worshipped would be unable to deliver him from the king's hands" (20.88). But, of course, God did intervene to spare Izates.

Thus, Josephus amply demonstrates his assertion that God rewarded Izates's commitment to a proper conversion (20.48). The convert Helena's memory is forever blessed, too, because of her benefactions (20.53).

To be sure, this lengthy story illustrates many consistent themes of the narrative: God rewards virtue and punishes wickedness, always maintaining control of history, in order to spare the righteous, in spite of human designs. But it is fair to ask whether the Gentile reader should not have learned somewhat more from this final major episode, namely, that full conversion to Judaism is a good thing. It frequently arouses the hatred of one's fellow nationals, and so it may cause great difficulty for the convert, but God rewards the faithful. If this is the story's message, then the royal house of Adiabene, at the end of *Antiquitates judaicae,* serves to fulfil the expectations created at the beginning of the narrative. Following in the footsteps of Epaphroditus, these persons, too, are persuaded of Judaism's beauty, embrace it fully, and are not disappointed. Note, incidentally, that the story assumes the ubiquity of Judeans who are willing to guide foreigners through conversion. It mentions three such individuals: Ananias, Eleazar, and the unnamed figure who first coached Helena (*A.J.* 20.35).

We conclude, therefore, that the scope and the tone of *Antiquitates judaicae* are not adequately explained by an apologetic motive, although that motive is surely present. Rather, Josephus effectively provides here a primer in Judean culture for interested Gentiles. He even shows how God rewards sincere converts. Of course, Josephus does not punctuate each volume of *Antiquitates judaicae* with forthright exhortations to conversion; the appeal is subtler and operates at various levels. Nevertheless, Josephus's appeal is unmistakable and, in view of the fact that he wrote this work in Rome under Domitian's reign, when Judaizing was particularly hazardous, it seems even courageous.

AIMS OF *CONTRA APIONEM*

The preface to *Contra Apionem* (1.1–5) makes it a sequel to *Antiquitates judaicae.* The valuable little work is often mined for its quotations of otherwise lost sources, but seldom read in light of Josephus's aims, which are admittedly difficult to understand on most accounts. Had the twenty-volume *Antiquitates judaicae* been intended, as most critics think, as a defensive work, yet failed in its apologetic aim, then it is odd that the weary Josephus (*A.J.* 1.7–8) would continue his exercise in futility by writing another two volumes on the same theme. Did he really think that he would change the minds of those who slandered Judean origins, if they remained still not persuaded by his twenty-volume history?

Those scholars who see Josephus as a quisling who wrote *Bellum judaicum* as a lackey of Rome and *Antiquitates judaicae* as an opportunistic work of repentance or self-promotion, have a particularly hard time explaining this extra expenditure of effort in the service of Judean tradition. Cohen (1987b, 425) and Schwartz (1990, 23, 56n. 127) are forced to conclude that *Contra Apionem* is not really a production of Josephus at all, but their proposal is untenable. Again, the work is replete with Josephan language and themes, and the author's systematic refutation of slanders about Jewish antiquity (summarized in *C.Ap.* 2.228–290) was already woven into the fabric of *Antiquitates judaicae.*

I would argue that both the form and the content of the tract, not to mention the creative energy that it reflects, are best understood if Josephus was here continuing his effort to further interest in Judean culture—including a recommendation of conversion. Lacking space for an analysis of the whole text, I will focus first on the preface and structure, then on a few key passages, and finally on the question of genre.

Preface and Overview

Josephus dedicates *Contra Apionem* (1.1; 2.1, 196) to the patron of the *Antiquitates judaicae* and *Vita*. Epaphroditus, a Gentile with a deep interest in Judean culture, continues to serve as a paradigm of the implied reader. That Josephus has such an image in mind is confirmed by his closing address: "To you, Epaphroditus, who are a devoted lover of truth [cf. *A.J.* 1.12], and for your sake to any who, like you, may wish to know the facts about our race" (*C.Ap.* 2.196). Although Josephus complains about the fact that certain people continue to slander Judean history in spite of his *Antiquitates judaicae,* neither that work nor the present one were written for the slanderers themselves; Josephus still expects a well-disposed and curious Gentile audience.

As the older title of *Contra Apionem* suggests ("Concerning the Antiquity of the Judeans"; cf. Eusebius, *Hist. eccl.* 3.9.4), this work shares the same theme as *Antiquitates judaicae.* Josephus now summarizes the purpose of that earlier work as having been threefold: to show the extreme antiquity of the Judean race (over 5,000 years), its unique foundation and character, and the way in which it came to inhabit Judea (*C.Ap.* 1.1). At least, these are the aspects of *Antiquitates judaicae,* which Josephus now wishes to develop further; if asked about that work in general, he might have said more.

Although his audience and general theme remain the same, Josephus changes his approach and genre. We have seen that *Antiquitates judaicae* basically told the Judean story, Josephus occasionally punctuating the narrative with appeals to the reader and refutations of slander but almost always otherwise allowing his judgments, both positive and negative, to remain implicit. What changes in *Contra Apionem* is that Josephus now places his historical material directly in the service of his forthright positive and negative appeals. He claims that he will now refute Judaism's detractors, correct the ignorance of others, and "teach all those who wish to know the truth concerning the antiquity of our race" (*C.Ap.* 1.3). *Contra Apionem* is therefore a streamlined, methodical chapter, which may be schematized as follows:

Introduction (1.1–59) [*exordium*]
>   General Introduction: recapitulation of *Antiquitates judaicae;* reasons for writing now (1.1–5)
>   Programmatic Digression: Greek and Oriental Historians [*narratio?*]; Oriental historians are the best, and the Judeans are the best of them (1.6–59)

Body (1.60–2.286)
>   I. Proof of Judean Antiquity [*probatio*]
>   (a) Reasons for Greek Silence about Judeans (1.60–68)
>   (b) Oriental Evidence for Judean Antiquity: Egyptian, Phoenician, Chaldean (1.69–160)
>   (c) Overlooked Greek Evidence for Judean Antiquity (1.161–218)
>   II. Refutation of Slanders, including Apion's, concerning Judean antiquity (1.219–320; 2.1–144) [*refutatio*]

Conclusion (2.145–296) [*peroratio*]
>   Positive Portrayal of Judean Culture (2.145–286)
>   Summary and Epilogue (2.287–296)

After an opening digression, in which he challenges the notion that Greek writers should be privileged as the source of all knowledge, Josephus moves to the main argument. First, he will show that Judean culture is old, even though that point is not widely understood. Second, he will refute, one by one, the Judeans' chief literary opponents. Finally, he will offer a positive synopsis of Judean culture on its own terms—in effect, an extended and highly charged peroration. On the face of it, then, about half of the work (the middle part) is denunciative, and half persuasive. On closer analysis, however, even the denunciative material attempts to show the superiority of Judean culture. Throughout, Josephus makes use of polemical contrast (*sygkrisis*) between Judean and Gentile cultures. We shall take up the main units in order, but focus our attention on the final section.

Body of **Contra Apionem**

Josephus introduces his positive appeal into his so-called "digression" (*C.Ap.* 1.57), which anticipates some important features of the later argument, when Josephus asserts that (i) Oriental historians in general have older and more trustworthy historical records than the Greeks; and (ii) among Orientals, the Judeans have excelled in record-keeping (1.29). The Judean records have long been completed, whereas the Greek records are late and contradictory. Since "old is good" in the Roman world (Feldman 1993a, 177–78), this proof of antiquity amounts to high praise. Moreover, the Judean laws, unlike those of other nations, demonstrably enable their advocates to hold death in contempt (1.43), which was a critical test of authenticity for ancient philosophy (MacMullen and Lane 1992, 63–69).

Josephus's proof of Judean antiquity (*C.Ap.* 1.60–218) is also a vehicle for his positive claims about Judaism. For example, when Josephus claims that Judeans have seldom been mentioned in the literature of other people because they are not a maritime nation but have traditionally devoted themselves to quiet agriculture (1.60–64), he is—in addition to making a rational explanation—evoking the old Roman bucolic ideal. Greek lawgivers and philosophers, he says, have long admired and imitated aspects of Judean culture: "Not only did the Greeks know the Judeans, but they admired any of their number whom they happened to meet" (1.175). So the venerable Pythagoras incorporated Judean principles into his philosophy (1.162, 165); Aristotle was deeply impressed by, and learned from, a Judean whom he met (1.176–182); and Hecataeus of Abdera wrote an entire book about the Judeans in which he admired their resolve to observe their laws in the face of opposition, their imageless worship, their freedom from superstition, and the fertility of both their people and their land (1.191–204).

Even in the most obviously defensive section of the work—his refutation of anti-Judean slanders (*C.Ap.* 1.219–2.144)—Josephus assumes a position of superiority. First, he isolates the source of the slanders as Egypt, and then argues that Egyptian hatred of the Judeans stems from envy, since the Judeans formerly ruled that country (1.222–224). He sarcastically cites the difference between Egyptian and Judean religion, which is as great as the difference between irrational beasts and the real nature of God. He continues: "These frivolous and utterly senseless specimens of humanity, accustomed from the first to erroneous ideas about the Gods [i.e., regarding animals as Gods], were incapable of imitating the solemnity of our theology, and the sight of our numerous admirers filled them with envy" (1.225). In effect, then, Josephus dismisses all the slanders heard in Rome in his day as derived from envious and spiteful Egyptians. Cohen's point (1988, 4–9) that some of Josephus's assumptions would not have convinced a critical Greek reader only reinforces the conclusion that Josephus expected a benevolent, already partially committed audience.

After summarizing each Egyptian author's comments on the Judeans, Josephus ridicules their statements by pointing out internal contradictions. He also takes every opportunity to reiterate the shortcomings of Egyptian culture (*C.Ap.* 2.139). But he reserves his sharpest barb for Apion, who had exercised some influence in Rome under Claudius: this lying troublemaker, Josephus claims, who had taken so much pleasure in deriding circumcision, was himself forced to be circumcised late in life, for medical reasons, and eventually died of ulcerated genitals. J.G. Müller notes (1969, 9) that, in spite of its failings by modern standards (cf. Cohen 1988), this section reflects a literary-critical ability of the highest order for the first century CE; its cleverness must have been impressive. But in all of his witty refutation of Egyptian writers and their religion, Josephus assumes a benevolent readership already predisposed to Judean culture and its ineffable deity. He is attacking Judaism's detractors in a safe atmosphere.

Positive Summary and Appeal

Josephus's assumptions about his audience and his own aims become clearest in the second half of Volume 2. Here Josephus gives his most forceful statement of Judaism's virtues: it is a way of life that is vastly superior to any other, and it welcomes converts. In *Contra Apionem* 2.145–286, Josephus states that the Judean laws cultivate piety (*eusebeia*), friendship (*koinonia*) with one another, humanity (*philanthrôpia*) toward the world, justice, steadfastness, and contempt of death (2.146). And Judeans not only possess the most excellent laws; they also observe them most faithfully (2.150).

What comes next is disarmingly frank. Josephus admits that every nation tries to make a case for the antiquity of its own laws, because everyone agrees that the oldest is best: the one who introduced the concept of ordered life is more admirable than those who merely imitated him. But this premise only sets up Josephus's claim: "I maintain that our legislator is the most ancient of all legislators in the records of the whole world. Compared with him, your Lycurguses and Solons and Zaleukos, the legislator of the Locrians, and all those who are so admired among the Greeks, seem to have been born just yesterday" (*C.Ap.* 2.154). And again: "But the question, who was the most successful legislator, and who attained to the truest conception of God, may be answered by contrasting the laws themselves with those of others" (2.163). We can only appreciate the boldness of this exercise when we recall that Josephus is writing for Gentiles: he is trashing their own native traditions, and he expects to get away with it. He expects, then, a benevolent readership.

The principal points of this polemical contrast deserve careful attention from the perspective of our question: Is Josephus appealing to potential converts? In *Contra Apionem* 2.164–171, we read that Moses rejected other forms of government in favour of "theocracy," making God the only sovereign, and inculcated the noblest possible concept of God as one, eternal, omnipresent, uncreated, ineffable. Moses' views have been adopted by some eminent philosophers, admittedly, but they have failed to make them into a cultural norm as Moses did.

According to *Contra Apionem* 2.172–183, the comprehensiveness of Moses' legislation is without parallel. It is comprehensive in scope, in method (because, for Judeans, theory is inseparable from practice, whereas others have difficulty uniting theory and practice), and in constituency (for even women and children know and observe the laws). The pervasive legal literacy of the Judeans produces a unique harmony of outlook among them. The supreme value in Judean culture, overriding all others, is life in accord with the laws.

In *Contra Apionem* 2.184–189, Josephus asks rhetorically concerning the Judean Law: "What could one change in it? What more beautiful Law could have been found?…Could there be a more beautiful or just Law than one that makes God the Governor of all things, assigns the administration of the greatest matters to the collective body of priests, and then entrusts the government of the other priests to the high priest?" The whole administration of the state, he says, "resembles some sacred ceremony." Again, the law is perfect and complete.

The lengthy section in *Contra Apionem* 2.190–219, which comes next, is a radiant summary of the Judean Law's content, emphasizing its humaneness. It teaches a philosophical conception of the one true God, who is worshipped by the practice of virtue, not by sacrifice; the cult is practised at one temple only, with great restraint and dignity, and with prayer only for the common good, not for selfish ends; rites of passage (marriage, birth, and death) are all regulated so as to encourage virtue and humanity; filial piety ranks very highly; all social relationships are ordered to ensure justice; aliens are welcome to join the culture; merciful treatment of others, even declared enemies and animals, is required of Judeans; penalties for transgression are severe—in many cases, death (this is evidently an attractive feature!); and the promise of a new and better life awaits those who are faithful to the Law.

Incidentally, it is a mistake to see Josephus's notice that the Pharisees are lenient in punishment (*A.J.* 13.294) as some kind of commendation. Leniency in applying laws was no more popular in his day than it is in ours. In Josephus's view, the inexorable severity of the Law toward wrongdoers, and its serviceability as an instrument of public order, were an important part of its great appeal (cf. *A.J.* 1.14, 20, 22, 23; *C.Ap.* 2.178, 187, 194); he assumed that his readers would agree, because they perceived their age as a time of rampant lawlessness (see especially *C.Ap.* 2.276–278).

It is most interesting for our purpose that, in such a brief survey of the laws, which deals only with those elements that would attract the reader, Josephus should so conspicuously feature the treatment of aliens:

> It is worth considering how the lawgiver gave attention to the fair treatment of foreigners. It is obvious that he took the best possible precautions so that we should neither corrupt our own customs nor jealously keep them from those who elect to share them with us. For those who wish to come and live under the same laws with us, he welcomes generously, holding that a community consists not in race alone but also in the selection of a way of life. Nevertheless, he did not desire that those who come by with only a minor interest should be involved in our special way of life. (*C.Ap.* 2.209–210)

Several aspects of this passage merit comment. First, Josephus distinguishes between those who are merely interested in some part of Judean culture (casual visitors) and those who, like Helena and Izates, come and live under the laws. Arguably, Josephus is trying here to influence his readers to move toward a full commitment. Second, there is a noteworthy coincidence of language between this passage and the preface to *Antiquitates judaicae:* just as the high priest Eleazar did not wish "jealously to hoard" the Judean Law (*A.J.* 1.11) and so led the translation of the Septuagint for Gentiles, so also here Josephus's Moses insists that Judeans not jealously hoard their treasures. This coincidence of language underlines Josephus's consistency of purpose in both works. Third, the language has a philosophical tinge: to choose Judaism is to choose (*proaireomai*) a way of life (*bios*) and not simply another national cult. It is therefore like conversion to philosophy in Arthur Darby Nock's analysis (1933).

In *Contra Apionem* 2.220–286, Josephus turns again to a polemical contrast of the Judean constitution with other systems. The Judean Law is superior to all others because it is more practical and, therefore, more practised than Plato's laws; it inspires more commitment than Sparta's famous laws; Judeans have a famous willingness to die for their laws; and the

Judean laws do not depict gods in human form or as having human passions, as do the traditions of other nations.

In *Contra Apionem* 2.255–278, Judeans are said to agree with the very best Greek philosophers in both maintaining laws and refusing to associate with lawbreakers. But they are much more open than others to adopted foreigners. Significantly, in view of the common perception of Judean clannishness, Josephus concedes that, "we do not wish to have fellowship with those who select another way of life" (2.258). Nevertheless, he continues, "We, on the contrary, though we do not consider it worthwhile to pursue the customs of others, still we receive with pleasure [or: offer a warm reception to] those who decide to share ours with us. And this should be a clear sign, I think, of both our humanity and our magnanimity" (2.261).

As in the preface to *Antiquitates judaicae,* the willingness to share the benefits of Judean culture with others, as Josephus himself did by following the example of the high priest Eleazar, is said to be a sign of magnanimity. Judeans cannot keep secret the good things that they enjoy. As in *Antiquitates judaicae,* Josephus stresses simultaneously the separateness of Judean culture and its openness to converts. This is, really, the positive face of the points criticized by Juvenal and Tacitus: even though the Judeans hold themselves separate from others, they welcome converts, who then become part of a tightly knit community.

Josephus follows up on the point (*C.Ap.* 2.262–278): if the Judeans are charged with misanthropy because of their adherence to their own laws and rejection of foreign practices, then the legendary Athenians and Spartans should be so charged as well; every self-respecting country fosters its own laws. On the other hand, those other nations—including the nations of Josephus's readers—have long since given up this admirable practice and allowed their laws to fall into disuse. Indeed, they have become so lax in enforcement that fines are now accepted in cases of adultery, and "violation of the laws has with most nations become a fine art. Not so with us" (2.276–277). We see Josephus, here again, appealing to the law-and-order instincts of readers who see lawlessness all around them.

In stark contrast with the failure of tradition among other peoples, the Judeans' laws are not only observed by themselves, but have for a long time been borrowed by others as well (*C.Ap.* 2.279–286). In particular:

> The masses have for a long time shown great eagerness for our piety, and there is not one city, whether Greek or barbarian, nor a single nation, which the custom of the seventh day, which we keep free of work, has not infiltrated, and where the fasts, and burning of lamps, and many of our prohibitions with respect to meats are not observed. They try further

to imitate our harmony (*homonoia*) with one another, distribution of goods....The most marvellous thing is that it is without the alluring bait of sensual pleasure, but only because of its intrinsic merit, that the Law has proven so effective; and, just as God permeates the universe, so the Law has found its way among all humanity. Each person who considers his own country and his own household will not disbelieve what I am saying. (*C.Ap.* 2.282–284)

If we leave aside the historical (im)plausibility of this oft-cited passage and ask only about its force within the text, we see that Josephus has pulled together a variety of particular conditions to serve his general point concerning the global influence (and therefore the vitality) of Judean culture. In good rhetorical fashion, he employs all available means of persuasion, from alleged imitation of Judean harmony and charity (impossible to prove), to borrowing of the weekly rest-day custom (which may indeed have been growing in his day), as well as the specific adoption of Judean fasts, food laws, and Sabbath rituals, which could be expected only of God-fearers and proselytes. Leaving aside his more far-fetched claims of imitation, we may still find here understandable cause for celebration on Josephus's part (cf. his earlier enthusiasm about Daniel) in the wide spectrum of attraction to Judean ways. These same phenomena are cause for complaint by Seneca, Juvenal, and Tacitus. Although Josephus here acknowledges, for rhetorical purposes, many levels of imitation, his consistent position in *Antiquitates judaicae* and *Contra Apionem* is to prefer full conversion.

This rousing celebration of Judean culture forms the extended peroration of *Contra Apionem.* As in *Antiquitates judaicae,* this has the effect of subordinating the defensive material to a positive appeal. A brief epilogue in the proper sense (*C.Ap.* 2.287–296) reprises both the denunciative and persuasive positions of the tract. Josephus reiterates that Judean laws represent the very highest of human aspiration; they cannot be surpassed; and Judeans deserve credit for first introducing these beautiful ideas to humanity.

What response should all of this provoke in the friendly (interested) Gentile reader? Should the reader respond: "Well, I'm glad to hear that you Judeans are not as guilty and depraved as I might have thought on the basis of what I had heard from your detractors"? No! This is not primarily an exercise in forensic rhetoric, debating the truth about the past, but it hovers between the epideictic (confirming shared ideals) and deliberative (requiring further action) species. The proper response to Josephus's appeal, I suggest, would be to explore Judean culture more intensively and to consider choosing its *bios* as one's own, accepting Josephus's invitation to share its laws completely.

Genre of Contra Apionem

We move now to considerations of genre. Genre is a notoriously slippery concept, but in the case of *Contra Apionem* hardly anyone has even attempted a classification. This is a guarded way of saying that I do not know of such a classification at all. Müller's commentary on *Contra Apionem* (1969) does not attempt to define its genre. Thackeray (1967) spoke only of one section as an "encomium"—a term widely adopted by others. Bilde (1988) believes that he is the first even to propose a complete outline or "disposition." He proposes that the whole work is "missionary literature." I essentially agree, but wonder whether the genre can be more precisely defined. I shall argue that the most plausible generic affiliation has direct implications for our assessment of the work's aim.

Like *Antiquitates judaicae, Contra Apionem* portrays Judaism in philosophical terms. Judaism is a philosophical culture, whose founding philosopher was Moses, and it was recognized as such by Pythagoras, Plato, and Aristotle. That is why Judaism's God is somewhat like the God of the philosophers. Fulfilling the aspirations of Greek philosophers, Judaism also places a premium on the ascetic life. So it is not like other national cults, with their temples and many sacrifices, visible images of God, and esoteric rituals. Whereas Roman writers tended to group Judaism with Egyptian, Syrian, and Chaldean superstitions, Josephus—along with other Greek-speaking Judeans such as Artapanus, Aristobulus, Philo, and the author of 4 Maccabees—presents Judaism as a national philosophy. But this presentation serves, among other things, to facilitate the notion of conversion, for conversion to a comprehensive way of life or *bios* was more appropriate to the international philosophical schools than to the ethnically rooted Mediterranean cults (Nock 1933). This observation raises the question whether *Contra Apionem* should not be considered an example of the genre *logos protreptikos,* which had wide currency among the Hellenistic philosophical schools.

Definition of logos protreptikos

Definition of **logos protreptikos**   Marrou defines the *logos protreptikos* as "an inaugural lecture that tried to gain converts and attract young people to the philosophic life" (1956, 206–207). Although scholars have found examples of the genre in part of Plato's *Euthydemus*, the chief exemplar is widely thought to have been Aristotle's *Protrepticus* (Diog. Laert. 5.22.12), which is preserved only in fragments. According to Diogenes Laertius, philosophers of all schools wrote *protreptikoi*—Aristippus (2.85.5), Plato (3.60.4), Theophrastus (5.49.18), Demetrius of Phaleron (5.81.13), Antisthenes (6.2.1), Monimus (6.83.14), Persaeus the student of Zeno (7.36.15), Posidonius (7.91.8), Ariston of Chios (7.163.7), Cleanthes (7.175.9), and Epicurus (10.28.13)—but none of these texts has survived either. Cicero's fragmentary *Hortensius* is known largely for its role in persuading the young Augustine to take up philosophy (*Conf.* 3.4.7). An extant Greek inscription mentions a competition for composing *logoi protreptikoi* in the Athenian ephebate (*IG* II 2119). The evidence is thus enough to indicate that *logoi protreptikoi* constituted a recognized class of philosophical writing long before Josephus's time, even though our most complete examples come from his time and later.

Unfortunately, the dearth of early examples is matched by a complete absence of theoretical discussion in both the handbooks of rhetorical theory and the *progymnasmata* (manuals of rhetorical exercises). To be sure, the rhetors discuss *to protreptikon* in the general sense of persuasion, as a parallel technique to *to apotreptikon* or dissuasion, but they do not discuss a kind of discourse or dialogue aimed at encouraging conversion to the philosophic life (Aune 1991, 279). Aune (1991, 280) reasonably suggests that this deficiency results from the ancient standoff between rhetors and philosophers: the rhetors simply did not recognize as noteworthy exhortations to philosophical conversion. Whatever the cause of this lack may be, however, the best we can do now is to rely on contemporary scholars who have made inductive analyses of particular texts and the phenomenon as a whole.

A seminal article is Mark D. Jordan's attempt (1986) to eke out a generic definition of philosophic protreptic from four examples: the Socratic "interludes" in Plato's *Euthydemus*, Aristotle's *Protrepticus* (hypothetically reconstructed from fragments), Seneca's 90th epistle (which sets out to correct Posidonius's lost *Protrepticus*), and Iamblichus's fourth-century CE *Protrepticus*. Also helpful is the summary portion of David Aune's recent chapter arguing that the Christian letter to the Romans is a *logos protreptikos* (1991). Neither Jordan nor Aune has an interest in *Contra Apionem,* and neither identifies it as an example of the genre. Nevertheless, a survey of their observations concerning the genre incline me toward such an association.

Jordan does not consider it possible to define the genre either by a characteristic structure or by a set of concrete aims, since representatives of all schools wrote *protreptikoi* in different forms and for somewhat different audiences, and defined their aim (the highest good) differently. Jordan settles for a situational definition, namely: "each author confronts a hearer whose choice is the target of many other persuasions. The unity of philosophic protreptic...would seem to lie in the [*sic*] this 'exigence,' in the hearer's moment of choice before ways-of-life....Protreptics are just those works that aim to bring about the firm choice of a lived way to wisdom." (1986, 330).

On the way to this generic definition, Jordan makes some particular observations that bear on *Contra Apionem*. He notes that the address to an individual, such as Aristotle's *Protrepticus* for Themison the King of Cyprus, "gives the treatise that concrete urgency appropriate to protreptic" (Jordan 1986, 321). And Jordan shows the importance of *synkrisis* (polemical contrast) in repudiating all claims to knowledge other than those being advocated by the author (1986, 321).

Aune puts it this way: "The central function of *logoi protreptikoi,* within a philosophical context, was to encourage conversion….However, *logoi protreptikoi* also characteristically included a strong element of dissuasion (*apotrepein*) or censure (*elenchein*) aimed at freeing the person from erroneous beliefs and practices" (1991, 280). After noting that the genre could take either discursive or dialogical forms, Aune quotes a fragment of Philo of Larissa (Stobaeus, *Flor.* 2.7.2) to the effect that all protreptic consists of two parts: demonstration of the value of philosophy and refutation of its detractors. At least in the abstract, then, *Contra Apionem* seems to correspond well to the thrust of the *logos protreptikos.* A brief consideration of *protreptikoi* from the century following Josephus's floruit will clarify the issue.

***Examples of* logos protreptikos**   It is noteworthy that the largest number of surviving examples comes from Christian apologists in the mid-second century CE and beyond, i.e., from the time at which Christianity consciously began to present itself to the world as a philosophical school. But if Christian authors seized upon this genre for attracting converts, once they had begun to think of Christianity as a philosophy, then one must ask whether Judean writers who had long before conceived of Judaism as a philosophy did not also employ the form. Aune mentions several Hellenistic-Roman and Christian examples of the genre, but does not discuss them in detail. We shall consider three of the clearest cases: Lucian's *Wisdom of Nigrinus,* the so-called *Epistle to Diognetus,* and Clement of Alexandria's self-styled *Exhortation (Protrepticus) to the Greeks.*

Although Lucian frames *Nigrinus* as a dialogue at the beginning and the end, the bulk of this writing is given to the speech of Character B (as A.M. Harmon in the Loeb edition helpfully labels him). Character B has just returned from Rome, where he met the Platonist philosopher Nigrinus, otherwise unknown. The encounter has suddenly changed the life of Character B, transforming him into a happy and blissful man (*eudaimon te kai makarion*). Recall Josephus's promise of *eudaimonia* to those who would embrace the Judean laws. Then, Character B says: "Don't you think it wonderful, by Zeus, that instead of being a slave, I am free; instead of being poor,

I am truly wealthy; instead of being ignorant and blind, I have become sound?" (1). Character A then implores him not to hoard jealously from a friend the source of such bliss; this is, of course, the same language that Josephus used to characterize his and Eleazar's motives (see above).

In response to this request, Character B recalls in detail the speech of Nigrinus, which pierced his soul and led him to embrace philosophy (35–37). That speech is essentially a *synkrisis*, contrasting the disgusting worldly values so prevalent in Rome with the philosophical life, free of luxury and sham, which prevails in Athens. To choose the Athenian life is to choose a life of toil (14, 33), but one that alone brings happiness. Interestingly, Character B's praise of the philosophic life and repudiation of false living does not include an explicit appeal for the conversion of Character A; but we are not surprised when Character A insists at the end that he must join his friend in a "change of heart" (38). I submit that Josephus expected the same response from many hearers in the light of his presentation.

Our second example of the protreptic genre is the Christian *Epistle To Diognetus,* which is variously dated to the mid- or late second century CE. This document has a structure that in many ways parallels *Contra Apionem.* For example, the epistle opens with a prologue addressed to "most excellent Diognetus"—the same title used by Josephus of Epaphroditus—who is identified as a deeply interested outsider making active inquiries concerning Christian piety (1.1). After ridiculing pagan worship of handmade gods in human form (2), as did Josephus, the Christian author disparages Judaism as an option. He does this by rejecting the notion that God needs sacrifices (a point pre-empted by Josephus!) and by repeating common objections to Sabbath observance, circumcision, and dietary laws (3–4).

Having thus refuted false sources of knowledge, the author of *Diognetus* moves to his positive portrayal of Christian piety (5–6), which again parallels Josephus at many points: Christians do not expose their infants, and they are happy to suffer for their faith, holding death in contempt. Just as Josephus repeatedly cited Judean suffering as proof of this point, so the Christian author recalls Christians "flung to the wild beasts to make them deny their Lord, and yet remaining undefeated" (7, end). We even find this remarkable parallel: whereas Josephus had suggested that as God permeates the cosmos, so the Law permeates all humanity, the author of *Diognetus* proposes that, "As the soul is diffused through every part of the body, so are Christians through all cities of the world" (6.1). And where Josephus had credited Moses with constructing a constitution that time could not weaken, our Christian author appeals to the divine authentication of Christ's revelation. The epistle ends with a direct appeal to Diognetus to believe and to emulate God's goodness (10.4), just as Josephus had claimed that Judaism teaches participation in God's virtue (*A.J.* 1.23).

With Clement of Alexandria's *Protrepticus,* we see the complete "nativization" in Christian circles of aggressive philosophical protreptic. Clement knew of Josephus's work (*Strom.* 1.21.147) but clearly relies on his own learning for *Protrepticus.* It is a much more rambling, detailed, and anecdotal treatise than *Contra Apionem,* and Clement feels little need to include as much refutation of slander as Josephus. Clement takes the offensive throughout. Still, we are in the same kind of literary world: he writes for benevolent Gentile readers who are willing to tolerate a sustained attack on their native traditions.

After a proleptic *synkrisis* that contrasts popular Greek with Christian views (1), Clement writes four chapters (2–5) in which he savagely ridicules common notions of the gods and their activities, along with the gullibility and superstition of the masses. Included among his targets are also the most popular philosophical positions (5). Like Josephus, Clement allows that the better philosophers long ago taught the truth, but they derived their knowledge from the Hebrew Scriptures (6.60p), which are the best source of (Christian) truth (8–9).

Having made his theoretical case, in the final three chapters (10–12) Clement draws out the practical consequence that, knowing now the only true source of knowledge and happiness, his readers ought to convert to Christianity. This section is particularly interesting in social terms because, like Josephus with the story of Adiabene, Clement faces head-on the social obstacles to conversion. He must show that the benefit is great enough to warrant the overthrow of the universal principle, "It is not proper to overthrow a way of life (*ethos*) passed down to us from our ancestors" (10.72p; cf. *C.Ap.* 2.144). Clement closes with repeated appeals to choose life over death.

Contra Apionem *as* logos protreptikos   These three examples are obviously different in setting, length, and internal structure (dialogue or discourse, autobiographical or abstract), as were also the examples considered by Jordan. But they suffice to confirm the vitality of philosophical protreptic during the century following Josephus. They also show that the genre was so well known that it could be used subversively, to draw people away from traditional philosophy and into Christian groups that now understood themselves as philosophies. But one might reasonably ask whether the widespread Christian employment of this genre, once Christianity was conceived along philosophical lines, had not been anticipated by Judean authors who, similarly, considered Judaism to be a philosophy.

It seems to me that no generic distinction can be drawn between these examples of philosophic protreptic and Josephus's *Contra Apionem*. All three of the sample texts presuppose a benevolent reader in search of happiness. All of them identify the highest, truest, noblest source of knowledge and way of life (*bios*). All of them polemically contrast this most desirable life with available alternatives (according to Philo of Larissa, refutation of slander was also a standard part of protreptic, though it is not as prominent in the sample texts as it is in *Contra Apionem*). And all of them conclude with either the explicit or implicit prospect of conversion to the way of life that has just been advocated. If these other texts are admitted as *logoi protreptikoi*, then Josephus's *Contra Apionem* should be admitted as well. This generic affiliation would provide support for our assessment based on context and content that Josephus writes to encourage conversion.

CONCLUSION: *CONTRA APIONEM* IN CONTEXT

My goal in this chapter has been to understand better the aim of Josephus's *Contra Apionem*. My proposal is that the work means to encourage potential converts to Judaism. First, I have attempted to reread the work's content within its immediate social and literary environment. Conversion to Judaism was a well-known phenomenon in Rome during the first century CE, and attraction to Judean culture continued after the great war. At the same time, the revolt rekindled anti-Judean sentiments among the literati, and postwar conditions would necessarily have made conversion to this way of life more problematic. Josephus's first literary effort (*Bellum judaicum*) aimed to relieve anti-Judean sentiment in Rome and elsewhere. During the reign of Domitian (81–96 CE), which proved to be even more difficult for converts to Judaism, Josephus composed a primer in Judean culture to meet the needs of Gentiles who were eager to learn it. He closed the *Antiquitates judaicae*, which presents Judean philosophy as the only sure path to *eudaimonia*, with a stirring conversion story.

This social and literary context provides important clues for understanding *Contra Apionem*, which Josephus wrote during the reign of Nerva (most likely) as a sequel to *Antiquitates judaicae*. It is addressed to the same interested Gentiles. Josephus now takes the opportunity, while triumphantly refuting the Judeans' slanderers, to contrast Judean culture with all others, concluding that Judaism is the best possible system of laws under which one could live. He closes with an extended encomium on the laws, which once again features the prospect of conversion. The net effect of Josephus's remarks should be to make readers dissatisfied with anything but Judaism. The conclusion seems unavoidable that Josephus wished his

Gentile readers not to remain "casual visitors," as he says, but to come and live under Judean laws.

Second, I have argued that *Contra Apionem* has the generic features of philosophic protreptic: it exhorts an interested outsider to find happiness in one option on the philosophical landscape through conversion to that way of life (*bios*). It uses polemical contrast (*synkrisis*) to disqualify other options under consideration, thus confirming the hearer's preliminary direction. It would be difficult to distinguish *Contra Apionem,* generically, from such an undisputed *logos protreptikos* as Clement's *Protrepticus.*

We may now note Bilde's independent suggestion that *Contra Apionem* is "primarily a work of missionary literature" aimed at "those who were interested in Judaism" (1988, 120). Although he has not, as far as I know, developed this suggestion, the foregoing argument would support his claim. Here is a text that was undeniably written by a prominent Judean for Gentiles, it was very probably read by Gentiles, and it recommends conversion. Whether Judaism was a missionary religion or not, Josephus tried to be a Judean missionary in Rome.

I am aware that this reading of *Contra Apionem* sits uncomfortably with common views regarding both Judean proselytism and Josephus's own character. The question of Judean proselytism we must leave with the observation that, no matter how strange it may seem that people would abandon their native traditions for a markedly different regimen of life, it is difficult to explain in any other way the Roman evidence concerning such a possibility. As for Josephus's character, it is basically unknown, since all we have are highly rhetorical writings from his hand. Whatever his real character may have been, his literary legacy moves in a single direction: from urgent refutation of postwar anti-Judaism (in *Bellum judaicum*) to leisurely advocacy of Judean tradition (in *Antiquitates judaicae*) to forthright appeal in *Contra Apionem.* Josephus was famous among Gentiles not as a traitor to his country but as the Judean historian (Suetonius, *Vesp.* 5.6.4; Dio, *Hist. Rom.* 65.1.4). Lacking any direct access to his mind, we may nevertheless be sure of at least two things that he really did believe: (a) the God of the Judeans controlled and predicted all of world history, and (b) philosophically-minded pagans were now steadily moving toward the ethical monotheism that Judean culture had always taught. If he believed these two points alone, we may understand something of his eagerness to share the benefits of his tradition with outsiders.

8

On Becoming a Mithraist
New Evidence for the Propagation
of the Mysteries

Roger Beck

INTRODUCTION

Against the charge of proselytizing, no religion of antiquity can mount a more credible defence than Mithraism. It was the most self-effacing and retiring of the "dynamic" cults (to use MacMullen's term [1981, 112], where it seems almost a misnomer). Unlike Isism or the cult of the Magna Mater, Mithraism had no public presence or persona, and appears rigorously to have denied itself all opportunities for self-promotion and display which might win it adherents or at least the acquaintance and passive admiration of the masses. How, then, did it recruit, or, if that is too proactive a term, accrete?

The contrast could not be more extreme: on the one side, the conspicuous temple thronged by the devout or the merely curious (one thinks, for example, how remarkable in appearance and how frequented was the complex of Iseum and Serapeum in the Campus Martius at Rome; see Turcan [1992, 109 f.] for a good description); and on the other, the typical urban mithraeum tucked away in a suite in some apartment or business block and clearly intended, like modern club rooms, "for the use of members only" (see White's descriptions [1990, 47–59]).

In its withdrawal from the public arena, Mithraism likewise denied itself those occasions of pomp and ceremony, pageantry and procession, of which perhaps the best example, despite its fictional setting, is the Isiac procession to the Ploiaphesia at the climax of Apuleius's *The Golden Ass* (11.7–11; see, further, Turcan 1992, 104–20). These were the events by which typically the dynamic cults advertised themselves and proclaimed (I use the word advisedly) their gods. They were also the occasions of recruitment, or so at least they were represented. Again, the example from *The Golden Ass* is instructive. The miracle wrought on Lucius (11.12–13) may have gained only a single Nockian "convert," but it—and the entire pageant in which it is set—won something of more abiding importance: the acknowledgement by the awestruck crowd of the goddess' majesty and effectiveness. Isism was sustained in good part by that admiring but personally uncommitted corona.

What drew and retained the corona (since miracles are unreliable) was, in a word, spectacle—the more exotic, the better (see MacMullen 1981, 18–34). Even the culturally alien and rebarbative, like the *galli* of the Magna Mater, could play their part. The aim was the promotion of the deity, and the means was showmanship; which should not be seen as detracting from the seriousness of the enterprise. Alexander of Abonutei-chos, we may accept, was no less sincere for being a brilliant impresario (Remus 1983, 159–73, 203f.). All of which is to say that cults of this type may not have proselytized systematically, but they certainly proclaimed systematically. No mission, but plenty of public message.

It is worth recalling that great public events of miracle or of confrontation, if not of pageantry, are ascribed to Christianity by the ancient sources and postulated by modern critics as a major cause of its transmission and growth (see MacMullen 1984, 25–29; also M. Smith 1978). I leave it to others to judge whether this was actually so or not. Rodney Stark's demonstration (1996, 3–27) that growth through family and social networks at the rate of 40 per cent per decade (a mere 3.42 per cent per year) will account for the increase in the number of Christians over the first three centuries, renders the great conversion occasions redundant as a causal explanation; though this is not to say that they didn't take place. The more important point, however, is that, as related, the scenario of the acknowledgement of the deity's power by witnesses to great public encounters is essentially the same for Christianity as for the self-advertising pagan cults.

I am persuaded by Richard I. Pervo (1987) that the accounts have more to do with meeting a benchmark of edification, excitement, and proper form in the narratives of the faith's propagation than with how the faith was actually propagated. Pervo's thesis is that, in this regard, the canonical Acts are indistinguishable from the apocryphal. Their episodes are of the sort that Christian, no less than pagan, readers expected in prose narratives about heroic figures. Hence they are no different in kind from the episodes of the analogous pagan literature, the genre of the ancient novel (see Hägg 1983, 154–65; Heiserman 1977, 183–219).

Whether it is a matter of actuality or of image, there is in this matter of anticipated and elicited crowd reaction no functional difference between the doings (and sufferings) of Christian apostles as reported in the various Acts, on the one side, and, on the other, the preachings, confrontations, and miracles of an Apollonius of Tyana as reported by Philostratus, the performances of an Alexander or a Peregrinus as pilloried by Lucian, or the spectacular cures worked on an Aelius Aristides as recorded by himself. Martyrdom was, of course, unique to Christianity as a mode of publicity and hence of propagation (see Bowersock 1995). But it belongs with scenes of miracle and confrontation as large-scale and dramatic public events in which spectator reaction was an integral part (see MacMullen 1984, 29f.; Lane Fox 1986, 419–92).

The culmination of these activities is the aretalogy, or wonder at and acknowledgement of the manifest power and virtues of the god expressed in the cries of the bystanders (M. Smith 1971; Merkelbach 1994; Beck 1996a). As the vindicated priest of the Delian Serapis aretalogy concludes, "the entire people marvelled that day at your prowess" (Totti 1985, no. 11, lines 90f.); or Apuleius's Lucius, "the crowd was amazed, and the devout paid homage to this clear manifestation of the power of the mighty deity.... With one clear voice, stretching their hands toward heaven, they bore witness to the marvellous beneficence of the goddess" (*Metam.* 11.13, trans. Hanson; cf. *Metam.* 16).

Such high drama and its players are quite simply irrelevant to Mithraism. The cult did not commend itself or its god to the public, and so had no need of charismatic figures to make the commendation. Accordingly, we must place Mithraism at the extreme low end of a spectrum of self-advertisement, acknowledging that in this respect it is as remote from, say, Isism as it is from Christianity. The moral is that the dynamic cults of paganism cannot be reduced to a single pattern of propagation or a single set of growth strategies. Mithraism's absence from the public arena makes talk of competition or of rivalry, whether with other pagan cults or with Christianity, somewhat problematic; likewise, success based on victory in competition. It takes two to start a fight, and by accident or design Mithraism never put itself in a position to pick one.

This is not to suggest that these concepts and terms—competition, rivalry, success—are altogether inappropriate, just that they require some caution when applied to Mithraism. For example, what is said by Leif E. Vaage (chapter 1) about the need to acquire a limited number of [participants] as one's "own" in order to assure the group's ongoing social reproduction is germane—crucially so, as we shall see—to Mithraism. But to present this reproductive imperative as motivated by, or leading to, heightened prestige and/or power for the group or as an aspect of a generalized steady state of constant struggle or agonistic competition with other groups, would not, I think, be true for a cult that demonstrably stood apart from the agonistic arena and eschewed all public display of group or individual prestige. Mithraists displayed their secular accomplishments epigraphically within the temple; outside the temple, there is not a whisper of their religious allegiance to reflect credit on their cult.

MITHRAISM AND CONVERSION

It would be a mistake to conclude that Mithraism's reticence had anything to do with lack of substance as a religion; that it did not proclaim itself because it had nothing much to proclaim, no product worth advertising in the public domain. That view of the cult is indeed held. On the basis of the known profile of Mithraism's membership and in reaction against certain untenable theories about its creed, the cult is sometimes presented as little more than a club for Roman "good ol' boys." I quote, for example, N. M. Swerdlow (1991, 62) as an extreme proponent of this view: "a rude fraternal cult of soldiers on the frontier," "perhaps not a serious religion after all." Likewise, although much more complex and altogether more plausible, MacMullen's model of Mithraism nonetheless centres on the sociability of a backyard barbecue—with spiritual fixings:

> The attraction of the cult lay rather in a broad range of feelings and experiences: in roasting sacrificial hens and pork ribs on the sidewalk or somewhere above ground, with one's friends; descending into the barrel-vaulted dusk of the chapel, into the very presence of the god, for a long meal with much wine; thereafter (it may be imagined) communal chanting of a prayer, fortifying thoughts, perhaps some special verses or paean pronounced by the priest. When and how often the priest spoke of the god's gifts to men and drew worshipers in to a knowledge of the soul's necessary passage to a higher home, there to abide for all eternity, we do not know. (MacMullen 1981, 124)

Interesting here is the contrast between the sureness about the cult's social life and the uncertainty about its mysteries.

Its naïveté aside, such a view can only be maintained by ignoring or discounting some part of the evidence. The archaeological, iconographic, and even the fragmentary literary record of Mithraism reveals the outlines of a mature cosmology, theology, and soteriology. I have argued this case elsewhere in discussing the form and function of the mithraeum (Beck 1992, 4–7; 1995, 106ff.; 2000, 160–64). Archaeology amply confirms the text of Porphyry (*Antr. nymph.* 6) to the effect that the mithraeum is a cavelike structure because it is intended as a "model of the universe" and because the Mithraists there induct their initiates into the mystery of the soul's descent into and exit from the world of mortality (see below). The details of the cosmic model given by Porphyry (*Antr. nymph.* 24) are found exemplified in the excavated mithraea. It is far from unsophisticated. Yet both the cosmology and, even more, the soteriological intent and function of the mithraeum are frequently ignored. Neither L. Michael White (1990, 59) nor Manfred Clauss (1990, 51–70), for example, mentions more than the basic datum, mithraeum=cave. Why the mithraeum should be so designed and how that design was worked out in detail appear to be non-questions, despite extant evidence, literary and archaeological, to answer both. These are strange silences in these works, the first of which explores the sacred spaces of ancient religions, while the second purports to offer a comprehensive description of the cult in question.

   Instead, let me touch briefly on Mithraic ethics, because they suggest that in becoming a Mithraist one might indeed undergo a change of life, which bears all the hallmarks of a conversion. This is as good a way as any of showing that the cultists were involved in a profoundly religious enterprise. I need cite only a single text of Porphyry and two graffiti from separate mithraea.

1. Porphyry tells us that the proper medium of ablution for Mithraic Lions was honey (since honey is liquid yet fiery) and that the Lions had their hands washed with it on initiation with the instruction to "keep them pure from everything distressing, harmful, and loathsome" (*Antr. nymph.* 15, trans. Arethusa).

2. A well-known painted text in the Sa. Prisca Mithraeum pleads "receive, Father, receive, Holy One, the incense-burning Lions, through whom we offer incense and through whom we ourselves are consumed" (Vermaseren and Van Essen 1965, 224, lines 16f., Wall K2, lower layer).

3. A graffito in the Dura Europos Mithraeum invokes the "fiery breath which for magi too is the ablution of the holy" (Rostovtzeff et al. 1939, 127, no. 865). Together, these three testimonies speak of induction into a life of service to the deity and one's fellow initiates, characterized by a special purity, both ritual and moral, and sanctioned by a highly idiosyncratic sacramental symbolism of fire, liquid, and breath. If this isn't conversion in the fullest sense, I don't know what is.

Whether or not real-life Mithraists behaved any differently as a consequence of their initiation, or whether they fully understood and entered wholeheartedly into the world of their mystery, is immaterial. No doubt some did, some didn't. This is merely a truism about life in any religion with an ethical component. What matters is that the model of a converted life was set before the initiates as something to which to aspire or, at the very least, as an ideal to be acknowledged.

In chapter 1, Leif E. Vaage rightly questions Arthur Darby Nock's contention that Mithraism (*pace* Renan) could never have taken Christianity's place because it was an altogether different religion, since unlike Christianity it did not demand "the adhesion of the will to a theology, in a word faith, a new life in a new people" (Nock 1933, 14). All those things (theology, faith, new life) are in fact demonstrable in Mithraism, and again Vaage is right—and shrewdly right—in seeing the distinction not in body-and-soul commitment per se but rather in the champions and enforcers of that commitment, namely, their high profile and survival in the annals of Christianity, on the one hand, versus their low profile and disappearance from the records of Mithraism, on the other. Nock was right, though, on one point: that Mithraism, in Christianity's default, "could not have founded a holy Mithraic church" (Nock 1933, 14). That is so, however, not because of the nature of Mithraism, that it was not a faith to which a man could "belong . . . body and soul," but because there was never in Mithraism the centripetal will to create such an entity. What it did create, the very different matrix in which it perpetuated itself, we shall see in due course.

MITHRAISM'S POPULARITY

Mithraism, then, was a cult which not only (a) did not proselytize but also (b) did not publicly advertise itself, yet (c) did offer a religious experience both profound and peculiar. It is difficult to explain how such a cult could have sustained itself without adducing a fourth characteristic: (d) its social conformity. It is agreed by all that Mithraism flourished because it appealed to, and so could reproduce itself within, the structures and networks of Roman society, most obviously, of course, the military, but also the civil service (see, for example, the customs bureaucrats at Poetovio in Pannonia; Beskow 1980) and the *familiae* of the great (see Gordon 1972a; also Liebeschuetz 1994). Mithraism as a loyalists' religion is well emphasized in Merkelbach's study of the cult (1984, 153–88). We infer this understanding, of course, not directly from the testimonies of the initiates, but from the known facts of the status and occupations of the members, as preserved in the epigraphy of mithraea across the length and breadth of the empire. We are fortunate now to have this record thoroughly tabulated and expertly analyzed in Manfred Clauss's *Cultores Mithrae* (1992).

What it was about the Mysteries of Mithras that attracted conformists in the middle and lower echelons of the empire's key structures, we do not know. On the face of it, Mithraism's popularity is strange. The Mysteries were devoted to a foreign god of a dangerous people; indeed, one of the few facts that the Mysteries divulged to outsiders was that they were "Persian"—and unapologetic about it. Moreover, they were full of esoteric learning which one might suppose to be of little appeal to such a clientele. It may be that we should seek the attraction of the Mysteries not so much in the Mysteries as in the initiates themselves, in the appeal of like to like. One joined because people one knew, respected, and trusted had joined. Similarly, one invited others to join whom one knew, respected, and trusted. For recruitment, propagation, and accretion, the network of "good ol' boys" may after all be a sufficient model (cf. Stark 1996, 15–21).

Even so, the appeal of the Mysteries is, finally, a rather unscientific question, for one can never demonstrate that it was one feature rather than another which attracted people. That people were attracted is a fact, but as to what feature in particular drew them, they have left us no testimonials and are forever beyond the reach of our questionnaires (and even if they weren't, we would be deeply sceptical of their response—or at least we ought to be, if we may retroject into antiquity what Stark has to say about the unreliability of expressed, after-the-fact reasons for conversion [1996, 15–21]). However, it is not unlikely that the "unconquered" (*invictus*) nature of the god was attractive especially to the cult's military clientele, soldiers being professionally averse to defeat. Mithraism's notorious exclusion of women is impossible to factor in. On the one hand, the cult thereby denied itself half the human race—although it never aspired to be a universal religion and therefore cannot be judged unsuccessful on that account. On the other hand, males working in an all-male environment would routinely expect the exclusion of women, which might thus be seen not merely as a strategy for success but as a necessary condition. There are no grounds for construing Mithraism as a particular haven for misogynists, although there are traces in the cult's ideology of more than classical antiquity's routine misogyny (see Gordon 1972a, 42–64).

ORIGINS AND SPREAD OF MITHRAISM

To appreciate that network in operation, we may look at some striking recent evidence that has come to light in Virunum, the administrative capital of the province (formerly kingdom) of Noricum. It belongs, however, to the stage of the cult's maturity, its steady state rather than its initial burst of growth. I should first say something, then, about the stage at which Mithraism was a real novelty, when presumably those who were co-opted into it had for the most part no prior knowledge of its existence.

The origins and spread of the Mysteries are matters of perennial debate among scholars of the cult. I have recently contributed a new scenario (Beck 1998a), in which I suggest diffusion from a founding group consisting of the military and household followers of the last ruling king of Commagene, Antiochus IV (deposed 72 CE). The high mobility of this group, following its patrons first in the Civil and Judaean Wars and then into exile in Rome, would account for the wide geographical spread of the earliest evidence for Mithraism. The group's military and civilian composition would account for the emergence of Mithraism both in the Roman army and in bureaucratic and household structures (the *familiae* of the great). Lastly, the attested mixture of Greek and Persian theology (together with much astrology) in the Commagenian dynastic traditions would account for that same ideological blend (the content undergoing a sea change into the new religion) in the Mithraic Mysteries. There is, incidentally, no evidence for the existence of typical Roman Mithraism prior to the very late first century CE. Most accounts of Mithraism place its genesis in the mid-first century CE. My late foundation scenario avoids the awkward evidential silence over the interval.

Nonetheless, to preclude suspicions of idiosyncrasy, let me simply sketch here what is probably today the dominant model.[1] The Mysteries, it is thought, were fashioned in Rome in the late first century CE. They were carried thence by Italian soldiers north to the Rhine and Danube, where they are first attested within a relatively brief time span in several widely separated locations. The cult then spread, during the second century CE, from the frontiers to the hinterlands of the European provinces, to the non-military European provinces, to North Africa, and throughout Italy; also, though it seems only spottily and to a very limited extent, in the Orient as well.

It is impossible to trace the exact course of this expansion. Iconography, it used to be thought, furnished a key. The composition of the tauroctony (the icon of the bull-killing Mithras), in particular its frame and the arrangement of side-scenes around the central scene, was used to establish

---

1 See Merkelbach 1984, 146–49; Clauss 1990, 31f.; 1992, 253–55; Turcan 1993, 31–37; for an excellent up-to-date overview and critique, Gordon 1994. The old Cumontian model of formation in, and diffusion from, Anatolia (see Cumont 1956a, 11–32; cf. pp. 33–84 on propagation in the West) is by no means dead—nor should it be. On the role of the army in the spread of Mithraism, see Daniels 1975.

a filiation, much like a manuscript stemma, in which groups of monuments could be ordered as to their derivation and an archetype postulated. The spread of the cult, it was thought, must have replicated the filiation of the monuments (Beck 1984, 2074–78; Saxl 1931; Will 1955).

Although this quest proved unsuccessful and in its simplest form was misconceived, it did rest on an important truth about Mithraism. Visual art was always and everywhere the prime medium of the Mysteries. That art, despite its complexity, is remarkably uniform. Clearly it is not an epiphenomenon, not simply a local or regional expression of myth and doctrine received in other forms, i.e., by word of mouth or sacred text. Rather, it was part and parcel of the mysteries transmitted, the physical sign, together with the mithraeum itself, of the authentic Mysteries of Mithras.

How was that iconography transmitted? The problem was thrown into sharp relief by the discovery of the Dura Europos mithraeum. Here was a mithraeum widely separated from the cult's zones of concentration, yet which demonstrated in its array of side-scenes in the arch surrounding the tauroctony remarkable fidelity to European norms. It is hard to escape the conclusion that graphic designs of some sort were part of the baggage of those who brought the Mysteries to Dura. Pattern books or illustrated sacred texts have been suggested (Beck 1984, 2016).

Richard Gordon (1994, 463) has used the term *colporteurs* ("pedlars") to describe metaphorically the early carriers of the Mysteries. The term is apt, perhaps even in the literal sense of luggage carried. At any rate, the transmission of iconography is a factor not to be lost sight of when one models the propagation of Mithraism. It shows, moreover, how different must be the modes of propagation for the various religions of antiquity. The appropriate composition of icons was scarcely a concern of the Christian *colporteurs.*

NEW EVIDENCE FROM VIRUNUM

We may turn now to the principal subject of this chapter: how the new evidence from Virunum illustrates recruitment into the Mysteries of Mithras in their mature phase. The new evidence is a bronze plaque containing a complete *album,* or membership list, of a mithraeum. The find yielded an additional dividend, in that it shows that a previously known list of a selection of the same names on a fragmentary stone is also Mithraic. More will be said about this second *album* in due course.

The bronze plaque from Virunum was discovered in 1992, and ably published by Gernot Piccottini in 1994 (*AE* 1994, 1334; Clauss 1995; Gordon 1996a). It had been deliberately hidden in antiquity, but unfortunately not in its proper mithraeum. Though Virunum is fairly rich in Mithraic finds, the sites of its mithraea have not yet been discovered.[2]

The plaque, dedicated to Mithras (in the formula *D[eo] I[nvicto] M[ithrae]*) and for the well-being (*pro salute*) of the emperor Commodus (the name was erased at his *damnatio memoriae*), lists the names of thirty-four men, "*qui templum vii (sic) conlapsum impendio suo restituerunt*," i.e., those who at their own expense restored the mithraeum, which had collapsed in some (probably natural) catastrophe. As the inscription across the bottom records, one of these men, Ti. Claudius Quintilianus, donated the plaque for the dedication of the mithraeum and "embellished the ceiling with paintings" (*et camaram picturis exornavit*).

The names fill the first one and one-third columns of a space that potentially held four columns. In other words, twice as much space as was filled was left for future names. It is unlikely that this space was reserved, optimistically, for an influx of after-the-event contributors to the building fund, so one must assume that it was intended for the names of future initiates and thus to serve as the *album* of the mithraeum in the coming years. That is indeed the use to which it was put.

From Commodus's title, the *terminus post* for the dedication can be deduced to be early in the year 183 CE (Piccottini 1994, 15). Within a year and a half at most, two lines of preamble were added to the right of the top of the second column where, otherwise, the third and fourth column of names would in due course have commenced. These two most unusual lines tell us that the original group, or what was left of it, "came together because of the mortality" (*et mortalitat[is] causa convener[unt]*) on a date which translates as June 26, 184 CE. (*Marullo et Aeliano co[n]s[ulibus] VI K[alendas] Iulias*). The "mortality," whatever it was, appears to have carried off five of the original thirty-four, for the Greek letter *theta* (for *thanôn*, = 'deceased') has been set against their names. Piccottini (1994, 22–25) reasonably suggests the plague as the cause, and a commemoration of their deceased fellow initiates as the event for which the Mithraists assembled.

---

2 The Mithraic finds of Virunum are nos. 1430–1440 in Vermaseren 1956–1960 (in the province of Noricum as a whole, nos. 1401–1461). Hereafter, Mithraic monuments, etc., in Vermaseren's corpus will be cited by number prefixed by "V." In Schön 1988, the Virunum Mithraic finds are nos. 165–175 (in Noricum as a whole nos. 131–176); see also Alföldy 1974, 195–97. V1438 and 1431 both record the rebuilding of a mithraeum, in 239 and 311 CE, respectively. There is no reason why those two dedications and the bronze plaque should not all belong to the same mithraeum at different dates in its institutional life, although, as we shall see below (A New Mithraeum?), at least one other Virunum mithraeum is probable.

In a separate article, I have explored the doctrinal implications of the festival of the "mortality" and the coincidence, if such it is, that it was held at the time of the summer solstice, which, in Mithraic cosmology and soteriology, is the gate through which souls enter and descend into the mortal condition (see Beck 1998b). Interestingly, the dedication of the Virunum mithraeum recorded in V1438 (see above, n. 2) also took place at this time of year (June 25). That, together with the fact that the dedication also mentions a "painting" (*cum pictura*), makes it probable that we are dealing with the same mithraeum rebuilt some 56 years later. The aforementioned article concerns the utopian side of the cult (to use J.Z. Smith's polarity [1990, 121–42]). Here I am concerned more with the locative side, or the response of the Virunum Mithraists to the exigencies of the here and now, in particular with their strategy for self-perpetuation.

Celebrating (or deploring) the "mortality" is not the only recorded reaction of the Virunum Mithraists. They also co-opted eight new members, who were duly registered in the next block of names in the second column. Thereafter, as Piccottini infers from the different and progressively deteriorating hands of the inscribers, there were another sixteen additions, concluding with L. Quar(tinius?) Quartus, appended inelegantly below the last word of the lower part of the dedication (Piccottini 1994, 25ff.; see the dividing lines drawn there on Abb. 15, p. 27).

Piccottini argues that these were annual additions, and that the plaque accordingly records recruitment into the mithraeum from 184 CE, the year of the "mortality," to 201 CE. What warrants this inference is the second *album*,[3] to which I alluded earlier. Its two marble fragments contain names that appear in the second, third, and fourth columns of the bronze plaque. They appear, moreover, in the same order in both documents. Finally, no names appear in the marble *album*, which do not appear on the bronze. Enough of the introductory text of the marble *album* remains to tell us that those named there built some edifice "from the ground up at their own expense" (*a s]olo impen[dio] suo extruxer[unt*), and that they built it between 198 and 209 CE (Piccottini 1994, 41). The inference is inescapable that they are the same group of Mithraists, building again some fifteen to twenty-five years later.[4] Into this time slot comfortably fits the terminus of

---

3 Piccottini 1994, 44ff. Its two fragments (found more than a century apart) are (1) *CIL* III 4816 (= *ILLPRON* 15, 16) and (2) *ILLPRON* 748, 773, 774.

4 The marble *album* is thus the fourth Mithraic building dedication to be recovered from Virunum (see above, n. 2). In A New Mithraeum? (see below), I recapitulate Piccottini's plausible case that this represents a new and separate building undertaken by a group from the original mithraeum when the membership had outgrown the mithraeum's capacity.

the bronze *album,* on the assumption that its blocks of names represent annual recruitment.

MITHRAISM AND THE MITHRAEUM

The principal lesson that the Virunum *alba* teach us about the propagation of Mithraism seems at first one of almost breathtaking banality: it was a matter not of spreading the word but of topping up the membership. The Mysteries of Mithras were mediated in and through a mithraeum, which was both a physical structure of limited size and the group of individuals that assembled there (*qui convenerunt*). Accordingly, the first responsibility of a mithraeum was to perpetuate itself, to keep the numbers up, to keep the roof over its head (bronze *album: vi conlapsum impendio suo restituerunt;* marble *album: a solo impendio suo restituerunt*). The bronze *album* gives us an unprecedented view of one mithraeum's recruitment, annually recorded over a span of eighteen years, in pursuit of this end.

The cult of Mithras (i.e., the Mysteries of Mithras considered as an institution rather than a road to salvation, though, parenthetically, it was just as much the latter as the former) was the sum of its mithraea, neither more nor less. The mithraeum was the unit both of propagation and of self-perpetuation. Here, then, is the matrix within which Mithraism renewed itself. Here, too, is the real reason why Nock was right in scouting the possibility of a "holy Mithraic church" (see above, Mithraism and Conversion). On a second look, therefore, the lesson of the Virunum *alba* is not banal at all.

Again, I emphasize that the mithraeum was a physical structure, no less than a group of members. This is by no means a trivial or adventitious matter. Rather, at issue is the role of the mithraeum in the ideology of the Mysteries. The mithraeum, as Porphyry informs us, was "a model of the universe," and it was designed on that principle so that initiates could be inducted there into the mysteries of the soul's entry into and departure from mortality (see above, Mithraism and Conversion). The mithraeum was thus no mere container of the Mysteries and their initiates, but part and parcel of the mysteries transmitted, an indispensable instrument of initiation—one might even say, of salvation itself. Literally keeping the roof over one's head meant symbolically keeping the universe in place. Hence, I suggest, the importance of the painted ceiling in our *alba,* probably the very same one renewed in the rebuilding of 239 CE (V1438; see above, n. 2 and New Evidence from Virunum). Ceiling decorations of mithraea are cosmic or celestial, e.g., the stars of the Capua Mithraeum (V180) and, especially, the zodiac of the Ponza Mithraeum (Beck 1976–1978).

Here again, then, we have a radical difference from early Christian communities, in whose propagation physical structures played no obvious part, because they were not an essential component of the thing propagated. It is interesting, too, to note how with Mithraism both the practical (locative) consideration of sustaining a certain number of participants, which determined a particular room size, and the ideological (utopian) consideration of what that room was all about, go hand in hand. Ignore either, and the propagation of the Mysteries remains indeed a mystery.

A NEW MITHRAEUM?

In the two Virunum *alba*, do we have an example of the propagation of a new mithraeum out of its parent? Piccottini (1994, 50) argues plausibly that we do: that the marble *album* represents the translocation of a number of members of the original mithraeum and the foundation of a new mithraeum built "from the ground up" (*a solo*). The reason for the translocation would be simply that the old mithraeum was oversubscribed. The new mithraeum was not intended for new recruits (there are no new names on the marble *album*) but to accommodate the overflow. No missionary zeal here!—but, rather, a steady accretion through kin and social networks of precisely the sort that Rodney Stark (1996, 14–21) now postulates for early Christianity and which scholars of Mithraism have all along assumed for this cult (see below on the recruitment of kin).

Piccottini's account (1994, 44ff.) rests on the reconstruction of the marble *album,* which severely limits the number of names in its columns. The remains of only three columns are actually preserved on the two fragments. An initial column must be postulated to the left in order to accommodate selected members from years prior to 184 CE. Q. Septimius Speratus is the first name in the third column. At the end of the preserved part of the second column are traces of M. Marius Zosimus. Since a mere three names separate these two men in the bronze *album,* and since the marble *album* follows the order of the bronze without exception (disregarding the names omitted), it follows that the second column of the marble *album* could have contained at most, below Zosimus, the three names that separate him from Speratus in the bronze *album.* The other columns must have been proportionately limited, leading to the conclusion that the marble *album* represents a selection of the membership of the bronze and not the surviving membership ca. 202 CE.

Nevertheless, the possibility that the marble *album* might represent the surviving membership in 202 CE cannot be entirely excluded. On this scenario, there would have been no migration, no new mithraeum, and no net increase in the Mithraic community in Virunum. Simply, a new *album*, the marble one, was started, when the old one, the bronze, was full. Coincidentally, the existing mithraeum was rebuilt. There may have been more than one mithraeum in the course of Virunum's history, but the evidence so far has not established the fact conclusively.

The weakness in Piccottini's account is that it does not address emigration from Virunum or deaths subsequent to the great "mortality." Presumably, some members did die in the eighteen years between 184 and 202 CE; and just as it is likely that several new members came from out of town (see below), so it is likely that one or two moved away. The annual cohorts of recruits might well have been intended to balance these losses, to keep the mithraeum in a steady state; in which case, recruitment was an even more mundane matter than in Piccottini's account.

Piccottini's account can accommodate attrition at a maximum average rate of very little more than one member per year: 98 members listed, minus 5 dead in the "mortality" = 93; minimum number on the marble *album*, i.e., the founding group of the postulated new mithraeum = 40; 93–40 = 53; assume that the optimum capacity of the old mithraeum was no less than the original group of the bronze *album* (= 34); 53–34 = 19, which in turn = the maximum number of deaths and departures over the eighteen years in question. Even if attrition was comprised entirely of deaths, the mortality rate seems surprisingly low.

MITHRAISTS OF THE VIRUNUM *ALBA*

There is, of course, much to be said about the ninety-eight Mithraists of the Virunum *alba*; about their civil status (freeborn citizen, freedman, peregrine, or servile), their family relationships, their ethno-cultural origins (Latin, Greek, or native Celt), their other attested affiliations and activities, their leaders (insofar as these can be identified); and about the cult of Mithras in Virunum as known from the considerable remains previously discovered there. All but the last of these matters are fully explored by Piccottini (1994, 28–44; cf. Gordon 1996a),[5] so there is no need to review them extensively here, except for two which particularly concern propagation: the mithraeum's leadership, and recruitment of kin and within *familiae*. First, though, I will make some general observations.

---

5 On Mithraism in Virunum, see *AE* 1994, 1334; Clauss 1995; Gordon 1996a; on Mithraism and the oriental cults in Noricum, see Alföldy 1974, 194–97; Schön 1988. There was a Dolichenium in Virunum (Schön 1988, nos. 198–212). Interestingly, the donor of our mithraeum's ceiling painting, Ti. Claudius Quintilianus, also made a dedication to Jupiter Dolichenus (Schön 1988, no. 210).

The great majority of members in Virunum were Roman citizens, whether freeborn or freed. Indeed, among the ninety-eight, there is only one identifiable peregrine, Calend(inus) Successi f(ilius), and one slave, Speratus s(ervus). It is impossible to distinguish freedmen from freeborn citizens by name alone, although Greek cognomina tend to be indicative of freedmen. Piccottini (1994, 29–31) finds twenty-four Greek cognomina, as against fifty-six Latin (seventy-one individuals) and four indigenous Celtic. Again, there are ninety-eight members, but ninety-nine individuals are mentioned, since Calendinus's father, Successus, is named.

In this context, a fairly high proportion (ca. 25 per cent?) of freedmen among Mithraists is not unexpected. The low proportion of indigenous Celtic names is remarkable, though likewise not unexpected. Many of the prosopographical links made by Piccottini are necessarily tentative, but we may say with certainty that at least one of the Mithraists was a person of some consequence in the larger community: L. Lydacius Ingenuus, known from *CIL* III 4813 f. as *IIvir iure dicundo in Virunum* and *sacerdos* and *flamen* (presumably of the imperial cult) and as dedicator of altars to the "Imperial Victory" (*Victotiae Augustae*). All in all, then, the picture is just what one has come to expect of Mithraists: modest worldly success (enough disposable cash to rebuild their mithraeum without, it seems, assistance from a patron) set within the context of a provincial administrative centre (a religion not of Noricum but of the Roman presence in Noricum).

MITHRAEUM LEADERSHIP

The leadership of a mithraeum was exercised by its Father or Fathers (*Pater/Patres*). The Father was the highest of seven grades in a hierarchy of initiations (see, e.g., Beck 1992, 8–10). There is currently some controversy over whether the grades, and particularly the Father, were priestly offices; also, whether they were normative, in the sense that all or most Mithraists in all or most mithraea would be expected to enter the *cursus* (on both questions, see Gordon 1994, 465–67). There could be more than a single Father in any mithraeum, as we shall see was the case at Virunum.

The bronze *album* notes six *Patres* at one time or another (on the Virunum *Patres,* see Piccottini 1994, 34–36; I see no reason to entertain the possibility that the abbreviated form *pat,* used for four of the six, might mean *pat[ronus]*). The original pair, Iulius Secundinus and Trebius Zoticus, were given pride of place at the head of the first column, though their rank was not actually inscribed until later, in fact by the hand which added the cohort of 184 CE. A different hand added the grade title to the name of Atticius Sextus at the bottom of the first column. Given his position in the

list, we may infer that he was not yet a *Pater* at the time of the original dedication, but he must have been elevated to that rank not long afterwards
since he, like his colleague Trebius Zoticus, fell victim to the "mortality." It
is possible that he was elevated to replace Trebius but quickly succumbed
to the same fate.

Most interesting is the arrival of the next Father, Trebius Alfius. He is
the first listed of the cohort which in 184 CE brought the membership up
to strength after the "mortality." Since his rank was inscribed by the same
hand that inscribed his name (as well as the rank of the two original
Fathers), we must infer that he brought his rank with him, or at least sufficient seniority as a Mithraist to render him immediately *papabile.* The
same appears to be true five years later (189 CE) of C. Fl(avius) Nectareus.[6]
His title, too, was inscribed by the same hand that inscribed his name.
Interestingly, precedence in the list for that cohort of two was given not to
him but to his fellow initiate, Q. Baienius Ingenu(u)s. In contrast, the last
listed *Pater,* M. Mar(ius) Severianus, appears to have reached the grade
some time after his induction into the mithraeum in 192 CE, since his title
appears to have been added subsequently. Severianus is the only *Pater* to
appear on both *alba,* but unfortunately his name is not well enough preserved on the marble to know whether his rank was also given there. What
can be said with certainty is that his rank did not promote him to the head
of the new list. Unlike the bronze, the marble *album* seems to have ignored
such precedence or, rather, to have defined precedence strictly by year of
entry.

The bronze *album,* one must admit, is not very informative about the
dynamics of leadership in the Virunum mithraeum. Starting in the second year, it duly registers the title of *Pater* for those who held it. The fact that
two of the four added Fathers joined from outside might suggest that the
mithraeum was at pains to ensure that there was no lacuna in this senior
grade. But it might equally well mean no more than that two Mithraists of
this rank had arrived in town during the nineteen years of the *album*'s
span.

My guess would be that the practice at Virunum was to have a pair
of colleagues as *Patres.* Iulius Secundinus and Trebius Zoticus were the
Fathers when the new mithraeum building was dedicated, and they are
set at the head of the list. Atticius Sextus succeeded Trebius Zoticus, and
Trebius Alfius succeeded Trebius Zoticus, each on his predecessor's death.

---

6 Nectareus, given the cult's interest in honey (Porphyry, *Antr. nymph.* 15–20, and see
   above, Mithraism and Conversion), is a suspiciously apposite name for a senior Mithraist;
   cf. Melichrisus ("honey-anointed"), the dedicant of V2268/9 (Moesia Inferior).

Five years later, Flavius Nectareus was co-opted, already a *Pater*, to succeed Iulius Secundinus or Trebius Alfius, whichever one had died or moved away. Not less than two years after that, the recently joined Marius Severianus was created *Pater* in succession to Secundinus, Alfius, or Nectareus. Several years later, when the new (marble) *album* is drawn up, Severianus is still a member and presumably a *Pater*. His colleague cannot be ascertained. It is possible, on this scenario, that Severianus, like Alfius and Nectareus, held the grade of *Pater* on arrival but was made a Father of the Virunum mithraeum only when there was a vacancy in the diarchy.

Whatever the case, one does not get the impression that these *Patres* were the "Pauls" of the Virunum community, and one might take this impression as yet another index of the difference between the propagation of Mithraism and the propagation of early Christianity. Caution, though, is needed. As Richard Gordon has pointed out (1994, 466 f.), formal inscriptions are not the written medium through which the Mysteries of Mithras expressed their inner dynamics. That function belongs rather to graffiti and *dipinti*. What inscriptions reveal for the most part is external, not internal, status.

No doubt, in this highly respectable cult association, external precedence was duly respected. Speratus the slave would not be giving orders to Lydacius Ingenuus the duumvir. Superficially, one might assume from the Virunum bronze that all Mithraists were more or less equal; but it is just as apparent that more equal than the others was the one who could pay not merely for his share of the building but also for the plaque to dedicate it and the pictures on its ceiling, Ti. Claudius Quintilianus (see above, n. 5, on this person's votive dedication to Jupiter Dolichenus as well).

It would, however, be dangerous to project that secular precedence deep into the life of the mithraeum as a religious enterprise. Neither Claudius Quintilianus the donor nor Lydacius Ingenuus the duumvir was a Mithraic *Pater*. It seems to me that this is precisely what distinguishes classic Mithraism of the second and third centuries CE from the otherwise (as far as we can tell) identical form practised in Rome in the late fourth century CE by certain members of the pagan nobility. The Mithraism of the latter was clearly their creature. They held the high cult offices, and they controlled initiation into its grades (see, e.g., V400–406). Mithraism was an instrument of the pagan revival of the elite; and so, like most cults of this sort when they command no popular base, evanescent.

FAMILY RELATIONSHIPS

One would like to know whether family relationships played much of a role in the recruitment of the Virunum Mithraists. Obviously, they cannot have done so in the same way as they did among contemporary Christians, for the simple reason that Mithraism excluded women. A family, then, could not become Mithraic in the same sense that it could become Christian. But was there a pattern of Mithraists recruiting their sons or other male relatives?

Potentially, among the shared Gentile names, there could be numerous close family relationships. But it is, of course, no more likely that all the Aelii on the bronze *album* were related than it is that all the Smiths would be, on the membership list of a modern small town club. Piccottini does not make exaggerated claims; rather, he finds (1994: tables between 28 and 29) four fairly certain father-son pairs, one fairly certain pair of brothers and one fairly certain trio of brothers, with another twenty-two possible relationships of either the father-son or the brotherly variety. It is likely, then, that close kinship among males did play a considerable, though not crucial, role in Mithraic recruitment at Virunum. Again, we would scarcely expect it to be otherwise.

Shared *nomina* can also indicate a patron-freedman relationship (or freedmen of the same *familia*), especially when Greek cognomina are involved (see above, Mithraists of the Virunum *Alba*). It is likely, though unable to be proved, that there are instances of this relationship among the shared Gentile names of the *alba*. For example, Piccottini (1994, 41–43) makes Trebius Zoticus the freedman of Trebius Alfius, one of the Fathers. He identifies the latter with the equestrian M. Trebius Alfius of *CIL* III 4788. This latter person was *conductor* (contractor) of the Noricum iron industry. The position became that of an imperial procurator under M. Aurelius, so *CIL* III 4788 predates the Mithraic *album*. Richard Gordon (personal letter) dates it to 157 CE. For this reason, I hesitate to follow Piccottini in his identification of the Mithraic *Pater*. If Piccottini were right, Trebius Alfius would, of course, replace Lydacius Ingenuus (see above, Mithraists of the Virunum *Alba*) as the mithraeum's greatest success story. In the ancient context, the patron-freedman relationship should, of course, also be classified as a family relationship.

The Lydacii furnish an interesting case (Piccottini 1994, 38f.; and see above, Mithraists of the Virunum *Alba*). Lydacius Ingenuus was on the original list of thirty-four members, as was a certain Lydacius Charito. It is not an unreasonable assumption that the former, the "Freeborn" (Ingenuus) Lydacius, was the son of the latter, and that the latter, with his Greek cognomen, was a freedman. We know that there was a third generation of male Lydacii, since one of Ingenuus's dedications is for the well-being of his son, L. Lydacius Honoratus. Interestingly, this son did not join his father's mithraeum in any of the subsequent eighteen years (it would be even more interesting to know whether he chose not to be initiated or was prevented by some other cause such as death). It is possible that his uncle was a member, since his mother, the co-dedicant of one of the altars, was a Rufia Severa, and a Rufius Severinus was, like the two Lydacii, one of the original thirty-four.

CONCLUSION

One concludes that Mithraism grew, or maintained itself in a steady state, not by proselytizing or by "spreading the word" to strangers, but by the commendation of friend to friend, by co-option among like-minded adult males in delimited social contexts; also that, in all likelihood, recruitment among kin and via the patron-freedman relationship played a significant part. This is not a new or surprising finding. In fact, it is what we have known or sensed all along for Mithraism. The Virunum *alba* merely present this picture on a fuller canvas with some of the details fleshed out. The similarity with what Rodney Stark (1997, 13–21) describes relative to recruitment to new religious movements in the present, and what he postulates for early Christianity, is striking. It's not so much what you believe or can be persuaded to believe that counts; it's whom you know.

Lastly, I shall briefly review some of the implications, for the Mithras cult, of Jack Lightstone's exciting theoretical and methodological suggestions in chapter 5. In particular, I shall take a quick look at Mithraism through the lens of Lightstone's first proposition: "religious rivalry is a subset of a larger category, namely, differentiation of the social world." In Lightstone's model, religions, through their spokespersons, map out their own ideal social worlds, including principles and rules of conduct within those worlds. Actual behaviour in the real world may or may not correlate with the ideal behaviour so constructed. Externally, one form of religious rivalry occurs when *your* actual behaviour fails to conform to *my* expectations of your behaviour within my construct of the social world. At the same time, no doubt, *my* actual behaviour fails to conform to its expected pattern in *your* social world.

On Lightstone's paradigm, I should present Mithraic ethics more in terms of the construction of an ideal world, in which, for example, initiates of the Lion grade *assent to* (though they do not necessarily practice outside the mithraeum) an ethic of pure, austere, and thus appropriately "fiery," behaviour. The external case is more interesting. Were there occasions when the Mithraists' ideal world conflicted either with the actual common world of Greco-Roman society or with the ideal constructions of other religions? The latter question is more easily answered. Mithras in the myth steals the bull that he slays: he is *boöklopos,* the cattle thief. He is also worshipped in "caves," in places of darkness, even though he is a sun god, a god of light. Christian polemicists turned both of these elements in the Mithraists' constructed world against them (see, e.g., Firmicus Maternus, *Err. prof. rel.* 5.2).

The former question, about conflicts between the Mithraic world and the real social world, has to be answered with an argument from silence. There are no reports of any friction, any collisions, at all. No one has suggested that this is simply due to the paucity of external evidence concerning the cult. The Mithraists made no secret of their construction of themselves as "Persians" worshipping a "Persian" god. Yet Persia, historically, was Rome's most formidable enemy. This can only mean that the Mithraists were such transparently loyal citizens of the Roman Empire that they and their constructed world posed no threat, whether in reality or in perception, to the common social order. In Lightstone's terms, in its values and in its postulated social relationships, the world of the Mithraists was entirely congruent with the normative world of the Empire.

Part III

RISE?

9

Rodney Stark and "The Mission to the Jews"

Adele Reinhartz

INTRODUCTION

Unlike most books, Rodney Stark's *The Rise of Christianity* appeared with two different subtitles. Taken together, these offer a succinct and accurate description of Stark's approach and subject matter. "A Sociologist Reconsiders History," the subtitle borne by the hardbound edition, labels Stark's field and signals his use of sociological principles in the service of historical reconstruction. "How the Obscure, Marginal Jesus Movement Became the Dominant Religious Force in the Western World in a Few Centuries," the subtitle that graces the paperbound edition, describes the specific historical questions addressed in the book.

Stark's argument is that the spread of the early Christian movement was due not to mass conversions or the persuasive power of the Christian message but, rather, to "the arithmetic of growth" (1996, 4). To grow from approximately one thousand members in the year 40 CE to close to thirty-four million adherents in 350 CE required an expansion rate of 40 per cent per decade (1996, 7 [Table 1.1]). While this rate may sound high, it is consistent with the patterns of other movements, such as the Mormon community, which has grown 43 per cent per decade over the past century (see Stark 1996, 7; cf. Donaldson, chapter 6).

Stark's fundamental question is: "How was it done?" (1996, 3). Historians' approaches to this question consider the complexities of the Roman Empire, its specific political, economical, theological, and social conditions, particular personalities and events in Christian and Roman history, and a host

of other factors. By contrast, Stark draws inferences from modern social scientific theories, particularly his own formal theorizing about the growth of
religious movements in the modern period, and then tests them in rather general terms against the historical record to the extent that this is possible.

One component of Stark's overall argument is that Diaspora Jews continued to be a significant source of Christian converts until much later
than many historians of early Christianity have suggested. In the third
chapter of his book, entitled "The Mission to the Jews: Why It Probably Succeeded," Stark (1996, 49–71) offers a critique of the commonly accepted view
that mission to the Jews failed after 70 CE and argues instead that Diaspora
Jewish communities were a major source of Christian converts until the fifth
century CE.

Stark's third chapter begins with a brief assessment of the evidence that
is often cited to support the prevalent view: the presence of a large and
obdurate Jewish population after the rise of Christianity; the existence of
large synagogues in the Diaspora in the second through the fifth centuries
CE; hostile textual references from both sides, in which Christians portray
Jews as stubborn and wicked, and Jews mock Christians and attempt to
exclude them from their midst—"And that's all" (1996, 51). By the conclusion of the chapter, Stark has countered all these points: there were far
more than enough Diaspora Jews to fill out the ranks of Christianity as well
as to maintain a sizable non-Christian presence (1996, 69); many large
Diaspora synagogues provide evidence for—rather than against—an ongoing successful mission to the Jews (1996, 68–69); hostile textual references
may reflect the attempt of Christian leaders to wean their followers from
Judaism rather than hostility toward the Jews as a group that had largely
rejected Christian preaching (1996, 66).

Stark's argument does not focus on these points, however. The body of
his third chapter explains a number of social-scientific principles that account
for the growth of new religious movements: that conversion takes place primarily through prior social networks; that new converts tend to come from
groups that are marginal to the mainstream; and that a successful movement
provides continuity with the ethnic or religious identity of the target group.
From these principles, Stark develops an understanding of "what *should
have happened*," that is, "why the mission to the Jews of the diaspora should
have been a considerable *long-run* success" (1996, 70; emphasis his). Although
Stark recognizes the gap between "should" and "did," he cautiously concludes that "a very substantial conversion of the Jews actually did take
place" (1996, 70). But he does not offer a detailed and comprehensive discussion of the relevant textual and other sources to support this conclusion.

My starting point, in this chapter, is the assumption that, if a successful Christian mission to the Jews continued until the fifth century CE, it should be discernable in the textual evidence for specific Christian communities—and not only an inference from sociological principles. I take as a test case the early Christian group with which I am most familiar, namely, the Johannine community.

THE JOHANNINE COMMUNITY

There is no direct textual, archaeological, or inscriptional evidence for the existence of the Johannine community. Nonetheless, on the basis of the Gospel of John and of the canonical letters ascribed to John (1–3), it is supposed that such a group did exist in the late first and early second centuries CE. Although scholars differ regarding specific details, there is a consensus that the Johannine literature was written within a particular group, and that the demography, history, and theology of the group are reflected in some way in these texts.

The community is thought to have flourished in an urban centre within the Jewish Diaspora, in close proximity to a Jewish community. If so, then, according to Stark, this community would fulfill an important criterion for successful Jewish missionary activity to the Jews (1996, 62). Efforts to pinpoint the location more precisely have not resulted in a definitive and universally accepted provenance, due to the meagreness of the evidence. Early Christian writers locate the Gospel of John in Ephesus (R.E. Brown 1966, 1:ciii). Because Ephesus is also associated with the Book of Revelation, Revelation 2:9 and 3:9 may suggest tension between the Jewish and Christian populations in that city. The island of Patmos, which is mentioned in Revelation (1:9) as the location of its author, is approximately 100 km southwest of Ephesus. Raymond E. Brown suggests that the author of Revelation left Palestine for Ephesus after 70 CE. From Ephesus he was exiled to Patmos. Although the author was likely not a member of the Johannine community, he may have had some contacts with the Johannine writings, either in Palestine before 70 or in Ephesus during the last two decades of the first century CE (R.E. Brown 1997, 804). The fact that Acts 19:1–7 names Ephesus as the only spot outside of Palestine where John the Baptist engaged in baptizing activity may provide further support for this suggestion, since John 1–3 is frequently seen as a polemic against John's baptizing activities (R.E. Brown 1966, 1:lxvii–lxx).

Another possibility is Alexandria. Perceived affinities between Johannine and Philonic thought on such matters as the Logos have supported this possibility (R.E. Brown 1966, 1:ciii). The relatively large number of Johannine fragments found in Egypt suggests that the Gospel of John may have circulated widely there. C.H. Dodd states that "whatever other elements of thought may enter into the background of the Fourth Gospel, it certainly presupposes a range of ideas having a remarkable resemblance to those of Hellenistic Judaism as represented by Philo" (1953, 73). Though, more recently, scholars have viewed the Jewish background of the Fourth Gospel more broadly (see W.D. Davies 1996).

Some scholars suggest Antioch, on the grounds that Ignatius of Antioch, whom Latin writers considered to be a disciple of John, may have drawn on the Fourth Gospel (R.E. Brown 1966, 1:ciii). More recently, it has been argued that the Gospel of John was written in the tetrarchy of Herod's son Philip, in the region of Batanea and Gaulanitis (modern Golan Heights), where the spoken language was Greek and where Jewish Christians constituted a significant portion of the population (Wengst 1983). Any of the above-mentioned cities would have provided the conditions in which the Johannine community would have encountered a sizable number of Jews among whom to recruit new adherents.

The history of Johannine scholarship adds to the appeal of the Johannine community as a test case for Stark's approach. The prevailing understanding of the community's demography and general history conforms to the model that Stark is criticizing. That is, most scholars argue that although the originating members of the Johannine community were Jews, the mission to the Jews had largely been abandoned by the time the Gospel of John reached its present form near the end of the first century CE (cf. Culpepper 1998, 46, who comments on the large influx of non-Jewish believers into the Johannine community after its expulsion from the synagogue). By this point in time, the Johannine community included Samaritan and Gentile converts, and directed its outreach primarily to the Gentiles. The pivotal moment in the history of the community is thought to have been a traumatic expulsion of Jewish Christians from the synagogue in approximately 85 CE. This event marked a severe downturn in the relationship between the Johannine Christians and the Jewish community, which would have precluded missionary outreach. Most important scholars of the Johannine tradition view the community's history along these lines (see, e.g., Barrett 1970; R.E. Brown 1979; Martyn 1979; D.M. Smith 1984; Culpepper 1998; cf. Reinhartz 1998a).

At the same time, a small but vocal number of Johannine scholars disagree with this construction and argue that the community continued to seek Jewish converts and that the Gospel of John was intended as a missionary document aimed at convincing Diaspora Jews that Jesus is the

Messiah of Israel (e.g., van Unnik 1959; Robinson 1959–1960; Carson 1987). This position is based on a number of points, including the precise wording of the Gospel's statement of purpose in John 20:30–31 and the identification of the "Greeks" in John 12:20 as Greek-speaking Jews (van Unnik 1959, 408; Robinson 1959–1960, 121; Kossen 1970; cf. the counterargument in R.E. Brown 1966, 1:314, 466).

Both of these positions, and their many variations, are supported by intricate arguments regarding the sources and composition history of the Gospel of John, the nuances of particular terms, the larger background of Jewish sectarianism, and a host of other factors, which are far removed from Stark's sociological approach. Nevertheless, Stark's principles may provide another vantage point from which to consider the demography and history of the Johannine community.

The Gospel of John is the primary witness regarding the Johannine community towards the end of the first century CE. The letters of John are used in the reconstruction of the community's internal conflicts at the very end of the first century (R.E. Brown 1979, 94–144; Culpepper 1998, 251–53). What follows is an attempt to read the Gospel of John through the lenses provided by Stark. The purpose is twofold: to assess the strengths and weaknesses of Stark's arguments regarding the mission to the Jews, and to consider the Gospel of John in the light of Stark's sociological principles.

For the purposes of this exercise, we shall make two methodological moves that are pragmatic (insofar as they allow a brief and relatively nontechnical treatment of the topic), if not unassailable. First, we shall adopt the approach advocated by J. Louis Martyn (1979), which is to view the Gospel of John not only as a story of Jesus, expressing the viewpoint of a particular evangelist, but also as the story (if not the historical record) of the Johannine community itself (cf. Reinhartz 1998a; also 1998b). Second, we shall assume that meaningful, if incomplete, conclusions can be drawn on the basis of the Gospel of John in its final form, that is, without resolving the thorny issues of its sources and composition history.

Social Networks

The cornerstone of Stark's theory of the rise of Christianity is the principle that religious groups, cults, and sects spread through existing networks. The power of the message per se (including the Christology of the Gospel of John) is less significant than the social connections between believers and other members of the various familial and other social networks of which believers are a part. As Stephen Wilson points out (chapter 3), it is likely that at least some converts came to Christianity through personal curiosity and inner impulse. This does not exclude, however, the possibility that even such individualists may have heard about or been attracted to Christianity through other members of their own family or other social networks.

Several sections of the Gospel of John portray the role of social relationships in the growth of Jesus' following. The "call of the disciples" sequence in John 1:35–51 presents a series of episodes, most of which follow a common pattern: a person has a direct encounter with Jesus and then brings a friend or a relative to meet Jesus. In 1:36, John the Baptist tells two of his disciples: "Look, here is the Lamb of God"; these two then follow Jesus. In 1:40–41, one of these two disciples, namely, Andrew, calls his brother, Simon Peter. Andrew testifies to Simon Peter concerning Jesus' identity and then brings Simon Peter to Jesus. In 1:43, Jesus calls Philip, who, in turn, finds Nathaniel and brings him to Jesus. Similarly, the Samaritan woman testifies of her encounter with Jesus to her community. The Samaritans then invite Jesus to stay with them and become believers themselves (4:28, 39–42). Towards the end of Jesus' public ministry, an unspecified number of Greeks come to Philip. Philip then approaches Andrew, and both disciples try to arrange for these Greeks to meet Jesus (12:20–22).

Also relevant is John 11:1–44, which portrays the sisters, Mary and Martha, in mourning after the death of their brother, Lazarus, and concludes with Lazarus's resurrection. Though apparently known to be "beloved" of Jesus and plausibly recognized as Jesus' followers or even disciples (Schüssler Fiorenza 1992, 63), these women are comforted in their mourning by "many of the Jews" (11:19). Not only are the Jews who surround Mary and Martha behaving as if these women were still part of their community (although, according to the consensus view, Mary and Martha would have already been excluded from the synagogue on the basis of their belief that Jesus is the Messiah; cf. 11:21–27), but they are also curious about Jesus and his possible identity as the Messiah. John reports that the chief priests planned to execute Lazarus, "since it was on account of him that many of the Jews were deserting and were believing in Jesus" (12:11).

According to these passages, Jews, Samaritans, and possibly also "Greeks" came to follow Jesus through established kinship or social relationships. According to a two-level reading of the Gospel of John, the disciples, the Samaritan woman, the Greeks, and the Bethany siblings represent individual and group members of the Johannine community. One could read the Gospel of John, therefore, as supporting Stark's assertion that adherence to this new movement took place through existing social networks, and that most (though not all) of these adherents were Jewish.

This reading, however, ignores the strong possibility that the composition of the community as reflected in the Gospel of John changed over time and in response to historical circumstances. R.E. Brown's theory, for example, posits a correspondence between the order in which characters are introduced in the Gospel narrative and the order in which particular groups joined the community. Thus the call of the disciples (John 1:35–50) evokes the community's founders, the inclusion of the Samaritans an intermediate stage (4:1–54), and the influx of the Greeks (12:20) a late stage after the expulsion from the synagogue (9:22; see R.E. Brown 1979, 166–67 and passim; also R.E. Brown 1997, 374–76; Martyn 1979, 102–107). While the Gospel of John therefore provides strong support for Stark's claim about the essential role of social networks in the growth of religious movements, it does not necessarily indicate an ongoing Jewish mission past the foundational period in the community's history.

Marginalization

A second principle is that converts to a new religious movement come primarily from the inactive, discontented, and secularized segments of society (Stark 1996, 54). For early Christianity, according to Stark, the prime pool of potential converts was to be found among Hellenized Diaspora Jews. These Jews were on the margins of "traditional orthodox" Judaism, which Stark apparently identifies as the Judaism of Jerusalem (1996, 57). Their marginality with respect to Judaism is demonstrated most vividly by their general lack of Hebrew knowledge, which required a Greek translation of the Bible (Stark 1996, 57); and by the fact that many embraced some elements of pagan religious thought (Stark 1996, 58). Though Stark does not provide any examples; perhaps he has Philo in mind. At the same time, these Jews were set apart from mainstream Greco-Roman society by an ethnicity intrinsic to the Law, which enclosed them in a spiritual ghetto (Stark 1996, 58). Though, again, Stark provides no definition of ethnicity, which seems unlikely to have been merely a matter of observance of the Law.

Stark's description of Hellenized Diaspora Judaism relies heavily on Philo. In subordinating divine authority to reason and to symbolic or allegorical interpretation, Philo accommodated faith to the exigencies of time and place (Stark 1996, 61). Stark acknowledges that Philo is not "everyman." Nevertheless, the fact that Philo publicized his views through his treatises while apparently retaining public esteem suggests to Stark that Philo represented fashionable opinion and therefore can be used as evidence for the extensive accommodation of Hellenistic Judaism (1996, 60).

Stark further speculates that socially marginal Diaspora Jews would not have been easily put off by the facts of crucifixion. Not only did they know that Roman justice was opportunistic, but they also would have believed reports concerning the machinations of the high priests in Jerusalem (Stark 1996, 62). In addition, it "seems reasonable to suppose" that escalating conflict between Rome and various Jewish nationalist movements would have added to the burden of marginality experienced by Hellenized Jews (Stark 1996, 62). On the other hand, there is no evidence that the Jewish revolt in 70 or the Bar Kochba revolt in 132–135 CE had any serious impact on relations between Christian and Jewish communities in the Diaspora. Rather, these wars might have added to the growing weakness of "traditional Orthodoxy" in the Diaspora and therefore would have increased the potential appeal of Christianity (Stark 1996, 64).

For marginal Jews such as these, Stark argues, the God-fearers, Gentile "fellow-travellers" who did not take the final step of fulfilling the Law, might have represented an attractive model of "an alternative, fully Greek Judaism" (1996, 59). Of course, Jews were unable to cast aside ethnicity to become God-fearers. But the decision of the Apostolic Council against requiring converts to observe the Law created a religion free of ethnicity, a religion that would have satisfied the desires of Hellenized Jews as Stark has described them (1996, 59).

In fact, states Stark, early Christianity offered the same things to Hellenized Jews that the Reform movement gave to emancipated Jews in nineteenth-century Europe (1996, 54). The processes of emancipation allowed these Jews to move outside their tightly knit and homogeneous communities within the Jewish ghettos and opened up new professional, political, and social opportunities. When Jews left the ghetto, they found it more difficult to maintain Jewish law as well as less desirable to do so. Emancipation fostered a desire to shed the highly distinctive aspects of Jewish dress and appearance as well as to relax dietary and other restrictions that prevented free association. In these ways, emancipation caused hundreds of thousands of European Jews to become socially marginal, that is, to enter into a situation in which their membership in two groups posed a contradiction or cross-pressure, such that their status in each group was lowered by their membership in the other (Stark 1996, 52). Some Jews tried to resolve this pressure by converting to Christianity; others considered conversion distasteful after centuries of Christian hostility to and persecution of Judaism (Stark 1996, 69). Of the latter group, many turned to Reform Judaism. The Reform movement within Judaism was designed to provide a non-tribal, non-ethnic religion rooted in the Old Testament and the European enlightenment through a focus on theology and ethics rather than custom and practice. Judaism was no longer to be considered a nation but a religious community (Stark 1996, 54).

In Stark's view, the factors that made Reform Judaism an attractive option to marginalized nineteenth-century European Jews are the same as those that would have made Christianity appealing to Hellenized Diaspora Jews of the first five centuries CE. This analysis of both Hellenistic Jews of the first century CE and emancipated Jews of the nineteenth century illustrates a point made previously by Jack Lightstone (chapter 5). Lightstone argues that group identity is forged not only over against other social groups but also through patterns of interaction with them. The potential for conflict among such groups is greatest when one group takes members of another group into social arenas, which the latter group has not mapped out as areas where co-participation is acceptable.

Although Stark is likely correct in portraying Diaspora Jews as being caught between two cultures, his portrait is problematical in several respects. First is the use of Philo, a first-century Alexandrian Jew, as typical or representative of Diaspora Jews throughout the Roman Empire in the first through fifth centuries CE. It may be the case that Diaspora Jews outnumbered Palestinian Jews by at least four to one—Stark (1996, 57) estimates four to six million Diaspora Jews as compared with one million Palestinian Jews—and that these several million Jews lived in numerous communities covering a large geographical area throughout the Roman Empire. If so, it seems reasonable to posit some variety in Jewish identity.

Following Stark, we may consider a modern analogy. There are palpable differences among the handful of Jews in South Porcupine; members of a small Jewish but well-organized community in Hamilton, Ontario; the sizable but declining Jewish community in Montreal, Quebec; and the million-strong and prominent Jewish population of New York City, New York. An assessment of North American Jewry based on a single one of these communities might discover certain common concerns, such as intermarriage, and identify areas of accommodation to non-Jewish culture and society, but would err in generalizing about more subtle matters such as the receptiveness to new ideas and adherence to tradition or the particular tensions within the Jewish community or between the Jewish and non-Jewish populations. The specific settings affect the ways in which Jewish identity is configured and expressed, and they also define the range of Jewish expression available. If this is true in our own day, how much more so for an era without newspapers, air travel, the telephone, or the Internet! On this basis, we are justified in our reserve about taking Philo as representative of Diaspora Judaism as such.

A second difficulty lies in Stark's assumption that there existed in first-century Judaism a "traditional orthodoxy," against which Hellenized Diaspora Jews would have been considered to be, and would have felt themselves, marginal. Stark does not provide any support for this assumption; this aspect of his argument testifies to his reliance on scholarly works that predate, or do not take into account, the significant work of the last several decades, which suggests a variety within first-century Judaism and a rather lengthy and by no means linear process by which one particular type of Judaism eventually became recognized as normative (Cohen 1987a, 134–37). While one may speak more confidently of a normative Judaism in the fourth and fifth centuries CE, even this normative Judaism should not be described as "orthodox" in the modern sense of the term (Rackman 1987, 682).

Third, it is unclear whether the Apostolic Council did, in fact, create a Judaism that was free from ethnicity, to which Jews flocked in droves. Following Conzelmann, Stark argues that the Jewish Christians were the first to avail themselves of freedom from the Law (1996, 61; cf. Conzelmann 1973, 83). Nonetheless, as both Conzelmann and Stark acknowledge, it is uncertain exactly when it became unacceptable for Christians to observe the Jewish law (see Stark 1996, 66). Conzelmann (1973, 84–86) attempts to resolve this point by arguing that, while there were Jewish Christians for whom the Law was still in effect, the Law itself as a way of life was called into question by the Apostolic Council. The Council set in motion a conflict regarding Jewish Christian obligation to keep the Law, and also raised questions about how Jewish and Gentile Christians might live together in community. Certainly, the evidence suggests that Jewish Christians continued to observe many of the visible aspects of Jewish law and custom; and, indeed, according to another of Stark's principles, this continuity of both thought and practice itself would have contributed to the success of the mission to the Jews. But if this is the case, the argument that Christianity appealed to Jews precisely because it offered an accessible belief system free from Jewish ethnicity is considerably weakened.

Finally, despite our own earlier recourse to a modern analogy, the principle behind using such analogies to illuminate ancient history may be called into question. Stark's defence of this methodological move is based on the conviction that the principles that govern religious movements transcend the particularities of time and space (1996, 22). Stark's defence of this argument entails a lecture on the use of "proper scientific concepts," which is addressed to historians who "seem to have considerable trouble with the idea of general theories because they have not been trained in the distinction between concepts and instances" (1996, 22). This may be so. But it is difficult to shake the feeling that, in drawing such a straight line between Diaspora Judaism in the Roman Empire and Diaspora Judaism in post-emancipation Europe, one is inevitably overlooking cultural and social differences that are far from trivial. Similar reservations have been expressed by Harry O. Maier, who suggests that Stark's network analysis would have benefited from a closer study of the hierarchical structure of ancient society. In Maier's words, "The application of general laws or concepts to account for particular behaviours ignores context-specific determinants of differing historical phenomena" (1998, 331).

Let us leave these reservations aside, however, in order to consider whether the substance of Stark's argument regarding the appeal of Christianity to marginalized Jews can be supported from the Gospel of John; or, conversely, whether it can shed light upon the Johannine community. The Gospel of John implies a division between the Jewish leadership, which is centred in Jerusalem, and the Jewish populace. In John 7, for example, this division is expressed by the crowds in Jerusalem, who speak of their leaders in the third person: "Now some of the people of Jerusalem were saying, 'Is not this the man whom they are trying to kill?' And here he is, speaking openly, but they say nothing to him! Can it be that the authorities really know that this is the Messiah?'" (7:25–26). A similar division is implied in John 12:10, which records the chief priests' plan to execute Lazarus, "since it was on account of him that many of the Jews were deserting and were believing in Jesus" (12:11). The Pharisees and the chief priests use their power to question John the Baptist (1:19–25), to exclude from the synagogue the parents of the man born blind (9:22), to interrogate Jesus and to deliver him to Pilate (18:19–28). The crowds, on the other hand, are attracted to Jesus (12:19), weigh the arguments for and against Jesus' Christological claims (7:25–43), and even believe in him (12:11). Among those sympathetic to Jesus, only Nicodemus has some position within the authoritative group (3:1; 7:50); his association with Joseph of Arimathea suggests that his pro-Jesus sympathies are not directly known to others within his social group (Tanzer 1991, 285–300).

On a two-level reading of the Gospel of John, it might be argued that these divisions demarcate two groups of Jews, with the Jewish authorities representing mainstream Judaism based in Jerusalem and the crowds representing marginal, accommodated Diaspora Judaism attracted to the Christian message. This has been argued, for example, by van Unnik, who accounts for the presence of both positive and negative characterizations of the Jews in the Gospel of John by suggesting that "there is a distinction made between the Jews in Jerusalem and in the diaspora" (1959, 408). Yet it cannot easily be argued that the division between the authorities and the common people represents a conflict between Jerusalem-centred Judaism and the Diaspora. Although Jesus initially receives a warm reception from the Galileans, who also travel to Jerusalem for the Passover (John 4:44–45), it is subsequently not clear that the Jews who are attracted to Jesus' message are all or even primarily from the Galilee. The Jews who comforted Martha and Mary and those who became followers of Jesus in the aftermath of Lazarus's raising were likely to be Judeans, since John 11 is situated in Bethany on the outskirts of Jerusalem.

Cultural Continuity

A third principle affecting the growth of religious movements is cultural continuity. Stark argues that "people are more willing to adopt a new religion to the extent that it retains cultural continuity with conventional religion(s) with which they are familiar" (1996, 55). In Stark's view, Christianity offered far more cultural continuity to Hellenistic Jews than it did to Gentiles (1996, 59), for it allowed these "accommodated Jews" to retain much of the religious content of both Jewish and Greek culture and at the same time to resolve contradictions between them.

A two-level reading of the Gospel of John suggests that Johannine Christianity would have offered cultural continuity to potential Jewish converts along the lines suggested by Stark. The Fourth Gospel, like the Synoptic Gospels, places Jesus in Palestine, has him interacting with a variety of characters, most of whom are Jewish, and portrays Jesus as a participant in major Jewish activities such as the pilgrimage festivals. John's Jesus is repeatedly called "rabbi" (1:38, 49; 3:2, 26; 4:31; 6:25; 9:2; 11:8). Although this title may simply mean "teacher" in these contexts (R.E. Brown 1966, 1:74), Jesus also displays a use of scripture—in the form of biblical quotation (7:38), interpretation (10:34–36), and allusion (3:14)—similar to the Tannaitic rabbis known to us from post-Johannine sources (cf. Schuchard 1992). Johannine Christology presents Jesus in Jewish messianic terms as the Christ, the Son of Man, divine wisdom, and King. Even the challenging soteriological claims of John 6, that believers must drink the blood and eat the body of Christ, are phrased in the context of the manna that God had provided from heaven and place Johannine theology firmly within the context of the Passover, the Jewish season most closely associated with redemption (see 6:35–51).

These elements would have been familiar to Palestinian and Diaspora Jews alike. Other aspects may have appealed more specifically to Diaspora Jews. Most obviously, the Gospel of John is written in Greek, the lingua

franca of Jews in the Greco-Roman Diaspora (though knowledge of Greek
was not unknown among Palestinian Jews). In addition, there are some
points of contact, such as the Logos doctrine, which has affinities to Greek
philosophical traditions as well as to Jewish wisdom literature, even if C.H.
Dodd (1953, 263–85) has overstated the degree to which Johannine theology is similar to Philo's thought (cf. M. Scott 1992, 83–115).

Nevertheless, the very existence of a new religious movement implies
some degree of discontinuity in relationship to other groups, and the language of conversion implies a rupture in the relationship of the new adher-
ent to his or her community of origin. Although Stark consistently uses
"conversion" to describe the adherence of Jews to the Christian movement, Stark does not discuss discontinuity as a factor in the development
and spread of Christianity. The reason for this omission may be that Stark
is not so much interested in a detailed description of how and why Jews
would have joined the Christian movement, as he is simply to argue that
it is plausible that they continued to do so for the first few centuries CE. Yet
it would seem pertinent at least to acknowledge that areas of discontinuity also need to be considered.

The Gospel of John itself draws attention to at least one element of this
discontinuity, namely, the confession of Jesus as the Messiah; which,
according to John 9:22, was the grounds for expulsion from the synagogue.
It might be argued that, in the context of a first-century Judaism in which
messianic speculation was rife, the belief in the coming of a Messiah is
not necessarily a mark of discontinuity. Stark addresses this point obliquely
when he comments that, due to their reverence for Jerusalem, Diaspora
Jews would be less dubious than Gentiles about claims that the Messiah
comes from Palestine, which Gentiles regarded as a backwater (1996, 62).
The Christology of the Gospel of John and its consistent portrayal of this
perspective as the stumbling block to Jesus' Jewish audiences suggest,
however, that the confession of Jesus as Christ and Son of God was central
to the identity of the Johannine Christians, and marked the boundary
between the Johannine and Jewish communities. For a Jew to cross that
boundary therefore provided both continuity and discontinuity with his
or her Jewish heritage and identity.

Discontinuity may also be found in those passages that imply a critique
or replacement of the temple in Jerusalem and its place in Jewish worship
and belief. The Johannine Jesus declares to the Samaritan woman that
"the hour is coming and is now here" when worship will no longer be
associated with the temples in Gerizim and Jerusalem (John 4:21), but
"the true worshippers will worship the Father in spirit and truth" (4:23).

Jesus does go up to the temple in Jerusalem during the first and third Passover described in the Gospel of John. But if we read the Gospel of John as the community's story, the fact that Jesus and thousands of other Jews with him spend the middle Passover in the Galilee (John 6) may hint at a critique of aspirations, in the post-70 CE period, for the restoration of the temple in historical or eschatological time. On the other hand, if the Johannine community included a substantial number of Jews opposed to the temple in Jerusalem, as Oscar Cullmann has argued (1975, 53, 87–89; cf. also Rensberger 1988, 25–26), then this element, too, might be continuous with the belief system to which they may have adhered before joining the Johannine community.

Finally, a word must be said about the anti-Jewish rhetoric of the Gospel of John. The descriptions of "the Jews" as Jesus' enemies, who expel believers from the synagogues and persecute them even unto death (John 9:22; 16:2), are arguably indicative of the major source of discontinuity that Jewish converts to Johannine Christianity would have experienced. Although Johannine Christianity used some familiar messianic titles, relied on the Jewish scriptures, and reinterpreted well-known Jewish symbols, the anti-Jewish invective suggests that Jewish adherents would have had either to renounce their identity as *Ioudaioi* or to risk being associated with the negative pole of this rhetoric in the Gospel of John.

The anti-Jewish language of the Gospel of John has generally been seen as evidence that the community no longer was interested in converting Jews in the late first century CE. As Burton Mack points out in a review of Stark's work, "No Jew worth his salt would have converted when being told that he was guilty of killing the messiah" (Mack 1999, 134). All the more so, perhaps, if she is told that she is a child not of Abraham nor of God but of the devil (John 8:44). On the other hand, as Bruce Malina and Richard Rohrbaugh point out, such statements may be read as a kind of "anti-language" that "creates and expresses an interpretation of reality that is inherently an alternative reality…to society at large" (1998, 10–11). Anti-languages "are generally replications of social forms based on highly distinctive values. These values are clearly set apart from those of the society from which antisocietal members derive" (Malina and Rohrbaugh 1998, 11). If so, the anti-Jewish rhetoric of the Gospel of John, though evidence of, and a contributor to, discontinuity, would not necessarily be an argument against Stark's theory. If Johannine anti-language takes Jewish norms as its point of departure, then it may have been intended precisely for potential Jewish adherents to the Johannine community.

CONCLUSION

Despite the flaws in some of Stark's arguments, the Gospel of John and, by extension, the history and demography of the Johannine community provide some support for Stark's three main sociological principles. Adherents to Johannine Christianity appear to have been gathered through the lines of existing social and familial networks; they seem to have come from segments of Greco-Roman society, which were marginal to the institutions of Jewish authority; and the Johannine community provided some measure of continuity with the cultural groups from which these new adherents may have come.

Stark's argument for an ongoing successful mission to the Jews supports the theory that the Johannine community, through the Gospel of John, intended to reach out to Diaspora Jews as potential new recruits. As we have seen, the evidence in favour of this argument is problematic. First, not only Jews but also Samaritans and Greeks are portrayed as coming to Jesus through defined social networks. Second, Stark's approach does not allow one to distinguish between the various stages in community growth. Thus the evidence in favour of an influx of Jewish adherents may, in fact, pertain only to an early stage in the life of the Johannine community, and thus may not support the theory that the mission to the Jews continued to be successful in the latter part of the first century CE. Finally, there is no real basis on which to argue that the Jewish crowds who listened to Jesus' speeches and may distinguish themselves from the Jewish authorities indeed represent Diaspora Jews; or that the "Greeks" of John 12:20 are Hellenistic Jews and not Gentile Greeks.

Most problematic for the notion of an ongoing successful mission to the Jews on the part of the Johannine community is the theory of its expulsion from the synagogue. As noted at the outset of this chapter, in order to read the Johannine community out of the Gospel of John and in order to apply Stark's sociological principles to the history of this community, we must rigorously—perhaps, even slavishly—apply Martyn's two-level approach to interpretation of the text, by viewing the Gospel of John as the story of the community. In doing so, however, we must also read the expulsion passages (John 9:22; 12:42; 16:2) as referring to historical events that occurred within the recent memory of the community, namely, the expulsion of Johannine Christians from the synagogue. Most scholars view this event as the definitive and hostile split between the Jewish and Christian communities. By solidifying the boundary between these two communities, such a split would have disrupted the social networks, as well as the opportunities for contact, that active missionary activity would require.

Stark offers us a way around this stumbling block indirectly. Although Stark does not address the Gospel of John directly, he does provide a brief interpretation of John Chrysostom's anti-Jewish polemics, which we may adapt for our present purpose. According to Stark, we should view Chrysostom's emphatic attacks on Judaism as an attempt to wean Christians away from contacts with Jews and to consolidate a diverse and splintered faith into a clearly defined catholic structure. In a similar vein, the expulsion motif may reflect not the memory of expulsion but, rather, the tension engendered by ongoing social contacts between Jews and the Johannine community. In fact, some scholars suggest that one purpose of the rhetoric of the Gospel of John was to discourage its readers from further contacts with Jews and Judaism. R.E. Brown, for example, reads John 12:11 as "a tacit invitation to those Jews who believe in Christ to follow the example of their compatriots who had already left Judaism to follow Jesus" (1966, 1:459).

Although Stark argues that Chrysostom's anti-Jewish rhetoric was not motivated by a concern that Christians would "backslide" into Judaism, there is evidence to suggest that this did occur (see Wilson, chapter 3). Hebrews 10:29 promises dire consequences for "those who have spurned the Son of God, profaned the blood of the covenant by which they were sanctified, and outraged the Spirit of grace." The context of this warning compares Jesus' sacrifice with those offered, year after year, in the temple, implying that it is the possibility of backsliding into Judaism which is being addressed. The letter of Ignatius to the Philadelphians (6) warns, somewhat more explicitly: "if anyone expounds Judaism to you, do not listen to him; for it is better to hear Christianity from a man who is circumcised than Judaism from a man uncircumcised; both of them, if they do not speak of Jesus Christ, are to me tombstones and graves of the dead, on which nothing but the names of men are written..." (Schoedel 1985, 200).

The Gospel of John could also be a tacit warning to Johannine Christians, whether of Jewish or of Gentile origin, not to seek to return to the Jewish fold; which, from the Johannine perspective is incompatible with full faith in Jesus as the Messiah, as R. Alan Culpepper suggests (1987, 281; also Kimelman 1981, 235). Indeed, Reuven Kimelman raises the possibility that "the whole charge [of exclusion and persecution] was concocted to persuade Christians to stay away from the synagogue by making them believe that they would be received with hostility" (1981, 234–35). This argument for exempting the expulsion passages from a two-level reading is not entirely convincing. Nevertheless, it points to the complexity of reconstructing the demography and history of a community on the basis of a document in which it is described only indirectly, if indeed at all.

10

"Look How They Love One Another"
Early Christian and Pagan Care for the Sick and Other Charity

Steven C. Muir

INTRODUCTION

The American sociologist Rodney Stark and the early third-century Christian apologist Tertullian (*Apology* 39) each contrast early Christian charity with the heartlessness of the pagan world. In *The Rise of Christianity* (chapter 4), Stark asserts that a significant factor in the success of Christianity was the care of the sick voluntarily undertaken by Christians, particularly during crisis situations. Stark considers empire-wide plagues that occurred during 165–180 and 251 CE. He finds that the conventional institutions of Greco-Roman society—medicine, civic religion, the philosophical schools— were unable to deal with these plagues as effectively as the simple palliative care of Christians, who were a new religious movement in the empire. In this chapter, I evaluate Stark's thesis and examine charity in the Roman Empire. While Stark's idea has merit, the situation is not as black-and-white as he and Tertullian have claimed.

ANALYSIS OF STARK'S WORK

Overview

Drawing upon the work of several historians (McNeill 1976; Zinsser 1934; Boak 1955), Stark estimates that two plagues in the second and third centuries CE were major turning points in the history of the Roman Empire. Stark admits (1996, 75) he is closely following William H. McNeill's brief discussion (1976) of the plagues and the evidence of Cyprian and Dionysus of Alexandria. Despite Stark's implied claim to the contrary (1996,

74–75), this type of analysis *has* been done in scholarship on early Christianity (see, e.g., Harnack 1908, 1:171–73; Phillips 1930, 113; Dodds 1965, 136–37; G.W.H. Lampe 1966, 48, 52; Lane Fox 1987, 323–24, 590–91). Stark asserts that not only did those plagues wipe out large segments of the population, but they also taxed and permanently shattered the conventional social and religious coping mechanisms of the Greco-Roman world, and in fact were leading contributors to the Empire's decline. In sharp contrast to mainstream society, Christian groups during this period had a clearly articulated ethic of charity and an equally well-developed practical system to deliver nursing care and other good deeds to both members and outsiders. It is Stark's thesis, in chapter 4, that cataclysmic plagues provided a critical growth (or "market") opportunity for early Christian groups. Here Stark (1996, 75, 78–79) uses ideas from sociology about revitalization movements. In this view, new religious movements arise in response to social crises that have not been successfully met by current religions (see also Stark and Bainbridge 1985, 177, 360–62; 1987, 188–89).

Stark proposes three points to support his thesis. He asserts that Christian beliefs provided more satisfactory explanations of the meaning of the disasters than did paganism (thus producing a more attractive religious "product"); that Christian practices of charitable health care were more effective than anything offered by non-Christian groups (resulting in lower mortality rates among Christians and an influx of pagans into the group); and that constraints against a pagan's converting to Christianity were lessened as that person's non-Christian friends and relatives died and attachments and obligations to charitable Christians increased. As Stark (1996, 75) notes, the first two points are taken from McNeill (1976, 108–109), who makes an interesting comparison between the spread of Christianity, on the one hand, and, on the other, the contemporary spread of Buddhism during plague years in China during the Han Empire in the first century CE (1976, 121). Although this point provides a parallel situation in support of Stark's position, he does not comment on it. In what follows, I will examine Stark's thesis and each of his three points.

Severity of the Plagues

How serious were the aforementioned plagues, and how widespread? Opinion varies on these issues. Stark views the plagues as being exceptionally severe and widespread. He says that the plague was "devastating… lethal…from a quarter to a third of the empire's population died from it" (Stark 1996, 73; also pp. 76–77). Stark assumes that the plagues were smallpox and measles, diseases that *can* have very high mortality rates in virgin populations. However, the diagnosis of which diseases occurred in the ancient world is a notoriously difficult task. If the mortality rates were high, this would support Stark's claim of the importance of these events. Ancient writers depict these plagues as severe (e.g., "the worst ever"), but an examination of accounts of other plagues shows that this was a common rhetorical statement (Gilliam 1961, 249). In general, the scholarship used by Stark accepts the ancient writers at face value and, like them, paints a dramatic and perhaps inflated picture of the effect of these epidemics.

Other scholarship is more cautious concerning the severity of these plagues. In an oft-cited article, J.F. Gilliam provides a thorough summary and analysis of the ancient evidence for the plague of 165 CE. Gilliam (1961, 247–48) finds that there is no ancient account of the plague which is comprehensive, precise, and reliable. Many of the accounts are of dubious value, and some are probably not relevant. The most striking and sweeping statements about the plague were made in the fourth and fifth centuries CE, long after the event, and the fame of the plague may be due more to credulous acceptance of hyperbole than to actual effect (Littman and Littman 1973, 253).

Stark considers but rejects the estimates of Gilliam (1962, 249: 1–2 per cent) and R.J. Littman and M.L. Littman (1973, 255: 7–10 per cent). Gilliam (1961, 249) finds that, while the plague likely was severe, infectious diseases in general were an important factor in the high death rate of the ancient world. Epidemics were nothing new. The Roman Empire developed and expanded during a constant succession of pestilence and other calamities. Hector Avalos (1999, 4) notes, for example, that, in the first and second centuries CE, the Roman Empire was marked by rapid urbanization, population surges, and increased travel (troops and merchants). These factors contributed to both the growth of Christianity and the increase in infectious disease.

It is certain that the aforementioned plagues occurred. The question is whether they provided the dramatic turning points in the Roman Empire's history that some ancient writers, and Stark, suggest. If these plagues were more typical events among the many diseases and calamities of the era, rather than outstanding examples, then, while they may have contributed to the growth of Christianity, they may not have played the pivotal role proposed by Stark. Stark (1996, 3) recognizes that there likely were *many* factors involved in Christianity's success.

Explanatory Capacities

Stark (1996, 74; also pp. 77–82) proposes that paganism (here, as elsewhere in Stark, a deliberately broad and loosely defined term—critiqued by Castelli 1998, 230) offered no satisfactory explanation regarding the cause(s) of these plagues. This failure provided early Christianity, which did provide an explanation, with a window of opportunity to attract new members. There are several points to be evaluated here.

A basic principle of data collection is to have as large a sample as possible: it is a pity that Stark did not follow this practice in his survey of historical information. Stark's three-sentence assessment of the entire range of pagan religions draws upon a single citation of the early twentieth century German scholar Adolf von Harnack (see Stark 1996, 79, citing Harnack 1908, no page given). Stark lets Cicero (quoted from a secondary source) speak for Greco-Roman philosophy. Ancient science and medicine get similarly short shrift. Even for an author so admittedly impatient with historical specificity (Stark 1998, 261, 265; critiqued by Mack 1999, 133; also Leyerle 1997, 308; Porpora 1997, 773; J.Z. Smith 1997, 1165) and reliant upon experts in the field (Stark 1996, xi–xiv), such breathtaking generalizations by Stark are sure to make historians and classicists shudder. The Greco-Roman world is worth a more informed and nuanced assessment, if it is not to be a caricature or a straw man (cf. Beck, chapter 11). Stark adopts the dualistic view of his Christian sources, finding that Christianity is completely different from all other religions (see Stark 1996, 82; critiqued by Castelli 1998, 230, 237; also J.Z. Smith 1997, 1164; Braun 1999, 130, who comments on the theme of the "triumph of virtue," which is common in Christian historical self-narration, a point also raised by Vaage, chapter 1).

Were cognitive explanations the overriding concern for people in antiquity, which they are for moderns? In stating that "humans are driven to ask why," does Stark (1996, 79) anachronistically project a twentieth-century view onto the first century CE? Would crises have caused a pagan to question and possibly to abandon his or her faith? Did the ancients even have faith as we understand the term? The so-called failure of pagan religions to provide conceptual answers may be a modern identification of an issue that was not significant to ancient people (cf. Mack 1999, 135).

Stark likely is closer to the mark when he notes that people may form new religious affiliations when their old religion seems to be unavailing in a practical way against disasters (1996, 77). For example, we know that the Asclepius cult was introduced in Rome during the great plague of 293 BCE, when appeals to the conventional state gods and all other measures had failed (Walton 1894, 15). Amundsen and Ferngren (1982a, 83) note that widespread pestilence was responsible for the introduction of a number of foreign deities from Greece and elsewhere, when Rome's own gods failed to avert disease. But even here the matter is not so cut and dried. The fact that a pagan formed new religious alliances usually did not entail his or her abandonment of old ones. For example, we have the case of Aelius Aristides, who, like most pagans of the first century CE, was an eclectic worshipper of many gods. Although he switched primary allegiance from the Olympians (Zeus, Apollo, etc.) and Egyptian gods (Sarapis and Isis) to Asclepius, when the latter god seemed most effective in his personal cures, Aristides always remained reverent toward the many other gods of his society, and offered them the usual worship, consisting of specific acts of piety such as sacrifice, prayer, and inscriptions (Behr 1968; Muir 1995). In other words, religion in the ancient world was more manifest in one's actions than one's inner thoughts. Modern scholars often overlook this fact.

In fact, there were explanations for plagues on both the pagan and the Christian side of things. As Stark notes, the Christian explanation was that their own sufferings were trials and tests and, sometimes, a speedy ticket to the blessed afterlife. Christians usually saw pagan suffering as a judgment or punishment visited by God on outsiders for their impiety and persecution of Christians. Like Christians, pagans thought that plagues and disasters were the result of the gods punishing humans for some act of impiety or breach of social-religious laws, for example, neglect of proper sacrifices and prayers, polluting acts, sacrilege (Walton 1894, 50; Amundsen and Ferngren 1982a, 70, 72, 83).

Was Christianity alone in offering a hopeful view of the future? Stark assumes that this is the case. Stark's statement (1996, 88) that "the pagan gods offered no salvation. They might be bribed to perform various services, but the gods did not provide an escape from mortality," nonetheless does not jibe with what we know of Greco-Roman religion, particularly the Mysteries. Admittedly, people in the Greco-Roman world held a variety of views regarding the afterlife. The average person saw life after death as a shadowy existence. Heroes and the elite might expect a more glorious existence in a paradise. Nonetheless, the initiates of various mystery religions hoped for a better-than-average afterlife, and this benefit appears to have been one of the attractions of the Mysteries.

Similarly, Stark's assertion (1996, 86) that "the Christian teaching that God loves those who love him was alien to pagan beliefs," is an inaccurate generalization. The pagan religions likely offered practitioners all the affectively satisfying aspects we associate with any deeply religious experience: as Stark himself suggests, "paganism, after all, was an active, vital part of the rise of Hellenic and Roman empires and therefore *must* have had the capacity to fulfill basic religious impulses—at least for centuries" (1996, 94; emphasis his). We have examples of personal devotion in mysteries (for example, Apuleius/Lucius in the Isis cult) and in healing cults (Aristides in the cult of Asclepius). Stark relies here on MacMullen's (1981) portrait of Greco-Roman religion as a system of exchanges between the divine and human realms: the gods give blessings; humans give worship and sacrifice. While this is generally an accurate view, we should not overlook the affective or devotional dimension of this exchange system (see below; also Beck, chapter 11). For example, consider this beautiful second-century prayer inscribed to the healing god, Asclepius:

> Asclepius, child of Apollo, these words come from your devoted servant.
> Blessed one, god whom I yearn for, how shall I enter your golden house
> unless your heart incline towards me, and you will to heal me and restore
> me to your shrine again, so that I may look on my god, who is brighter
> than the earth in springtime? Divine, blessed one, you alone have power.
> With your loving kindness you are a great gift from the supreme gods to
> mankind, a refuge from trouble. (J. Ferguson 1970, 110).

In general, the initiate in the Mysteries seems to have had a closer, more experiential and personal relationship with the deity than the average person in the Greco-Roman world (Burkert 1987, 7–11; Meyer 1987, 8–9). In some cases, members of healing cults (for example, Aristides) also had a close relationship with the deity. They considered that they had been "touched by the god" during their healing. The deity had acted as their patron, dispensing valuable advice and health. There is an affinity between healing/votive cults and the Mysteries, as Walter Burkert notes (1987, 12–19; cf. Beck, chapter 11). Burkert emphasizes that both are expressions of personal religion in the Greco-Roman world, they are religious activities governed by private decision rather than public or civic obligation, and they seek salvation or deliverance through personal relationships with a deity. This assessment does much to enrich our estimation of healing cults as being full-fledged religious groups in the Greco-Roman world. Stark likely would characterize these healing cults as "client cults" (1996, 205–208): that is, transaction-oriented religions that offered little, if any, sense of community (cf. R. Collins 1999, 138–39). Such an assessment is too limited.

Superior Charity of Christians

There is no disputing that Christian charity was an ideology put into practice. Such activity was widespread and it is well attested in early Christian texts. Nevertheless, in some groups or at some times, we get the sense that encouragement was needed! Several early Christian writers stress the theme of charity and almsgiving as a means of sanctification and heavenly reward (see, e.g., Cyprian, *Works and Almsgiving*—written at the same time as *Mor-*

tality during the plague of 250 CE; also Phillips 1930, 89; Budde 1931, 572; G.W.H. Lampe 1966, 53). Similarly, threats of eternal punishment are promised those who fail to act charitably toward the needy (see, e.g., *Apocalypse of Paul*, NTA 2.733). Christian charity is a topic difficult to discuss adequately in a single chapter (cf. Harnack 1908, 1:120–23, 149–83; Phillips 1930, 20–39, 79–82, 99–100, 121–23; Budde 1931, 562–72; Ste. Croix 1975, 25–27; R.M. Grant 1977, 127–33; Banks 1983, 312–19; Mullin 1984; Osiek 1981; González 1990, 93–125). Here I will summarize only a few key general points.

The New Testament injunctions to practise charity and to love one another are well known. Christian writers from the first to fourth centuries CE reiterate the importance of almsgiving, individual and group care for the sick and the poor, and love of the community (e.g., *1 Clem.* 54.4; 55.2; Justin Martyr, *1 Apol* 1.67; *Herm. Sim.* 1.5, 8–9; 3.7; *Herm. Mand.* 8.10; Aristides, *Apol. ANF* 277; *Diogn.* 10.6; Hippolytus, *Trad. ap.* 20, 25–27, 30; Tertullian, *Apol.* 39.5–6, 16; 42.8; *Scap.* 4; Clement of Alexandria, *Quis div.; Apost. Const.* 3.4; Lactantius, *Div. Inst.* 6.12). From an early date, specific roles within the Christian community were established for the performance of practical service to the sick and needy. In Christian discourse, we find many references to deacons (*hoi diakonoi,* who likely served men primarily) and to "widows" (*hai cherai,* a group of older single women, who were in service to other women and children) (Cranfield 1966, 37–39; G.W.H. Lampe 1966, 48–63). An interesting and little-known post-Constantinian service group is the *parabolani,* a Christian order of male nurses in Alexandria, who tended the sick, and which probably originated in response to a plague (Anonymous [ODCC] 1997; Venables 1908).

Charitable activities within Christianity were seen as a religious act and a duty. They were thought to be pleasing to God, a means of sanctification, a way of repaying the debt owed to Christ, and they were enacted both informally (in an *ad hoc* manner) and formally within liturgical and ritual settings (stressed by G.W.H. Lampe 1966). Such charitable acts were community-building and community-maintaining activities, and they put the group in a good public light. Bruce W. Winter (1994) argues that the good works urged in the New Testament were public benefactions. The aim of early Christians was to be judged well by outsiders in view of their public generosity. Stark's (1996, 78–79) comments about revitalization movements mobilizing people to attempt collective action are therefore appropriate vis-à-vis early Christianity. Nonetheless, would such charity automatically have made for a more attractive religious product in the ancient world (cf. McCutcheon 1999, 128)?

There are cases of Christian responses to large-scale calamity, not mentioned by Stark, which provide additional evidence for Stark's thesis. First are the events of a plague and famine during the reign of Maximinus Daia (early fourth century CE), as described by Eusebius:

> the testimonies of the zeal and of the piety of the Christians in all things became quite clear to all the heathen. For example, they [the Christians] alone in such evil surroundings exhibited their sympathy and humanity by actual deeds: all during the day some persevered diligently with the last rites and the burial of the dead (for there were countless who had no one to care for them); others gathered in one assemblage the multitude of those who throughout the city were wasting away from famine, and distributed bread to them, so that the matter became noised about by all men, and they glorified the God of the Christians, and, convinced by the facts themselves, they confessed that these alone were truly pious and righteous. (Eusebius, *Hist. eccl.* 9.8)

Robin Lane Fox (1987, 591) provides examples of how Christian charity stood in contrast to that of the pagan world. In the 250s, it was Christian groups, not the pagan cities, which undertook collections to ransom their members from barbarian captors. During the siege of Alexandria in 262 CE (concurrent with the plague!), two Christian leaders arranged to rescue many old and weak people, both Christians and pagans. During the great famine of 311–312 CE, rich pagan donors at first gave but then withheld dole funds, fearing they themselves would become poor. Christians, on the other hand, offered last rites to the dying and buried them, and distributed bread to all others who were suffering from hunger.

Stark (1996, 75, 88, 90) claims that the palliative care practised by Christians would have led to a higher survival rate among the sick. That may be the case, although, in the case of highly infectious diseases, caregivers run the risk of becoming infected themselves and dying. Christian charity may have been counterproductive from a demographic perspective. Granting Stark's claim, however, an improved survival rate over time could translate into increased group numbers. Stark (1996, 75, 90–91) further suggests that Christians who recovered from plagues due to their group's superior health care would have acquired immunity from the disease, and that this condition would have appeared "miraculous" to outsiders. With Stark, we may suppose that such an air of invincibility and growth would contribute to the attractiveness of the group: Christians would seem favoured by their god. This is an imaginative (in a positive sense) reconstruction of an ancient situation. Nonetheless, these are credible speculations, not proven facts.

A fly in the ointment is the fact that no Christian writer on the subject—and there are not many who wrote on this subject—boasts of superior survival rates. We assume that they would have done so, if matters
were as dramatic as Stark suggests. It would have been good publicity.
Instead, the texts we have show Christians dying off in as large numbers
as their pagan neighbours. Let us, then, revisit the sources used by Stark
and look at them more closely.

Writing about the plague of 250 CE, Cyprian suggests that the high
mortality among Christians was causing a crisis of faith: "Now *it troubles some*
that the infirmity of this disease carries off our people equally with the
pagans, as if a Christian believes to this end, that, free from contact with
evils, he may happily enjoy the world and this life, and, without having
endured all adversities here, may be preserved for future happiness. *It troubles some* that we have this mortality in common with others" (*Mort.* 8,
emphasis mine; see also *Mort.* 15: "Many of us are dying in this
mortality…without any discrimination in the human race, the just are also
dying with the unjust"). In *Mortality* 1, Cyprian notes that, although most
Christians are confident, a few are not standing firm in the faith, hence
Cyprian's pastoral tract to encourage his flock and interpret the situation
for them. Stark (1996, 77, 81) notes, but does not address, this issue.

Dionysus of Alexandria, also writing about the plague of 250 CE, similarly notes that Christians and non-Christians were being stricken:

> [The plague] did not keep away *even from us,* but it came out against
> the heathen in force…[Christians are] fearlessly visiting the sick and
> continually ministering to them, serving them in Christ, most cheerfully
> departed this life with them, *becoming infected with the affliction of others,
> and drawing the sickness from their neighbours upon themselves,* and willingly
> taking over their pains. And *many,* after they had cared for the sickness
> of others and restored them to health, themselves *died,* transferring
> their death to themselves…*the best of the brethren among us departed from
> life in this manner,* some presbyters and deacons and some of the
> laity…this form of death, which had its origin in much piety and strong
> faith, seemed to be a little short of martyrdom. (Dionysus of Alexandria,
> cited in Eusebius, *Hist. eccl.* 7.22, emphasis mine)

Stark (1996, 82–83) quotes this passage, but emphasizes the mortality dif-
ferential suggested in the first sentence: "it came out against the heathen
in force." We are probably justified, however, in looking behind this text and
imagining that the deaths of "the best of the brethren" caused a crisis in
the Alexandrian Christian community. The phrase "even from us" suggests an expectation (also seen above in Cyprian) among some early Chris-

tians that they should be exempt from disaster, and disappointment when they were not spared. Dionysus seeks to address this issue by portraying the dead Christians as paradigms of faith and heroic martyrs. We can also hear echoes of a similar crisis in the taunts of a pagan critic of Christians, as recorded by Minucius Felix:

> Some of you, the greater half...go in need, suffer from cold, from hunger and toil. And yet your god allows it, he connives at it, he will not or cannot assist his own followers....You have dreams of posthumous immortality, *but when you quake in the face of danger,* when you burn with fever or are racked by pain, are you still unaware of your real condition? Do you still not recognize your human frailty? Poor wretch, whether you like it or not, you have proof of your own infirmity, and still you will not admit it. (Minucius Felix, *Oct.* 12, emphasis mine)

The word "danger" (*periculo*) can refer to a bodily illness or some kind of external affliction. Like Dionysus, Minucius Felix counters this crisis by portraying the afflictions of the Christians as a kind of testing (*Oct.* 36). The evidence suggests that the Christians' superior survival abilities were not always evident either to pagans or to Christians.

Was paganism deficient in dealing with illness and calamity? Stark (1996, 156) admits that healing was a central aspect of both paganism and early Christianity. Stark cites some secondary sources, but essentially leaves this statement unexplained. Presumably, he is referring, at least in part, to healing cults. This vital side of Greco-Roman religious life is left unexplored in Stark's work.

We know that the Asclepius cult reached its peak in the second to fourth centuries CE. The healing/mystery cult of Isis and Sarapis also was extremely popular during this period (Kee 1986, 67–70; Avalos 1999, 49–53). Apart from these large-scale healing cults, we have abundant evidence that many gods, heroes, and daimons were propitiated in sacrifices and votive offerings throughout the empire. Healing was foremost among the benefits that people sought through these offerings. Further, we must keep in mind that the people of the ancient world generally saw the gods as being effective in dealing with illness, even plague. Such is the evidence of thanksgiving inscriptions and *ex votos*, and the growth of the large-scale cults bears out such an assertion. When plagues came, the usual response was to step up the performance of ritual acts. Sacrifices, offerings, prayers, petitions, hymns, vows, acts of purification, and special festivals were performed regularly and lavishly. Oracles and magicians were busy during plague periods, dispensing advice and amulets (Rouse 1902, 189–91; Gagé 1955, 69–83; Amundsen and Ferngren 1982a, 70–83; Beck, chapter 11).

Stark (1996, 84–85) brings in Thucydides' *History of the Peloponnesian War,* although from a much earlier period (the Athenian plague of 431 BCE), as evidence of a Greco-Roman tendency for persons to avoid helping the sick during a plague. There are problems, however, with Stark's treatment of Thucydides' text. Stark quotes portions of the text which support his thesis, but omits other sections that do not, and he misinterprets yet other parts. Admittedly, Thucydides notes the ineffectiveness of both medicine and religion in coping with the plague, but this rhetorical statement is intended to prove the assertion (so typical of ancient plague accounts) that "no pestilence of such extent nor any scourge so destructive of human lives is on record anywhere" (2.47). In other words, Thucydides is more concerned with making a dramatic point than with critiquing the failure of medicine or religion, as Stark would have it. Stark then quotes from a section of Thucydides (2.51) which describes how people who were afraid of contagion abandoned the sick. The result was that they died with no one to look after the sick. What Stark has left out of this excerpt is that Thucydides is describing a Catch-22 scenario, in which many notable persons who had made a point of visiting their sick friends also lost their lives to the plague— an example of the aforementioned counterproductive side of altruism. The text in full reads:

> they became infected by nursing one another and died like sheep. And this caused the heaviest mortality; for if, on the one hand, they were restrained by fear from visiting one another, the sick perished uncared for, so that many houses were left empty through lack of anyone to do the nursing; or if, on the other hand, they visited the sick, they perished, especially those who made any pretensions to goodness. For these made it a point of honour to visit their friends without sparing themselves at a time when the very relatives of the dying, overwhelmed by the magnitude of the calamity, were growing weary even of making their lamentations. (Thucydides, *Hist.* 2.51)

In addition, Stark quotes, from the same section, some lines that seem to state that people had stopped worshipping the gods. But Thucydides is not saying that out of despair the people absolutely rejected the gods. Rather, Thucydides relates how people, in the extremity of crisis, became careless of certain socio-religious conventions, such as burial customs, public decorum, and self-restraint. Part of the problem is that the English translation Stark uses narrowly renders *sebein* as "worship." The Loeb edition translates this word as "piety" (performance of traditional acts honouring the gods), which gives a meaning more fitting to the sense of the passage. Stark also ignores a passage (Thucydides, *Hist.* 2.52) that describes corpses piled up in the temples: this image suggests that many of the sick and dying did seek the aid of the gods up until the very end.

Early Christians contrast their charity with the heartlessness of the pagan world (Francis and Sampley 1975, 265; Winter 1994). We should accept this testimony with caution, since it is polemical (cf. Lane Fox 1987, 591). Note that both Cyprian and Dionysus are writing in-house material, sermons and epistles. Stark recognizes that Dionysus's text is a "tribute" (1996, 82) and a "pastoral letter" (1996, 83). It is quite likely that such literature would not only comment on but also exaggerate the differences between Christian and pagan behaviour. Stark asserts, somewhat ingenuously, that "it seems highly unlikely that a bishop would write a pastoral letter full of false claims about things that his parishioners would know from direct observation" (1996, 83). On the contrary, people like to hear positive things about themselves and their group, and spoon-fed stereotypes often are easily digested. While we should not reject the evidence in question, neither must we accept it at face value. Stark has been criticized for his uncritical acceptance of the testimony of ancient texts (see Castelli 1998, 237; Mack 1999, 134; cf. Stark 1998, 259–67).

Stark (1996, 83–84) is on firmer ground when he brings in Julian's testimony (cf. G.W.H. Lampe 1966, 52; R.M. Grant 1977, 124). When a mid-fourth-century pagan emperor, hostile to Christianity, paints an unflattering picture of his own religious world and grudgingly admits the superiority of Christian charity toward the poor and the sick, this is telling evidence. Julian contrasts the charity of Christians with the failure of paganism, hoping to inculcate similar values in his revival of paganism (see Julian, *Works* 289A-293A; 424C; 429D; 453A). The post-Constantinian date of the emperor, however, must be kept in mind. The institutionalized Christian charity against which Julian rails is almost certainly more developed and extensive than that which was practised by Christians in the previous three centuries. Stark (1996, 84) only quotes Julian in part, failing to note Julian's second statement, which also would be helpful to Stark's case: "For when it came about that the poor were neglected and overlooked by the priests, then I think the impious Galileans [i.e., Christians] observed this fact and devoted themselves to philanthropy. *And they have gained ascendancy in the worst of their deeds through the credit they win for such practices*" (Julian, *Letter to a Priest* 337, emphasis mine).

The satirical portrait of Christian charity by another unsympathetic outsider, Lucian of Samosata (*Peregr.* 12–13), also deserves mention (cf., further, Phillips 1930, 82; Ste. Croix 1975, 25; Osiek 1981, 375; Mullin 1984, 58). In Lucian's account, widows and church officials (perhaps deacons) visit a jailed Christian leader. Meals, books, and money are sent to him, and the local Christians spare neither expense nor effort to assist him. We may also see an outsider's view of Christian activities reflected in Tertullian's polemical boast against the pagans: "The practice of such a special love brands us in the eyes of some. *"See,"* they say, *"how they love one another"* (for they hate one another) "and how ready they are to die for each other" (they themselves would be more ready to kill each other)" (*Apol.* 39.7, emphasis mine; see, further, *Apol.* 42).

In order to assess the difference between Christian and pagan charity, we have to consider what pagan charity was like (see Hands 1968; also Phillips 1930, 8–14; R.M. Grant 1977, 100–101; Countryman 1980, 25–26, 103–14; Banks 1983, 317–18; Mullin 1984, 19–21; Garnsey and Woolf 1989, 154; Mitchell 1993, 2:81–83). There are two aspects to this issue: general charity in the Greco-Roman world, and charity specifically in response to illness. A simplification, but one that is basically true, is that the various forms of Greco-Roman charity were motivated by *philotimia* (love of public honour) rather than altruism; however, some philosophers (Cicero, Seneca) advocated lack of concern for personal gain in philanthropic acts, and some groups (Pythagoreans, Essenes, Therapeutae) had communal sharing and common property. Nonetheless, whether we are considering philanthropy, euergetism (doing good deeds), public benefactions and various sponsorships (e.g., doles, feasts, festivals and games, buildings), or gifts from a patron to a dependent client, the evidence overwhelmingly suggests that the majority of people undertaking these things did so for the acclaim they would receive. Even the mutual support of voluntary associations was based on the principle of reciprocal return. Thus, L. William Countryman (1980, 26) makes the interesting observation that the *nouveaux riches* sought to imitate the established elite by demonstrating that they, too, were public-spirited. Those who were not eligible for public office still could benefit small groups of their fellow citizens by becoming patrons of clubs.

The conventional modern assessment is that these people achieved their reward in this life (honour, support in personal causes) whereas the Christians expected heavenly (i.e., deferred) rewards. True enough, but to a needy person receiving subsidized grain, a free meal, or access to the gymnasium or baths, the benefits were as tangible as they would have been if a Christian had done them. While the sick and the poor were not targeted as recipients of Greco-Roman charity, they would have benefited from these efforts from time to time. A pervasive expectation in Greco-Roman society was that the wealthy and elite should contribute generously to civic affairs (see Harland, chapter 2; Beck, chapter 11). The evidence from literary and inscriptional sources suggests that upper classes were indeed generous.

Turning to the issue of health care, doctors were expensive and used primarily by the elite, although there may have been state-subsidized or privately endowed medicine available in some locations of the Greco-Roman world. Redmond Mullin (1984, 19) notes that doctors and teachers might receive tax relief in return for free service to the towns (for doctors in public service [*iatros dêmosieuôn*] and the availability of health care to the poor, see Edelstein and Edelstein 1945, 2:175; Hands 1968, 131–35, 139; Avalos 1999, 91–93). There are inscriptions that praise doctors for treating the poor and rich alike or for accepting no fee (Hands 1968,133). Nonetheless, the main recourse for the poor who had become sick was to seek religious assistance, in miracle or magic, which was often combined with a dose of practical advice.

In particular, temples devoted to Asclepius, the pre-eminent healing god of the Greco-Roman world, specialized in such activities. By the second century CE, many Asclepieia, particularly the large and influential one at Pergamum, had changed from sites simply devoted to religious rituals, such as sacrifice and incubation, into large-scale complexes resembling modern sanitoria, with baths, gymnasia, hostels, and attendant physicians who would act as health consultants and dream-interpreters. In some cases, these centres would offer limited treatment, for example, potions and prescriptions, exercise, massage, cleansing (Walton 1894, 36, 39; Hands 1968, 132–38; Mullin 1984, 19; Remus 1996).

The evidence indicates that the lower classes were not excluded from these sites, nor were fees usually charged: time available for recovery was likely the only restriction on attendance. Arthur Robinson Hands (1968, 138) notes that if a poor person could not obtain a quick cure, he (or she) likely went back to work and either recovered or died. Only the rich could afford to nurse their illness through long periods of convalescence. Ramsay MacMullen (1981, 42n. 43) discusses *hoi katoikountes*—"hangers-on" and dependents of temples—who likely were paupers and fugitives. Evidence for these persons comes from inscriptions from Asia Minor. Emma J. Edelstein and Ludwig Edelstein (1945, 2:173–80) argue extensively and persuasively that the Asclepieia would have offered some degree of health care to the needy. Avalos (1999, 91–93) suggests the opposite, but he may be conflating the fees charged by temples with the generous donations made by wealthy patrons. Finally, it has been a long-standing assumption in scholarship that many of the extant inscriptions at Asclepieia were made by persons of low social and economic rank, such as courtesans and slaves (e.g., Walton 1894, 58; Rouse 1902, 206–207). In a recent study, Sara B. Aleshire (1992, 85–92) reviews the evidence and finds that the dedicants were a heterogeneous group (from many social classes).

Attachments and Constraints

Stark's insight (1996, 75) on the opportunities for new patterns of attachment resulting from Christian ministry to the sick is fascinating, as is his intuitively credible observation that obligations to Christian caregivers and healers could have brought in new members (cf. Luke 8:2–3; the women who had been healed or exorcised by Jesus became his sponsors—and disciples?). This issue relates to Stark's observation (1996, 16) drawn from modern sociological studies of conversion: interpersonal attachments, rather than theological or ideological persuasion, are often the instigating factor in a convert's attraction to a group. Many scholars of early Christianity, surveying second- to fourth-century Christian evangelistic success, would agree with Stark's application of this observation to that situation.

Was Christian charity intramural, or was it also directed toward outsiders, i.e., pagans? If the latter, then there would be an influx of pagans forming new attachments to the Christians who had offered them charitable health care. Speaking of conversion in the second and third centuries CE, MacMullen observed that a likely setting was "the room of some sick person" (1984, 41). This would be an example of what Stark calls an "open network" (1996, 20), one where members reach outside the group boundary to draw in newcomers. According to Stark: "an epidemic would have caused chaos in pagan social relations, leaving large numbers with but few attachments to other pagans, meanwhile greatly increasing the relative probabilities of strong bonds between pagans and Christians" (1996, 91).

This, however, is a difficult issue to assess. It is likely that the majority of Christian charity was directed toward Christians (Lane Fox 1987, 591). Stark (1996, 92) admits that the care offered by Christians to outsiders would necessarily have been selective (offered to neighbours, friends, and relatives) rather than comprehensive. Thus we have a network based as much on pre-existing social relations (kinship, friendship) as on healing. Early Christian communities simply did not have the resources to carry out wide-scale public charities—at least, not until after Constantine.

One underlying problematical assumption in Stark's discussion is the notion that religion was a distinct entity in the ancient world, in fact, a social commodity, which could be chosen or discarded (see, e.g., 1996, 37). Is this an anachronistic (modern) view? The current standard assessment is that religion in the ancient world was embedded in society and was not dis-crete from other areas of life. Some scholars of early Christianity assert that religion was not an independent institution at all in the ancient world (e.g., Malina 1997, 594).

Stark assumes exclusivity in religious affiliation. This assumption stands behind Stark's discussion of "control theories of conformity" (1996, 75). From the pagan point of view, is constraint against joining other reli-gious groups even an issue? Paganism generally was a tolerant and non-exclusive world view, one in which "the more gods, the better" could well have been a slogan. Constraint and exclusivity belong more to a Christian agenda (see Beck, chapter 11). In examining Stark's theses, Keith Hop-kins makes an insightful assessment of many a pagan convert's likely degree of commitment to Christianity:

> Ancient Christian leaders (and modern historians) may have chosen to consider as Christian a whole range of ambiguous cases: occasional vis-itors to meetings, pious Jewish god-fearers who also attended syna-gogue, or ambivalent hypocrites who continued to participate in pagan sacrifices and who saw nothing particularly wrong in the combination of paganism and Christianity, or rich patrons, whose help Christians wanted, and whose membership they claimed. (Hopkins 1998, 187)

What would the picture be if we applied this insight to pagans attracted to Christianity because of Christian healings and ministry to the sick? Would pagans have converted, in the sense of exclusive allegiance to one group, as Stark suggests? Would they merely be hangers-on, treating Christianity as a client cult, and dropping out once they were healed? Or, as was typi-cal in the ancient world, would they have accepted Christian teachings and praxis, cheerfully combining rituals to a new god with their already existing religious activities? Would such persons properly be called Chris-tians?

Other Issues

As Stark sketches possible scenarios for Christian growth based on mortal-ity rates, he crunches the numbers impressively (1996, 89–90, 91–92). Even-tually the numbers take on a life of their own, and assume a solidity they simply cannot have. We have to remember that, unlike usual statistical presentations, Stark's discussion is not based on data that have been sci-entifically collected and analyzed. Rather, this is admittedly hypothetical material (Stark 1996, 89, 91), based on estimates rather than hard data, which have been put on the table in order to see if Stark's assertions about

Christian growth are plausible. Some scholars have noted the ephemeral foundation of this edifice (see Klutz 1998, 169; Bryant 1997, 191; also Leyerle 1997, 306–307). Robert M. Grant (1996, 1082) is correct when he states that Stark has raised some important questions and provided some tentative theoretical answers. Hard evidence, however, in favour of these theories is still wanting.

Chapter 4 of *The Rise of Christianity* ("Epidemics, Networks, and Conversion") should be read in conjunction with chapter 7 ("Urban Chaos and Crisis: The Case of Antioch"). The two subject areas are related to one another, and more integration could have been done between them. In chapter 7, for example, Stark (1996, 149–56) discusses the poor health and sanitation conditions in the Greco-Roman urban centres that were the primary site of early Christian missionary efforts. In a word, the cities were unhealthy. The poor would have felt these conditions most acutely, since they were living in cramped quarters in the worst parts of town. Disease and, in particular, epidemics would have been exacerbated by the physical conditions of the cities (Littman and Littman 1973, 256; Carney 1975, 83–136, esp. pp. 84–89 on population density and health conditions in the cities; also Harland, chapter 2). Furthermore, the ancient world had its share of other disasters and calamities, each of which would have provided an opportunity for Christian charity. For example, Stark (1996, 159) lists an impressive array of natural and human-caused disasters in ancient Antioch: invading armies, often sacking and plundering, sieges, large-scale fires, riots, earthquakes, epidemics, and famines. This pattern could be repeated for many cities, especially in Asia Minor. The situation is summarized well in the following statement:

> Christianity arose as a revitalization movement that arose in response to the misery, chaos, fear, and brutality of life in the urban Greco-Roman world....Christianity revitalized life in Greco-Roman cities by providing new norms and new kinds of social relationships able to cope with many urgent urban problems. To cities filled with the homeless and impoverished, Christianity offered charity as well as hope. To cities filled with newcomers and strangers, Christianity offered an immediate basis for attachments. To cities filled with orphans and widows, Christianity provided a new and expanded sense of family. To cities torn by violent ethnic strife, Christianity offered a new basis for social solidarity. And to cities faced with epidemics, fires and earthquakes, Christianity offered nursing services.

CONCLUSION

Rodney Stark has provided us with a provocative new way to consider why Christianity grew from a small Jewish sect to an empire-wide religion. As a sociologist, Stark looks to social factors rather than theological, philosophical, or ideological explanations for a group's growth. He suggests that interpersonal relations, such as those seen in care of the sick, were instrumental in early Christianity's growth. Some practical considerations may also have played a role, such as reduced mortality rates in the group, due to basic health care (especially after major calamities such as plagues).

As scholars of early Christianity, we may applaud this insight, even as we question some of Stark's arguments. Stark's theories about the attractiveness of Christianity because of its superior capacity to explain disasters and the reduction of constraints for pagans entering Christianity during crisis periods are problematical. They reveal an inadequate understanding of Greco-Roman religion and of the ways in which persons in antiquity thought and acted. We struggle to find evidence of the role of interpersonal relations in the limited data from the period in question. Our sources (mostly Christian) want to portray the success of Christianity as part of the inevitable plan of God, due more to divine intent than to human action. In many texts, it is evident that early Christian writers ignore and even suppress the role played by social factors in the growth of Christianity (Theissen 1982a, 175). We have to dig deeply and carefully to find the mundane causes behind early Christianity's expansion.

Stark has laid a foundation for further questions that we may address to the ancient texts. His lack of critical engagement with ancient sources need not deter us; in fact, it gives us impetus to explore the issue in greater depth. Avalos (1999, 99–107) suggests that Christianity offered decentralized (in every city) and, at times, mobile (itinerant) health care, which would have been an inducement for the sick to affiliate with Christians. R.J.S. Barrett-Lennard (1994) reviews extensive textual evidence of Christian healing from the second to fourth centuries CE, but does not examine the social dimensions of the issue.

It seems likely that one reason for Christianity's growth was the charitable activities of its members. Stark concentrates on two plagues as turning points in the history of the group (and of the Roman Empire). Less dramatically but more realistically, Christianity in the second to fourth centuries CE likely grew out of hundreds of opportunities to minister to the poor and the sick. Charity in the Greco-Roman world was largely at the discretion of individuals. Rich benefactors who sought to fulfill their role as elite members of society and gather public acclaim performed generous acts. The scope and amount of these acts varied according to the donor. On the other hand, charity was, in effect, an institutionalized policy of Christianity from its beginning. Christians had an organized and efficient mutual support network. They looked after one another in times of crisis, and their efforts toward outsiders may have attracted some new members to the group. The pooled efforts of Christians likely resulted in a healthier-than-average group, and over time their numbers would increase significantly. While this situation was not the sole reason for the group's growth, it was a significant factor. Thus, though Christian charity was not a totally new "product" in the religious marketplace of the Greco-Roman world, it was likely mass-marketed by Christians and easily available to others.

11

The Religious Market of the Roman Empire
Rodney Stark and Christianity's Pagan Competition

Roger Beck

PAGANISM AND STARK'S MARKET MODEL OF RELIGION

In the penultimate chapter of *The Rise of Christianity* (1997, 191–208), after explaining much of Christianity's growth in its first three centuries with little reference to rival religions other than Judaism, Rodney Stark properly turns to the pagan competition. What weaknesses in paganism, he asks, facilitated Christianity's remarkable success? Stark proposes a number of factors, none of them particularly new. What is novel is the way in which he shows these factors at work within an economic model of religions competing as quasi-firms in a quasi-market (Stark 1997, 193–94). Religions thrive or go under for essentially the same reasons as businesses: they succeed or fail in attracting and retaining consumers of their "product lines."

Stark rightly points out that his approach allows him to "focus on the behaviour of religious *firms* rather than only upon religious *consumers*" (1997, 194). In my view, Stark should have pushed his market analogy here further than he does. He could have given the *coup de grâce* to that old incubus on the study of competing religions of antiquity, namely, the deep spiritual malaise that was supposed to have afflicted Roman society in the imperial age (see Harland's deconstruction of this myth, chapter 2) and to have been remedied, *inter alia,* by the mystery cults, Judaism, and Christianity. A hard-headed business approach suggests, however, that product often precedes need and actually creates it. Which of us ten years ago needed a computer of the power, speed, and versatility now deemed essential to our trade? Likewise, might it not have been the production and marketing of (e.g.) salvation by new firms in bigger and better brand packages, which generated the demand for it in the Greco-Roman world?

Before deploying this market metaphor, Stark sets out a paradigm of social behaviour, in which individuals choose between competing religions and their products by assessing their benefits against costs (1997, 167–72). This choice is as rational in the religious sphere as in the economic: hence "rational choice" theory as the matrix for Stark's analysis of religious affiliation. It is a measure of the success of Stark's explanation of the rise of Christianity that the paradigm of rational choice remains persuasive even in the extreme life-and-death case of the martyr (1997, 163–89).

An important criterion of religious markets is the degree to which they are regulated by the state (Stark 1997, 194–95). This is not simply a matter of tight or lax policing by the authorities. Rather, tightly regulated economies are those that display a state-sanctioned religious monopoly; loosely regulated economies are those that manifest religious pluralism. The Roman Empire clearly belongs among the latter: the multiplicity of its religions (and gods) is one of its most striking features, and even at the height of the persecutions its policy was to convert the Christians *from* Christianity, not *to* some other specific religion (Stark 1997, 205). At the same time, just as in a financial market there may be complete freedom to choose which stocks and bonds to buy, but very tight control over how they are traded, so in ancient paganism, for all its polytheistic options, the *conduct* of the cults was regulated, usually at city level, in minute detail. Any sourcebook of ancient society will confirm this with a selection of typical statutes (e.g., F.C. Grant 1953, 3–32). In this sense, the religious market of the empire was actually very tightly regulated. For Stark, then, the question becomes: since a free market tends to foster efficient, client-responsive firms and therefore makes it difficult for new firms to enter and gain market share, what were the weaknesses in the pagan firms, which allowed their Christian competitor to "wedge out" such a sizable and solid share (1997, 197)? What, in sum, were the shortcomings of the pagan firms as market performers?

To the distinction between markets Stark adds another between types of firms. This second distinction is twofold: firms that are "exclusive" and "engaged in the *collective production* of religion" versus firms that are "nonexclusive" and "cannot sustain collective production and therefore specialize in *privately produced* religious goods" (1997, 203–204; Stark's italics). Christianity, like Judaism, is obviously an exclusive religion: you cannot be a Christian (or a Jew) and worship the gods of other firms; just as, obviously, the multifarious cults of paganism are non-exclusive: other gods and other firms are recognized and you may even select, on your own mix-and-match agenda, several of the options. We should keep in mind, however, the obvious danger of the twofold criterion: were there really no sort-crossers in the pagan section, i.e., non-exclusive cults that nevertheless produced religion collectively?

By the "collective production of religion" Stark intends the building and fostering both of the actual religious community and of the sense of community, which the religion imparts as one of its most valuable dividends; also achieving, through the community, the religious goals of its individual members. The demonstration of how these religious goals were realized in early Christianity and how, in sociological terms, they functioned as growth factors occupies the bulk of *The Rise of Christianity.* Undoubtedly, it is the book's finest accomplishment.

"Privately produced religious goods," in contrast, are services purchased (most often literally so) from a religious specialist without the purchaser's ongoing commitment. Appropriately, such providers are termed "client cults." The one-off purchase of a magician's services is typical of their operations (Stark 1997, 205). Other typical (modern) products are "New Age crystals," "astrological charts," and "psychic healing" (Stark 1997, 204).

Stark accordingly concludes that the non-exclusive, privately oriented cults of the Roman Empire proved themselves to be poor competitors in that they were incapable of building and maintaining brand loyalty. Since there was nothing in market regulation or in the nature of the firms themselves to inhibit shopping around, investors did precisely that, diversifying their portfolios to minimize risk (Stark 1997, 204). Paganism's competitive weaknesses were the mirror image of Christianity's strengths.

THE PROBLEM

Given its effectiveness in accounting for the rise of Christianity, Stark's solution would be wholly persuasive if Greco-Roman paganism was indeed as he describes it. It was not. Unfortunately, Stark's characterization is both simplistic and inaccurate. The problem, moreover, is not simply one of misrepresenting the data or of failing to indicate the full range. It lies equally in the construction of the model and paradigms of religious behaviour, which are supposed to cover pagan and Christian alike, indeed, any and every individual exercising her or his religious options in any human society.

Stark, to his credit, does not offer just a new and better empirical account of the rise of Christianity. Rather, as Stark explicitly states, his aim is to show how an historical process should be viewed as the consequence of the operation of certain principles of socio-economic behaviour, which are analogous in their stringency to the laws of physics and which can be expressed as a series of universally valid propositions (1997, 21–27, 45–46). What is sauce, then, for the Christian goose must also be sauce for the pagan gander. But the paradigms of pagan behaviour which Stark advances are a travesty of actual paganism: witness the trivial array of private religious goods, cited above, which are said to typify the product lines of its characteristic firms, or their modern equivalents. Real, actually existing paganism was an altogether more formidable and complex thing. As we shall see when we come to look at the public cults, it cannot readily be accommodated to the model of free market religious competition, which Stark propounds. So the model itself, as would-be universal theory, falls seriously into question.

PAGANISM OF THE PRIVATE SECTOR: THE ASSOCIATIVE CULTS

Stark's paradigm of pagan religion, as we have seen, is the client cult. Certainly, paganism frequently operated in this mode, as so-called votive religion. One contracted with the chosen god for a service (e.g., recovery of health) at a cost (typically an animal sacrifice or dedicated artifact); if the god delivered, so did you. A crisp transaction for religious services took place, with no ongoing relationship with priest or god or cult community. It is non-exclusive (one may patronize any relevant and accessible firm), and it is aimed at a private good. If this were all there was to paganism, then paganism would indeed fit with Stark's model of the religious market.

There were, however, pagan firms that were both non-exclusive and aimed at the collective production of religious goods. In Stark's model, this ought not to be, for it is a contradiction: "nonexclusive firms cannot sustain collective production and therefore specialize in *privately produced* religious goods" (1997, 204; Stark's italics). Theory, however, must yield to fact; and fact it is that numerous pagan firms engaged—and engaged successfully—in collective religious production, sustaining thereby high levels of enduring commitment among their members. Yet these were all instances of non-exclusive religion, which placed no impediment on honouring deities external to the particular cult.

Far from exhibiting an "inability…to generate *belonging*" (Stark 1997, 206; his italics), the pagan cults demonstrate, time and again, that forming and maintaining groups for the achievement of common goals, whether narrowly religious or more broadly social, was precisely their purpose and *modus operandi*. Before reviewing some of these groups, let me first cheerfully concede Christianity's competitive edge. Its success in generating brand loyalty is undeniable, and Stark's demonstration of how this was achieved, both through sharing and caring in the harsh environment of the ancient cities (1997, chapters 4 and 7; cf. Muir, chapter 10) and through the rewards and even the demands of the Christian life (1997, chapters 2 and 8), is masterful and moving. Somewhat confusingly, both the otherworldly rewards extended by Christianity and the terms and conditions set for their achievement are termed "compensators." But Stark's analysis of the way in which compensators (in both senses) functioned to enhance group coherence, to mitigate the "free rider" problem, and to drive up the perceived value of Christian membership (its market capitalization, as it were), is both elegant and convincing. My point is simply that certain pagan firms were similar, if finally less effective, competitors in the market; they, too, put collective goods on offer, though in most cases their product lines were more limited than Christianity's.

It is increasingly now recognized that much of religion in Greco-Roman society, outside of the public cults (a huge other world that we shall look at later), was mediated through local non- or sub-elite groups known (to use a modern label) as voluntary associations (see Kloppenborg and Wilson 1996; especially Kloppenborg 1996; Wilson 1996; also Beck 1996b; Remus 1996). Philip Harland (chapter 2) has admirably described these associations and their role in the vigorous religious life of the post-classical *polis*. Essentially, voluntary associations were clubs, instituted for a common purpose, sometimes for clearly religious ends, such as the cells of Mithraism, sometimes for more secular (or what we would call secular) ends, such as the trade guilds. It would be a mistake, however, to discount all the latter on the grounds that they were not real religious phenomena (cf. Harland 1999). Granted, the self-styled "worshippers of Diana and Antinous" at Lanuvium constituted a savings society for the funerals of its members (*CIL* XIV 2112, trans. MacMullen and Lane 1992, 66–69), and the Iobacchoi at Athens a dining club (*IG* II 1368, trans. MacMullen and Lane 1992, 69–72). Nevertheless, these things were done under divine patronage. Consequently, to their participants they were self-evidently religious enterprises. Besides, in the former, a decent funeral is itself a religious product; so, in the latter, is partying—when the god so honoured is Dionysus. There is more than a whiff of puritan disapproval in Stark's characterization of pagan good cheer; likewise pagan "lack of public reverence" (1997, 198–201). Reprehensible though these features of paganism may have been—and reprehended they certainly were by Christian contemporaries—they are not *ipso facto* signs of competitive weakness. The Iobacchoi, moreover, did not meet merely to carouse; their activities included a sermon, a sacrifice, and quite possibly the performance of mystery plays, with the members assuming roles drawn from cult myth—sacred charades, as it were. The collective production of religious goods by a myriad of non-exclusive firms, far from being the impossibility that Starkian theory makes it, was a norm permeating Greco-Roman society.

Most of the firms of paganism represented by the voluntary associations did what one would call a specialist or niche business. There were, however, some full-service firms or religious department stores (Stark's metaphor, 1997, 206), which offered more or less complete product lines, including all the benefits of belonging. They recruited, moreover, as did early Christianity, through social networks. The most obvious and best-documented example is Mithraism, where a considerable mass of epigraphic data concerning its members, mostly recovered from their own mithraea and thus attached to known and precise contexts (e.g., a particular military camp), has allowed us to reconstruct the social networks in and through which the cult grew and flourished.

The data, empire wide, are impeccably displayed in Manfred Clauss's *Cultores Mithrae* (1992; almost one thousand Mithraists extant, with many career details) and admirably evaluated there by Clauss and in important articles by Richard Gordon (1972a) and J.H.W.G. Liebeschuetz (1994; see also Beck 1992; 1996b; 1998a—a reconstruction of Mithraism's founding group; and Clauss 1990, 42–50). Shortly after *Cultores Mithrae* was published, the names of a further ninety-eight Mithraists were recovered on the bronze *album* (membership list) of the Virunum community, which was the subject of the preceding chapter 8.

Of all this evidence and its scholarly analysis Stark makes no mention.[1] In some ways, it would have been helpful to him, for it would have supported his fundamental thesis in the first chapter of *The Rise of Christianity* concerning Christianity's growth, namely, that new religious movements spread through social networks (see Stark 1997, 13–21). The ultimate

---

1 The omission, though unfortunate, is understandable. Paganism, after all, is a very minor concern in Stark's inquiry, and assimilating sufficient scholarship on Christianity over the first three centuries from a standing start was surely enough of a challenge. For his broad picture of paganism, Stark relied primarily on MacMullen 1981, a sensible choice at the time for the single most informative work. I would now recommend Beard, North and Price 1998, whose primary virtue is a sensible articulation of the development of the Roman Empire's multiplicity of religions within a single historical process. On the mystery cults specifically, Stark cites only Cumont 1956b, now terribly out of date (the original French edition appeared in 1911). A better guide, especially to the social aspects of the mysteries, is Burkert 1987.

intent of the first chapter is to demonstrate that this mode of growth, sustained at the rate of 40 per cent per decade, will account for the numerical "rise of Christianity." Mass conversion need not be postulated. Adele Reinhartz (chapter 9) confirms for the Johannine community Stark's paradigm of growth through social networks, not only as a matter of fact but also as the community's own recognized mode of increase. Stark uses his familiarity with modern movements such as the "Moonies" with great effectiveness to establish this principle; but there is also ample evidence, whose import is not in dispute, among the cults contemporary with early Christianity. To the student of ancient paganism, Stark's principle of dissemination through social networks is very old news indeed.

In another way, however, this evidence from pagan antiquity would have proved something of an embarrassment to Stark. If Mithraism, to retain the example, was disseminated through social networks much as was Christianity, and if Mithraism was likewise in the business of generating collective religious goods for its members, wherein lies the difference? Stark (1997, 203–208) offers one further distinction: a radically different level of commitment. But that is just a deduction from the supposed characteristic of non-exclusive religions: they are geared to private ends; therefore commitment to faith and group is neither demanded nor given. As we have seen, however, the premise is simply false when applied to ancient cult associations.

Is there, nevertheless, empirical evidence that cult initiates lacked commitment to their groups? Stark offers none. Thomas Robbins is quoted to the effect that one was *"converted* to the intolerant faiths of Judaism and Christianity while one merely *adhered* to the cults of Isis, Orpheus, or Mithra" (1988, 65 = Stark 1997, 205; italics *sic*). But Robbins is simply echoing the distinctions made by Nock in *Conversion* (1933, 7) half a century earlier, distinctions grounded not in fact so much as in lingering Judeo-Christian assumptions about worthy objects of commitment. These postulated attitudinal differences are, at bottom, just the sort of unprovable "historical psychologisms" that Stark, as a social scientist, properly condemns (1997, 200).

How does one evaluate a pagan initiate's commitment to his or her cult group and its mystery? They were not tried in the fires of persecution, the ultimate test. Testifying voices are mostly silent (the sole substantial exception, Lucius in *The Golden Ass* of Apuleius, while valuable, is fiction), and few group records have survived. Among the latter, however, is the recently discovered Mithraic *album* or membership list from Virunum, which was the subject of chapter 8. It is worth a second look here because, unusually, it documents an extended period (some two decades) in the life of this Mithraic community.

Briefly to review the data from the *album,* it records initially the 34 names of those who "restored at their own expense" their mithraeum, which had been wrecked, probably in some natural disaster (*templum vii* [sic] *conlapsum*). One of the members donated the plaque for this reded- ication and "embellished the ceilings with paintings." Soon after, a second, less happy occasion was recorded: the members "came together because of the mortality" (*mortalitat[is] causa convener[unt]*) on a date that trans- lates as June 26, 184 CE. The "mortality" was likely the plague then rav- aging the empire (Breitwieser 1995). Against five of the names is inscribed a Greek *theta,* meaning *thanôn* = "deceased," and eight new names are added to the list. The Mithraists, it appears, met to mourn and commem- orate their dead and, perhaps on the same occasion, to co-opt new mem- bers. Fresh blocks of names, inscribed in different hands, appear thereafter, until the *album* is full. Piccottini (1994, 25–26) argues convincingly that these represent annual cohorts. If this is so, the record of cult membership, comprising ninety-eight names in all, extends over nineteen years. Many of the names appear, in the same order, in another fragmentary list that has long been extant (Piccottini 1994, 44–50). Clearly, these, too, were Mithraists, and they, too, as this second *album* records, "built [their edi- fice] from the ground up at their own expense." Piccottini argues that they established a new and separate community; i.e., they were not sim- ply the surviving members of the old community transcribed when the first *album* was full.

The Virunum *alba* furnish unambiguous evidence of the *collective* pro- duction of religious goods, sustained over a number of years, including a time of crisis at the beginning of the record, when the "collapse" and rebuilding of the cult meeting place was rapidly followed by the havoc of the plague, a disaster that bore especially heavily on the group's leadership (two of the five dead held the senior rank of "Father"). Yet the group sol- diered on. Their commitment to their common enterprise is indisputable. What was their commitment to each other? What care did they give their dying colleagues and the sick who survived? We cannot tell. But why assume that it was any less than the care given by an average Christian com- munity to its own?

Or, again, to turn to peculiarly religious goods, what hope of salvation, what confidence in their saviour god, did those dying Mithraists and their surviving brethren carry with them? Here we have at least some footing, for we are not totally uninformed on Mithraic soteriology and the cult's principal doctrines regarding the destiny of souls. This is not the place for the specifics.[2] Suffice it to say that the Mithraists had within their belief system ample reason to die in "sure and certain hope." For Stark (1997, 35–36, 167–73), this is the ultimate religious good. The Mithras firm undeniably dealt in it, namely, the rewards of "victory over death" or "eternal life," which cannot be obtained in the present secular order. More precisely, such a good are the "compensators" of trust and expectation that these rewards will be realized in the life to come; they are warrants, as it were, to be exercised in the hereafter. Their value is enhanced and their perceived risk lessened, as Stark shrewdly argues, when they are produced collectively—just as we see the Mithraists of Virunum doing.

There is, then, no objective reason for supposing that our exemplary pagan initiates, the Mithraists of Virunum, were any less committed to their group, to each other personally, and to their saviour god, than were, say, Paul's Christians at Corinth or John's seven churches in Asia. To claim that the Mithraists and the devotees of other mystery gods adhered to their communities (as if temporarily stuck there until something better came along) while the Christians were converted to theirs, is unwarranted—and belittling. Conversion versus adhesion is finally just another *a priori* strategy, empirically bogus and methodologically lazy, for explaining Christianity's triumph. One would not have expected a social scientist to adopt it so uncritically.

PAGANISM OF THE PUBLIC SECTOR

The pagan firms, especially the voluntary associations and the mystery cults, which exhibit community life, could no doubt be accommodated within Stark's model of a religious economy by re-characterizing them more accurately as collective producers of religious goods of the same type as Christianity. Christianity's eventual market dominance could then be explained, in part, by demonstrating that the pagan firms were less efficient or, more tellingly, less ambitious producers of these same goods. Much more problematic are the public cults, the religion of state and city, which

---

2 Our evidence for Mithraic soteriology mostly concerns the mystery of the soul's descent and return, into which, Porphyry tells us (*Antr. nymph.* 6), the initiate was inducted within the "cosmic model" of the Mithraic "cave." I have repeatedly argued for the cogency of this evidence (e.g., Beck 1992, 4–7; 1996b, 183). In Beck 1998b, I relate these matters to the meeting of the Virunum Mithraists *mortalitatis causa*. In Beck 2000, 158–65, I argue that one of the ritual scenes depicted on a recently published Mithraic cult vessel is precisely that initiation into the mystery of cosmic soul travel, of which Porphyry speaks.

Stark virtually ignores when he treats of Christianity's pagan rivals.[3] Public religion, as it functioned in the Roman Empire, simply cannot be accommodated within a model of a market economy of competing religious firms,
whether loosely or strongly regulated.

At the heart of the problem is the fact that the state was not, as the
model implies, merely the market regulator, a regulator that happened to
favour and subsidize certain pagan firms. Rather, the state itself, through
the public cults, was directly engaged in the business of religion. It generated a religious product. That product, the goal of public religion, is simply stated: the *pax deorum,* the "peace of the gods" or their goodwill, from
which communal prosperity and harmony would flow. In the production
of this communal good, principally through sacrifices to the gods and the
due observance of their festivals in the calendar, the cults of public paganism did not function as stand-alone religious enterprises—let alone competing enterprises—distinct from the secular state enterprise. Rather,
public paganism in its totality was the state itself operating in the religious mode.

This is quite different from the sort of monopoly situation exemplified in historic Christendom, where church and state remained distinct
entities, however Christian the state claimed to be and however all-encom-
passing and exclusive the authority of church over society might have been.
The pope was not the emperor, nor the emperor the pope. But in ancient
Rome the emperor was Pontifex Maximus, and that high religious office was
and always had been an office of state. The essentially lay nature of the
Roman priesthoods, largely mirrored in the priesthoods of the cities of the
Greco-Roman world, cannot be overemphasized. Priests, by and large, were
citizens of the elite political class performing public functions, not a professional clergy, even a very worldly one (Beard and North 1990). Conversely, at Rome the most important religious functions connected with
ongoing public business were performed not by priests at all but by magistrates acting *ex officio.* The great priestly colleges were advisory rather
than executive. Thus there was no distinct institutional state religion as we
would understand it—that was the joint invention of Christianity and the
Christianized empire—but, rather, merely the myriad regulated cults and

---

3 Again, this follows from Stark's reliance on MacMullen (1981) as Stark's primary guide
to paganism. MacMullen, of course, does not ignore the workings of traditional official
paganism, but it is not his focus. Better guides on this score would have been Liebeschuetz
1979; Wardman 1982. The full picture is now admirably presented in Beard, North and
Price 1998. A local cross-section (for the city of Carthage, then a Roman *colonia*), equally
well displayed, is presented in Rives 1995 (cited by Stark).

rites of the *publica sacra* designed to link Rome and the communities of the empire in proper relationship with their gods.

Stark's market model treats the pagan cults indiscriminately as firms competing for customers with religious products. For the public cults, this makes no sense. First, as we have seen, the firms of public paganism were not in competition. They were complementary elements in the religion of Rome and its communities, each playing its necessary part in securing the *pax deorum*. If we wish to retain the commercial metaphor, we might liken public paganism in the Roman Empire structurally to some vast conglomerate, dedicated to a common mission (in the business sense) but operating through numerous local branches or franchises differentiated by their particular deities—a sort of empire-wide "Gods-R-Us." Organizationally, this mega-firm was no rigid top-down hierarchy. Team management and local branch-plant initiative in delicate negotiation with head office were its characteristics. Its true leaders in product development were the city councils, provincial assemblies (the functions of which were mostly religious), and individual aristocrats, not the emperor or the governors (Rives 1995, 96–99). This holds even for CEO-worship in the imperial cults (Price 1984).

Second, the product of public paganism was not primarily aimed at the individual consumer. To be sure, an individual could generally use a public cult for private ends, making a vow to the god and redeeming it with a sacrifice or dedication as appropriate. But first and foremost, the users of the public cults were the communities. Priests and magistrates performed sacrifices, and the cult festivals were duly held on behalf of the commonwealth. Religion was collectively produced for collective ends. For all his emphasis on collective production in Christianity (a mode equally germane, as we have seen, to the cult associations of paganism), Stark's religious consumer is an individual, and the definitive religious products of his firms, such as the promise of victory over death, are personal. In rational choice theory with a classic market model, it cannot be otherwise. The player is the autonomous individual exercising choice, even when a monopoly situation drastically curtails the options.

In chapter 2, Philip Harland argues persuasively that an anachronistic concept of individualism underlies the old scenario of *polis* religion in decline. Nuancing Harland's perception, I would suggest that it was Christianity, together with certain of the mystery cults, notably, Mithraism and Isism, which brought the mentality of radical personal choice and religious self-definition into being, so that Stark's paradigm of religious behaviour in due course becomes germane. But, on the whole, the religious environment of the Roman Empire in the first three centuries of Christian growth is not best characterized as a market, in which autonomous individuals choose products. The paganism of the public cults, i.e., most of what a contemporary would recognize as religion, worked in an altogether different fashion. A different economic metaphor is required. I suggest—no great novelty—that of the exchange.

The ancients would have had no difficulty understanding the metaphor of exchange. Certainly, it would not have scandalized them; for the cult of the gods, whether undertaken publicly by the state or in private votive religion, was in fact and in essence an exchange. Its aim was reciprocity, as encapsulated in the simple Roman formula, *do ut des*: "I, the mortal, give, so that you, the immortal, might give in return." The standard medium of exchange, the human currency for divine favours done or anticipated, was animal sacrifice; in addition, temples, statues, humans, and all the apparatus of public worship played their part as tangible items of value. In this exchange, however, the players were humans and their communities, on one side, and the gods, on the other—not, as in Stark's model, religious firms and their clients. The operations of that ancient exchange, moreover, are not susceptible to academic analysis (except as a purely human social and mental construct), since it is predicated on the actuality of the gods as real market players. For most Christian contemporaries, incidentally, the exchange was real enough: it was simply a corrupt and corrupting market that trafficked with demons.

There was, though, at work in the empire's religion an exchange more amenable to social scientific analysis. It has long been recognized that much of what drove public paganism was the competition of the city elites for prestige—in a word, *philotimia* (love of honour). Prestige was acquired by conspicuous activity in the religious sector, especially by large-scale endowments (e.g., building and dedicating a temple or funding a festival). In this way, an exchange of material wealth into social status and thence into political power was realized. Central to these activities, and very much geared to their timocratic goals, was the elite's participation in the cults as principal functionaries, i.e., as priests performing sacrifice. At the heart of the entire apparatus, ideologically and locatively, as head of the religion of the empire's ruling city state was the Biggest Priest of them all, the Pontifex Maximus, the emperor himself—so pre-eminent a figure, in fact, that he was himself the object of veneration in the imperial cults, in which regional and civic aristocrats vied for the honour of holding his priesthood (Price 1984).

This vast empire-wide enterprise, in which piety was harnessed to philanthropy for the production of timocratic capital, is termed euergetism (literally, benefaction). Certainly, its good works included what we would call charity (in the practical sense) or welfare. But its principal product line, which devoured much of antiquity's economic surplus, was temples, statues, games, anything that could be gazed on or witnessed by the citizenry in awe at the benefactor's munificence and piety: circuses before bread, to adapt the old phrase that Paul Veyne took as the title of his fundamental study of the phenomenon (1976). Here, too, we see an exchange at work, as private wealth and the personal wealth of the emperor are transmuted into public amenities available to all—or, at least, to a much wider circle than the civic elite (for further description and examples of euergetism, see Harland, chapter 2).

Stark's classic market model is incapable of accommodating the social and political realities of this religious economy based on philanthropic exchange. Generally, Stark's terms and concepts, such as "compensators" or "free riders," do not apply, and many of his propositions, which fit ancient Christianity and the religious movements of modern Western society to a "T," are not so much false as beside the point when ancient paganism is measured against them. This is particularly so when the propositions concern social class.

First, the tripartite classification of religious rewards in Stark's second chapter is not germane to public paganism, and consequently its correlation with social class according to three propositions has little relevance in the ancient context. The three propositions, rephrased here for the sake of brevity, are: (1) the worldly rewards of religion tend to accrue to the upper classes; (2) compensating religious rewards tend to be sought disproportionately by the lower classes; and (3) the quest for rewards not attainable in this life is class-neutral (Stark 1997, 34–37). To take the last proposition first, public paganism was not in the business of posthumous rewards. In so far as it concerned itself with the hereafter, its concern was that the dead of the community be kindly disposed, or at least not hauntingly hostile, to the community of the living; hence festivals of the dead and care for proper burial. As to the second proposition, public paganism was not in the business of compensating religious rewards, either. As we have seen, the religious good sought was the "peace of the gods" and the corresponding prosperity and harmony. All profited from the goodwill of the gods, though the rich had the larger stake in a stable society and so profited more than the poor. Only the first proposition, then, that the worldly rewards of religion accrue disproportionately to the upper classes, appears both relevant and true. Even here, however, we should recall that materially elite *philotimia* served to transfer amenities down the social scale. In the philanthropic exchange, what the rich got as output from the input of their wealth was respect, and hence, in that intensely deferential society, political power that required relatively little coercive force to maintain (Gordon 1990, 224).

A later proposition, concerning the worldly rewards of religious leadership, is true only to the letter of public paganism, not to its spirit. Stark proposes that "religious leaders have greater credibility when they receive low levels of material reward in return for their religious services" (1997, 174). What Stark has in mind is the greater credibility of "impoverished ascetics" over "affluent clergy." Now it is true, by and large, that the expenditure of the elite of the Roman Empire as religious leaders was greater than the material income from their religious offices. Of course, there are exceptions. In the Greek cities, certain priesthoods could be purchased as a capital investment, with the temple and sacrificial revenue furnishing an income stream (see the fine example in F.C. Grant 1953, 30 = SIG^3 1009). Nonetheless, the priest's "credibility" would not have been diminished by buying and profiting from such a priesthood. Quite the contrary: an investor was necessary for the cult to function at all. In fact, the more the elite invested in religious production, the greater their credibility. It is no accident that membership in the Roman priestly colleges was one of the most expensive honours that there was, involving payment of the appropriately named *summa honoraria* at the highest level (Gordon 1990, 223–24). It was not, however, expected of the elite that they spend their way into poverty, still less than they adopt voluntarily an "impoverished asceticism." They were and remained extremely wealthy people.

Indeed, the elite had to remain conspicuously wealthy, precisely in order to retain their credibility as people favoured by the gods. In a "theodicy of good fortune," poverty is not a sign of grace. Quite the opposite: philanthropy drawing on boundless wealth signifies both piety and the gods' reciprocal favour. The biggest player in these stakes was naturally the emperor: maximum wealth, maximum philanthropy, maximum respect, maximum piety, Pontifex Maximus. It is no use protesting that the emperor and the elite were not exactly what one has in mind as religious leaders. They had the priesthoods to prove it. Their piety is an objective fact, almost quantifiable and documented painstakingly in the epigraphic record. Literally, it is set in stone. In the case of the emperor, this image of public piety is consolidated by more or less monopolizing the depiction of sacrifice on relief sculpture and coinage (Gordon 1990, 202–19). Neither "impoverished ascetics" nor "affluent clergy" is a meaningful category in assessing public paganism; it makes no sense to measure the credibility of religious leadership in the Roman Empire on this bipolar scale.

Of equally dubious relevance to public paganism is the concept of "compensators," whether used in the sense of the peculiar rewards or of the sacrifices demanded of the religious life. The rewards of public paganism were all direct, mostly material, and realized in the here and now: the pay-out of the philanthropic exchange and communal prosperity consequent on propitiation of the gods. Sacrifice in the metaphorical sense of self-denial, the acceptance of stigma, and perseverance even to a martyr's death, was not an option, still less a requirement.

There are almost no exceptions where we can observe a religious life played out within a public cult according to the Starkian paradigm of the choice and acceptance of compensators. Significantly, the clearest case occurs in the context of a healing cult, where religion is most obviously personal. In the *Sacred Tales* (Behr 1968), the aristocratic orator and valetudinarian Aelius Aristides has left us a record of his endlessly sought cures at the great shrine and medical arts establishment of the god Asclepius at Pergamum. The cult was a high-profile public institution, but within it Aristides forged a deeply personal and (as he sensed it) reciprocal relationship with Asclepius. Eric Robertson Dodds (1965, 39–45) has drawn a wonderful portrait of this "anxious pagan," showing, by reference also to his dream life, how Aristides religion functioned as compensation for the ruin by ill health of a promising career (see also Remus 1996). Even his ill health was converted to religious ends, for it sanctioned his dependency and claims on Asclepius's services. Through it all, Aristides loved, and felt himself loved by, his saviour god.

In the Starkian sense, Aristides received as "compensator" a properly religious reward. Compensators in the sense of tough demands were also part of the deal. Granted, nothing in his relationship with Asclepius required loss of wealth, worldly status, or life. Though, in a strange way, loss of life was indeed called for—and met, but by substitution. As Aristides tells us in the *Sacred Tales* (*Or.* 48.27), a finger could be substituted for the whole body and, in turn, a ring for the finger. Likewise, the deaths of two of his foster kin were interpreted as substitutes for his own death (*Or.* 48.44; 51.19–25). The required sacrifice was he himself, but the compensator could be off-loaded. Even so, physical ordeals were called for, and although these can easily be dismissed as prescribed cures (doctor's orders), the more accurate view is to see in them the conditions of Asclepius's favour, for directly or indirectly the god was the prescribing physician. Here is a not untypical example:

It was the middle of winter and the north wind was strong and it was icy cold, and the pebbles were fixed to one another by the frost so that they seemed like a continuous piece of ice....When the divine manifestation [i.e., Asclepius' to Aristides, commanding the ordeal/cure] was announced, friends escorted us, and various doctors...And there was also another great crowd, for some distribution happened to be taking place beyond the gates. And everything was visible from the bridge....When we were at the river, there was no need for anyone to encourage us. But being still full of warmth from the vision of the God, I cast off my clothes, and not wanting to be massaged, flung myself where the river was deepest. Next, as in a pool of very gentle and tempered water, I passed my time swimming all about....When I came out, all my skin had a rosy hue and my body was comfortable everywhere. And there was a great shout from those present and those coming up, shouting that celebrated phrase, "great is Asclepius!" (Aristides, *Or.* 48.19–21; trans. Behr 1968, 227)

Note the way in which even the rigorous compensator becomes a joyful duty. Note, too, how the admiring throng endorses both compensator and reward, boosting through its collective response the value of the Asclepian firm and its products. Here, indeed, pagan religious behaviour within a major public cult does appear to conform to the Starkian model. But it does so only because, exceptionally, cult activity is here a matter of personal religious option. An autonomous religious consumer makes his choices, pays the price, and enjoys the product. The necessary conditions and players are in place for the classic economic model to work.

The incident just described also illustrates to perfection why the "free rider problem" is an irrelevance to public paganism. In Stark's model, free riders pose a problem because they consume a religion's product opportunistically as occasion serves and without real commitment (1997, 174–76). The agnostic's church wedding is a classic modern example. In ancient public paganism, however, the "free ride" was precisely the point. Ordinary folk were not expected to play an active, committed role. Instead, what was required was that one should honour the gods by participating, passively, in their festivals: attend, admire, applaud, and consume; in other words, accept the free ride proffered by a munificent patron. We should observe the exemplary behaviour of the crowd on the bridge and the river banks at Pergamum, much of which had turned out, as it was supposed to, for a "distribution," one of those ubiquitous dividends of the euergetic machine. The free rider, far from being a problem, was an essential component of Greco-Roman religion. After all, the entire timocratic enterprise breaks down if there is no grateful populace to admire and applaud the philanthropy.

Only once did the system require the active commitment of its users. The edict of the emperor Decius in 249 CE commanded that all inhabitants of the empire, presumably with the exception of the Jews, not only sacrifice but also acquire statements (*libelli*) certifying that they had done so. Usually, a negative construction is placed on this requirement: it was a police measure designed to identify Christians and by the test itself to get them to desist or face the consequences. Recently, however, James B. Rives (1995, 258–61; 1999) has forcefully reopened the alternative case that it was a genuine attempt to institute a common empire-wide cult of the gods, not by posting a slate of official deities to be worshipped (a hopeless task) but by making the traditional mode of accessing them, i.e., sacrifice, a universal participatory requirement, thus a "compensator" in the full Starkian sense. It was not sufficient just to opt out of Christianity; one must opt into paganism or, rather, into religion as a contemporary would have seen it. Whatever its intent, the experiment did not work and soon lapsed. Nevertheless, as Rives argues, it was the shape of things to come—in the Christian empire.

My final demonstration of the ill fit of Stark's model of religion with public paganism concerns, again, the issue of class. Class distinction, as we have seen, was paramount in the workings of public paganism: the (minute) upper class monopolized the priesthoods and paid the shot; the (huge) lower class reciprocated with honour to the gods—and to the elite. Class is also crucial to Stark's explication of the rise of Christianity; he devotes his second chapter to this theme.

For Stark, early Christianity is a good proving ground for the proposition that cults, in the modern sociological sense of new religions, draw their membership from higher social levels than do sects or reform movements within existing religions. These correlations work admirably in modern society, and Stark (1997, 30–31) uses the recent tendency to locate early Christianity in the higher, if not tip-top, reaches of society to demonstrate that the correlation works also in antiquity, since Christianity was a new religion (i.e., a cult) and not a reform movement (i.e., a sect).

Stark's ultimate purpose in chapter 2, made explicit in its conclusion (1997, 45–47), is to make a point about the generalizability of theory, whether it be the laws of gravity (his analogy) or sociological principles concerning religious phenomena. One does not really need to demonstrate empirically the class composition of early Christianity; one can infer it from the principle that "cult movements overrecruit persons of more privileged backgrounds," once it has been determined that Christianity was a "cult" in the defined sense and not a sect. In sum, "[t]he whole point of theories is to *generalize* and hence to escape the grip of perpetual trial and error" (Stark's italics).

This is all very liberating, but can we really shuffle off so easily our plodding habit of case-by-case empiricism? I suggest not, and my reluctance stems from a concern about the universe of cults and sects. The physicist's confidence in gravity (to follow Stark's analogy), and his consequent inattention at a baseball game to a fly ball's monotonous habit of coming back down to earth, rests on innumerable observed instances that what goes up does indeed come down—and not just at the ballpark. There are, however, in absolute terms, not that many "cults" and "sects." Therefore, especially when moving into the different arena of ancient society, I require more than a single instance before placing much reliance on the applicability of Stark's generalization concerning class, cult, and sect. In particular, I wish to see the principle operating within the majority religion of the times with an example of a "sect" or sect-like movement recruited from the proletariat. But as soon as this modest desideratum is formulated, it becomes apparent that it cannot be met. Try to imagine a class-based reform movement in public paganism: the mental experiment simply cannot be achieved. This is not because public paganism was not amenable to reform, or because reforms were never undertaken. Rather, it is because reform or renewal within public paganism was not a matter of group formation.

What, then, does "reform" mean in the context of public paganism? What was the perceived problem, what was to be done, and by whom? Here is what the Augustan poet Horace says about it in the opening of the sixth of his great state odes:

> *Delicta maiorum immeritus lues,*
> *Romane, donec templa refeceris*
>   *aedesque labentis deorum et*
>   *foeda nigro simulacra fumo* (Horace, *Carm.* 3.6.1–4)

> "You'll pay for your fathers' crimes, Roman, though you don't deserve it, until you restore the god's collapsing temples and their images polluted with black smoke."

Horace's answers could not be clearer: the gods are punishing Rome (witness foreign threats and the late civil wars) for neglect of their cult (in the original ancient sense of that word). The solution: restore the *publica sacra,* i.e., the apparatus of temples, priesthoods, festivals, sacrifice, etc., by which the gods are served as they require, and by so doing renew the *pax deorum.*

Leadership in the renewal lay, of course, squarely with the emperor.[4] Horace was as close to a government spokesperson as one could get, and we may be sure that he here reflects Augustus's agenda. To confirm it, we need only look at the emperor's own political testament, the *Res Gestae Divi Augusti,* with its heavy emphasis on temple building and reconstruction (see, e.g., F.C. Grant 1957, 169–72, where it appears first among a number of documents that well illustrate the "Augustan Restoration" on pp. 169–214). Reform was necessarily top-down. In this, as in other episodes of pagan renewal, for example, the almost single-handed efforts of the emperor Julian to reform paganism, in part along Christian lines, by injecting a measure of pastoral care (cf. MacMullen and Lane 1992, 266–73), there is simply no room for a "sect" or sect-like group, still less one recruited disproportionately from the proletariat.

And what was the attitude of the lower class to reform? For our final example, let us listen to a voice calling from the crowd for a change of heart vis-à-vis the official gods and their worship. It is a fictional voice, but it comes from Petronius's *Satyrica,* one of the few sources where we can have some confidence that we are hearing the authentic cadences of the non-elite. The speaker is Ganymede, a freedman dining with his peers (some are well off, others less so, at least to judge from their complaints):

> Whatever is to happen if neither the gods nor man will take pity on this town? As I hope to have joy of my children, I believe all these things come from heaven. For no one now believes that the gods are gods. There is no fasting done, no one cares a button for religion: they all shut their eyes and count their own goods. In old days the mothers in their best robes used to climb the hill with bare feet and loose hair, pure in spirit, and pray Jupiter to send rain. Then it used promptly to rain by the bucket…and they all came home wet as drowned rats. As it is, the gods steal upon us with woolly feet because we are sceptics.[5] So our fields lie baking. (Petronius, *Sat.* 44.16–18; trans. Heseltine)

It is a classic statement of problem and solution as seen by the common man with a maudlin hankering for the good old days when religious action, sincerely undertaken, got results: (1) no rain, (2) pray, (3) rain; the gods used to be on side and now they're not. From our perspective, what matters is that the misfortunes are public, and likewise their remedies.

---

4 On the Augustan reforms, see now Beard, North and Price 1998, 167–210. Whether the religious crisis was real or a politically convenient fiction or a bit of both, the actions taken were real enough and the underlying assumptions were widely shared.

5 The precise significance of the gods' *pedes lanatos* is unknown, although the sense is clear: the gods are as careless of humans as humans now are of the gods.

There could be no question of Ganymede and his peers banding together in some sect-like movement to reform the cult of Jupiter on the colony's capitol, in order to make it somehow a more meaningful religion. The very idea is absurd. One notes, however, that proper religion, in Ganymede's view, is not solely a matter of performance. Right attitude (*mentibus puris*) also plays a part. There is also a modest "compensator": the pilgrimage to the capitol is to be barefoot.

CONCLUSION

On the issue of cult, sect, and class, Stark's principle fails because its categories of "cult" and "sect" do not apply across the board in the religious world of Greco-Roman society. Why, then, does the principle hold, or appear to hold, for early Christianity? What holds, I suspect, is not a principle at all, but merely a comparison—an illuminating one, to be sure, for it is precisely the sort of interesting comparison that Jonathan Z. Smith encourages scholars in the study of religion to make, the essence, indeed, of our "drudgery divine" (1990, 53)—that early Christianity is like modern cults and unlike modern sects in that it over-recruited among the (relatively) privileged. When all is said and done, Stark's generalizations are not universal laws of human religious behaviour within any social context, but analogies that happen to work well in the comparison of early Christianity and new religious movements in modern Western society. The mystery and other associative cults of Greco-Roman antiquity might be fitted, with some adjustments, onto the same comparative grid, but not the paganism (or paganisms) of public religion.

ACKNOWLEDGMENT

An earlier version of this chapter was presented to the Religious Rivalries Seminar of the CSBS at its 1999 meeting. I am grateful to members of the seminar for numerous helpful comments, and especially to the session's respondent, Peter Beyer, for his lively and lucid explication of rational choice theory, which underlies Stark's book. I am likewise indebted to Joseph Bryant for his sage advice and for sharing with me his critical perspective on rational choice theory (see Bryant 1997).

12

Why Christianity Succeeded (in) the Roman Empire

Leif E. Vaage

INTRODUCTION

This chapter aims to sharpen some of the notions I advanced in chapter 1 in the light of the intervening discussion. Again, my interest here has primarily to do with earliest Christianity. The latter's apparent aptitude for success as a religion of empire is the issue that most concerns me now. The fact that Christianity came to triumph as it did is not something I personally find appealing—neither historically nor otherwise. Indeed, if there is a larger purpose to this chapter, it is to remind those who yet remain identified with this legacy (as many of our social institutions still do) of Christianity's latent and lymphoid lust for social dominance. Unlike Ethelbert Stauffer (1955, esp. p. 275) I do not consider the establishment of Constantine's *imperium gratiae* versus Rome's *imperium naturae* to represent a significant change in kind. In fact, while describing the supposed difference between the two, Stauffer himself speaks of the former as "the renewed empire," although he also claims, incredibly, that the Christian version was "an empire which practised forgiveness."

I do not think that Christianity was destined, in any way, to succeed (in) the Roman Empire. Neither, however, do I think that Christianity's eventual success in this realm was merely a function of fortune: the result of a happy mix of accident or opportunity and propitious habits. Without denying the role that such factors undoubtedly played in constructing the historical script of emerging Christian hegemony, these factors were able to contribute to this outcome, I suggest, only because such a script was

253

already sufficiently composed and operative in the centuries before titular domain was achieved.

That such dominance has never been entirely successful is, of course, the other story to be told. Nonetheless, my focus here shall be on earliest Christianity's innate pretension to hegemonic power. Not that I think this pretension was necessarily unique to Christianity. It may be that early Judaism and other ancient religious traditions also possessed such tendencies and aspirations. If so, why they failed to realize them in the face of Christianity's rise is a question that needs to be addressed by a more comprehensive explanation of events in late antiquity. Again, my purpose in this chapter is merely to demonstrate why Christianity's eventual emergence as a religion of empire is an outcome thoroughly consistent with (much of) earliest Christianity's constitutive discourse and not so obviously a transformation or deviation from its original nature.

Obviously, there are many and various ways in which earliest Christianity can be seen, retrospectively, to have anticipated in its developing social practices and defining mental habits an imperial destiny. Some of these are briefly noted below. My main argument, however, will be that it was especially the manner in which earliest Christianity *resisted* Roman rule, which made it such a probable successor to the eternal kingdom.

DISCOURSE AS A SOCIAL FACTOR

In his book *The Rise of Christianity,* Rodney Stark (1996; 1997) provides a sociological explanation why the new religious movement of Christianity was able to succeed as quickly as it did in the context of the Roman Empire. It is not my purpose here to contradict Stark's general thesis or its possible improvements (see, e.g., chapters 9, 10, and 11). Nonetheless, in contrast to Stark and his theoretical co-religionists, I want to suggest an essentially discursive reason for Christianity's eventual success as the chosen faith of Roman rule. In my opinion, it was the expressly political tenor of earliest Christianity's various offers of salvation, which made its subsequent coronation hardly a surprise.[1] I am aware that this proposal may seem to be a statement of the obvious or, perhaps, an exaggerated emphasis of a few features that certainly are true as far as they go, but which hardly tell the whole story. Nonetheless, I think that Christianity's cultural destiny was,

---

1 Cf. the claim made by the Stoic philosopher M. Cornelius Fronto to the Roman emperor Marcus Aurelius: "Now *imperium* is a term that not only connotes power but also speech, since the exercise of *imperium* consists essentially of ordering and prohibiting" (*Ad verum imp.* 2.1; LCL 2:139, trans. Haines).

in fact, decisively shaped by the fact that so much of its core religious vocabulary is expressly political and so frankly imperial.

Consider, for example, the common early Christian invocation of Jesus as Lord (*kyrios*), the promise of incorporation through Jesus into a divine kingdom (*basileia*) or higher "heavenly" household, and the description of those affiliated with Christ as the official assemblies (*ekklêsiai*) of such a realm. Richard A. Horsley (1998, 170) tries to distinguish, in the historically authentic Pauline writings, between "the primary sense of political ruler" for the title *kyrios* and its other possible meaning as "slave-master." Horsley's main concern is to challenge any suggestion that early Christian self-understanding was a form of slave-consciousness. But this strikes me as wanting to have your cake and eat it, too. Could one be recognized in antiquity as politically *kyrios* without a corresponding slave-body (*doulos*), since the term *kyrios* (*dominus*) denotes precisely domination over someone else? Even the term "gospel" (*euaggelion*), as Helmut Koester has underscored (with other scholars before him), was part of the discourse of Roman (Augustan) imperial propaganda. Thus Koester writes:

> All these inscriptions [using the term *euaggelion*] result from the religio-political propaganda of Augustus in which the rule of peace, initiated by Augustus' victories and benefactions, is celebrated and proclaimed as the beginning of a new age. This usage of the term [*euaggelion*] is new in the Greco-Roman world. It elevates this term and equips it with a particular [imperial] dignity. Since the Christian usage of the term for its saving message begins only a few decades after the time of Augustus, it is most likely that the early Christian missionaries were influenced by the imperial propaganda in their employment of the word.[2]

Whatever we might wish to conclude about the influence of imperial propaganda on early Christian discourse originally—as Koester notes (1990, 4n. 2), most scholars have been "very hesitant" to imagine such a direct connection—the imperial inscriptions to which Koester refers make it clear that early Christian self-presentation in these terms certainly would have been heard as "talking the talk" of Rome. The same holds true for other vocabulary as well: for example, the description of Jesus Christ *kyrios* as Saviour (*sôtêr:* Luke 2:11; Acts 5:31; 13:23; John 4:42, etc.) or offering salvation (*sôtêria:* 1Thess. 5:8–9; Phil. 1:28; 2:12; Rom. 1:16; 10:1; 11:11; 13:11, etc.);

---

2 See Koester 1990, 4; cf. Deissmann 1927, 366–67; Schniewind 1927, 87–93; Friedrich 1964, 721–25; Stuhlmacher 1968, 196–206. For the best known of these inscriptions, namely, the calendar inscription from Priene, see Mommsen and von Wilamowitz-Moellendorff 1899, 275ff; Dittenberger 1960, 2:48–60 (#458); also Wendland 1904, 335ff; Pfohl 1966, 134–35.

the promise of peace in this name (Luke 2:14, 29; John 14:27; 16:33; 20:19, 21, 26; Acts 10:36, etc.); the recollection of the same person's erstwhile fateful appearance (*epiphaneia:* 1 Tim. 6:14; 2 Tim. 1:10; 4:1, 8; Tit. 2:13; also 2 Thess. 2:8); and, of course, the prospect of his proximate *parousia* (Matt. 24:3, 27, 37, 39; 1 Thess. 2:19; 3:13; 4:15; 5:23; 1 Cor. 15:23; Jas. 5:7, 8; 2 Pet. 1:16; 3:4, 12; 1 John 2:28; also 2 Thess. 2:1, 8; though *parousia* could also be used more literally to refer to someone's physical presence: see, e.g., 1 Cor. 16:17; 2 Cor. 7:6, 7; 10:10; Phil. 1:26; 2:12; also 2 Thess. 2:9). To this list Dieter Georgi (1991) and R.A. Horsley (1998, 162) would add *pistis* and *dikaiosyne.* In fact, these are not the only other early Christian terms characteristic of ancient imperial speech. One could also include, for example, the discourse of patronage-clientism and of the well-ordered household. My point is merely to underscore the patently political nature of key aspects of early Christian speech.

With these observations, I mean to note the same sort of ideological complicity for early Christianity in the context of the Roman Empire, which Edward Said has demonstrated for nineteenth-century English literature and related works of art in the context of the modern British and other contemporary empires. Said does not deny or even question that such cultural products might also be instruments of aesthetic pleasure and refined reflection. Nonetheless, he writes:

> Now the trouble with this idea of culture [as essentially aesthetic pleasure or refined reflection] is that it entails…thinking of [one's own culture] as somehow divorced from, because transcending, the everyday world. Most professional humanists as a result are unable to make the connection between the prolonged and sordid cruelty of practices such as slavery, colonialist and racist oppression, and imperial subjugation on the one hand, and the poetry, fiction, philosophy of the society that engages in these practices on the other….Culture conceived in this way can become a protective enclosure: check your politics at the door before you enter it. (Said 1994, xiii-xiv)

According to Said, the "facts" of the British and other modern European empires belong, intrinsically and significantly, to the otherwise decidedly literary and imaginary world of the Victorian novel (see, e.g., the writings of Jane Austen, Rudyard Kipling, Joseph Conrad) and other aesthetic works (e.g., Verdi's *Aida*). Likewise, in my opinion, earliest Christianity's core religious vocabulary frankly betrays its own imperial matrix of origin. Telling, too, is how thoroughly the interpretation of this language by modern biblical scholarship has served primarily to obscure such a fact. Typically, this has been accomplished by declaring the so-called true or proper meaning of the terminology in question, when used by one or another early Christian, to be ultimately a higher (theological) or more universal (religious) or more narrowly specific (historical) one. In this regard, R.A. Horsley is neither fish nor fowl, since he aims on the one hand to challenge such a scholarly tradition, only to replicate it on the other hand by drawing a series of excessively facile oppositions (see, e.g., 1998, 164). Whatever transcendent truth the different writings of the New Testament might genuinely aim to project, the defining language of their vision remains rooted in the conventional rhetoric of Roman hegemony.

EARLY CHRISTIANITY AS GOOD IMPERIAL CITIZEN

That early Christianity quickly accommodated itself to life within the Roman Empire is hardly a novel insight; though, perhaps, a truth yet worth repeating. Charting the different mechanisms by which Christianity became progressively assimilated to the standard social structures of the Roman Empire, such as the properly ordered patriarchal household, is what scholars have been doing whenever they have discussed the business of its institutionalization. Again, more research certainly could be done to reveal all the ways in which Christianity was and became ever more culturally conventional. None of this, however, helps to explain why it not only survived but soon proved to be so ably suited to take over as imperial underwriter, once the Roman Empire ceased to function as a purely Roman venture (except, of course, to underscore the degree to which much less actually changed with Constantine than often has been supposed). Nonetheless, before pursuing the question of Christianity's aptness for empire, it may be important to consider first the extent to which the New Testament, especially in its final canonical form, simply makes of this tradition a good imperial citizen.[3]

Exemplary, if not constitutive, of the canonical perspective is the work of Luke-Acts. It is helpful to recall that whatever modern scholarship might choose to say about Luke-Acts as originally a single two-volume work, in the manuscript tradition of the New Testament not only is Acts always

---

3 In part, this may be due to the fact that some writings in the New Testament are politically disinterested, being either imaginatively above and beyond or hermetically enclosed within the reigning world order (see, e.g., the Gospel of John, Ephesians, 1–3 John; cf. 1 Thess. 4:12). Otherwise, it would be instructive to consider the degree to which the historical creation not only of the New Testament but, with it, of the Christian Bible as a whole was originally a Roman project: in other words, a book produced in Rome for a Roman "catholic" audience out of the specifically Roman experience of early Christianity. Cf. Trobisch 1996.

separated from Luke but it is also typically conjoined with the Catholic Epistles. Thus, of the four main subunits—i.e., the four Gospels, the Pauline Corpus (including Hebrews), the Catholic Epistles (with Acts), and the Book of Revelation—in which the New Testament typically was published and disseminated before the Protestant Reformation, at least two of these (the four Gospels and the Catholic Epistles) include the perspective of Luke-Acts. Moreover, through the addition of the Pastoral Epistles to the Pauline Corpus, which manifest a social vision very much akin to that of Luke-Acts (and 1 Peter)—indeed, to such an extent that Stephen Wilson (1979) has suggested that "Luke" himself may have been responsible for the composition of these writings, not to mention the interpolation of other like-minded materials into the historically authentic writings of Paul (see, e.g., 1 Cor. 14:33b-36, viz. 14:34–35)—it becomes clear that virtually the entire New Testament, in its principal manuscript divisions, is marked by a view that, at best, deserves to be seen as politically accommodating.

According to Paul W. Walasky (1983), Luke has written, in his two-volume account of Christian beginnings, an *apologia pro imperio*—and not, as other scholars have suggested, an *apologia pro ecclesia*. Thus the implied audience of the work would not be a Roman magistrate or some other external authority but, rather, early Christians who apparently (mistakenly) thought that their faith required or implied an anti-imperial stance. Walasky is correct, I believe, in characterizing Luke-Acts as an *apologia pro imperio* (cf. Conzelmann 1964; Cassidy 1978; 1987; Esler 1987; Yoder 1988; also Strobel 1973, 97–106, esp. p. 100). Walasky's conclusion, however, or assumption that this was good and wise counsel on the part of the evangelist, is less obviously apt. Walasky would have Luke make a necessary accommodation of the early Christian project to earthly reality; but Walasky describes this earthly reality all too superficially as basically benign. Moreover, Luke is supposed thereby to have safeguarded the spiritual truth of the Christian gospel against an excessively countercultural or antinomian understanding. This, too, begs more questions than it answers.

Nonetheless, Walasky is basically correct, I think, that Luke's understanding of early Christianity effectively renders it a (Stoic) type of personal ethics (à la Seneca), which promised its practitioners a greater measure of individual well-being and contentment but always entirely within the bounds of the existing social order. If occasionally one might be obliged to "serve God rather than man," such service was typically a threat only to one's own existence as a martyr or witness to the truth in question. In this regard, Luke's representation of Jesus and his disciples, including the figure of Paul, as men of (ascetic) valour is quite compatible with the evangelist's larger political vision of early Christian accommodation and submission to Roman rule. At the same time, such a depiction of exemplary personal virtue would soon be able to be read, by a later generation, as a warrant for its right to exercise imperial power, just as Virgil understood his depiction of Aeneas's rigours of renunciation in the *Aeneid* to represent part of the formative *paideia* and now proper claim of the Roman people to universal hegemony (see Keith and Vaage 1999).

COMMUNICATIO IDIOMATUM POLITICORUM

More instructive for the purposes of this essay are those texts that appear to contravene the preceding interpretation of Luke-Acts because they would speak against or compete with the claims of Roman rule. Such texts are the focus of this next section, beginning with the birth narratives in Luke 1–2 and the account of Jesus' ascension to heaven in Luke 24:50–52; Acts 1:1–11. Extending this analysis, I shall then go on to discuss the seven letters to the seven churches in Revelation 2:1–3:22; and, finally, a number of writings of the Pauline Corpus, most especially 1 Thessalonians, 1–2 Corinthians, and Philippians.

My principal purpose in reviewing seriatim these different forms of early Christian self-representation is to assess their collective thrust. However much each text is plainly quite unlike the others in this or that regard, what kind of (political) discourse do they nonetheless constitute when taken together as a whole? Does an early Christian style of pronouncement become apparent, which is sufficiently continuous or coherent in its mode of programmatic articulation to explain the subsequent cumulative effect of imperial success by Christianity? In the language of pharmacology, does the canonical combination produce a certain unforeseen "potentiation" of effect, however much, in retrospect, this now seems predictable?

Of course, one could always try to show that the apparent challenge to Roman rule in these texts does not, in fact, occur. This is, for example, the interpretation of Luke-Acts by Klaus Wengst (1986, 89–105), according to whom Luke not only depicts Jesus and his followers as being respectful of Roman rule because of such fair treatment by it, but the evangelist also underscores that the kingdom whose ruler Jesus is, is essentially a spiritual one. Hence the removal to heaven in Luke 19:38 of the peace that Jesus' birth is said to inaugurate in Luke 2:14, as well as Jesus' own departure to heaven at his ascension in Luke 24:50–52; Acts 1:1–11, are both supposed by Wengst to make clear to the early reader of Luke-Acts that the kingdom of God that Jesus preached was not, ultimately, a threat in any way to Roman rule or the Augustan peace (see, further, Janzen 2000).

Again, this may be true as far as it goes. Nonetheless, Jesus' ascension to heaven (together with the peace his birth inaugurated) does not merely signify in Luke-Acts Jesus' removal from life on earth but also equally his elevation to the highest level of cosmic authority, which is the realm of the gods. Jesus now sits in Acts at the right hand of divine glory, which in ancient understandings of the constitution of political power, also says something about governance on earth. For this reason, if not directly challenging Roman imperial rule (by placing Jesus and the kingdom of God beyond Rome's immediate sphere of influence), Acts simultaneously installs both Jesus and the kingdom of God cosmologically above the Roman Empire and thereby, implicitly, in a position whence eventually to assume the prerogatives of such a reign.

The Birth Narratives in Luke 1–2

It is often suggested that the explicit reference in Luke 2:1 to (a decree of) Caesar Augustus, which not only defines when but also why Jesus was born in Bethlehem, helps to articulate the Gospel's opposition between the *Pax Romana* that officially began with Augustus's birth and the early Christian realm of peace "on earth...among persons of good will," which is heralded by the angels in Luke 2:14 (cf. R.A. Horsley 1989, 32–33). Thus, for example, Raymond E. Brown writes:

> It can scarcely be accidental that Luke's description of the birth of Jesus presents an implicit challenge to this imperial propaganda, not by denying the imperial ideals, but by claiming that the real peace of the world was brought about by Jesus. The testimony to the *pax Christi* was not a man-made altar such as that erected to the *pax Augusta*; rather, there was a heavenly host that proclaimed peace to those favoured by God. The birthday worthy of divine honor and marking the true new beginning of time took place not in Rome but in Bethlehem. The claim in the Priene inscription of Augustus, "The birthday of the god has marked the beginning of the good news for the world," has been reinterpreted by an angel of the Lord with the heraldic cry: "I announce to you good news of a great joy which will be for the whole people: To you this day there is born in the city of David a Saviour who is Messiah and Lord" (Luke 2:10–11). (R.E. Brown 1977, 415–16)

Once more, all of this may be true as far as it goes. But notice how, in Brown's own reading of the narrative of Jesus' birth in Luke, the evangelist's "implicit challenge to this imperial propaganda" is accomplished, as Brown puts it (with my emphasis), *"not by denying the imperial ideals,* but by claiming that the real peace of the world was brought about by Jesus." In other words, Jesus would represent the "true" realization of the project otherwise identified with Augustus. Similarly, regarding Luke 2:10–11, Brown writes: "I shall point out below that Luke derived the titles 'Saviour, Messiah, Lord' from the early Christian kerygma, as indicated by his use of them in Acts; but here [in Luke 2:10–11] he has recast them into *a solemn formula imitative of imperial proclamation*" (1977, 416n. 23; emphasis mine). Fighting fire with fire the evangelist may be, but the result of this is often simply more fire.

Other aspects of Luke 1–2 echo the fourth eclogue of the Roman imperial poet Virgil (see R.E. Brown 1977, 564–70). This poem was an eschatological hymn of hope, promptly proven premature, which heralded the end of the hundred years of civil war that had so crippled the Roman republic during the first century BCE. Written under the consulship of Asinius Pollio (40 BCE), whose mediation helped to forge the Peace of Brundisium, ostensibly reconciling Octavian (Augustus) and Mark Antony, the competing heirs of Julius Caesar, Virgil's fourth eclogue describes the arrival of the anticipated new age, embodied in the figure of "the boy about to be born, under whom the race of iron will cease and a golden race will spring up over the whole world…He will receive divine life…And he will rule over a world made peaceful by the virtues of his father" (*Ecl.* 4.8–9, 15, 17; cf. also *Ecl.* 4.53–39 and Luke 2:25–32; Janzen 2000, 87–89; Erdmann 1932).

It makes little difference to my thesis whether we conclude that Luke actually knew Virgil's poem or that both Virgil and Luke employed the same or a similar (Semitic) tradition of messianic prophecy in their respective compositions. It does matter, however, that early readers of the gospel of Luke would have heard in the evangelist's narrative of Jesus' birth a declamation like Virgil's poem. It is clear that early Christians soon read Virgil's poem as a declamation like Luke's birth narrative. According to R.E. Brown: "The earliest attestation of the Christian messianic interpretation of the Fourth Eclogue seems to be in Lactantius's *Divinae Institutiones* VII 24; PL 6:810, written *ca.* 313. The interpretation was [subsequently] popularized in Constantine's *Oratio ad sanctorum coetum* 19–21; PL 8:455ff" (R.E. Brown 1977, 564n. 1). Lactantius was likely not the first Christian to have read Virgil's poem in this way.

Most important, however, is simply the fact that Luke's description of Jesus' birth—for the sake of argument, let us say that originally it was meant to register an absolute alternative to the rule of Augustus; nonetheless, notice how it fits so easily within the tradition of Roman imperial writing: specifically, works celebrating the person and *res gestae* of a given emperor. Indeed, the more clearly Luke in his description of Jesus' birth is

deemed purposefully to have opposed the Christian saviour to Augustus, the
more directly such a description would serve, under other circumstances,
to portray Jesus as the quintessential Roman ruler. In other words, by
depicting the birth of Jesus, in Luke 1–2, as the advent of the universal
sovereign, soon enough there would be no reason not to understand this
text as, in fact, the beginning of the *res gestae* of the Christian emperor par
excellence. Note that the final scene from Jesus' childhood, in Luke 2:41–52,
which has the twelve-year-old boy-man teaching prodigiously in the temple, reflects a standard feature of many imperial biographies (Wiedemann
1989, 54ff.).

The Ascension Narratives in Luke 24:50–53; Acts 1:1–11

The same holds true, *mutatis mutandis,* for Luke's account of Jesus' ascension (not to mention his death: see Kloppenborg 1992, esp. 111–13, 115–16).
The account of Jesus' departure into heaven in Luke 24:50–53; Acts 1:1–11
obviously removes Jesus from the plane of earthly history. At the same
time, the narrative asserts his enthronement at the right hand of universal majesty (cf. Acts 7:55). Incidentally, this assertion that Jesus' post-
mortem destiny entailed prompt promotion *ad dexteram* appears to be the
only item of early Christian conviction on which all confessions agree (see
Barn. 15:9; *Gos. Pet.* 55–56; the Christian interpolation in *T. Benj.* 9:5; Tertullian, *Adv. Jud.* 13.23; Eusebius, *De eccl. theol.* 3.5; Fitzmyer 1985, 1589). In the
ascension, through which Jesus now becomes installed as viceroy of the
heavenly monarch, Jesus is established as supremely *kyrios.* However Chris-
tologically "stunted" Jesus might remain here in the eyes of later orthodox
theology, not being yet "of one substance with the Father," no doubt exists
regarding his new role in world governance. Must one therefore not
acknowledge a decidedly anti-imperial posture, at least in this instance, for
the author of Luke-Acts?

It is Jesus' ascension that editorially defines the evangelist's own view
of Jesus (see Luke 9:51; 24:31, 51; Acts 1:2, 9, 11, 22). Certainly not the resurrection! A.W. Zwiep (1996) claims that, in the Gospel of Luke, Jesus'
post-mortem exaltation already occurs as part of the resurrection. This
strikes me as tacit recognition of the fact that, in Luke, Jesus' resurrection
does not actually mean much as such: it requires the inclusion of a post-
mortem exaltation in order to make any difference. Nonetheless, by explaining the significance of Jesus' ascension in Luke-Acts through the concept
of the resurrection, i.e., as an extension or elaboration of it, Zwiep keeps
intact the traditional Christian theological conviction of the resurrection as
the critical *novum* (for an even more harmonizing interpretation of the
ascension narrative in Luke 24:50–53, see Fitzmyer 1985, 1588–89: "Hence

the 'ascension' is nothing more than this appearance of the risen Christ to his assembled disciples.").

At most, to speak as Paul, the resurrection of Jesus represents, in Luke-Acts, the first occurrence of a general event (cf. 1Cor. 15:20). In this regard, Jesus in Luke-Acts would be simply *primus inter pares* eschatologically. Luke continues early Christian and Jewish discourse about the resurrection of the dead as one of the signs of the end of the world in its current manifestation. But—this is my main point—Luke does not use the language of resurrection in order to characterize what would be unique or even especially notable about Jesus. Rather, it is Jesus' ascension that renders him a singular figure in Luke-Acts. In fact, it seems to me that, for the evangelist, Jesus' resurrection merely serves to undo the evident injustice of his death; just as previously in the gospel, Jesus, and subsequently in Acts, the apostles occasionally bring dead people back to life in order to rectify their undeserved or premature demise.

Consider, then, the extent to which Jesus' ascension in Luke-Acts is recounted as a Roman imperial apotheosis. It is hardly identical (cf. Bickermann 1929). Not merely the soul, in Jesus' case, is supposed to have gone skyward, but the whole carnal carriage. No bird (eagle) was on hand to register the successful transfer. Jesus is supposed to have undergone his translation when (once again) alive. On the other hand, the whole point of apotheosis was to claim a greater ongoing life for the (ostensibly) deceased.

In claiming that Jesus' ascension in Luke-Acts is like a Roman imperial apotheosis, I understand both ascension and apotheosis to be forms of the ancient notion of assumption versus any attempt to distinguish between the latter and ascension (cf., e.g., Plevnik 1984, esp. p. 278n. 16; D.A. Smith 2001, 89). Jesus is described here, in the standard language of ancient assumption narratives, as having been "borne up to heaven" (*anephereto eis ton ouranon,* Luke 24:51; see, further, Acts 1:9: *epêrthê kai nephelê hypelaben auton;* 1:11: *houtos o Iêsous ho analemphtheis…eis ton ouranon*); after which the disciples, who were with Jesus at his take-off site, are said to have "worshipped him" (*proskynêsantes auton*) before returning to Jerusalem (Luke 24:52; cf. Lohfink 1971, 48f.). Most importantly, once Jesus' farewell speech has been delivered in Acts 1:9, it is underscored that the disciples "saw him" as he was "lifted up" (*kai tauta eipôn blepontôn autôn epêrthê*) until a cloud obscured their view. In fact, it could hardly be underscored more emphatically that indeed Jesus was *seen* ascending into heaven: "And… while they were watching (*blepontôn autôn*)…a cloud took him away from their eyes (*apo tôn ophthalmôn autôn*) and as they were staring (*atenizontes*) into heaven…why do you stand looking (*blepontes*) into heaven…in the same manner you observed (*etheasasthe*) him going into heaven" (Acts 1:9–11). Such eyewitness testimony was considered essential for ratification of any imperial apotheosis (Bickermann 1929, 8f; cf. Suetonius, *Aug.* 100.4; Dio Cass. 56.46.2; 59.11.4; Justin, *1 Apol.* 1.21; Tatian, *Ad Gr.* 10; Tertullian, *Spect.* 30.3). Indeed, so essential, or stereotypical, a feature of Roman imperial apotheosis was such confirmation by eyewitness that this became the stuff of satire (see, e.g., Seneca, *Apocol.* 1; Sullivan 1986, 221). Finally, another aspect of Jesus' ascension in Luke-Acts, which corresponds to accounts of Roman imperial apotheosis, is the concluding "heavenly confirmation" of the translation in Acts 1:10–11 (cf. Lohfink 1971, 45f.).

Use of the verb *anapherein* (Luke 24:51 together with *diistênai;* also, in Luke-Acts, *analambanein:* Acts 1:2, 11; Luke 9:51, and *epairein:* Acts 1:9) as well as the language of disappearance (*nephelê hypelaben auton apo tôn ophthalmôn autôn:* Acts 1:9; cf. Luke 24:31: *aphantos*) are typical of the *topos* of heavenly assumption in antiquity (Lohfink 1971:41–42; for use of *anapherein* plus the prepositional phrase *eis ton ouranon,* see Plutarch, *Num.* 2.3; Antoninus Liberalis 25; scholion on Apollonios Rhodios, *Argon.* 4.57, ed. Keil; also Dio Cass. 56.42). Lohfink notes, however, that the verb *analambanein,* which is "Luke's own *terminus technicus* for the ascension of Jesus, plays no role in Greek assumption texts" (1971:42).

Daniel A. Smith (2001, 88, 108n. 44) claims that the category of assumption should not include Roman imperial apotheosis. Nevertheless, as Smith himself otherwise argues (2001, 88f and passim), since assumption was possible not only before or escaping death but also after death, I fail to understand why Roman imperial apotheosis would not be another type of post-mortem assumption. This is, in fact, the perspective of Lohfink (1971, 37–41).

It has been debated whether the phrases, *kai anephereto eis ton ouranon* and *proskynêsantes auton,* were originally found respectively in Luke 24:51 and 24:52. Scholars who favour their absence, i.e., the shorter reading or Western "non-interpolation" as the more original text, include Mikeal C. Parsons (1986; 1987, 29–52) and Bart D. Ehrman (1993, 227–33; cf. Zwiep 1996, 220n. 9). Against this position in favour of both phrases or the longer Alexandrian reading as the more original text, Zwiep has argued that the Western reviser removed these phrases together with other modifications in order to eliminate "any suggestion that Jesus ascended physically— with a body of flesh and bones—into heaven," reflecting second- and third-century criticism of "belief in a physical, observable ascension…in gnostic and docetic circles" (1996, 243). The motive for these emendations, however, may not have been only theological but also political, namely, to eliminate any suggestion that Jesus' ascension was a Roman imperial apotheosis. In this case, the *"heretical* corruption of Scripture" (Zwiep 1996, 244) would be the more "progressive" ideological critique.

While the disciples' question to Jesus in Acts 1:6, whether "at this time you will re-establish Israel's kingdom," is immediately rebuffed in Acts 1:7 with the disclaimer that "it is not yours to know the *chronous* or *kairous,* which the father has determined by his own *exousia,"* the statement also takes for granted that, in fact, it is this father—namely, God, to whose right hand Jesus is about to ascend and whence he is scheduled to return "just as you saw him go" (Acts 1:11)—who indeed determines by his authority (*exousia*) the duration of every kingdom on earth. The effect is equivalent to Jesus' concluding pronouncement in the Gospel of Matthew, where Jesus declares that now "all authority [*exousia*] has been given to me in heaven and on earth" (28:18). Although Luke-Acts does displace the concrete meaning of the imperative "to serve God rather than humans" away from imperial politics into the realm of personal virtue, the narrative of Jesus' ascension nonetheless provides all the ideological elements necessary to understand such service as ultimately realized within the elevated one's earthly empire.

The Book of Revelation (2:1–3:22)

One does not normally associate Luke-Acts with the Book of Revelation. Accommodation to Roman rule is hardly the key in which the latter work sings its hymn of diehard resistance. Even the revolutionary understatement that some scholars have surmised for the birth narrative and other parts of Luke-Acts stands in sharp contrast to the fierce polemic of Revelation, which all too obviously opposes the Roman Empire as the quintessential embodiment of everything that the visionary of the apocalypse considered to be evil in the ancient world. In celebrating the impending fall of the Great Whore, a.k.a. Babylon or Rome, and the concomitant marriage feast of the Lamb in Revelation 17:1–19:10, it can hardly be ignored how utterly the author of this work desired the Roman Empire's full destruction. Indeed, such an understanding has now become the standard interpretation.

Noteworthy, therefore, is the way in which this total opposition to the Roman Empire nonetheless finds expression in Revelation through Rome's own language of empire. Take, for example, the repeated invocation of God, viz. Lord God (*kyrios ho theos*) as *pantokratôr.* Except for 2 Corinthians 6:18, this way of referring to God (*pantokratôr*) only occurs in the New Testament in the Book of Revelation (1:8; 4:8; 11:17; 15:3; 16:7, 14; 19:6, 15; 21:22). Similarly, in Revelation 19:16, immediately after the fall of Babylon and the marriage feast of the Lamb, the rider on the white horse, whose

appearance marks the beginning of the end of the end of things, is explicitly an imperial figure, having written on his garment (as the hippest label)
and on his thigh (as the sexiest tattoo) the title, "King of kings and Lord
of lords" (for "king of kings" as part of ancient imperial speech, see Rudberg 1911). Previously in Revelation 17:14, the same title, "Lord of lords
and King of kings," belonged to the Lamb, which fights the ten kings or
horns of the beast that carries the Great Whore that is Babylon or Rome.
This Lamb is the same one that, in Revelation 5:8–14, was acclaimed and
invested from on high with all the attributes of total hegemony. The horizon of redemption in Revelation is a *coup d'état:* one emperor replaces
another.

Revealing in this regard are the textual variants for the final phrase in
Revelation 5:10. While a good variety of manuscripts state that those whom
the Lamb has made a *"basileian* and *hiereis* for our God...shall rule [*basileu-
sousin*—notably, still] on the earth," a second group of manuscripts asserts
that it is "we" who shall do this (*basileusomen*). Another set of variants
claims that the former group of persons already rule in the present tense
(*basileuousin*). Obviously, there was some interest in the details of the projected takeover.

Also notable in this regard is the fact that the new Jerusalem serves,
in the end, to replace the hated imperial city of Babylon or Rome. Though
certainly different from it in many respects, the heavenly city nonetheless
comes to occupy the very space that the latter once had filled.

Most telling, however, is, in my opinion, the literary style of the seven
letters to the seven churches in Revelation 2:1–3:22. For the voice that
speaks here is explicitly one of imperial authority. Already in 1911 Gunnar
Rudberg explored the formal correspondence that exists between these
celestial *communiqués* and "the well-known stone copy of a letter or rescript
of King Darius I to his Asia Minor official (governor) Gadatas" (1911, 171f.).
The inscription was found in 1886 in a village of Magnesia on the Maean-
der. Especially significant for Rudberg is the similar use, in both cases, of
the opening formula *tade legei,* together with a description of the imperial
subject who speaks and the specified reference to the intended recipient.
Rudberg also notes the similar juxtaposition of praise and censure in both
writings (1911, 172–73; for the *tade legei* formula, see also Stauffer 1955,
181; Lähnemann 1978, 200). Rudberg reviewed biblical and other ancient
evidence for such phraseology and found it to be specifically the language
of high (political) authority (1911, 173–78). At the same time, Rudberg
tried to explain the minor internal differences between these traditions.
Finally, after briefly discussing a few other inscriptions, Rudberg specu-

lated: "In the home region of the apocalyptic seer [of Revelation] there were probably Persian inscriptions, perhaps partly of the same sort as the letter of Darius in Magnesia. He also appears to have had ample opportunity to become familiar with them, since some of them were refurbished in the first century A.D." (1911, 179).

More recently, affirming and amplifying Rudberg's argument, David E. Aune (1997, 117–32, esp. pp. 126–29) similarly proposes that the seven proclamations to the seven churches reflect the form and content of ancient imperial edicts. Aune thinks that these proclamations also can be identified with a "paraenetic salvation-judgement oracle" (1997, 126)—a proposal I find far less compelling. Using especially the work of Margareta Benner, *The Emperor Says: Studies in the Rhetorical Style in Edicts of the Early Empire* (1975; see also Winterbottom 1977, 419–20; Fridh 1956), Aune makes the following comparisons:

> The *praescriptio,* with the verb of declaration, [i.e., the title(s) and name(s) of the issuing magistrate(s) or emperor plus *dicit/dicunt* or *legei/legousi*] is the only formal characteristic consistently recurring in imperial edicts. Each of the seven proclamations [in Revelation] begins with a *praescriptio* similar to those found in imperial edicts, except that in them the verb of declaration *precedes* the christological predications, while in imperial edicts it *follows* the name(s) and title(s) of the issuing magistrate(s) or emperor....
>
> While no counterpart to the *prooemium* [i.e., the preface, which was supposed to produce benevolence and interest on the part of the addresses] is found in the seven proclamations, its absence is appropriate in eastern provinces where the traditions of absolute sovereignty, first of the Persian monarchs and then of the Hellenistic kings, were predominant.
>
> The *narratio,* which occurs with some frequency in Roman edicts, often has the character of reported information (*renuntiatum est nobis*). The *narratio* has a functional counterpart in the [*oida*] clauses in each of the proclamations....
>
> The *dispositio* [expressing decisions] occurs in each proclamation, except that it is not introduced with the usual ordaining verb meaning "I command," but is influenced by the conditional style of prophetic speech consisting of ethical exhortations usually matched by conditional threats....
>
> Finally, statements with a function similar to the *sanctio* or *corroboratio* of Roman edicts [intended to bring about obedience to the enactment] are regularly found at the close of each proclamation in the conditional promise of victory. (Aune 1997, 128–29)

On the basis of this comparison, Aune concludes: "The author's use [in Revelation] of the royal/imperial edict form is part of his strategy to polarize God/Jesus and the Roman emperor, who is but a pale and diabolical imitation of God. In his role as the eternal sovereign and king of kings, Jesus is presented as issuing solemn and authoritative edicts befitting his status" (1997, 129). One might just as easily conclude, however, on the basis of the same comparison, that God and Jesus in Revelation are mirror-imitations of the Roman emperor. For this reason, to repeat the previous citation: "In his role as the eternal sovereign and king of kings, Jesus is presented [in Rev. 2:1–3:22] as issuing solemn and authoritative edicts befitting his status" (Aune 1997, 129). Such language, originally of resistance, soon would serve equally well as the discourse of succession.

The Pauline Corpus

The writings of Paul present a more puzzling paradigm, though not at the level of the Pauline Corpus itself. The complete presentation of the apostle and his thought in the fourteen writings that together make up his canonical legacy underscores very much as Luke-Acts does the good character of Christianity as imperial citizen. Thus, for example, 1 Timothy establishes as the first order of business in arranging the affairs of "the household of God...which is the assembly [ekklêsia] of the living God" (3:15), that one should "before all else make requests, prayers, petitions, thanksgivings on behalf of all persons, [which is to say,] on behalf of kings and all who are in positions of authority, so that we might lead a peaceful and quiet life in all piety and veneration" (2:1–4; cf. 1 Pet. 2:13–17). Similarly, the author of Ephesians makes it clear that "our struggle is not against enemies of blood and flesh," including presumably the present imperial order; rather, Christians are supposed to struggle against "the cosmic powers of this present darkness, against the spiritual forces of evil in heavenly places," and other things equally invisible and ethereal (6:12). The canonical reader is thereby encouraged to understand comparable pronouncements elsewhere in the corpus paulinum such as Romans 13:1–7 or 1 Thessalonians 4:12 as also advocating unswerving civil obedience.

Again, it does not really matter what the original meaning of these texts now is said to be. For example, Neil Elliott (1997b) struggles valiantly to make Paul not mean in Romans 13:1–7 everything that these verses have been understood to demand in the subsequent history of their interpretation. Elliott's concluding claim that "[o]nly the most pernicious twists of fate would later enlist these verses in the service of the empire itself" (1997b, 204) fails to consider how the Pauline Corpus itself already provided the context for such a reading. Moreover, insofar as the various writings of the Pauline Corpus all were read soon in the light or under the auspices of the Book of Acts, it is precisely the politically compliant or quiescent features of these texts, which logically one might assume also to be normative or typical for Paul in his letters.

Again as with Luke-Acts, there are other texts in the Pauline Corpus which once may have registered resistance or opposition to Roman rule. Precisely, however, because of the imperial tenor of these texts, they, too, soon would function just as well to explain (the prospect of) Christian dominance. Thus, for example, the image of the Christian assembly (*ekklêsia*) as the body of Christ, with Christ as its head, makes use of a number of stock political tropes in antiquity to explain the specific nature of the church. The symbol of the human body and its head was, in fact, a regular feature of Roman imperial propaganda. Consider, for example, what Angela Standhartinger writes about Colossians:

> The image of the state as a body that needs a head, whose lack or competing possibilities lead to war and destruction, is variously used in the time after the republic to legitimate the Roman emperor....Also the image of the ligaments and sinews, whereby the body is joined to the head, is used in presentations of the Roman ruler....In contrast with Roman state philosophy, it is not the emperor but Christ, in Colossians, who is the head of the *ekklêsia*, viz. the body. Christ in Colossians takes the place of the emperor. Not only has his good news or gospel already been proclaimed throughout the whole world (Col 1:5f, 23); he is also the head of the body, through which growth is made possible. The *ekklêsia* is his body, as the imperium is the body of the emperor. Finally, in Colossians, the rule of Christ not only guarantees unity but also peace (Col 3:15). The ecclesiology of Colossians thus competes with contemporary state philosophy. (Standhartinger 1999, 227–28; my translation)

Yet again, all of this may be true, exactly as stated, as far as it goes. The author of Colossians understood the early Christian assembly to constitute an alternate body politic to the Roman Empire with Christ as ersatz ruler (in this sense, "Christ in Colossians takes the place of the emperor"); an equally universal gospel provided all the standard benefits—unity and peace—of imperial rule. At the same time, this form of competition with contemporary state philosophy ultimately represents merely another instance of it (in this sense, "Christ in Colossians takes the place of the emperor"), since the only clear difference between the two competing options would be Christ instead of Caesar. Such personalized competition for supreme command was, once more, a standard feature of Roman imperial politics. Thus, the main difference between Colossians and Constantine would finally be a matter of degree, not of kind (cf. R.A. Horsley 1998, 166).

Even if we were to restrict our discussion, quite ahistorically, to the undisputedly authentic letters of Paul, there is still a profoundly imperial logic at work in these writings. Take, for example, Pauline eschatology (including soteriology and Christology). The promise that Paul makes in the name of the kingdom of God to those who have become, through baptism or reception of the spirit (of God, viz. Christ), co-inheritors with Christ (viz. Israel) of God's ultimate favour, is integration into God's eschatological household. Indeed, this is finally what (Gentile) salvation means for Paul: adoption into the *familia* of the divine (Jewish) world monarch. Adoption means the right to enjoy all the benefits and privileges that go with belonging to the ruling (end-time) imperial household. Not the least of these is assured escape or probable pardon from the master's proverbial wrath and its destructive consequences.

While there are many things in this ancient Mediterranean understanding of the human situation *coram deis et hominibus,* which hardly imply the sempiternity of the Roman Empire, the new creation or aeon or order that was supposed to follow the demise of the current arrangement of things (*to schêma tou kosmou toutou,* 1 Cor. 7:31) yet remains, for Paul, life under imperial rule. This is because the key problem, for Paul, is, ultimately, how to find oneself on the winning side of the impending eschatological contest, which is presumed to be God's side, and not among those who contrariwise are destined to lose or become lost. In other words, Paul's scenario of salvation takes for granted the imperial makeup of the world. Apparently, Paul could not imagine human life without empire, however much the apostle may have been persuaded that the prevailing order was finally untenable because inherently skewed. As the Roman Empire became less and less specifically Roman in its complexion and more and more a "multinational" conglomerate, the Pauline promise of early Christian integration through "our *kyrios* Jesus Christ" into the next divinely ordered imperial household thus easily provided the rationale for an ever more explicitly Christian vision of political hegemony.

Certainly this is true for the earliest of Paul's extant letters. In 1 Thessalonians 4:15–17, the prospect of Jesus' imminent *parousia*—already announced in 1:10 as due "from heaven...[to] rescue us from the coming wrath"—is described as the arrival of an imperial representative at the gates of the city. According to Koester: "It has been a general assumption that the *parousia* is used as a technical term for the eschatological coming of Jesus or the Son of Man. However, there is no evidence in pre-

Christian apocalyptic literature for such technical usage. If there is any 'technical' use of *parousia* it appears in the terminology for the arrival of a king or an emperor" (1997, 158; cf. Rigaux 1956, 198; also Josephus, *A.J.* 11.327ff.). Likewise, the reference in 4:17 to "meeting" the Lord uses a term that typically was associated with the reception of an imperial visitor: "*Apantêsis* is a technical term describing the festive and formal meeting of a king or other dignitary who arrives for a visit of a city. It is the crucial term for Paul's description of the festive reception of the Lord at his coming. The united community, those who are alive and those who have died and have been raised, will meet the Lord like a delegation of a city that goes out to meet and greet an emperor when he comes to visit" (Koester 1997, 160; cf. Peterson 1929–1930; 1933, 14–15; Best 1972, 199, for further bibliography).

For Erik Peterson (1929–1930) the significance of this association is the logic it implies of a return to the place (city) whence the welcoming party first departed. In this case, the purpose of "being snatched up on clouds to meet the Lord in the air" would be to accompany him back down to earth, where "thus we shall be always with the Lord." Although Koester (1997, 160n. 8) agrees with Peterson's philology, Koester simply dismisses the other question of "where the believers will be after this festive meeting of the Lord as unnecessarily speculative" (1997, 160n. 10). The political implications of the issue, however, hardly are so.

Finally, regarding Paul's pronouncement in 1Thessalonians 5:3, which states: "Whenever they say, 'Peace and Security,' then sudden destruction will come upon them as birth-pangs to a pregnant woman and they will not escape," Koester contends: "As a political slogan, *eirênê kai asphaleia* = *pax et securitas* is best ascribed to the realm of imperial Roman propaganda. If this interpretation of the phrase is correct, it would imply that Paul points to the coming of the day of the Lord as an event that will shatter the false peace and security of the Roman establishment" (Koester 1997, 162; cf. Bammel 1960, 837; Frend 1965, 96, 124n. 69). "Shatter" is the operative word, for what is supposed to come next is, in fact, no less violent and coercive than the "false peace and security of the Roman establishment." At least, the subsequent reference in 5:5 to local Christians being as "children of light" and of day is taken by Koester as evidence that a Qumran-like "notion of eschatological battle lies much closer to Paul's thought here than some kind of baptismal piety." In addition, there is also Paul's "subsequent use of the images of the weapons of God" in 5:8f. (Koester 1997, 162f.). Indeed, the Thessalonians are exhorted in these verses to put on the armour of faith and love and the hope of salvation (*elpida sôtêrias*), for whose possession (*eis peripoiêsin sôtêrias*) they have been divinely destined "through our *kyrios* Jesus Christ" (cf. also 1 Thess. 1:3).

Koester thinks that the reference in 1 Thessalonians 5:8 to faith, hope, and love somehow transforms the "traditional apocalyptic language with which [Paul] had started the passage" into an affirmation of the Thessalonians as "the architects of the new eschatological community in which the future is becoming a present reality" (1997, 163). Whatever may be true in this statement vis-à-vis the early Christian experience of time, it is difficult to discern what is new about the eschatological community. Since in Koester's own description of this community it is constituted through the conventional conviction that its destiny will be established by the timely intervention—past and future—of a heavenly warlord, "our *kyrios* Jesus Christ," whose eventual appearance on the nimbused outskirts of the city the Thessalonians are urged to anticipate as the next imperial visitation.

Karl P. Donfried rehearses the same data, noting also the reference in 1 Thessalonians 2:12 to God's call "into his own kingdom" plus the use of *kyrios* in the eastern Mediterranean from the time of Augustus to refer to the Roman emperors, "although the first verifiable inscription of the *Kyrios*-title in Greece dates to the time of Nero" (1997, 217; cf. Deissmann 1927, 351–58). Donfried takes these correspondences or connotations to explain how Paul's preaching "could be understood or misunderstood in a distinctly political sense" (1997, 216). In fact, Paul's preaching in 1 Thessalonians is plainly political, whether this was the case naively—due to its use of apocalyptic traditions—or deliberately.

The triad of faith, love, and hope in 1 Thessalonians 5:8 merely registers the early Christian name for its form of ideal *oikodomê,* which the Romans called *pax et securitas* (cf. Koester 1997, 165). The ideological opposition between 1 Thessalonians 5:3 and 5:8f. is therefore essentially the contrast between them and us. Like Koester, Donfried also endeavours to discover a greater significance for the formula "faith, love, and hope." On the basis of the dual reference to "faith and love" in 1 Thessalonians 3:6 and the strong emphasis on hope elsewhere in the letter (1 Thess. 1:10; 2:19; 3:13), Donfried concludes that "it is likely that what is lacking in the faith of the Thessalonians is the dimension of hope" (1997, 220). Donfried thinks that the Thessalonians had suffered some sort of civic persecution, mainly on the basis of the references to affliction, struggle, and suffering in the letter (1 Thess. 1:6; 2:2, 14; 3:3, 4; cf. Phil. 1:30). None of this makes any difference politically. The Christian community in Thessalonica may have been, in Koester's words, "a utopian alternative to the prevailing eschatological ideology of Rome." But, again, it was alternative in form, not substance, since the salvation in view is essentially the same. In the end, Koester's claim is an empty one: a negative assertion, limited to the deconstruction of "traditional apocalyptic topics" and "postures" (1997, 166).

In the case of the early Christian community at Corinth, if Paul had determined initially to know nothing among them but "Jesus Christ and him crucified" (1 Cor. 2:2), opining subsequently that if "the rulers of this age" (*tôn archontôn tou aiônos toutou*) had known the preordained countercultural wisdom of God "they would not have crucified the Lord of glory" (2:8), the risen Christ nonetheless continues to be described by Paul in his correspondence with the Corinthians as a conquering general, whose own eventual submission to God will occur only after all other things have been made subject to him (cf. R.A. Horsley 1998, 162). Indeed, the eschatological scene in 1 Corinthians 15:20–28 unabashedly recalls the triumphal procession of a Roman military chief of staff returning to the imperial city, first, to display the evidence of his far-flung conquests before then submitting to the governing authority of the Senate. That this end-time scenario also might derive, in part, from Jewish apocalyptic speculation hardly diminishes its Roman imperial connotations.

Traces of the image of a triumphal procession are also present in 2 Corinthians 2:14. According to Klaus Wengst: "When Paul continues in II Cor. 2.14, 'And reveals the fragrance of his knowledge through us all everywhere,' he is retaining the image of the triumphal procession. For the mention of 'fragrance' might be made in this context against the background of the custom of carrying containers with incense alongside the triumphal chariot, from which clouds of incense ascended to heaven" (1986, 206n. 74; cf. Carr 1981, 62f). Conceivably, the thorn in Paul's flesh, which is immediately identified as an *aggelos Satanas* who beat Paul lest he should become overly inflated after his brief sojourn in paradise (2 Cor 12:7), similarly recalls, albeit sardonically, the slave who stood behind each general returning triumphantly to Rome in order to remind him that *sic transit gloria mundi*. Not surprisingly, in 1 Corinthians 15:23, Paul continues to anticipate with all the same connotations as before the *parousia* of the Lord Jesus Christ. The horizon of Paul's hope remains as imperial as ever.

Even so, Paul's so-called theology of the Cross, to which especially the statements in 1 Corinthians 2:2, 8 have seemed to so many scholars to bear witness, could represent a countervailing, if not wholly "anti-Roman-imperial," perspective on the part of the apostle. This presumes, of course, that Paul had a theology of the Cross. According to Neil Elliott: "It is impossible to exaggerate the importance of the cross of Jesus Christ to Paul" (1997a, 167). In my opinion, however, such a claim is, exegetically, a gross exaggeration. Reference to the Cross or its equivalent is hardly a leitmotif of the different Pauline writings: mention is made of it only in 1 Corinthians 1:13, 17, 18, 23; 2:2, 8; 2 Corinthians 13:4; Philippians 2:8; 3:18; Galatians 2:19; 3:1; 5:11, 24; 6:12, 14; Romans 6:6. Notice that any such reference is completely lacking in 1 Thessalonians and Philemon; in 2 Corinthians and Romans, the reference is almost incidental. Even in Philippians, I would argue, the two references to the Cross are essentially rhetorical flourishes. In the case of 1 Corinthians, only in the first two chapters does the Cross play any explicit role in Paul's argument. Every other issue in this letter Paul resolves by other means. Whatever, therefore, the particular significance might be of the more frequent references to the Cross in Galatians, this significance cannot simply be exported to the other Pauline writings. References to Jesus' death are not simply equivalent to a statement about the Crucifixion, if only because the more generic expression "death" lacks precisely the politically charged overtones of "crucifixion" as state-sponsored execution.

Paul obviously knew that Jesus had died on a cross and that such a death was not a noble one. Nonetheless, there is no evidence to suggest that Paul thought to make a political virtue out of this servile, criminal fact. To the extent that Jesus' death became increasingly a significant feature of Paul's understanding of the gospel he proclaimed to Gentiles, the saving dimension of Jesus' death reciprocally had less and less to do with the specific act of crucifixion. At least, I find the essential absence of any reference to the Cross in Romans a striking feature of this letter. Rather, it was both Jesus' erstwhile and Paul's own probable death—i.e., the most universal and ordinary experience of human vulnerability—which Paul increasingly incorporated into his own ever more fragile experience (albeit with enduring conviction) of God's new creation in Christ through the spirit.

For this reason I am not inclined to find in Paul's reference to "Jesus Christ and him crucified" in 1 Corinthians 2:2 or any of the other (relatively few) pronouncements regarding the Cross and Crucifixion in the Corinthian correspondence further evidence of the apostle's "anti-imperial" proclamation. In my judgment, none of these has much, if anything at all, to do with the political imaginary here at work. In 1 Corinthians 1–2 the references to the Cross and Crucifixion serve primarily as rhetorical counterpoint to the competing claims of greater wisdom and social standing as the defined benefits of the early Christian offer of salvation (see, further, Vaage 1994).

R.A. Horsley thinks that Paul's counsel in 1 Corinthians 5–6 is definitely "anti-Roman-imperial," because the apostle is supposed to advocate here autonomous adjudication of intramural conflict "in complete independence of 'the world,'" which is to say, among the "holy" confreres and not before the "unjust" civic authorities (1 Cor 6:1; R.A. Horsley 1997, 245). Nonetheless, R.A. Horsley claims, this "did not mean completely shutting themselves off from the society in which they lived"; "[t]he believers should thus not cut off all contact with 'the immoral of this world, or the greedy and robbers'" (1997, 245)—even though this is precisely what the rhetoric of 1 Corinthians 5–6 repeatedly implies. As R.A. Horsley himself contends: "The assembly's independence and autonomy, moreover, meant that members should work out *any and all* disputes within the community and have *no* relations with the dominant society, such as resorting to the established courts" (1997, 246; emphasis mine).

Likewise, in 1 Corinthians 8–10, regarding the consumption of food-offered-to-idols, R.A. Horsley writes: "Paul insists on political-religious solidarity *over against* the dominant society which was constituted precisely in such banquets or 'fellowship/sharing' with gods. For the members of the new alternative community that meant *cutting themselves off* from the very means by which their previously essential social-economic relations were maintained" (1997, 249; emphasis mine). According to R.A. Horsley: "The law and the courts in the Roman Empire were instruments of social control, a vested interest of the wealthy and powerful elite which operated for their own advantage over that of those of lesser status." Paul's insistence that "the assembly run its own affairs" would represent "a complete declaration of independence and autonomy" akin to other contemporary "[s]tatements of self-government" (R.A. Horsley 1997, 246–47; cf. Wengst 1986, 76–77, who underscores repeatedly that, in 1 Cor. 6:1–8, Paul "presupposes the recognition of law and norms," despite the inherent injustice of the Roman legal system).

In fact, Paul's outrage at the Corinthian community's practice expresses not diplomatic anxiety about imprudent behaviour or a strategic misstep but, rather, reflects the standard anxieties of ancient honour: "Or do you not know that the 'saints' will judge the world?…Do you not know that we shall judge angels, not to mention *biotica?*" (1 Cor. 6:2–3). The underlying rationale is the old-fashioned one of the hierarchy of superior over inferior: in R.A. Horsley's terms, the purview of an "elite [to wit, the 'saints'] which operated for their own advantage [to inherit the kingdom of God: see 1 Cor. 6:9–10] over that of those of lesser status," for example, all the "bad" people listed in 1 Corinthians 5:11; 6:9–10. There is little, if anything, in Paul's argument here to distinguish early Christian aspirations from those of the last legal lords.

In addition, R.A. Horsley proposes that (i) the prohibition of food-offered-to-idols in 1 Corinthians 8–10, (ii) Paul's refusal to accept economic support from the Corinthians, and (iii) the collection for the poor among the saints in Jerusalem, all manifest the same "anti-Roman-imperial" stance (1997, 247–51). Most of this, however, simply represents a tendentious or erroneous reading of the evidence. Regarding Paul's refusal to accept economic support, R.A. Horsley seems not to recognize how thoroughly he contradicts his own argument with the admission:

> Paul did not come up with *any* vision of an alternative political economy for his alternative society—which would have been extraordinary for antiquity. In his explanation of why he did not accept support, he simply resorted to the imagery of household administration...with the implied image of God as the divine estate owner and himself as the steward. Such imagery fits with similar controlling metaphors, such as God as a monarch, Christ as the alternative emperor, and himself as the Lord's 'servant' or 'slave.' He used his overall controlling vision of the 'kingdom' of God as a basis for rejecting the patronage system, but remained within that traditional biblical vision. (R.A. Horsley 1997, 250–51; emphasis mine)

In *Paul and Empire,* R.A. Horsley repeatedly claims: "in his mission Paul was building an international alternative society (the 'assembly') based in local egalitarian communities ('assemblies')" (1997, 8; further, R.A. Horsley 1998, 163, 176). The picture supposedly emerging from the Corinthian correspondence is "not one of a religious cult, but of a nascent social movement comprised of a network of cells based in Corinth but spreading more widely into the province of Achaia. That is surely indicated when Paul, writing later in coordination of the collection 'for the poor among the saints in Jerusalem,' refers not to Corinth alone but to Achaia more generally, just as he refers not simply to the Thessalonians or Philippians but to 'the assemblies of Macedonia' in general (2 Cor. 8:2; 9:2, 4)" (R.A. Horsley 1997, 245). R.A. Horsley, however, fails to consider the philological fact that Paul uses the singular *ekklēsia* only to refer to what *Paul* himself once sought to harass and destroy before his subsequent encounter with Christ (1 Cor. 15:9; Gal. 1:13; Phil. 3:6). Otherwise, Paul always refers to early Christian groups either as the local association or in the plural. The contrast, in this regard, with the vision of *the* church in Colossians and Ephesians could hardly be more striking or instructive. The difficulties, moreover, which Paul encountered in raising *his* collection for the poor in Jerusalem, suggest precisely not a sense of class solidarity or international consciousness on the part of the Pauline communities but, rather, the usual human reluctance to participate in projects of aid to total strangers. Paul's broad generalizations about support from Achaia and Macedonia are just that: rhetorical exaggerations.

In Philippians 3:20, Paul again speaks of "our *politeuma* in the heavens," whence early Christians were to await a saviour (*sôtêr*), in accordance with whose *euaggelion* Paul had exhorted the Philippians earlier in the epistle "worthily…[to] behave as citizens" (*axiôs…politeuesthe,* 1:27). The situation here recalls 1 Thessalonians. According to R.A. Horsley, Philippians 3:20 "sharply opposes Jesus Christ as Lord to the imperial saviour" (1997, 141). But, again, there is no indication that this "sharp" opposition finally means anything other than a Christian candidate for imperial champion: i.e., "Jesus Christ as Lord." Similarly, the early Christian hymn in Philippians 2:6–11, R.A. Horsley claims (citing Dieter Georgi), "must have suggested the events surrounding the [death] of a *princeps* and his heavenly assumption and apotheosis" (1997, 141). According to R.A. Horsley: "Paul's borrowing from and allusions to language central to the imperial cult and ideology reveal and dramatize just how anti-Roman imperial his own gospel was" (1997, 141). Yet again, however, the very same facts and line of reasoning explain just as easily why this discourse soon could authorize and even require Christian imperial pretensions.

The preceding discussion of the letters of Paul and the Pauline Corpus, together with the Book of Revelation and selected scenes from Luke-Acts, obviously cannot and does not claim to be exhaustive or even fully representative. My purpose here is merely suggestive: to propose an expressly political reading of the New Testament and, on this basis, an assessment of earliest Christianity as inherently imperial in its discursive formation. In this section, I have tried to demonstrate the degree to which a recurring pattern of reinscription of especially Roman codes of empire can be observed in a broad range of New Testament texts, whose original intention likely was precisely to resist this very thing. Indeed, it is exactly this curious combination of explicit antagonism and implicit imitation which made Christianity, in my opinion, particularly suited to succeed (in) the Roman Empire.

CONCLUSION

My proposal is quite simple, if far-reaching: earliest Christianity was inherently an imperial religion, which is to say, a social movement decisively shaped by the political culture of the Roman Empire, under whose aegis it first came into being (cf. R.A. Horsley 1997, 1: "Christianity was a product of empire"). The imperial essence of Christianity, however, is manifest neither uniquely nor even most tellingly in evidence of its accommodation to the dominant social structures and ideological expectations of the Roman Empire. Rather, I suggest, earliest Christianity's intrinsic will to rule is most evident, albeit paradoxically, in its initial modes of resistance to this regime. Hence, when R.A. Horsley writes: "Ironic as it may seem, precisely where he is borrowing from or alluding to 'imperial' language, we can discern that Paul's gospel stands counter primarily to the Roman imperial order, 'this world, which is passing away'" (1997, 7), Horsley is both right and wrong. It may be—indeed, I do not doubt—that Paul himself meant to oppose contemporary Roman rule. But precisely because his language of opposition was derived from the discourse of empire, the long-term legacy of such speech could hardly be anything other than a recurrence of the same.

In a sense, earliest Christianity is a type of cargo cult—albeit, in this case, the cargo in question was a certain political lexicon rather than a set of commercial commodities, and mindful of Jonathan Z. Smith's suggestion that cargo cults are finally not a general type of religion but a specifically Oceanic phenomenon, due to the regional mythology that defines the lost ancestors as white (1982b). Nonetheless, in practice, both traditions would be alike in worshipping the god that otherwise threatened to destroy them. Early Christianity is distinctive as a cargo cult simply because it worked as scripted, perhaps due primarily to the fact that its forms of utopian rewriting rehearsed with such resistance the language of succession.

Works Cited

Achtemeier, Paul J. 1996. *1 Peter: A commentary on First Peter.* Ed. Eldon Jay Epp. Hermeneia. Minneapolis: Fortress.

Aleshire, Sara B. 1992. The economics of dedication at the Athenian Asklepieion. In *Economics of cult in the ancient Greek world: Proceedings of the Uppsala Symposium 1990*, ed. Tullia Linders and Brita Alroth, 85–92. Stockholm: Almquist and Wiksell.

Alföldy, Géza. 1974. *Noricum.* Trans. Anthony Birley. London: Routledge and Kegan Paul.

Allen, Roland. 1962. *Missionary methods: St. Paul's or ours?* Orig. pub. 1912. Grand Rapids, MI: Eerdmans.

Amaru, Betsy Halpern. 1980–1981. Land theology in Josephus' *Jewish Antiquities. JQR* 71:201–29.

Amundsen, Darrel W., and Gary B. Ferngren. 1982a. Medicine and religion: Pre-Christian antiquity. In *Health-medicine and the faith traditions: An inquiry into religion and medicine*, ed. Martin E. Marty and Kenneth L. Vaux, 53–92. Philadelphia: Fortress.

———. 1982b. Medicine and religion: Early Christianity through the Middle Ages. In *Health-medicine and the faith traditions: An inquiry into religion and medicine*, ed. Martin E. Marty and Kenneth L. Vaux, 93–131. Philadelphia: Fortress.

Anonymous. 1997. Parabolani. In *Oxford dictionary of the Christian Church*, ed. E.A. Livingstone. 3rd ed. Oxford: Oxford University Press.

Applebaum, Shimon. 1976. The social and economic status of the Jews in the Diaspora. In *The Jewish people in the first century*, ed. Samuel Safrai and Moritz Stern, Vol. 1, 701–27. Assen: Van Goreum.

Ariès, Philippe, and Georges Duby, eds. 1987. *A history of private life.* Vol. 1. *From Pagan Rome to Byzantium*, ed. Paul Veyne. Trans. Arthur Goldhammer. Cambridge, MA: Harvard University Press.

Attridge, Harold W. 1976. *The interpretation of biblical history in the* Antiquitates Judaicae *of Flavius Josephus*. Missoula, MT: Scholars.

Aune, David E. 1991. Romans as a *Logos Protreptikos*. In *The Romans debate*, rev. and expanded ed., ed. Karl P. Donfried, 278–96. Peabody, MA: Hendrickson.

———. 1997. *Revelation 1–5*. WBC 52. Dallas: Word.

Aus, Roger D. 1979. Paul's travel plans to Spain and the "Full Number of Gentiles" in Rom. XI 25. *NovT* 21:232–62.

Avalos, Hector. 1999. *Health care and the rise of Christianity*. Peabody, MA: Hendrickson.

Bailey, J.L. 1987. Josephus' portrayal of the matriarchs. In *Josephus, Judaism and Christianity*, ed. Louis H. Feldman and Gohei Hata, 154–79. Detroit: Wayne State University Press.

Bakhtin, Mikhail Mikhailovich. 1968. *Rabelais and his world*. Trans. Helene Iswolsky. Boston: M.I.T. Press.

Balch, David L. 1981. *Let wives be submissive: The domestic code in 1 Peter*. SBL 26. Chico, CA: Scholars.

Bamberger, Bernard J. 1968. *Proselytism in the Talmudic period*. Orig. pub. 1939. New York: KTAV.

Bammel, Ernst. 1960. Ein Beitrag zur paulinischen Staatsanschauung. *ThLZ* 85:837–40.

Banks, Robert. 1983. The early Church as a caring community. *ERT* 7:310–27.

Barclay, John M.G. 1995a. Deviance and apostasy: Some applications of deviance theory to first-century Judaism and Christianity. In *Modelling early Christianity: Social-scientific studies of the New Testament in its context*, ed. Philip F. Esler, 114–27. London: Routledge.

———. 1995b. Paul among Diaspora Jews: Anomaly or apostate? *JSNT* 60:89–120.

———. 1996. *Jews in the Mediterranean Diaspora: From Alexander to Trajan (323 BCE–117 CE)*. Edinburgh: T. and T. Clark.

———. 1998. Who was considered an apostate in the Jewish Diaspora? In *Tolerance and intolerance in early Judaism and Christianity*, ed. Graham N. Stanton and Guy G. Strousma, 80–98. Cambridge: Cambridge University Press.

Barker, Ernest. 1927. Greek political thought and theory in the fourth century. In *The Cambridge ancient history*, ed. John Bagnell Bury et al., Vol. 4, 505–35. Cambridge: Cambridge University Press.

Barnes, Jonathan. 1986. Hellenistic philosophy and science. In *The Oxford history of the classical world: Greece and the Hellenistic world*, ed. John Boardman et al., 359–79. Oxford: Oxford University Press.

Baron, Salo Wittmayer. 1952. *A social and religious history of the Jews*. 2nd ed. New York: Columbia University Press.

Barrett, Charles Kingsley. 1970. *The Gospel of John and Judaism*. Philadelphia: Fortress.

———. 1994–1998. *A critical and exegetical commentary on the Acts of the Apostles*. 2 vols. International Critical Commentary. Edinburgh: T. and T. Clark.

Barrett-Lennard, R.J.S. 1994. *Christian healing after the New Testament.* Lanham, MD: University Press of America.

Bauckham, Richard. 1998. Jews and Jewish Christians in the land of Israel at the time of the Bar Kochba war, with special reference to the Apocalypse of Peter. In *Tolerance and intolerance in early Judaism and Christianity*, ed. Graham N. Stanton and Guy G. Strousma, 228–38. Cambridge: Cambridge University Press.

Beard, Mary, and John North, eds. 1990. *Pagan priests.* London: Duckworth.

Beard, Mary, John North, and Simon Price. 1998. *Religions of Rome.* 2 vols. Cambridge: Cambridge University Press.

Beck, Roger. 1976–1978. Interpreting the Ponza Zodiac. *JMS* 1:1–19; 2:87–147.

———. 1984. Mithraism since Franz Cumont. *ANRW* 2.18.4:2002–15.

———. 1992. The Mithras cult as association. *SR* 21:3–13.

———. 1995. Cosmic models: Some uses of Hellenistic science in Roman religion. *Apeiron* 27/4 [1994]:99–117.

———. 1996a. Mystery religions, aretalogy and the ancient novel. In *The novel in the ancient world*, ed. Gareth Schmeling, 131–50. Leiden: Brill.

———. 1996b. The Mysteries of Mithras. In *Voluntary Associations in the Graeco-Roman world*, ed. John S. Kloppenborg and Stephen G. Wilson, 176–85. London: Routledge.

———. 1998a. The Mysteries of Mithras: A new account of their genesis. *JRS* 88:115–28.

———. 1998b. *Qui mortalitatis causa convenerunt:* The meeting of the Virunum Mithraists on June 26, A.D. 184. *Phoenix* 52:335–44.

———. 2000. Ritual, myth, doctrine, and initiation in the Mysteries of Mithras: New evidence from a cult vessel. *JRS* 90:145–80.

Becker, Jürgen. 1993. *Paul: Apostle to the Gentiles.* Louisville: Westminster/Knox.

Begg, Christopher T. 1993. *Josephus' account of the early divided monarchy (AJ 8, 212–420): Rewriting the Bible.* Leuven: Peeters.

———. 1997. Solomon's apostasy (1 Kings 11, 13) according to Josephus. *JSJ* 28:294–313.

Behr, Charles A. 1968. *Aelius Aristides and the Sacred Tales.* Amsterdam: Hakkert.

Benner, Margareta. 1975. *The Emperor says: Studies in the rhetorical style in edicts of the early Empire.* Göteborg: Acta Universitatis Gothoburgensis.

Beskow, P. 1980. The *Portorium* and the Mysteries of Mithras. *JMS* 3:1–18.

Best, Ernest. 1972. *A commentary on the First and Second Epistles to the Thessalonians.* Black's New Testament Commentaries. London: A. and C. Black.

Betz, Hans Dieter. 1979. *Galatians.* Hermeneia. Philadelphia: Fortress.

Bevan, Edwyn. 1940. *Holy Images.* London: Allen and Unwin.

Bickermann, Elias. 1929. Die römische Kaiserapotheose. *ARW* 27:1–34.

Bilde, Per. 1988. *Flavius Josephus between Jerusalem and Rome.* JSPS 2. Sheffield: JSOT.

Blass, Friedrich, Albert Debrunner, and Robert W. Funk. 1961. *A Greek grammar of the New Testament and other early Christian literature.* Chicago: University of Chicago Press.

Boak, Arthur Edward Romilly. 1955. *Manpower shortage and the fall of the Roman Empire in the West*. Ann Arbor: University of Michigan Press.

Bonnard, Georges A., ed. 1966. *Memoirs of My Life*, by Edward Gibbon. London: Nelson.

Borgen, Peder. 1995. "Yes," "No," "How Far?": The participation of Jews and Christians in pagan cults. In *Paul in his Hellenistic context*, ed. Troels Engberg-Pedersen, 30–59. Minneapolis: Fortress.

Bornkamm, Günther. 1971. *Paul*. New York: Harper and Row.

Bowers, Paul. 1991. Church and mission in Paul. *JSNT* 44:89–111.

Bowersock, Glen Warren. 1995. *Martyrdom and Rome*. Cambridge: Cambridge University Press.

Box, George Herbert. 1929. *Early Christianity and its rivals*. London: Benn.

Bradeen, Donald W. 1975. The popularity of the Athenian empire. In *Problems in ancient history*, 2nd ed., ed. Donald Kagan, 404–11. New York: Macmillan.

Braude, William G. 1940. *Jewish proselyting in the first five centuries of the Common Era, the age of the Tannaim and Amoraim*. Providence: Brown University.

Braun, Willi. 1999. Sociology, Christian growth and the obscurum of Christianity's imperial formation in Rodney Stark's *The Rise of Christianity*. *RelSRev* 25:128–32.

Breitwieser, Rupert. 1995. Virunum und die "antoninische Pest." *Grazer Beiträger* 21:149–56.

Bringmann, Klaus. 1993. "The king as benefactor: Some remarks on ideal kingship in the Age of Hellenism." In *Images and ideologies: Self-definition in the Hellenistic world*, ed. Anthony Bulloch et al., 7–24. HCS 12. Berkeley: University of California Press.

Brown, Peter R.L. 1978. *The making of late antiquity*. Cambridge, MA: Harvard University Press.

Brown, Raymond E. 1966. *The Gospel according to John*. Vol. 1. Anchor Bible 29. Garden City, NY: Doubleday.

———. 1977. *The birth of the Messiah: A commentary on the infancy narratives in Matthew and Luke*. Garden City, NY: Doubleday.

———. 1979. *The community of the beloved disciple*. New York: Paulist.

———. 1997. *An introduction to the New Testament*. New York: Doubleday.

Browning, Robert. 1976. The crisis of the Greek city: A new collective study. *Philologus* 120:258–65.

Bruce, Frederick Fyvie. 1977. *Paul: Apostle of the heart set free*. Grand Rapids, MI: Eerdmans.

———. 1982. *The Epistle to the Galatians: A commentary on the Greek text*. New International Greek Testament Commentary. Grand Rapids, MI: Eerdmans.

Brunt, Peter Anthony. 1990. *Roman imperial themes*. Oxford: Clarendon.

Bryant, Joseph M. 1997. Review of Stark 1996. *Sociology of Religion* 58:191–95.

Buchholz, Dennis D. 1988. *Your eyes will be opened: A study of the Greek (Ethiopic) Apocalypse of Peter*. SBLDS 97. Atlanta: Scholars.

Budde, Gerard. 1931. Christian charity: Now and always. *Ecclesiastical Review* 85:561–79.

Burkert, Walter. 1987. *Ancient mystery cults.* Cambridge, MA: Harvard University Press.

Burton, Ernest de Witt. 1921. *A critical and exegetical commentary on the Epistle to the Galatians.* International Critical Commentary. Edinburgh: T. and T. Clark.

Burton, G.P. 1975. Proconsuls, assizes and the administration of justice under the empire. *JRS* 65:92–106.

———. 1993. Provincial procurators and the public provinces. *Chiron* 23:13–28.

Canetti, Elias. 1978. *Crowds and power.* Trans. Carol Stewart. New York: Seabury.

Carcopino, Jérôme. 1941. *Daily life in ancient Rome.* Ed. Henry T. Rowell. Trans. E.O. Lorimer. Harmondsworth, Middlesex: Penguin.

Carney, Thomas F. 1975. *The shape of the past: Models and antiquity.* Lawrence, KS: Coronado.

Carr, Wesley. 1981. *Angels and principalities: The background, meaning and development of the Pauline phrase* hai archai kai exousiai. Cambridge: Cambridge University Press.

Carson, Donald A. 1987. The purpose of the fourth Gospel: John 20:31 reconsidered. *JBL* 106:639–51.

Cassidy, Richard J. 1978. *Jesus, politics and society: A study of Luke's Gospel.* Maryknoll, NY: Orbis.

———. 1987. *Society and politics in the Acts of the Apostles.* Maryknoll, NY: Orbis.

Castelli, Elizabeth. 1998. Gender, theory, and the rise of Christianity: A response to Rodney Stark. *JECS* 6:227–57.

Clauss, Manfred. 1990. *Mithras: Kult und Mysterien.* Munich: Beck.

———. 1992. *Cultores Mithrae: Die Anhängerschaft des Mithras-Kultes.* Stuttgart: Steiner.

———. 1995. Review of Piccottini 1994. *Klio* 77:524–25.

Clay, Diskin. 1986. The cults of Epicurus. *CErc* 16:11–28.

Clerc, Michel. 1885. Inscription de Nysa. *Bulletin de correspondance hellénique* 9:124–31.

Cohen, Shaye J.D. 1979. *Josephus in Galilee and Rome: His* vita *and development as a historian.* CSCT 8. Leiden: Brill.

———. 1987a. *From the Maccabees to the Mishnah.* LEC 7. Philadelphia: Westminster.

———. 1987b. Respect for Judaism by Gentiles according to Josephus. *HTR* 80: 409–30.

———. 1988. History and historiography in the *Against Apion* of Josephus. *History and Theory* 27: 1–11.

———. 1991. Adolf Harnack's "The Mission and Expansion of Judaism": Christianity succeeds where Judaism fails. In *The Future of early Christianity: Essays in honor of Helmut Koester,* ed. Birger A. Pearson et al., 163–69. Minneapolis: Fortress.

————. 1992. Was Judaism in antiquity a missionary religion? In *Jewish assimilation, acculturation, and accommodation*, ed. Menahem Mor, 14–23. Lanham, MD: University Press of America.

————. 1993. "Those who say they are Jews and are not": How do you know a Jew in antiquity when you see one? In *Diasporas in antiquity*, ed. Shaye J.D. Cohen and Ernest S. Frerichs, 1–45. BJS 288. Atlanta: Scholars.

Collins, John Joseph. 1983. *Between Athens and Jerusalem: Jewish identity in the Hellenistic Diaspora*. New York: Crossroad.

————. 1985. A symbol of otherness: Circumcision and salvation in the first century. In *To see ourselves as others see us: Christians, Jews, "Others" in Late Antiquity*, ed. Jacob Neusner and Ernest S. Frerichs,163–86. Chico, CA: Scholars.

Collins, Randall. 1999. Applying contemporary religious sociology to early Christianity. *RelSRev* 25:136–39.

Conze, Alexander, and Carl Schuchhardt. 1899. Die Arbeiten zu Pergamon. *MDAI(A)* 24:164–240.

Conzelmann, Hans. 1964. *Die Mitte der Zeit: Studien zur Theologie des Lukas*. Tübingen: Mohr (Siebeck).

————. 1973. *History of primitive Christianity*. Trans. John E. Steely. Nashville: Abingdon.

Countryman, L. William. 1980. *The rich Christian in the Church of the early Empire: Contradictions and accommodations*. New York: Mellen.

Cranfield, Charles E.B. 1966. Diakonia in the New Testament. In *Service in Christ: Essays presented to Karl Barth on his 80th Birthday*, ed. James McCord and T. Parker, 37–48. Grand Rapids, MI: Eerdmans.

Cullmann, Oscar. 1975. *The Johannine Circle*. Trans. John Bowden. Philadelphia: Westminster.

Culpepper, R. Alan. 1987. The Gospel of John and the Jews. *RevExp* 84:273–80.

————. 1998. *The Gospel and letters of John*. Nashville: Abingdon.

Cumont, Franz. 1956a. *The Mysteries of Mithra*. Trans. Thomas J. McCormack. Orig. pub. 1903. New York: Dover.

————. 1956b. *The Oriental religions in Roman paganism*. Orig. pub. 1911. New York: Dover.

Daniel, Jerry L. 1981. Apologetics in Josephus. Ph.D. diss., Rutgers University.

Daniels, C.M. 1975. The Role of the Roman army in the spread and practice of Mithraism. *Mithraic studies: Proceedings of the first international conference of Mithraic studies*, 2 vols., ed. John R. Hinnells, Vol. 2, 249–74. Manchester: Manchester University Press.

Davies, John Kenyon. 1984. Cultural, social and economic features of the Hellenistic world. In *The Cambridge ancient history*, 2nd ed., ed. Frank William Walbank et al., Vol. 7, 257–320. Cambridge: Cambridge University Press.

————. 1995. The fourth century crisis: What crisis? In *Die athenische Demokratie im 4. Jahrhundert v. Chr.: Vollendung oder Verfall einer Verfassungsform?* ed. Walter Eder, 29–39. Stuttgart: Steiner.

Davies, W.D. 1996. Reflections on aspects of the Jewish background of the Gospel of John. In *Exploring the Gospel of John: In honor of D. Moody Smith*, ed. R. Alan Culpepper and C. Clifton Black, 43–64. Louisville: Westminster/Knox.

De Beer, Gavin, Sir. 1968. *Gibbon and his world*. London: Thames and Hudson.

Deissmann, Adolf. 1927. *Light from the ancient East*. Trans. Lionel R.M. Strachan. London: Hodder and Stoughton.

DeSilva, David A. 1996. Exchanging favor for wrath: Apostasy in Hebrews and patron-client relationships. *JBL* 115:91–116.

Devda, Tomasz. 1997. Did the Jews use the name Moses in antiquity? *ZPE* 115: 257–60.

Dill, Samuel. 1956. *Roman society from Nero to Marcus Aurelius*. Orig. pub. 1904. New York: World.

Dittenberger, Wilhelm. 1960. *Orientis Graeci inscriptiones selectae*. 2 vols. Hildesheim: Olms.

Dodd, Charles Harold. 1953. *The interpretation of the Fourth Gospel*. Cambridge: Cambridge University Press.

Dodds, Eric Robertson. 1959. *The Greeks and the irrational*. Berkeley: University of California Press.

———. 1965. *Pagan and Christian in an age of anxiety*. Cambridge: Cambridge University Press.

Donaldson, Terence L. 1997. *Paul and the Gentiles: Remapping the Apostle's convictional world*. Minneapolis: Fortress.

Donfried, Karl P., ed. 1991. *The Romans debate*. Rev. and expanded ed. Peabody, MA: Hendrickson.

———. 1997. The Imperial cults of Thessalonica and political conflict in 1 Thessalonians. In *Paul and empire: Religion and power in Roman imperial society*, ed. Richard A. Horsley, 215–23. Harrisburg, PA: Trinity Press International.

Droge, Arthur J., and James D. Tabor. 1992. *A noble death: Suicide and martyrdom among Christians and Jews in antiquity*. San Francisco: HarperCollins.

Dunn, James D.G. 1988. *Romans*. 2 vols. WBC 38. Waco, TX: Word.

———. 1998. Paul: Apostate or apostle of Israel? *ZNW* 89:256–71.

Edelstein, Emma J., and Ludwig Edelstein. 1945. *Asclepius: A collection and interpretation of the testimonies*. 2 vols. Baltimore: Johns Hopkins University Press.

Eder, Walter, ed. 1995. *Die athenische Demokratie im 4. Jahrhundert v. Chr.: Vollendung oder Verfall einer Verfassungsform?* Stuttgart: Steiner.

Ehrenberg, Victor. 1965. The fourth century B.C. as part of Greek history. In *Polis und Imperium: Beiträge zur Alten Geschichte*, ed. Karl Friedrich Stroheker and Alexander John Graham, 32–41. Zürich: Artemis.

———. 1969. *The Greek state*. 2nd ed. London: Methuen.

Ehrman, Bart D. 1993. *The Orthodox corruption of scripture: The effect of early Christological controversies on the text of the New Testament*. New York and Oxford: Oxford University Press.

Eisenbaum, Pamela M. 1998. Review of Stark 1996. *JAAR* 66:469–71.

Elliott, Neil. 1997a. The anti-Imperial message of the Cross. In *Paul and empire: Religion and power in Roman imperial society*, ed. Richard A. Horsley, 167–83. Harrisburg, PA: Trinity Press International.

———. 1997b. Romans 13:1–7 in the context of imperial propaganda. In *Paul and empire: Religion and power in Roman imperial society*, ed. Richard A. Horsley, 184–204. Harrisburg, PA: Trinity Press International.

Ellis, E. Earle. 1993. Coworkers, Paul and his. In *Dictionary of Paul and his letters*, ed. Gerald F. Hawthorne and Ralph P. Martin, 183–89. Downers Grove, IL: InterVarsity.

Elmslie, William Alexander Leslie, ed. 1911. *The Mishna on idolatry: Aboda Zara*. Cambridge: Cambridge University Press.

Erdmann, G. 1932. *Die Vorgeschichten des Lukas- und Matthäusevangeliums und Vergils vierte Ekloge*. Göttingen: Vandenhoeck and Ruprecht.

Esler, Philip Francis. 1987. *Community and gospel in Luke-Acts: The social and political motivations of Lucan theology.* Cambridge: Cambridge University Press.

Farnell, Lewis Richard. 1912. *The higher aspects of Greek religion*. London: Williams and Norgate.

Fee, Gordon D. 1995. *Paul's Letter to the Philippians*. Grand Rapids, MI: Eerdmans.

Feldman, Louis H. 1960. The orthodoxy of the Jews in Hellenistic Egypt. *Jewish Social Studies* 22:215–37.

———. 1986. How much Hellenism in Jewish Palestine? *HUCA* 57:83–111.

———. 1988. Use, authority and exegesis of *Mikra* in the writings of Josephus. In *Mikra: Text, translation, reading and interpretation of the Hebrew Bible in ancient Judaism and early Christianity*, ed. M.J. Mulder and H. Sysling, 455–518. Minneapolis: Fortress.

———. 1993a. *Jew and Gentile in the ancient world: Attitudes and interactions from Alexander to Justinian*. Princeton: Princeton University Press.

———. 1993b. Josephus' portrait of Balaam. In *The* Studia Philonica *annual: Studies in Hellenistic Judaism*, ed. David Runia, Vol. 5, 48–83. BJS 287. Atlanta: Scholars.

Feldman, Louis H., and Gohei Hata, eds. 1988. *Josephus, the Bible, and history.* Detroit: Wayne State University Press.

Ferguson, John. 1970. *The religions of the Roman Empire*. London: Camelot.

Ferguson, W.S. 1928. The leading ideas of the new period. In *The Cambridge Ancient History*, ed. S.A. Cook et al., Vol. 7, 1–40. Cambridge: Cambridge University Press.

Festugière, André-Jean. 1954. *Personal religion among the Greeks*. Berkeley: University of California Press.

———. 1972. Le fait religieux à l'époque hellénistique. In *Études de religion grecque et hellénistique*, 114–28. Bibliothèque d'Histoire de la Philosophie. Orig. pub. 1945. Paris: Vrin.

Figueras, Paul. 1990. Epigraphic evidence for Jewish proselytism in ancient Judaism. *Immanuel* 24/5:194–206.

Finley, Moses I. 1977. The ancient city: From Fustel de Coulanges to Max Weber and beyond. *Comparative Studies in Society and History* 19:305–27.

Fischel, Henry A. 1969. Story and history: Observations on Graeco-Roman rhetoric and Pharisaism. In *American Oriental Society, Middle West Branch, semi-centennial volume*, ed. Denis Sinor, 59–88. Bloomington: Indiana University Press.

———. 1973. *Rabbinic literature and Greco-Roman philosophy.* SPB 21. Leiden: Brill.

———. 1977. *Essays in Greco-Roman and related Talmudic literature.* New York: KTAV.

Fitzmyer, Joseph A. 1985. *The Gospel according to Luke (X–XXIV).* Anchor Bible 28A. Garden City, NY: Doubleday.

Francis, Fred O., and J. Paul Sampley. 1975. *Pauline Parallels.* Philadelphia: Fortress.

Franxman, Thomas W. 1979. *Genesis and the* Jewish Antiquities *of Flavius Josephus.* BibOr 35. Rome: Biblical Institute Press.

Fredriksen, Paula. 1986. Paul and Augustine: Conversion narratives, orthodox traditions and the retrospective self. *JTS* 37:3–34.

Freeman, Kathleen. 1950. *Greek city-states.* London: Macdonald.

Frend, W.H.C. 1965. *Martyrdom and persecution in the early Church.* Oxford: Blackwell.

———. 1997. Review of Stark 1996. *JEH* 48:515–16.

Freudenberger, Rudolf. 1969. *Das Verhalten der römischen Behörden gegen die Christen im 2 Jahrhundert, dargestellt am Brief des Plinius an Trajan und den Reskripten Trajans und Hadrians.* 2nd ed. Munich: Beck.

Fridh, Aa. J. 1956. *Terminologie et formules dans les Variae de Cassiodore.* Göteborg: Acta Universitatis Gothoburgensis; Stockholm: Almquist and Wiksell.

Friedrich, Gerhard. 1964. *euaggelizomai. TDNT* 2:721–25.

Friesen, Steven J. 1993. *Twice Neokoros: Ephesus, Asia and the cult of the Flavian imperial family.* Religions in the Graeco-Roman World 116. Leiden: Brill.

Frischer, Bernard. 1982. *The sculpted word: Epicureanism and philosophical recruitment in ancient Greece.* Berkeley: University of California Press.

Fuglum, Per. 1953. *Edward Gibbon: His view of life and conception of history.* Oslo: Akademisk Forlag; Oxford: Blackwell.

Furnish, Victor Paul. 1984. *II Corinthians.* Anchor Bible 32A. Garden City, NY: Doubleday.

Gafni, Isaiah. 1988. Josephus and I Maccabees. In *Josephus, the Bible, and history*, ed. Louis H. Feldman and Gohei Hata, 116–31. Detroit: Wayne State University Press.

———. 1992. *Jews in Babylonia in the Talmudic Period* [Hebrew]. Jerusalem: Magness.

Gagé, Jean. 1955. *Apollon romain.* Paris: de Boccard.

Garnsey, Peter, and Greg Woolf. 1989. Patronage of the rural poor in the Roman world. In *Patronage in ancient society*, ed. Andrew Wallace-Hadrill, 153–70. London: Routledge.

Gasparro, Giulia Sfameni. 1985. *Soteriology and mystic aspects in the cult of Cybele and Attis.* Études préliminaires aux religions orientales dans l'Empire romain 103. Leiden: Brill.

Gaston, Lloyd. 1987. *Paul and the Torah.* Vancouver: University of British Columbia Press.

Gauthier, Philippe. 1985. *Les cités grecques et leurs bienfaiteurs.* Bulletin de corre-spondance hellenique, Supplement 12. Paris: de Boccard.

———. 1993. "Les cités hellénistiques." In *The ancient Greek city-state: Symposium on the occasion of the 250th anniversary of the Royal Danish Academy of Sciences and Letters, July 1–4 1992,* 211–31. Historisk-filosofiske Meddelelser 67. Copenhagen: Royal Danish Academy of Sciences and Letters.

Geffcken, Johannes. 1978. *The last days of Greco-Roman paganism.* EMA 8. Trans. Sabine MacCormack. Amsterdam: North Holland.

Georgi, Dieter. 1986. *The opponents of Paul in Second Corinthians.* Orig. pub. 1964. Philadelphia: Fortress.

———. 1991. *Theocracy in Paul's praxis and theology.* Minneapolis: Fortress.

Ghosh, Peter. 1997. The conception of Gibbon's *History.* In *Edward Gibbon and empire,* ed. Rosamond McKitterick and Roland Quinault, 271–316. Cambridge: Cambridge University Press.

Gibbon, Edward. 1776–1788. *The history of the decline and fall of the Roman Empire.* London: Stahan and Cadell.

Gilliam, J.F. 1961. The plague under Marcus Aurelius. *AJP* 82/3:225–51.

Glad, Clarence E. 1995. *Paul and Philodemus: Adaptability in Epicurean and early Christian psychagogy.* Leiden: Brill.

González, Justo L. 1990. *Faith and wealth: A history of early Christian ideas on the origin, significance, and use of money.* San Francisco: Harper and Row.

Goodman, Martin. 1992. "Jewish Proselytizing in the First Century." In *The Jews among pagans and Christians in the Roman Empire,* ed. Judith Lieu et al., 53–78. London: Routledge.

———. 1994. *Mission and conversion: Proselytizing in the religious history of the Roman Empire.* Oxford: Clarendon.

Gordon, Richard L. 1972a. Mithraism and Roman society. *Religion* 2:92–121.

———. 1972b. Fear of freedom? Selective continuity in religion during the Hellenistic period. *Didaskalos* 4:48–60.

———. 1990. The veil of power: Emperors, sacrificers and benefactors. In *Pagan Priests,* ed. Mary Beard and John North, 199–231. London: Duckworth.

———. 1994. Who worshipped Mithras? Review of Clauss 1992. *JRA* 7:459–74.

———. 1996a. Two Mithraic albums from Virunum, Noricum. Review of Piccottini 1994. *JRA* 9:424–26.

———. 1996b. *Image and value in the Graeco-Roman world.* Collected Studies Series C551. Aldershot: Variorum.

Grabbe, Lester. 1992. *Judaism from Cyrus to Hadrian.* 2 vols. Minneapolis: Fortress.

Grant, Frederick C., ed. with an introduction.1953. *Hellenistic religions: The age of syncretism.* New York: Bobbs-Merrill.

———. 1957. *Ancient Roman religion.* New York: Bobbs-Merrill.

Grant, Robert M. 1966. *The Apostolic Fathers.* Vol. 4. *Ignatius of Antioch.* London: Nelson.

———. 1977. *Early Christianity and society: Seven studies.* San Francisco: Harper and Row.

————. 1980. The social setting of second-century Christianity. In *Jewish and Christian self-definition*, ed. E.P. Sanders, Vol. 1, *The shaping of Christianity in the second and third centuries*, 16–29. Philadelphia: Fortress.

————. 1996. Review of Stark 1996. *Christian Century* 113:1081–82.

Green, Henry A. 1985. *The economic and social origins of Gnosticism.* SBLDS 77. Atlanta: Scholars.

Green, Michael. 1970. *Evangelism in the early Church.* London: Hodder and Stoughton.

Green, Peter. 1990. *Alexander to Actium: The historical evolution of the Hellenistic age.* Berkeley: University of California Press.

Groag, Edmund, Arthur Stein, and Leiva Petersen. 1933. *Prosopographia imperii Romani Saec. I. II. III.* 2nd ed. Berlin: de Gruyter.

Gruen, Erich S. 1993. The *Polis* in the Hellenistic world. In *Nomodeiktes: Greek studies in honor of Martin Ostwald*, ed. Ralph M. Rosen and Joseph Farrell, 339–54. Ann Arbor: University of Michigan Press.

Guthrie, William Keith Chambers. 1950. *The Greeks and their gods.* London: Methuen.

————. 1955. *The Greeks and their gods.* Boston: Beacon.

Hadas-Lebel, Mireille. 1973. *De Providentia 1 & 2: Les oeuvres de Philon d'Alexandrie.* Paris: Cerf.

Hägg, Tomas. 1983. *The novel in antiquity.* Oxford: Blackwell.

Halbertal, Moshe, and Avishai Margalit. 1992. *Idolatry.* Trans. Naomi Goldblum. Cambridge, MA: Harvard University Press.

Hands, Arthur Robinson. 1968. *Charities and social aid in Greece and Rome.* London: Thames and Hudson.

Hansen, Mogens Herman. 1993. Introduction: The *Polis* as a citizen-state. In *The ancient Greek city-state: Symposium on the occasion of the 250th anniversary of the Royal Danish Academy of Sciences and Letters, July 1–4 1992*, 7–29. Historisk-filosofiske Meddelelser 67. Copenhagen: Royal Danish Academy of Sciences and Letters.

————. 1994. *Poleis* and city-states, 600–323 B.C.: A comprehensive research programme. In *From political architecture to Stephanus Byzantius: Sources for the ancient Greek polis*, ed. David Whitehead, 8–17. Historia Einzelschriften 87. Stuttgart: Steiner.

————. 1995. The autonomous city-state: Ancient fact or modern fiction. In *Studies in the ancient Greek polis*, ed. Mogens Herman Hansen and Kurt Raaflaub, 21–43. Historia Einzelschriften 95. Stuttgart: Steiner.

Harland, Philip A. 1996. Honours and worship: Emperors, imperial cults and associations at Ephesus (first to third centuries CE). *SR* 25:319–34.

————. 1999. Claiming a place in *Polis* and empire: The significance of imperial cults and connections among associations, synagogues, and Christian groups in Roman Asia (c. 27 BCE–138 CE). Ph.D. diss., University of Toronto.

————. 2000. Honouring the Emperor or assailing the beast: Participation in civic life among associations (Jewish, Christian and other) in Asia Minor and the Apocalypse of John. *JSNT* 77:99–121.

———. 2003. *Associations, synagogues, and congregations: Claiming a place in ancient Mediterranean society.* Minneapolis: Fortress.

Harnack, Adolf von. 1904–1905. *The expansion of Christianity in the first three centuries.* 2 vols. London: Williams and Norgate.

———. 1904–1905. *The expansion of Christianity in the first three centuries.* Trans. and ed. James Moffatt. 2 vols. New York: Putnam.

———. 1906. *Die Mission und Ausbreitung des Christentums in den ersten drei Jahrhunderten.* 2nd ed. 2 vols. Leipzig: Hinrichs.

———. 1908. *The mission and expansion of Christianity in the first three centuries.* Trans. and ed. James Moffatt. 2nd ed. 2 vols. London: Williams and Norgate; New York: Putnam.

———. 1961. *The mission and expansion of Christianity in the first three centuries.* Trans. and ed. James Moffatt. New York: Harper.

Harvey, Anthony Ernest. 1985. Forty strokes save one: Social aspects of Judaizing and apostasy. In *Alternative approaches to New Testament study,* ed. Anthony Ernest Harvey, 79–98. London: SPCK.

Hatzfeld, Jean. 1919. *Les trafiquants italiens dans l'orient hellénique.* Bibliothèque des Écoles Françaises d'Athènes et de Rome 115. Paris: de Boccard.

Hazelrigg, Lawrence. 1992. Individualism. In *Encyclopedia of sociology,* 901–907. New York: Macmillan.

Hengel, Martin. 1974. *Judaism and Hellenism: Studies in their encounter in Palestine during the early Hellenistic period.* 2 vols. Trans. John Bowden. Philadelphia: Fortress.

Heiserman, Arthur Ray. 1977. *The novel before the novel.* Chicago: University of Chicago Press.

Herford, Robert Travers. 1903. *Christianity in Talmud and Midrash.* London: Williams.

Herrmann, Peter, et al. 1978. Genossenschaft. In *Reallexikon für Antike und Christentum,* ed. Theodor Kluser et al., 83–155. Stuttgart: Hiersemann.

Hock, Ronald. 1980. *The social context of Paul's ministry: Tentmaking and apostleship.* Philadelphia: Fortress.

Hoenig, Sidney B. 1970. Oil and pagan defilement. *JQR* 61:63–75.

Holmberg, Bengt. 1978. *Paul and power.* Philadelphia: Fortress.

Hopkins, Keith. 1980. Taxes and trade in the Roman Empire (200 B.C.–A.D. 400). *JRS* 70:101–25.

———. 1998. Christian number and its implications. *JECS* 6:185–226.

Horsley, G.H.R. 1981–. *New documents illustrating early Christianity: A review of the Greek inscriptions and papyri.* 9 vols. North Ryde, Australia: Macquarie University.

———. 1987. Name change as an indicator of religious conversion in antiquity. *Numen* 34:1–17.

———. 1989. A fishing cartel in first-century Ephesos. In *New documents illustrating early christianity,* ed. G.H.R. Horsley, 95–114. North Ryde, Australia: Macquarie University.

Horsley, G.H.R., and John A.L. Lee. 1994. A preliminary checklist of abbreviations of Greek epigraphic volumes. *Epigraphica* 56:129–69.

Horsley, Richard A. 1989. *The liberation of Christmas: The infancy narratives in social context.* New York: Crossroad.

———. 1997. General introduction. In *Paul and empire: Religion and power in Roman imperial society*, ed. Richard A. Horsley, 1–8. Harrisburg: Trinity Press International.

———. 1998. Paul and slavery: A critical alternative to recent readings. *Semeia* 83–84: 153–200.

Hultgren, Arland J. 1985. *Paul's gospel and mission.* Philadelphia: Fortress.

James, William. 1902. *The varieties of religious experience.* New York: Longmans-Green; rpt. New York: University Books, 1963.

Janzen, Anna. 2000. Der Friede im lukanischen Doppelwerk vor dem Hintergrund der Pax Romana. Ph.D. diss., University of St. Michael's College, Toronto.

Jeffers, James S. 1991. *Conflict at Rome: Social order and hierarchy in early Christianity.* Minneapolis: Fortress.

Jewett, Robert. 1988. Paul, Phoebe, and the Spanish mission. In *The social world of formative Christianity and Judaism*, ed. Jacob Neusner et al., 142–61. Philadelphia: Fortress.

———. 1992. Ecumenical theology for the sake of mission: Romans 1:1–17 + 15:14–16:24. In *SBL 1992 Seminar Papers*, ed. Eugene H. Lovering, Jr., 598–612. SBLSP 31. Atlanta: Scholars.

Jones, Arnold Hugh Martin. 1940. *The Greek city from Alexander to Justinian.* Oxford: Clarendon.

———. 1971. *The cities of the eastern Roman provinces.* 2nd ed. Rev. Michael Avi-Yonah et al. Oxford: Clarendon.

Jones, Brian W. 1992. *The Emperor Domitian.* London: Routledge.

Jones, Christopher Prestige. 1978. *The Roman world of Dio Chrysostom.* Cambridge, MA: Harvard University Press.

Jordan, Mark D. 1986. Ancient philosophic protreptic and the problem of persuasive genres. *Rhetorica* 4:309–33.

Joyce, Michael. 1953. *Edward Gibbon.* London: Longmans-Green.

Kant, Laurence H. 1987. Jewish inscriptions in Greek and Latin. *ANRW* 2.20.2: 671–713.

Kee, Howard Clark. 1986. *Medicine, miracle and magic in New Testament times.* SNTSMS 55. Cambridge: Cambridge University Press.

Keith, Alison, and Leif E. Vaage. 1999. Imperial asceticism: Discipline of domination. In *Asceticism and the New Testament*, ed. Leif E. Vaage and Vincent L. Wimbush, 411–20. New York: Routledge.

Kerkeslager, Allen. 1997. Maintaining Jewish identity in the Greek gymnasium: A "Jewish load." *CPJ* 3.159 (= *P.Schub.* 37 = *P.Berol.* 134060). *JSJ* 28:12–23.

Kimelman, Reuven. 1981. *Birkat Ha-Minim* and the lack of evidence for an anti-Christian Jewish prayer in late antiquity. In *Jewish and Christian self-definition*, ed. E.P. Sanders, Vol. 2, 226–44. Philadelphia: Fortress.

Klebs, Elimar, Paul de Rohden, and Hermann Dessau. 1897–1898. *Prosopographia imperii Romani.* Berlin: Reimer.

Kleiner, Gerhard. 1970. *Das römische Milet: Bilder aus der griechischen Stadt in römischer Zeit.* Sitzungsberichte der Wissenschaftlichen Gesellschaft an der Johann Wolfgang Goethe-Universität Frankfurt/Main, 8.5. Wiesbaden: Steiner.

Kloppenborg, John S. 1992. *Exitus clari viri:* The death of Jesus in Luke. *TJT* 8:106–20.

———. 1996. Collegia and *thiasoi.* In *Voluntary associations in the Graeco-Roman world,* ed. John S. Kloppenborg and Stephen G. Wilson, 16–30. London: Routledge.

Kloppenborg, John S., and Stephen G. Wilson, eds. 1996. *Voluntary associations in the Graeco-Roman world.* London: Routledge.

Klutz, Todd E. 1998. The rhetoric of science in *The Rise of Christianity*: A response to Rodney Stark's sociological account of Christianization. *JECS* 6:162–84.

Knibbe, Dieter. 1978. Ephesos: Nicht nur die Stadt der Artemis. In *Studien zur Religion und Kultur Kleinasiens: Festschrift für Friedrich Karl Dörner zum 65. Geburtstag am 28. Februar 1976,* ed. Sencer Sahin et al., 489–503. Études préliminaires aux religions orientales de l'Empire roman 66. Leiden: Brill.

Knox, John. 1964. Romans 15:14–33 and Paul's conception of his apostolic mission. *JBL* 83:1–11.

Kolb, Frank. 1990. Sitzstufeninschriften aus dem Stadion von Saittai (Lydien). *EA* 15:107–19.

Koester, Helmut. 1990. *Ancient Christian Gospels: Their history and development.* Philadelphia: Trinity Press International.

———. 1997. "Imperial Ideology and Paul's Eschatology in 1 Thessalonians." In *Paul and empire: Religion and power in Roman imperial society,* ed. Richard A. Horsley, 158–66. Harrisburg: Trinity Press International.

Kossen, H.B. 1970. Who were the Greeks of John xii 20? In *Studies in John,* 97–110. Leiden: Brill.

Kraabel, A. Thomas. 1994. Immigrants, exiles, expatriates, and missionaries. In *Religious propaganda and missionary competition in the New Testament world: Essays honoring Dieter Georgi,* ed. Lukas Bormann et al., 71–88. Leiden: Brill.

Kreissig, Heinz. 1974. Die *Polis* in Griechenland und im Orient in der hellenistischen Epoche. In *Hellenische Poleis: Krise, Wandlung, Wirkung,* ed. Elisabeth Charlotte Welskopf, 1074–84. Berlin: Akademie.

Krieger, Klaus-Stefan. 1994. *Geschichtsschreibung als Apologetik bei Flavius Josephus.* Tübingen: Francke.

Lähnemann, Johannes. 1978. Die sieben Sendschreiben der Johannes-Apokalypse: Dokumente für die Konfrontation des frühen Christentums mit hellenistisch/römischer Kultur und Religion in Kleinasien. In *Studien zur Religion und Kultur Kleinasiens: Festschrift für Friedrich Karl Dörner zum 65. Geburtstag am 28. Februar 1976,* ed. Sencer Sahin et al., Vol. 2, 516–39. Leiden: Brill.

Lampe, G.W.H. 1966. Diakonia in the early Church. In *Service in Christ: Essays presented to Karl Barth on his 80th Birthday,* ed. James McCord and T. Parker, 49–64. Grand Rapids, MI: Eerdmans.

Lampe, Peter. 1987. *Die stadtrömischen Christen in den ersten beiden Jahrhunderten: Untersuchungen zur Sozialgeschichte.* 1st ed. Tübingen: Mohr (Siebeck).

————. 1989. *Die stadtrömischen Christen in den ersten beiden Jahrhunderten: Untersuchungen zur Sozialgeschichte.* 2nd ed. Tübingen: Mohr (Siebeck).

Lane Fox, Robin. 1986. *Pagans and Christians.* San Francisco: HarperSanFrancisco.

————. 1987. *Pagans and Christians.* New York: Knopf.

La Piana, George. 1927. Foreign groups in Rome during the first centuries of the Empire. *HTR* 20:183–403.

Laqueur, Richard. 1970. *Der jüdische Historiker Flavius Josephus.* Orig. pub. 1920. Darmstadt: Wissenschaftliche.

Laum, Bernhard. 1964. *Stiftungen in der griechischen und römischen Antike: ein Beitrag zur antiken Kulturgeschichte.* Orig. pub. 1914. Aalen: Scientia.

Le Bohec, Yann. 1981. Inscriptiones juives et judaïsantes de l'Afrique Romaine. *Antiquités africaines* 17:165–207.

Le Guen, B. 1995. Théâtre et cités à l'époque hellénistique : "Mort de la cité"—"Mort du théâtre"? *REG* 108:59–90.

Leon, Harry J. 1960. *The Jews of ancient Rome.* Philadelphia: JPSA.

Levi, Peter, trans. 1971. *Pausanias: Guide to Greece.* 2 vols. Harmondsworth, Middlesex: Penguin.

Leyerle, Blake. 1997. Review of Stark 1996. *JECS* 5:306–308.

Lieberman, Saul. 1950. The publication of the Mishnah. In *Hellenism in Jewish Palestine.* Texts and Studies of the Jewish Theological Seminary of America 18, 81–99. New York: Jewish Theological Seminary of America.

Liebeschuetz, John Hugo Wolfgang Gideon. 1979. *Continuity and change in Roman religion.* Oxford: Clarendon.

————. 1994. The expansion of Mithraism among the religious cults of the second century. In *Studies in Mithraism*, ed. John R. Hinnells, 195–216. Storia delle religioni 9. Rome: Bretschneider.

Lightstone, Jack. 1988. *Society, the sacred, and scripture in ancient Judaism.* ESCJ 3. Waterloo: Wilfrid Laurier University Press.

————. 1994. *The rhetoric of the Babylonian Talmud, its social meaning and context.* ESCJ 6. Waterloo: Wilfrid Laurier University Press.

————. 1997. Whence the Rabbis? From coherent description to fragmented reconstructions. *SR* 26:275–95.

Littman, R.J., and M.L. Littman. 1973. Galen and the Antonine plague. *AJP* 94:243–55.

Lohfink, Gerhard. 1971. *Die Himmelfahrt Jesu: Untersuchungen zu den Himmelfahrts- und Erhöhungstexten bei Lukas.* Munich: Kösel.

Luz, Menachem. 1989. A description of the Greek Cynic in the Jerusalem Talmud. *JSJ* 20:49–60.

Mack, Burton L. 1996. On redescribing Christian origins. *Method and theory in the study of Religion* 8:247–69.

————. 1999. Many movements, many myths: Redescribing the attractions of early Christianities. Toward a conversation with Rodney Stark. *RelSRev* 25:132–36.

MacMullen, Ramsay. 1970. Market days in the Roman Empire. *Phoenix* 24:333–41.

———. 1981. *Paganism in the Roman Empire*. New Haven: Yale University Press.

———. 1984. *Christianizing the Roman Empire, A.D. 100–400*. New Haven: Yale University Press.

MacMullen, Ramsay, and Eugene N. Lane, eds. 1992. *Paganism and Christianity, 100–425 C.E.: A sourcebook*. Minneapolis: Fortress.

Magie, David. 1950. *Roman rule in Asia Minor to the end of the third century after Christ*. 2 vols. Princeton: Princeton University Press.

Maier, Harry O. 1991. *The social setting of the ministry as reflected in the writings of Hermas, Clement and Ignatius*. Waterloo: Wilfrid Laurier University Press.

———. 1998. Review of Stark 1996. *JTS* 49:328–35.

Malina, Bruce J. 1997. Review of Stark 1996. *CBQ* 59:593–95.

Malina, Bruce J., and Jerome H. Neyrey. 1996. *Portraits of Paul: An archaeology of ancient personality*. Louisville: Westminster/Knox.

Malina, Bruce J., and Richard Rohrbaugh. 1998. *Social-science commentary on the Gospel of John*. Minneapolis: Fortress.

Marrou, Henri Irénée. 1956. *A history of education in antiquity*. Trans. George Lamb. London: Sheed and Ward.

Marshall, Howard. 1987. The problem of apostasy in New Testament theology. *PRS* 14:65–80.

Martin, Luther H. 1987. *Hellenistic religions: An introduction*. Oxford: Oxford University Press.

———. 1994. The anti-individualistic ideology of Hellenistic culture. *Numen* 41:117–40.

Martin, Ralph P. 1986. *2 Corinthians*. WBC 40. Waco, TX: Word.

Martyn, J. Louis. 1979. *The Gospel of John in Christian history: Essays for interpreters*. New York: Paulist.

Mason, Steve. 1988. Josephus on the Pharisees reconsidered: A critique of Smith/Neusner. *SR* 17:445–69.

———. 1991. *Flavius Josephus on the Pharisees: A composition-critical study*. SPB 39. Leiden: Brill.

———. 1992. Review of Schwartz 1990. *Ioudaios* 2.008.

McCutcheon, Russell. 1999. Introduction. *RelSRev* 25:127–28.

McKnight, Scot. 1991. *A light among the Gentiles: Jewish missionary activity in the Second Temple Period*. Minneapolis: Fortress.

McNeill, William H. 1976. *Plagues and peoples*. New York: Anchor.

Meeks, Wayne A. 1983. *The first urban Christians: The social world of the Apostle Paul*. New Haven: Yale University Press.

Meeks, Wayne A., and Robert Wilken. 1978. *Jews and Christians in Antioch in the first four centuries of the Common Era*. Sources for Biblical Study 13. Missoula, MT: Scholars.

Mendelson, Alan. 1988. *Philo's Jewish identity*. BJS 161. Atlanta: Scholars.

Merkelbach, Reinhold. 1984. *Mithras*. Königstein: Hain.

————. 1994. Novel and aretalogy. In *The Search for the Ancient Novel*, ed. James Tatum, 283–95. Baltimore: Johns Hopkins University Press.

Meyer, Marvin. 1987. Introduction. In *The ancient mysteries: A sourcebook*, ed. Marvin Meyer, 1–14. San Francisco: Harper and Row.

Millar, Fergus. 1977. *The Emperor in the Roman world (31 BC–AD 337)*. Ithaca, NY: Cornell University Press.

————. 1984. State and subject: The impact of monarchy. In *Caesar Augustus: Seven aspects*, ed. Fergus Millar and Erich Segal, 37–60. Oxford: Clarendon.

————. 1993. The Greek city in the Roman period. In *The ancient Greek city-state: Symposium on the occasion of the 250th anniversary of the Royal Danish Academy of Sciences and Letters, July 1–4 1992*, 232–60. Historisk-filosofiske Meddelelser 67. Copenhagen: Royal Danish Academy of Sciences and Letters.

———— et al. 1967. *The Roman Empire and its neighbours*. London: Weidenfeld and Nicolson.

Mitchell, Stephen. 1990. Festivals, games, and civic life in Roman Asia Minor. *JRS* 80:183–93.

————. 1993. *Anatolia: Land, men, and gods in Asia Minor*. 2 vols. Oxford: Clarendon.

Modrzejewski-Mélèze, Joseph. 1993. How to be a Greek and yet a Jew in Hellenistic Alexandria. In *Diasporas in antiquity*, ed. Shaye D. Cohen and Ernest S. Frerichs, 65–92. BJS 288. Atlanta: Scholars.

Mommsen, Theodor, and Ulrich von Wilamowitz-Moellendorff. 1899. Die Einführung des asianischen Kalenders. *MDAI(A)* 24:275–93.

Mossé, Claude. 1973. *Athens in decline, 404–86 B.C.* Trans. Jean Stewart. London: Routledge and Kegan Paul.

Muir, Steven C. 1995. Touched by a god: Aelius Aristides, religious healing, and Asclepius cults. In *1995 SBL Seminar Papers*, ed. Eugene H. Lovering, 362–79. SBLSP 34. Atlanta: Scholars.

Müller, J.G. 1969. *Des Flavius Josephus Schrift gegen den Apion: Text und Erklärung*. Orig. pub. 1877. Hildesheim: Olms.

Mullin, Redmond. 1984. *The wealth of Christians*. Maryknoll, NY: Orbis.

Munck, Johannes. 1959. *Paul and the salvation of mankind*. Trans. Frank Clarke. London: SCM.

Murray, Gilbert. 1935. *Five stages of Greek religion*. 2nd ed. Oxford: Clarendon.

Musurillo, Herbert. 1972. *The acts of the Christian martyrs*. Oxford: Clarendon.

Neusner, Jacob. 1964. The conversion of Adiabene to Judaism. *JBL* 83:60–66.

————. 1981. *Judaism: The evidence of the Mishnah*. Chicago: University of Chicago Press.

————. 1991. *The Bavli that might have been: The Tosefta's theory of Mishnah commentary compared with the Bavli's*. South Florida Studies in the History of Judaism 18. Atlanta: Scholars.

Nickle, Keith F. 1966. *The Collection: A study in Paul's strategy*. SBT 48. London: SCM.

Nilsson, Martin P. 1948. *Greek piety*. Trans. Herbert Jennings Rose. Oxford: Clarendon.

————. 1961. *Geschichte der griechischen Religion.* 2nd ed. Munich: Beck.

————. 1964. *A history of Greek religion.* 2nd ed. New York: Norton.

Nock, Arthur Darby. 1933. *Conversion: The old and the new in religion from Alexander the Great to Augustine of Hippo.* Oxford: Clarendon.

————. 1986. Conversion and Adolescence. In *Essays on religion and the ancient world,* 2 vols., ed. Zeph Stewart, Vol. 1, 469–80. Oxford: Clarendon.

North, J.A. 1976. Conservatism and change in Roman religion. *Papers of the British School at Rome* 44:1–12.

Noy, David. 1993–1995. *Jewish inscriptions of western Europe.* 2 vols. Cambridge: Cambridge University Press.

O'Brien, P.T. 1995. *Gospel and mission in the writings of Paul: An exegetical and theological analysis.* Grand Rapids, MI: Baker.

Ohlemutz, Erwin. 1968. *Die Kulte und Heiligtümer der Götter in Pergamon.* Orig. pub. 1940. Darmstadt: Wissenschaftliche Buchgesellschaft.

Oliver, James H. 1954. The Roman governor's permission for a decree of the *Polis. Hesperia* 23:163–67.

————. 1970. *Marcus Aurelius: Aspects of civic and cultural policy in the East. Hesperia* Supplement 13. Princeton: American School of Classical Studies at Athens.

Osiek, Carolyn. 1981. The ransom of captives: Evolution of a tradition. *HTR* 74:365–86.

Oster, Richard. 1976. The Ephesian Artemis as an opponent of early Christianity. *JAC* 19:24–44.

————. 1990. Ephesus as a religious center under the principate: I. Paganism before Constantine. *ANRW* 2.18.3: 1661–728.

Parke, Herbert William. 1985. *The oracles of Apollo in Asia Minor.* London: Croom Helm.

Parsons, Mikeal C. 1986. A Christological tendency in P75. *JBL* 105:463–79.

————. 1987. *The departure of Jesus in Luke-Acts: The Ascension narratives in context.* JSNTSup 21. Sheffield: JSOT.

Pecirka, Jan. 1976. The crisis of the Athenian *Polis* in the fourth century B.C. *Eirene* 14:5–29.

Pervo, Richard I. 1987. *Profit with delight: The literary genre of the Acts of the Apostles.* Philadelphia: Fortress.

Peterson, Erik. 1929–1930. Die Einholung des Kyrios. *ZST* 7:682–702.

————. 1933. *apantêsis. TWNT* 1:380.

Pfohl, Gerhard, ed. 1966. *Griechische Inschriften als Zeugnisse des privaten und öffentlichen Lebens.* Munich: Heimeran.

Phillips, Charles Stanley. 1930. *The new commandment: An inquiry into the social precept and practice of the ancient Church.* London: SPCK.

Piccottini, Gernot. 1994. *Mithrastempel in Virunum.* Aus Forschung und Kunst 28. Klagenfurt: Geschichtsverein für Kärnten.

Pleket, H.W. 1965. An aspect of the Emperor cult: Imperial mysteries. *HTR* 58:331–47.

Plevnik, Joseph. 1984. The taking up of the faithful and the resurrection of the dead in 1 Thessalonians 4:13–18. *CBQ* 46:274–83.

Poland, Franz. 1909. *Geschichte des griechischen Vereinswesens.* Leipzig: Zentral-Antiquariat der Deutschen Demokratischen Republik.

Pomeroy, Sarah B. 1977. TECHNIKAI KAI MOUSIKAI: The education of women in the fourth century and in the Hellenistic period. *AJAH* 2:51–68.

Porpora, Douglas. 1997. Review of Stark 1996. *Contemporary Sociology* 26:772–73.

Porton, Gary. 1988. *Goyim: Gentiles and Israelites in Mishnah-Tosefta.* BJS 155. Atlanta: Scholars.

Price, Simon R.F. 1984. *Rituals and power: The Roman imperial cult in Asia Minor.* Cambridge: Cambridge University Press.

Quandt, Guilelmu. 1913. De baccho ab Alexandri aetate in Asia Minore culto. *Dissertationes Philologicae Halenses* 21:101–277.

Rackman, Emmanuel. 1987. Orthodox Judaism. In *Contemporary Jewish religious thought*, ed. Arthur A. Cohen and Paul Mendes-Flohr, 679–84. New York: Scribner.

Rajak, Tessa. 1985. Jewish rights in Greek cities under Roman rule: A new approach. In *Approaches to ancient Judaism*, ed. William Scott Green, Vol. 15, 19–35. Atlanta: Scholars.

Ramsay, William Mitchell, Sir. 1895–1897. *The cities and bishoprics of Phrygia.* 2 vols. Oxford: Clarendon.

Rapske, Brian M. 1994. Acts, travel and shipwreck. In *The Book of Acts in its first century setting*, ed. Bruce W. Winter, Vol. 2, 1–48. Grand Rapids, MI: Eerdmans.

Reinhartz, Adele. 1998a. The Johannine community and its Jewish neighbors: A reappraisal. In *Literary and social readings of the fourth Gospel*, Vol. 2, *"What Is John?"* ed. Fernando F. Segovia, 111–38. Atlanta: Scholars.

———. 1998b. On travel, translation, and ethnography: Johannine scholarship at the turn of the century. In *Literary and social readings of the fourth Gospel*, Vol. 2, *"What Is John?"* ed. Fernando F. Segovia, 249–56. Atlanta: Scholars.

Remus, Harold. 1983. *Pagan-Christian conflict over miracle in the second century.* Patristic Monograph Series 10. Cambridge, MA: Philadelphia Patristic Foundation.

———. 1996. Voluntary associations and networks: Aelius Aristides at the Asclepieion in Pergamum. In *Voluntary associations in the Graeco-Roman world*, ed. John S. Kloppenborg and Stephen G. Wilson, 146–75. London: Routledge.

Rensberger, David. 1988. *Johannine faith and liberating community.* Philadelphia: Westminster.

Rhodes, P.J. 1994. The *Polis* and the alternatives. In *The Cambridge ancient history*, 2nd ed., Vol. 20, ed. D.M. Lewis et al., 565–91. Cambridge: Cambridge University Press.

Riesner, Rainer. 1994. *Die Frühzeit des Apostels Paulus: Studien zur Chronologie, Missionsstrategie und Theologie.* WUNT 71. Tübingen: Mohr (Siebeck).

Rigaux, Béda. 1956. *Saint Paul: L'Épitres aux Thessaloniciens.* Paris: Lecoffre.

Rives, James B. 1995. *Religion and authority in Roman Carthage from Augustus to Constantine.* Oxford: Oxford University Press.

———. 1999. The decree of Decius and the religion of empire. *JRS* 89:135–54.

Robbins, Thomas. 1988. *Cults, converts and charisma: The sociology of new religious movements.* Beverly Hills: Sage.

Robert, Louis. 1938. *Études épigraphiques et philologiques.* Bibliothèque de l'École des Hautes Études 272. Paris: Champion.

———. 1946. Un corpus des inscriptions juives. *Hellenica* 1:90–108.

———. 1969. Théophane de Mytilène à Constantinople. *CRAIBL*: 42–64.

Roberts, Colin, Theodore C. Skeat, and Arthur Darby Nock. 1936. The gild of Zeus Hypsistos. *HTR* 29:39–88.

Robinson, John A.T. 1959–1960. The destination and purpose of St. John's Gospel. *NTS* 6:117–31.

Rogers, Guy MacLean. 1991. *The sacred identity of Ephesos: Foundation myths of a Roman city.* London: Routledge.

———. 1992. The assembly of Imperial Ephesos. *ZPE* 94:224–28.

Rostovtzeff, Michael Ivanovitch, et al., eds. 1939. *The excavations at Dura-Europos: Preliminary report of the seventh and eighth seasons.* New Haven: Yale University Press.

Rouse, William H.D. 1902. *Greek votive offerings.* Rpt. New York: Arno, 1975.

Rudberg, Gunnar. 1911. Zu den Sendschreiben der Johannes-Apokalypse. *Eranos* 11:170–79.

Runciman, Walter Garrison. 1990. Doomed to extinction: The *Polis* as an evolutionary dead-end. In *The Greek city from Homer to Alexander*, ed. Oswyn Murray and Simon Price, 347–67. Oxford: Clarendon.

Safrai, Ze'ev. 1984. Fairs in the land of Israel in the Mishnah and Talmud periods [Hebrew]. *Zion* 49:139–58.

Said, Edward W. 1994. *Culture and imperialism.* Orig. pub. 1993. New York: Vintage.

Sanday, William, and Arthur C. Headlam. 1902. *A critical and exegetical commentary on the Epistle to the Romans.* 5th ed. International Critical Commentary. Edinburgh: T. and T. Clark.

Sandelin, Karl G. 1991. The danger of idolatry according to Philo of Alexandria. *Temenos* 27:109–50.

Sanders, E.P. 1992. *Judaism: Practice and belief 63 B.C.E.–66 C.E.* Philadelphia: Trinity Press International.

Sanders, Jack T. 1993. *Schismatics, sectarians, dissidents, deviants. The first one hundred years of Jewish-Christian relations.* Valley Forge, PA: Trinity Press International.

Sandnes, Karl Olav. 1991. *Paul: One of the prophets?* WUNT 2:43. Tübingen: Mohr (Siebeck).

Sartre, Maurice. 1991. *L'orient romain: provinces et sociétés provinciales en Méditerranée orientale d'Auguste aux Sévères (31 avant J.-C.- 235 après J.-C.).* Paris: du Seuil.

Saunders, Dero A., ed. 1952. *The portable Gibbon: The decline and fall of the Roman Empire.* New York: Viking.

Saxl, Fritz. 1931. *Mithras: Typengeschichtliche Untersuchungen.* Berlin.

Saxonhouse, Arlene W. 1996. *Athenian democracy: Modern mythmakers and ancient theorists.* Notre Dame: University of Notre Dame Press.

Schalit, Abraham. 1975. Evidence of an Aramaic source in Josephus' *Antiquities of the Jews. Annual of the Swedish Theological Institute* 4:163–88.

Schiffman, Lawrence H. 1985. *Who was a Jew? Rabbinic and Halakhic perspectives on the Jewish-Christian schism.* Hoboken, NJ: KTAV.

———. 1987. The conversion of the Royal House of Adiabene in Josephus and Rabbinic sources. In *Josephus, Judaism and Christianity*, ed. Louis H. Feldman and Gohei Hata, 293–312. Detroit: Wayne State University Press.

Schniewind, Julius. 1970. *Euaggelion: Ursprung und erste Gestalt des Begriffs Evangelium.* Orig. pub. 1927. Darmstadt: Wissenschaftliche Buchgesellschaft.

Schoedel, William R. 1985. *Ignatius of Antioch: A commentary on the letters of Ignatius of Antioch.* Hermeneia. Philadelphia: Fortress.

Schön, Dorit. 1988. *Orientalische Kulte im römischen Österreich.* Vienna: Bohlau.

Schuchard, Bruce C. 1992. *Scripture within scripture: The interrelationship of form and function in the explicit Old Testament citations in the Gospel of John.* SBLDS 133. Atlanta: Scholars.

Schürer, Emil. 1973–1986. *The history of the Jewish people in the age of Jesus Christ.* 3 vols. Ed. and rev. Geza Vermes et al. Orig. pub. 1890. Edinburgh: T. and T. Clark.

Schüssler Fiorenza, Elisabeth. 1976. *Aspects of religious propaganda in Judaism and early Christianity.* Notre Dame: University of Notre Dame Press.

———. 1992. *But she said: Feminist practices of biblical interpretation.* Boston: Beacon.

Schwartz, Seth. 1990. *Josephus and Judean politics.* CSCT 18. Leiden: Brill.

Scott, James M. 1994. Luke's geographical horizon. In *The Book of Acts in its first century setting*, Vol. 2, ed. Bruce W. Winter, 483–544. Grand Rapids, MI: Eerdmans.

———. 1995. *Paul and the nations.* WUNT 84. Tübingen: Mohr (Siebeck).

Scott, Martin. 1992. *Sophia and the Johannine Jesus.* Sheffield: JSOT.

Sedley, David. 1976. Epicurus and his professional rivals. In *Études sur l'Epicurisme antique*, ed. Jean Bollack and Andre Laks, 121–60. Lille: Publications de l'Université de Lille.

Segal, Alan. 1990. *Paul the convert: The apostolate and apostasy of Saul the Pharisee.* New Haven: Yale University Press.

Sheppard, A.R.R. 1984–1986. *Homonoia* in the Greek cities of the Roman Empire. *Ancient Society* 15–17:229–52.

Simon, Marcel. 1986. Verus Israel*: A study of the relations between Christians and Jews in the Roman Empire (135–425).* Trans. H. McKeating. Orig. pub. 1964. Oxford: Oxford University Press.

Smallwood, E. Mary. 1981. *The Jews under Roman rule: From Pompey to Diocletian. A study in political relations.* Leiden: Brill.

Smith, D. Moody. 1984. *Johannine Christianity: Essays on its setting, sources, and theology.* Columbia: University of South Carolina Press.

Smith, Daniel A. 2001. Post-mortem vindication of Jesus in the Sayings Gospel Q. Ph.D. diss., University of St. Michael's College, Toronto.

Smith, Jonathan Z. 1978. The temple and the magician. In *Map is not territory: Studies in the history of religions*, 172–89. SJLA 23. Leiden: Brill.

————. 1982a. In comparison a magic dwells. In *Imagining religion: From Babylon to Jonestown*, 19–35. Chicago: University of Chicago Press.

————. 1982b. A pearl of great price and a cargo of yams: A study in situational incongruity. In *Imagining religion: From Babylon to Jonestown*, 90–101. Chicago: University of Chicago Press.

————. 1990. *Drudgery divine: On the comparison of early Christianities and the religions of late antiquity.* Jordan Lectures in Comparative Religion 14; Chicago Studies in the History of Judaism. Chicago: University of Chicago Press.

————. 1997. Review of Stark 1996. *American Journal of Sociology* 102:1663–65.

Smith, Morton. 1956. Palestinian Judaism in the first century. In *Israel: Its role in civilization*, ed. M. Davis, 67–81. New York: JTSA.

————. 1971. Prolegomena to a discussion of aretalogies, divine men, the Gospels and Jesus. *JBL* 90:174–99.

————. 1978. *Jesus the magician.* New York: Harper and Row.

Smith, R.R.R. 1987. The imperial reliefs from the *Sebasteion* at Aphrodisias. *JRS* 77:88–138.

Sperber, Daniel. 1978. *Roman Palestine, 200–400. The Land.* Ramat-Gan: Bar-Ilan University Press.

Standhartinger, Angela. 1999. *Studien zur Entstehungsgeschichte und Intention des Kolosserbriefs.* Leiden: Brill.

Starbuck, Edwin Diller. 1915. *The psychology of religion: An empirical study of the growth of religious consciousness.* London: Scott.

Stark, Rodney. 1996. *The rise of Christianity: A sociologist reconsiders history.* Princeton: Princeton University Press.

————. *The rise of Christianity: How the obscure, marginal Jesus movement became the dominant religious force in the Western world in a few centuries.* San Francisco: HarperCollins.

————. E Contrario. *JECS* 6:259–67.

Stark, Rodney, and William Sims Bainbridge. 1985. *The future of religion: Secularization, revival and cult formation.* Berkeley: University of California Press.

————. 1987. *A theory of religion.* Toronto Studies in Religion 2. New York: Lang.

Stauffer, Ethelbert. 1955. *Christ and the Caesars: Historical sketches.* Trans. K. and R. Gregor Smith. London: SCM; Philadelphia: Westminster.

Ste. Croix, Geoffrey Ernest Maurice de. 1975. Early Christian attitudes to property and slavery. In *Church, society, and politics*, ed. Derek Baker, 1–38. Oxford: Blackwell.

————. 1981. *The class struggle in the ancient Greek world: From the archaic age to the Arab conquests.* Ithaca: Cornell University Press.

Stendahl, Krister. 1976. *Paul among Jews and Gentiles.* Philadelphia: Fortress.

Stern, Sacha. 1994. *Jewish identity in the early rabbinic writings.* Leiden: Brill.

Strobel, August. 1973. Die Friedenshaltung Jesu im Zeugnis der Evangelien— christliches Ideal oder christliches Kriterium. *ZEE* 17:97–106.

Stuhlmacher, Peter. 1968. *Das paulinische Evangelium.* Vol. 1. Göttingen: Vandenhoeck and Ruprecht.

———. 1991. The purpose of Romans. In *The Romans debate*, 2nd ed., ed. Karl P. Donfried, 231–42. Peabody, MA: Hendrickson.

Sullivan, John Patrick, trans. 1986. *Petronius, The Satyricon, and Seneca, The Apocolocyntosis*. Rev. ed. with introduction and notes. Harmondsworth, Middlesex: Penguin.

Swain, Simon. 1996. *Hellenism and empire: Language, classicism, and power in the Greek world AD 50–250*. Oxford: Clarendon.

Swerdlow, N.M. 1991. On the cosmical mysteries of Mithras. *CP* 86:48–63.

Tanzer, Sarah. 1991. Salvation is for the Jews: Secret Christian Jews in the Gospel of John. In *The future of early Christianity: Essays in honor of Helmut Koester*, ed. Birger Pearson, 285–300. Minneapolis: Fortress.

Tarn, William, and Guy Thompson Griffith. 1952. *Hellenistic civilisation*. 3rd ed. London: Arnold.

Taylor, Lily Ross. 1931. *The divinity of the Roman Emperor*. American Philological Association Monograph Series 1. Middletown: American Philological Association.

Tcherikover, Victor, ed. 1957. *Corpus papyrorum Judicarum*. Vol. 1. Cambridge, MA: Harvard University Press.

Thackeray, Henry St. J. 1967. *Josephus: The man and the historian*. Orig. pub. 1929.New York: KTAV.

Theissen, Gerd. 1982a. *The social setting of Pauline Christianity: Essays on Corinth*. Trans. John Schütz. Philadelphia: Fortress.

———. 1982b. Legitimation and subsistence: An essay on the sociology of early Christian missionaries. In *The social setting of Pauline Christianity: Essays on Corinth*, trans. John Schütz, 27–53. Philadelphia: Fortress.

Thomas, Carol G. 1981. The Greek *Polis*. In *The city-state in five cultures*, ed. Robert Griffeth and Carol G. Thomas, 31–69. Santa Barbara: ABC-Clio.

Thompson, Leonard L. 1990. *The Book of Revelation: Apocalypse and empire*. Oxford: Oxford University Press.

Tod, Marcus N. 1932. Clubs and societies in the Greek world. In *Sidelights on Greek History*, 71–96. Oxford: Blackwell.

Totti, Maria. 1985. *Ausgewählte Texte der Isis- und Sarapis-Religion*. Subsidia Epigraphica 12. Hildesheim: Olms.

Townsend, John T. 1985. Missionary journeys in Acts and European missionary societies. In *SBL 1985 Seminar Papers*, ed. Kent Harold Richards, 433–38. SBLSP 24. Atlanta: Scholars.

Trobisch, David. 1996. *Die Endredaktion des Neuen Testaments: Eine Untersuchung zur Entstehung der christlichen Bibel*. Freiburg, Switzerland: Universitätsverlag; Göttingen: Vandenhoeck and Ruprecht.

Turcan, Robert. 1992. *Les cultes orientaux dans le monde romain*. Paris: Les Belles Lettres.

———. 1993. *Mithra et le mithriacisme*. 2nd ed. Paris: Les Belles Lettres.

Turner, E.G. 1954. TIBERIVS IVLIVS ALEXANDER. *JRS* 44:54–64.

Urbach, Ephraim E. 1959. The rabbinical laws of idolatry in the second and third centuries in light of archaeological and historical facts. *IEJ* 9:189–205.

Vaage, Leif E. 1994. Redençâo e violencia: o sentido da morte de Cristo em Paulo. *RIBLA* 18:112–30.

Van der Horst, P.W. 1991. *Ancient Jewish epitaphs*. Kampen: Kok Pharos.

Van Unnik, Willem Cornelis. 1959. The purpose of St. John's Gospel. In *Studia evangelica: Papers presented to the International Congress on "The Four Gospels in 1957" at Oxford, 1957*, ed. Kurt Aland et al., Vol. 1, 382–411. Berlin: Akademie.

———. 1973. Der Ausdruck *heôs eschatou tês gês* (Apostlegeschichte I 8) und sein alttestamentlicher Hintergrund. In *Sparsa Collecta*, Vol. 1, 386–401. NovTSup 29. Leiden: Brill.

———. 1974. Josephus' account of the story of Israel's sin with alien women in the country of Midian (Num. 25:1ff.). In *Travels in the world of the Old Testament: Studies presented to Professor M.A. Beck on the occasion of his 65th birthday*, ed. M.S.H.G. Heerma van Voss et al., 241–61. Studia Semitica Neerlandia 16. Assen: van Gorcum.

Venables, E. 1908. Parabolani. In *Dictionary of Christian antiquities*, ed. Sir William Smith and Samuel Cheetham, Vol. 2. London: Murray.

Vermaseren, Maarten Joseph. 1956–1960. *Corpus Inscriptionum et Monumentorum Religionis Mithriacae*. 2 vols. The Hague: Nijhoff.

Vermaseren, Maarten Joseph, and Carl Claudius van Essen. 1965. *The excavations in the Mithraeum of the Church of Santa Prisca in Rome*. Leiden: Brill.

Veyne, Paul. 1976. *Le pain et le cirque: sociologie historique d'un pluralisme politique*. Paris: Seuil.

———. 1987 [1985]. The Roman Empire. In *A history of private life: From Pagan Rome to Byzantium*, ed. Paul Veyne, trans. Arthur Goldhammer, 5–234. Cambridge, MA: Harvard University Press.

———. 1990. *Bread and circuses: Historical sociology and political pluralism*. Trans. Brian Pearce. Abridged with an introduction by Oswyn Murray. London: Allen Lane (Penguin).

Walasky, Paul W. 1983. *"And so we came to Rome": The political perspective of St. Luke*. Cambridge: Cambridge University Press.

Wallace-Hadrill, Andrew. 1990. Roman arches and Greek honours: The language of power at Rome. *PCPS* 216:143–81.

Wallach, Luitpold. 1977. A Palestinian polemic against idolatry. In *Essays in Greco-Roman and related Talmudic literature*, ed. Henry A. Fischel, 111–26. Orig. pub. 1946. New York: KTAV.

Walton, Alice. 1979. *Asklepios: The cult of the Greek god of medicine*. Orig. pub. 1894. Chicago: Ares.

Wardman, Alan. 1982. *Religion and statecraft among the Romans*. Baltimore: Johns Hopkins University Press.

Ware, James. 1992. The Thessalonians as a missionary congregation: 1 Thessalonians 1, 5–8. *ZNW* 83:126–31.

Wedderburn, A.J.M. 1988. *The reasons for Romans.* Edinburgh: T. and T. Clark.

Weiss, Isaac Hirsch. 1904. *Dor Dor ve-Dorshav.* Part I. Vilna.

Weiss, H.-F. 1979. Pharisäismus und Hellenismus: zum Darstellung des Judentums im Geschichtswerk des jüdischen Historikers Flavius Josephus. *OLZ* 74: 421–33.

Welskopf, Elisabeth Charlotte, ed. 1933. *Hellenische Poleis: Krise, Wandlung, Wirkung.* Berlin: Akademie.

Wendland, Paul. 1904. SÔTÊR. *ZNW* 5:335–53.

———. 1972. *Die hellenistisch-römische Kultur in ihren Beziehungen zu Judentum und Christentum.* 4th ed. Tübingen: Mohr.

Wengst, Klaus. 1983. *Bedrängte Gemeinde und verherrlichter Christus.* Biblisch-Theologische Studien 5. Neukirchen-Vluyn: Neukirchener.

———. 1986. *Pax Romana and the peace of Jesus Christ.* Trans. John Bowden. London: SCM.

Westermann, Claus. 1969. *Isaiah 40–66: A commentary.* Philadelphia: Westminster.

White, L. Michael. 1990. *Building God's house in the Roman world.* Baltimore: Johns Hopkins University Press.

Wiedemann, Thomas. 1989. *Adults and children in the Roman Empire.* New Haven: Yale University Press.

Will, Edouard, and Claude Orrieux. 1992. *Prosèlytisme Juif? Histoire d'une erreur.* Paris: Les Belles Lettres.

Will, Ernest. 1955. *Le relief cultuel gréco-romain.* Paris.

Williams, Margaret H. 1990. Domitian, the Jews and "Judaizers": A simple matter of *Cupiditas* and *Maiestas? Historia* 39:196–211.

———. 1997. Jewish use of Moses as a personal name in Graeco-Roman antiquity: A note. *ZPE* 118:274.

Willoughby, Harold R. 1929. *Pagan regeneration: A study of mystery initiations in the Graeco-Roman world.* Chicago: University of Chicago Press.

Wilson, Stephen G. 1979. *Luke and the Pastoral Epistles.* London: SPCK.

———. 1992. Gentile Judaizers. *NTS* 38:605–16.

———. 1995. The Apostate minority. In *Mighty minorities? Minorities in early christianity: Positions and strategies,* ed. David Hellholm et al., 201–12. Oslo: Scandinavian University Press.

———. 1996. Voluntary associations: An overview. In *Voluntary associations in the Graeco-Roman world,* ed. John S. Kloppenborg and Stephen G. Wilson, 1–15. London: Routledge.

Winter, Bruce W. 1994. *Seek the welfare of the city: Christians as benefactors and citizens.* Grand Rapids, MI: Paternoster.

Winterbottom, Michael. 1977. Review of Benner 1975. *Gnomon* 49:419–20.

Wolfson, Harry Austryn. 1947. *Philo: Foundations of religious philosophy in Judaism, Christianity and Islam.* Cambridge, MA: Harvard University Press.

Woolf, Greg. 1996. Monumental writing and the expansion of Roman society in the early Empire. *JRS* 86:22–39.

Wörrle, Michael. 1988. *Stadt und Fest in kaiserzeitlichen Kleinasien: Studien zu einer agonistischen Stiftung aus Oenoanda*. Beiträge zur Alten Geschichte 39. Munich: Beck.

Yoder, John Howard. 1988. *The Politics of Jesus: Vicit Agnus noster*. 2nd ed. Orig. pub. 1972. Grand Rapids, MI: Eerdmans; Carlisle: Paternoster.

Ziebarth, Erich. 1896. *Das griechische Vereinswesen*. Stuttgart: Hirzel.

Zinsser, Hans. 1934. *Rats, lice and history*. New York: Bantam.

Zlotnick, Dov. 1988. *The iron pillar Mishnah*. New York: KTAV.

Zwiep, A.W. 1996. The text of the Ascension narratives (Luke 24.50–3; Acts 1.1–2, 9–11). *NTS* 42: 219–44.

Ancient Sources Index

5.41.6   142

Tatian, *Ad Graecos (Ad. Gr.)*
10   264

Tertullian
Adversus Judaeos (Adv. Jud.)
13.23   262
Apologeticum (Apol.)
39   213
39.5–6   219
39.7   225
39.16   219
40.1–2   37
42   103–104, 225
42.8   219
Ad Scapulam (Scap.)
4   219
De spectaculis (Spec.)
30.3   264

Graeco-Roman Literature

Aelius Aristides, *Sacred Tales (Or.)*
17.8   40
18   40
19   40
20   40
48.19–21   248
48.27   247
48.44   247
51.19–25   247

Antoninus Liberalis, *Metamorphoses*
25   264

Apollonios Rhodios, *Argonautika (Argon.)*
4.57   264

Apuleius, *The Golden Ass (Metam.)*
11.7–11   175
11.12–13   176
11.13   177
16   177

Aristotle, *Ethica Nicomachea (Eth. Nic.)*
10.6.1   150

Artemidoros, *Onirocriticus (Onir.)*
3.13   37
3.66   40

Cicero, *Oratio pro L. Flacco (Flac.)*
28.69   146

Dio Cassius, *Historia romana (Hist. Rom.)*
56.42   264
56.46.2   264
57.18.5a   144
59.11.4   264
60.6.6   144
65.1.4   173
67.14.1–3   70
67.14.2   143
68.1.1   144
68.1.2   143

Dio Chrysostom of Prusa, *Orationes (Or.)*
7.25–26   38
31.16   38
31.57   36
31.65   36
31.80–81   36
31.157   36
34.21–23   44
38–39   39
38.20   37
40.1   28n. 1
40.5–6   28n. 1
44   40
45.15–16   28n. 1
46   38
47.12–13   28n. 1

Diogenes Laertius
2.85.5   167
2.113–114   69
3.60.4   167
5.22.12   167
5.49.18   167
5.81.13   167
6.2.1   167
6.83.14   167
7.36.15   167
7.91.8   167
7.163.7   167
7.175.9   167
10.6–8   68
10.9–11   69
10.28.13   168

Epictetus, *Discourses (Diatr.)*
1.4.32   150
1.11.12–13   141
1.22.4   141
2.9.20   141

Ancient Names Index

Modern Names Index

Achtemeier, Paul J. 44
Aleshire, Sara B. 227
Alford, H. 17
Amundsen, Darrel W. 216
Applebaum, Shimon 57
Aune, David 168–69, 267–68
Aus, Roger D. 116–17, 122–25, 130
Austen, Jane 256
Avalos, Hector 215, 226, 230

Bakhtin, Mikhail Mikhailovich 73, 81
Barclay, John M.G. 57
Barker, Ernest 24
Barnes, Jonathan 34
Barrett-Lennard, R.J.S. 230
Basser, Reena xi, 89, 94
Beck, Roger xii, xiv, 49
Bengel, J.A. 16–17
Benner, Margareta 267
Best, Ernest 122
Bevan, Edwyn 79
Beyer, Peter 252
Beze, Theodore 17
Bilde, Per 167, 173
Box, George Herbert 32
Bradeen, Donald W. 24
Braun, Willi 216
Brown, Peter 33
Brown, Raymond E. 199, 203, 212, 260–61
Brunt, Peter Anthony 26

Bryant, Joseph 252
Burkert, Walter 35, 218
Burton, G.P. 26

Calvin, John 17
Canetti, Elias 73, 80–81
Clauss, Manfred 179–80, 238
Clay, Diskin 68
Cohen, Shaye J.D. 139, 145, 152–55, 159, 161
Conrad, Joseph 256
Conzelmann, Hans 206
Countryman, L. William 225
Cullmann, Oscar 210
Culpepper, R. Alan 212

Davies, John Kenyon 32
DeSilva, David A. 62
Devda, Tomasz 60
Dodd, Charles Harold 200, 209
Dodds, Eric Robertson 29, 31, 33, 247
Donaldson, Terrence xii, 139
Donfried, Karl P. 272
Dunn, James D.G. 115, 121, 131

Edelstein, Emma J. and Ludwig 226
Eder, Walter 25
Ehrman, Bart D. 264
Elliott, Neil 268, 273
Elmslie, William Alexander Leslie 76–77
Erasmus 17

322

Series Published by Wilfrid Laurier University Press for the Canadian Corporation for Studies in Religion/Corporation Canadienne des Sciences Religieuses

Series numbers not mentioned are out of print.

Editions SR

The Study of Religion in Canada / Sciences Religieuses au Canada

Studies in Women and Religion / Études sur les femmes et la religion

*Only available from Les Presses de l'Université Laval

SR Supplements

Series discontinued

Available from:
Wilfrid Laurier University Press
Waterloo, Ontario, Canada N2L 3C5
Telephone: (519) 884-0710, ext. 6124
Fax: (519) 725-1399
E-mail: press@wlu.ca
Website: http://www.wlupress.wlu.ca